Cambridge Studies in French

SENTENTIOUSNESS AND THE NOVEL

SENTENTIOUSNESS AND THE NOVEL

LAYING DOWN THE LAW IN EIGHTEENTH-CENTURY FRENCH FICTION

GEOFFREY BENNINGTON

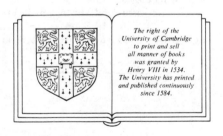

The right of the
University of Cambridge
to print and sell
all manner of books
was granted by
Henry VIII in 1534.
The University has printed
and published continuously
since 1584.

CAMBRIDGE UNIVERSITY PRESS

CAMBRIDGE

LONDON   NEW YORK   NEW ROCHELLE

MELBOURNE   SYDNEY

Published by the Press Syndicate of the University of Cambridge
The Pitt Building, Trumpington Street, Cambridge CB2 1RP
32 East 57th Street, New York, NY 10022, USA
10 Stamford Road, Oakleigh, Melbourne 3166, Australia

First published 1985

Printed in Great Britain at the University Press, Cambridge

British Library cataloguing in publication data
Bennington, Geoffrey
Sententiousness and the novel: laying down
the law in the 18th century French fiction. –
(Cambridge studies in French)
1. French fiction – 18th century – History
and criticism
I. Title
843'.5'09   PQ648

Library of Congress cataloguing in publication data
Bennington, Geoffrey.
Sententiousness and the novel.
(Cambridge studies in French)
Based on thesis (D. Phil.) – Oxford University.
Bibliography: p.
1. French fiction – 18th century – History and
criticism. 2. Didactic fiction, French – History and
criticism. 3. Rhetoric – 1500–1800. 4. Maxims in
literature. 5. Aphorisms and apothegms in literature.
I. Title. II. Series.
PQ648.B4   1985   843'.5'091   85-6700

ISBN 0 521 30246 3

308147

For e.g.

CONTENTS

Contents

Contents

Contents

FOREWORD

This book is concerned with a feature of discourse which I call 'sententiousness', with the effects produced by this feature in texts of narrative fiction, and specifically in some eighteenth-century French writing. Sententiousness is most clearly visible in texts in the form of maxims, aphorisms, and generalizing assertions, or, as I shall say later, in the form of sentences which *lay down the law*.

The analysis of this feature of discourse is formal up to the point where its formalism breaks down under the pressure of its own results. The effect of this breakdown is difficult for me to assess, but suggests at the very least that any 'results' obtained are 'provisional'. Just how radical a sense of the provisional is implied here will depend on whether such a breakdown can be formalized in a more powerful system, but the term is in any case not advanced in a spirit of empiricist modesty nor one of relativist self-righteousness. In the meantime (the time of the provisional) this breakdown does pose the problem of the book's genre. This genre is not that of traditional literary history, although I have not thought it necessary to rehearse yet again the arguments against this tradition of writing about literary texts – this work has already and convincingly been done in the area of the eighteenth-century French novel in excellent books by Peter Brooks, T.M. Kavanagh, Andrzej Siemek and Marian Hobson.[1] I assume that this debate is effectively over.

Nor is the genre that of the 'history of ideas': the breakdown of formalism does not here simply lead to an attempt to elucidate the *content* of sentious formulations, or to articulate that content in terms of 'world-views' or 'ideologies'. This is not to deny that some points are made which would be recognizable as pertinent within the terms of debate of such disciplines, but to suggest that any such points are subordinated to theoretical concerns. I should be only too pleased to be able to claim a modest place for this book in the heterogeneous genre recently characterized by Jonathan Culler as, simply, 'theory'.[2] One of the ways of reading what follows is as a narrative leading from 'structuralism' to 'post-structuralism', or, in a more oblique way, often via the notes, as an approach to a reading of the work of Jacques Derrida.

Claiming a status as both 'theory' and 'narrative', however, can scarcely identify a genre very confidently, for the narrative elements in the book return it to something like a history, and re-situate it in terms of the polarity of 'theory' and 'history' which dominates much current debate about literature. But in the present case, this situation is complicated by the fact that this polarity cannot in principle be discussed as simply a methodological protocol to the analyses, insofar as the basic binary opposition first addressed by those analyses (the opposition between sententious and narrative sentences) can itself be read as a version of that same polarity. When it makes theoretical claims, the book is obliged to produce sententious formulations and thus reproduce part of its object in a way which unsettles the pretension to theorize. But this complicity of the book with its object cannot simply imply a triumph of history and narratives, for sentences of this latter type, it is argued, are always informed by sententious force.

This complication of the polarity (in which the terms 'theory' and 'history' are often nowadays construed as rivals or opponents) will no doubt seem to be an unhappy compromise – but any such judgement could only be made from a position (which I believe to be mistaken) which expects the polemic between theory and history to result in victory for one of the terms. It is hard to imagine what such a victory might involve, for 'theory' and 'history' can *always* produce equally valid sentences about the referents (including the referents called 'theory' and 'history') positioned by their sentences: it is always possible to theorize a historical claim, as it is to historicize a theoretical pronouncement. Showing triumphantly that 'history' relies on at least one theoretical claim or demand (such as Jameson's 'Always historicize!'),[3] or that any theoretical sentence can be located in what is mysteriously called 'the historical real', allows local gratification but little more.

More ambitious attempts to 'transcend' altogether the opposition of theory and history[4] are only apparently more useful, and in fact are made possible only by a transcendental illusion that the referents positioned by the sentences of theory and history can be identified (from, or in, some third position) as 'the same'. The familiar operators of this type of approach (negativity, contradiction, *Aufhebung*) are not easy to escape, but are difficult to sustain in the light of recent work in philosophy (principally identified, in this book, with the names Derrida and Lyotard), which suggests that there is no *contradiction* between theory and history, but rather incommensurability. If there is a dialectic of theory and history, it is a dialectic in a non-Hegelian sense of the term, and it holds out no promise, beyond some 'seriousness, suffering, patience and labour of the negative', of ultimate resolution. More acutely, the relationship between theory and history can, following Lyotard, be termed a *différend*[5] (one effect, perhaps, of *différance* in Derrida's sense), and from a Hegelian standpoint, this will inevitably look like the 'unhapp compromise' referred to above.

But the pathos involved in such a characterization can be resisted or avoided, and 'post-structuralism' and 'post-modernism' (in Lyotard's sense)[6] are possible names for this resistance or avoidance. One of the re-discoveries prompted by this situation is that of fiction, humour, parody, travesty, the simulacrum. In the 'provisional meantime', which is simply *the time of the text*, clusters of sentences masquerade as books, however seriously they are written.

An earlier version of part of Chapter 5 appeared as 'Sade: Laying Down the Law', *Oxford Literary Review*, 6:2 (1984), pp. 38–56. Some of the comments on Paul de Man's reading of Rousseau are anticipated in 'Reading Allegory', *Oxford Literary Review*, 4:3 (1981), pp. 83–93.
I first came across the problem of sententiousness in an article by Robert Pring-Mill,[7] whom I thank for his warmth and encouragement during my days as an undergraduate. This book is based on my Oxford D.Phil. thesis, which would have been an impossible undertaking without the patient support and incisive criticisms of my supervisor, Ian Maclean. I also have debts of gratitude to Marian Jeanneret and Ann Jefferson, to Robert Young, Ann Wordsworth and Nick Royle of the *Oxford Literary Review*, and to friends and colleagues in Oxford, Paris, Cambridge and Sussex. Much of the original work on the thesis was carried out in Paris, and the final text bears many traces of the influence of Jacques Derrida and Jean-François Lyotard, whom I here thank for their inspiring teaching and rigorous example. Finally, I should like to thank the Fellows and Staff of Girton College, Cambridge, for graciously providing me with access to word-processing equipment which has greatly facilitated the preparation of the final typescript.

Cambridge, September 1984

Ce qu'il faut c'est sortir des détails pour parvenir aux idées générales très assises sur des lieux communs comme étayés de proverbes confirmés de bon sens baignant dans la science ruisselante de savoir.

– Jos Joliet,
L'Enfant au chien–assis,
p. 62

. . . sans même l'arête autoritaire d'un aphorisme.

– Jacques Derrida,
'Les Morts de Roland Barthes', p. 269

Part I
SENTENCES

1
APPROACHING
SENTENTIOUSNESS

1. Novel

'Soit un roman. Pour l'essentiel, il s'élabore d'une part dans l'ordre du récit, puisqu'il propose événements et actions, d'autre part dans l'ordre de la description, puisqu'il dispose objets et personnages.' Thus Jean Ricardou, at the beginning of a brilliant discussion of the formal problems raised by the coexistence in novels of these two 'orders'.[1] It would seem difficult to contest, at first sight, this characterization of the 'essential' elements of the novel.

If novels 'propose' events and actions, and 'dispose' objects and characters, they do so, and can only do so, by virtue of types of sentences. In a reductive but provisionally important sense, novels are made up *only* of sentences printed on paper: the only immediate 'given' (*datum*) of a novel is the text. Events, actions, objects, and characters are effects of that text: reading a novel means reading sentences.

The order of narrative can then be defined in terms of certain types of sentence, such as, 'Il se leva: sa casquette tomba. Toute la classe se mit à rire.'[2] The 'order of description', on the other hand, will be defined in terms of different types of sentence: 'Ovoïde et renflée de baleines, elle commençait par trois boudins circulaires; puis s'alternaient, séparés par une bande rouge, des losanges de velours et de poils de lapin.'[3] In the present case, one important criterion for distinguishing these types of sentences seems to be that of the tense of the verb (although this criterion would not work in all narratives): the preterite tense here marks narrative sentences, the imperfect descriptive sentences.

Ricardou does not want to suggest that this simple distinction is unproblematic, and the interest of his analysis stems from his awareness that the opposition is not one of clear-cut exclusion, but one of conflictual competition; and he can quite rightly go on to say that 'il n'y a pas de récit sans description', and 'il n'y a pas de

3

description sans récit'.[4] Exploration of these two 'essential' orders of the novel is important and productive.

1.1. The Sententious Proposition

It is not my immediate intention to contest Ricardou's results, nor to suggest that the types of sentence defined as 'narrative' and those defined as 'descriptive' are in fact not 'essential' to the novel. But it is clear that these are not the only types of sentence which make up the text of novels, and the following discussion will be concerned with a different type of sentence, which I shall call 'sententious', in its relationship with the narrative–descriptive complex. An example of this type of sentence in *Madame Bovary* would be the famous remark about language:

La parole humaine est comme un chaudron fêlé où nous battons des mélodies à faire danser les ours, quand on voudrait attendrir les étoiles.[5]

Whereas the narrative–descriptive opposition could in this case be characterized in terms of an opposition between preterite and imperfect tenses, here we have a verb in the *present* tense, and this is a first distinguishing mark of a sententious proposition. This use of the term 'present' is, however, misleading, and it would be more accurate to say that the sententious proposition is characterized by a verb which is *unmarked* in terms of tense: and this unmarked verb then tends to assume a value of eternality and universality.[6] Whereas sentences belonging to the narrative–descriptive complex tend to generate or present a *diegesis*[7] or 'universe' with a certain spatio-temporal coherence (in terms of which it is not nonsensical to ask questions of the type, 'When did he stand up?' and 'Where was his cap?'), the sententious proposition enjoys a freedom with respect to the coordinates of that 'universe', and if we ask the *text* to reply to the question, 'When and where is language like a cracked kettle?', it can only reply, 'Always and everywhere'. The sententious proposition is a generalization which is, in this sense, and quite independently of its being in this case a simile, independent of its diegetical context. This suggests that this third type of sentence in novels is not simply to be added to the list begun by narrative and descriptive types, but that it is of an order different from both. It is the conflictual coexistence of narrative and descriptive sentences which allows the elaboration of a diegesis, and such an elaboration requires both types, as Ricardou shows; sententious propositions as described so far do not contribute to the diegesis and seem to stand aloof from it.

In paying attention to sententiousness I am not then simply trying to complement Ricardou's description, nor, for the moment at least, contesting the idea that a novel is to be described as 'essentially' a narrative–descriptive complex. It is clear, for example, that a succession of narrative and descriptive sentences could make up a novel in the absence of any sententious proposition, whereas a series of sententious propositions could in no sense be described as a novel. This first formal approach to sententiousness suggests that if maxims, aphorisms and other sententious forms can indeed be found in abundance in novel texts, then they are no more than a non-essential adjunct to the 'essence' of the novel.

The apparently radical separation of sententiousness from this essence can be intuitively confirmed in a number of ways. For example, the 'translation' of a novel into a different narrative medium, such as film, immediately loses sententious propositions. Even if it is clear that narrative–descriptive propositions are never translated in this way without losses and additions, there is no great difficulty in imagining the proposition 'il se leva' as a (silent) sequence of film, whereas there is no easy way of imagining how the sententious example could be *shown* in this way. Sententiousness appears on a first approach to be more resolutely linguistic than narration or description, and could only survive our example of translation into film by reappearing in linguistic form, spoken by a character or a 'voice off', or written on the screen.

1.2. The Rest (I)

Sententious propositions seem then to be part of what we might call the 'rest' of the novel, the 'rest' that is left when the 'essential' narrative–descriptive elements have been taken into account. But this 'rest' displays a certain *resistance*, or 'restance',[8] to transformation. The rest remains. And this is indeed part of the pretension of sententiousness, its affirmation that what it says is valid 'always' and 'everywhere'. Sententiousness seems to want to transcend the contingency of the diegetical universe, and to be more 'essential' than what I have, following Ricardou, accepted as 'essential' to the novel. If a certain type of analysis of the novel tends to relegate sententiousness to the status of a non-essential adjunct, then sententiousness seems to take its revenge by insisting on its own universal validity, compared with which it is the narrative–descriptive complex that becomes the 'rest'. The apparently formal problem of the presence of sententious elements in novels thus becomes conflictual in its turn, and the

5

decision to describe either narrative–descriptive or sententious elements as 'essential' (and we have seen that in a sense sententious elements make this claim for themselves) involves taking sides in this conflict. Where Ricardou, and the 'structural analysis of narrative' in general, side with the narrative–descriptive complex, earlier traditions tended massively to side with sententiousness, and this was certainly the case, in general, in the eighteenth century in France.

This can conveniently be illustrated by a quotation from Marmontel, whose text shows nicely the logic of the 'rest' which I have sketched out. Marmontel is describing the result of the reader's contact with a novel:

Quand vient la réflexion, toute illusion est détruite. Que lui reste-t-il donc de cet enchantement? Ce qui lui reste est une vérité indestructible, inaltérable; qui se fixe dans l'âme, comme au fond d'un creuset, quand tout le reste est dissipé; et c'est en elle que consiste la moralité poétique, la moralité du roman.[9]

'Le reste reste', when its 'reste' disappears. The 'illusion' and 'enchantment' of the novel seemed to relegate 'truth' to a subordinate position (as 'the rest', precisely), but a final reversal reasserts that truth and dismisses the fiction as the 'rest'.

But the quotation from Marmontel does more than illustrate the formal points made so far, and introduces a new opposition, that between 'truth' and 'illusion', and a new term, that of 'moralité', into the discussion.

1.3. 'Truth' and 'Fiction'

Consider the following examples:

1. Caligula, ennemi de la vertu et jaloux des talents, avait surtout de la prétention à l'éloquence: il fut tenté de faire mourir Sénèque au sortir d'une plaidoirie où celui-ci avait été fort applaudi.

2. Les rois alliés partirent de Salente contents d'Idoménée et charmés de la sagesse de Mentor: ils étaient pleins de joie de ce qu'ils emmenaient avec eux Télémaque.

3. La tyrannie imprime un caractère de bassesse à toutes sortes de productions; la langue même n'est pas à couvert de son influence: en effet, est-il indifférent pour un enfant d'entendre autour de son berceau le murmure pusillanime de la servitude, ou les accents nobles et fiers de la liberté?

4. Un prince se déshonore encore plus en évitant les dangers qu'en n'allant jamais à la guerre. Il ne faut point que le courage de celui qui commande aux autres puisse être douteux. S'il est nécessaire à un peuple de conserver

son chef ou son roi, il lui est encore plus nécessaire de ne le voir point dans une réputation douteuse sur la valeur.

In terms of the discussion so far, it is clear that examples 1 and 2 belong to the narrative–descriptive complex, and that examples 3 and 4 are sententious. For the moment I shall not go into the problems raised by the fact that the second half of example 3 is in the form of a rhetorical question, and that the second sentence of example 4 is a prescriptive rather than a descriptive sentence.

Examples 1 and 3 are taken from a 'historical' text, Diderot's *Essai sur les règnes de Claude et de Néron;*[10] examples 2 and 4 from a 'novel', Fénelon's *Les Aventures de Télémaque.*[11] In principle this means that the narrative presented by example 1 should be true, or at least susceptible to a decision as to its truth or falsity according to certain more or less clearly defined criteria.[12] The proper names 'Caligula' and 'Sénèque' are proper names in the full Fregean sense of the term: they have reference, and thereby truth-value.[13] Example 2 is rather different, and the proper names 'Mentor' and 'Télémaque' (at least) have no reference: in Frege's terms this means not that the sentence is false, but that it is simply not susceptible to the true/false distinction. There is no question of truth-value here – the sentence is fictional.[14] This difference between the true/false on the one hand and the fictional on the other is not formally marked in the sentences concerned, and the assignation of sentences to one or other class involves the appeal to difficult notions of reference and verification. Whatever the value of these notions, the fact remains that some distinction between the two classes is possible in principle and is made in practice.

But the attempt to transfer even the *principle* of this distinction to examples 3 and 4 immediately runs into difficulties. These difficulties are not here due to the inability of the so-called 'verification principle' to account for universal and general propositions (which inability presumably immediately qualifies the principle itself as 'meaningless'),[15] but simply to the resistance of sententious propositions to the label 'fictional'. Even if we decide that such propositions are sloppy, difficult to verify or hopelessly pretentious and better avoided, it is difficult to imagine how they could be neatly removed from problems of truth and falsity and described as 'fictional'. There is no great problem, at this level of description, in accepting that narrative propositions in novels are fictional, but it is not easy to see how a sententious proposition in a novel is any more or less fictional than a similar proposition in a historical text.

The point of these remarks is simply to stress the incompatibility between sententiousness and the narrative–descriptive complex. The formal qualities of the sententious propositions are such that it inevitably 'remains' when the 'illusion' of the fictional narrative is 'destroyed' by reflection. In a certain sense, the sententious proposition *is* that 'reflection' which destroys, or at least commands and controls, that 'illusion'.[16] For a whole tradition of writing about the novel in the eighteenth century (and beyond in both directions), this survival of the maxim as reflection is the only possible justification for the temporary creation of the fictional 'illusion'.

It is, then, easy to see why Ricardou is right to claim that the narrative–descriptive complex is 'essential' to the novel (although of course that claim does nothing to help distinguish the novel from other narrative texts): sententiousness inevitably exceeds its situation in novels, not only cutting across generic boundaries, but challenging the distinction between true or false sentences on the one hand, and fictional sentences on the other. By disqualifying the predicate 'fictional', the sententious proposition accords itself a privilege with respect to 'truth' to which no narrative–descriptive sentence can pretend. The 'always' and 'everywhere' implied in the sententious proposition lifts it out of the text in which it appears, and in this important sense it is impossible to speak of sententiousness 'in' the novel.

The narrative–descriptive complex 'proposes' or 'disposes' events or objects in a circumscribed 'universe'; in the first instance, and whatever later considerations of exemplarity will be necessary, this complex deals with particulars. The sententious proposition refuses any such limitation. The incompatibility of the two classes of sentence is so great that it would appear reasonable to be surprised at their coexistence in novels, and to give up any attempt to articulate them. Sententious propositions stand out from their context and seem to invite extraction: they can quite happily be read in isolation from their surroundings. This partly explains why sententious propositions are so eminently *quotable*, and why they seem to invite what I shall later describe as an 'anthologizing' reading.

This isolation and detachability of sententious propositions is paradoxical: on the one hand they stand as fragments of the whole from which they are detached, but on the other they seem to aspire to the status of wholes in their own right, independent of any determined context. This would suggest that sententious propositions in fact form an independent genre in themselves, and that their appearance in novels (for example) is a case of the insertion of one genre into another.[17] Before suggesting various ways in which this apparently radical exteriority of sententiousness and narrative–descriptive sentences can and should be reduced, I shall therefore accept provisionally the characterization of sententiousness as a genre, and examine various attempts that have been made to analyse the structure of that genre and of the types of sentence that make it up.

2. Sententiousness as Genre (I): Two Models

Two ways of describing sententiousness as a genre suggest themselves. The first of these involves assembling all the 'co-hyponyms' with respect to which 'sententious proposition' is 'superordinate',[18] and distributing those terms within the conceptual space dominated by that superordinate: this is the procedure adopted by F. Rodegem in an attempt to clarify terminology.[19] The second procedure is to select a corpus of sentences intuitively recognized to be sententious, and to produce a grammar for the generation of these and other sentences respecting the rules thus elaborated: this is attempted by Serge Meleuc in an article based (almost inevitably) on the corpus provided by La Rochefoucauld's *Maximes*.[20]

2.1. The Distribution of Terms

Rodegem offers some general comments on his field of 'locutions sentencieuses', serving as peripheral fences around that field and preparing its internal division. This provides the following: 'Jugement de valeur – au sens large – [la locution sentencieuse] résume une sagesse pragmatique sous une forme concise, stéréotypée, le plus souvent rythmé à des degrés divers' (p. 679); 'La locution sentencieuse est une mise en garde, un avis plus ou moins contraignant, ou même un ordre impératif énoncé dans un but didactique, dialectique, ou catartique' (p. 685). Sententious formulations imply a value-judgement grounded in social norms; they transmit a cultural heritage and are inherently conservative: 'Les locutions sentencieuses assurent la permanence d'un ordre moral où la résistance à la nouveauté est le propre d'une mentalité conservatrice figée' (p. 686); 'Basé sur l'acquis antérieur, l'énoncé sentencieux fournit une solution toute faite aux problèmes et il évite de recommencer les tâtonnements des générations passées' (p. 687). Within this general field, Rodegem proposes a grid of nine possibilities corresponding to available terms. This grid is generated by two axes of three elements, the one concerned with

9

whether the field of application of the utterance is 'general', 'restrained', or 'specific', and the second whether the utterance is 'concrete', 'mixed', or 'abstract'. This produces the following table:

Enoncé	Général	Restreint	Spécifique
Concret	1. Proverbe	2. Locution proverbiale	3. Dicton
Mixte	4. Maxime	5. Slogan	6. Adage juridique
Abstrait	7. Aphorisme	8. Apophthegme	9. Devise
Norme	'Règle de vie'	Directive	Précepte

This system of classification is supplemented by a subsidiary assignation of the elements 'rhythm', 'metaphoricity', and 'normative thrust' to each of the nine cases. Thus, for example, all three of these elements are present in the proverb, whereas the 'locution proverbiale' retains only the aspect of metaphoricity. The 'adage juridique' is characterized by a strong normative thrust, and may possess an element of rhythm, but is distinguished at this level from the slogan only in that the slogan is more likely to contain this element of rhythm, and from the aphorism only in the strength of the normative thrust.

Despite the pertinence of some of Rodegem's general comments, and the attraction of an attempt to describe at once general characteristics and specific differences, there are some problems involved in this enterprise. For example, it is not clear why a slogan need be less 'specific' than an 'adage juridique', or less concrete than a 'locution proverbiale'. And Rodegem's later description of the apophthegm as a sententious quotation from a famous figure introduces difficult problems of enunciation and signatures into a field which his grid determines according to formal properties of utterances. Do aphorisms and apophthegms contain an element of 'sagesse pragmatique' assigned to all sententiousness? What is meant by the 'field of application'? Do *all* sententious formulations pass on the stereotyped knowledge of a cultural heritage? The problem seems to be that not all of the criteria brought to bear are of the same logical order: this means that even in cases intuitively characterized with reference to their enunciation, the axes of the grid force all the terms into relationships based on a vague notion of positive content or 'field of application'. A basic assumption here is that of the continuity and homogeneity of the space represented by the grid: these classical presuppositions[21] commit Rodegem to a certain view of linguistic functioning which is difficult to sustain. Any attempt to describe sententiousness as a genre in this way (and no such attempt will be made here) would no doubt have to accept the possibility of what Foucault calls a 'principle of discontinuity',[22] in order to avert the danger of assuming that sententious discourse can be thought of as a unified 'space' adequately covered by the terms available for designating individual sententious utterances, and the consequent apriorism implicit in the assumption that each of the available terms must correspond to a distinct position in the matrix. This is one of the basic difficulties involved in the constitution of sententiousness as a genre. Further, this type of 'mise en ordre' creates a problem which will return insistently: in order to characterize the sententious field (to fix its boundaries), Rodegem is *himself* obliged to produce sententious statements (as well as narrative–descriptive ones), which his model thus does not, and cannot, dominate.

2.2. A Generative–Transformational Model

Meleuc's method (the establishment of rules on the basis of a corpus) is more fruitful and avoids the problems encountered by Rodegem. From intuitive notions about what constitutes a maxim, supported by dictionary definitions (I shall return to the problem of definition below (§5.2)), Meleuc retains the ideas that a maxim states a universal, and that it is didactic. The first of these properties corresponds to my earlier location of the 'always' and 'everywhere' implied in sententious discourse, the second to what I shall develop at greater length in a later chapter in terms of the 'scene of education' implied by the pragmatics of sententiousness. The notion of universality is dealt with in the first part of Meleuc's article, subtitled 'Grammaire de la proposition', and that of didacticism in the second part, subtitled 'Syntaxe interpropositionnelle: la transformation négative'.

In the first section Meleuc is concerned to locate the restrictions imposed by the genre of the maxim on the production of sentences. Given the elements 'always' and 'everywhere', to which are added the elements 'il' and 'affirmation', certain forms are excluded. For example, given the fact that, as we have seen, a sententious proposition is resistant to contextual determination (and in La Rochefoucauld's *Maximes* this separation is of course a given, typographically marked by the spaces separating each maxim from the next, both inviting and frustrating the reader's desire to establish coherent strings of maxims), the various determiners of the noun lose any referential or anaphoric value.[23] Thus in maxims the subjects of which are 'l'homme', 'la jalousie', 'l'intérêt', 'la fortune', and so on

11

(Meleuc's examples, Maxims 43, 32, 40, 380) the article serves only to refer the noun to the linguistic code, and not to any specific referential situation. The article is imposed by a purely grammatical constraint. Similarly, the indefinite article ('un sot', 'un honnête homme': Maxims 387, 353) refers to the whole class concerned and not to specific individuals. Further, according to Meleuc, the demonstratives 'ce/cette/ces' constitute only a stylistically marked form of the article, except insofar as they refer anaphorically, not to an earlier segment of text, but to a *presupposed* prior statement which the maxim attempts to refute. It should be noted immediately that here the 'except' refutes the 'only': this presence of deictics in maxims already compromises their apparent autonomy, and this is one of the points at which the apparently radical separation of sententious propositions from the narrative–descriptive complex can be challenged.

If the class of demonstratives thus suggests that the maxim's self-sufficiency is not so great as may have appeared at first sight, then the other major class of deictics, the personal pronouns, will support that suggestion. Although Meleuc shows that the genre of the maxim allows only the forms *il(s)*, *elle(s)*, *on* and *nous*, thus excluding the most obviously deictic forms (*je* and *tu*),[24] the widespread use of the form *nous* is of the greatest importance. Meleuc suggests that the *il(s)* and *elle(s)* forms are to the *on* and *nous* as the merely general to the purely universal. But the *nous*, explicitly marking the presence of a subject of the enunciation in the utterance, and retaining an ambiguity with respect to the *destinataire* of that utterance, poses a pragmatic problem which will have effects throughout the analyses to come.

Still within the grammar of the proposition, the verbal system is controlled and reduced by the genre of the maxim. Meleuc shows that the only opposition retained here (apart from that between singular and plural, of no interest for the definition of the maxim) is the aspectual accomplished/unaccomplished opposition, as shown, for example, in Maxim 229: 'Le bien que *nous avons* reçu de quelqu'un veut que nous respections le mal qu'il nous fait' (Meleuc's emphasis, p. 77). When maxims are replaced in their cotextual[25] surroundings, this peculiarity of their verbal system becomes one of their principal distinguishing features.

A further feature of the maxim's verbal system located by Meleuc, one which will be of importance in the context of classical theories of language, is the predominant role of the verb 'to be', which has both a copulative and an existential role in maxims (i.e. both binding the sentence together and asserting the existence of the state of affairs described by the maxim), and which also, at least for the grammatical theory of the late seventeenth and early eighteenth centuries, marks the presence of the subject of the enunciation.

The first part of Meleuc's analysis thus isolates a number of limiting conditions determining maxims. I take these conditions to be applicable not just to the corpus chosen by Meleuc but in general to the type of sentence I refer to as 'sententious'. The second part of his article is perhaps more interesting, but also perhaps less easily generalizable. Starting from his assumption that the maxim is 'didactic', Meleuc states that 'l'énonciateur vise à persuader le récepteur; le premier étant le maître, l'autre l'élève' (p. 69). He then identifies these two positions with those of author and reader, and proceeds to find that in the rhetoric of the maxim the most common structure is one in which the maxim contradicts (corrects, demystifies) a previous statement attributed to the reader. This may appear to be a surprising assertion, but it is given a good deal of support by Meleuc's transformational analysis. As a preliminary example, Meleuc takes not a maxim, but the proverb 'Pauvreté n'est pas vice': by arguing that the non-identity of poverty and vice is already inscribed in the system of *langue* (in Saussure's sense), and that therefore the proverb tells us nothing new, Meleuc can infer that the sense of the proverb lies in its contradiction of an implied statement which denies that distinction:

Le proverbe ne prend donc son sens que s'il est mis en relation avec l'énoncé complet dont il est la négation. On peut dire qu'ici le proverbe rétablit la distinction de deux classes linguistiques (pauvreté différente de vice), qu'un autre énoncé, celui produit par un certain code socio-culturel, avait abusivement abolie; il rétablit donc une distinction de la *Langue* pervertie par un discours.   (pp. 83–4)

There is an immediate and important reservation to be made here, which suggests among other things the essential limitations of a purely linguistic approach to the problem of sententiousness. Meleuc postulates the existence of a pure state of *langue* in some logical priority to its possible contamination by discourse or a 'code socio-culturel': but clearly *langue* is only accessible *through* discourse, and if there is indeed a discourse which identifies poverty and vice, then that identification cannot simply be challenged by an appeal to *langue*. 'Vice' might be described as a superordinate term with a number of possible co-hyponyms which vary from discourse to discourse: any contradiction will take place between two rival discourses and not between a given discourse and the language-system. Meleuc falls into the error of hypostatizing the language-system and forgetting that it can be constituted as a theoretical fiction only through further acts of *parole* which draw on it, displace it, and reconstitute it.

This does not remove the interest of Meleuc's argument, but resituates it to some extent. It indeed seems necessary to analyse the numerous maxims which might be reduced to the form '(Ce qu'on appelle) X n'est que Y' (e.g. Maxims 1, 15, 20, 44, 82, 83, etc.) in terms of the model of negation suggested by Meleuc. On the other hand, it is difficult to accept his broadening of this type of analysis to practically the whole of the corpus (Meleuc attempts this generalization on page 89, arguing that explicit marks of the negation of the contested 'reader's statement' – of which the 'ne . . . que' formulation would be an example – are merely elements of surface structure) and difficult to agree with a concluding remark to the effect that 'la syntaxe générale de la Maxime, en tant que type de discours, peut être représentéé par la formule:

Enoncé du lecteur + NEG.   (p. 96)

This is no more interesting than the idea that *any* utterance can be described as a negation of a supposed contrary or contradictory utterance. On the basis of an undeniable empirical feature of his corpus (although Philip Lewis is certainly right to point out that if the 'ne . . . que' formula is indeed frequent in the first part of the *Maximes*, the examples become much less frequent as the book progresses),[26] Meleuc produces an untenable assertion; and in this he falls into the trap opened by the form of sententiousness itself, which can often be accused (except in the limiting case of analytic universal propositions) of over-generalization and intolerance of exceptions and difference.

On the other hand, the undeniable fact that there exists a *class* of sententious utterances which do display this feature (of negating a statement which they in some sense quote) again threatens the autonomy of the sententious proposition, making it partially dependent on a generally accepted prior discourse of accepted wisdom. I shall call such a discourse a 'doxa', borrowing this classical Greek term from Roland Barthes.[27] It is an essential point that the statements of the doxa are themselves sententious. It is tempting to suggest that sententiousness falls into two classes, and to label these 'doxal' and 'paradoxal', with only the second type corresponding to Meleuc's definition of the maxim. The analyses of the discourse of worldliness, in a later chapter, will attempt to show both the necessity and the insufficiency of such a distinction.

This extended summary of Meleuc's attempt to ground the maxim theoretically as a genre has allowed me to stress the specificity of sententious propositions with respect to the narrative–descriptive complex (which obeys none of the constraints isolated for the maxim by Meleuc), but also to suggest three points at which the apparent autonomy of sententious propositions might be placed in doubt: these three points involve the status of the ostensive deictics *ce*, *cette*, or *ces*, the personal pronoun *nous*, and the suggestion of a possible dependence of sententiousness on an accepted collective discourse which I have called the doxa. It is immediately obvious that the first and third of these points are versions of the same problem. Once we decide that the ostensive deictic is, even in La Rochefoucauld, *not* merely a stylistically marked form of the definite article, then it is clear that its function is to make anaphóric gestures towards statements from the doxa: thus 'Cette clémence dont on fait une vertu . . .' (Maxim 16) assumes a statement from the doxa to the effect that 'La clémence est une vertu'. That the problem presented by the *nous* is also to be linked to the question of the doxa is less immediately clear, insofar as it implies a problematic of the *enunciation* of sententious propositions which we shall have to consider at greater length before it is possible to agree with Lewis, who states that 'the fundamental problem of the maxim . . . becomes . . . the problem exposed by the first-person plural'.[28]

3. Sententiousness as Genre (II): Types

Before returning to this difficult problem, however, it will be worthwhile clarifying further the ground covered so far, to locate broad particularities of certain types of sententious discourse and to approach more nearly some of the questions to come, in the light of the following examples:

1. John, dressed in jeans and sweater, went out and bought a packet of cigarettes.
2. Too many cooks spoil the broth.
3. Every body continues in its state of rest, or uniform motion in a straight line, unless it is compelled to change that state by force impressed upon it.
4. In polite society one does not wipe one's fingers on the tablecloth.
5. 'Les sots ne comprennent pas les gens d'esprit.' (Vauvenargues)[29]
6. 'Qu'est-ce qu'un philosophe? C'est un homme qui oppose la nature à la loi, la raison à l'usage, sa conscience à l'opinion, et son jugement à l'erreur.' (Chamfort)[30]
7. 'La modestie, qui semble refuser les louanges, n'est en effet qu'un désir d'en avoir de plus délicates.' (La Rochefoucauld)[31]

Sentences

3.1. Narrative–Descriptive

Example 1 is included partly as a reminder of the narrative–descriptive complex. It is also worth pointing out that despite the differences I am stressing between this type of sentence and the following examples, this statement has in common with the rest its grammaticality and 'acceptability'. This notion of acceptability might be extended here to include an idea of verisimilitude.[32] This means that example 1, in its banality, is more 'neutral', not only than a sentence of the type 'colourless green ideas sleep furiously', but also than a sentence such as 'John, dressed in climbing-boots and dinner-jacket, ate the last octopus and scored a goal'.

3.2. Proverbs

It would be difficult to read example 2 as a narrative. The present tense of the verb does not of course necessarily disqualify this reading, but the absence of contextual reference for the 'Too many cooks' prompts a reading of the verb as an 'eternal' present, or as unmarked in terms of tense. Further, and this is a less trivial point than it may perhaps appear, the sequence is taken up (or can be taken up) by a 'cultural competence' in the reader, and recognized as a proverb. This involves a recognition of *repetition*: as Jean Paulhan suggests in a very interesting article, 'le proverbe est à la fois moins et plus qu'un raisonnement ou une métaphore: il est l'un et l'autre à l'état figé; il exige pour demeurer proverbe que les mêmes mots, qui le composent, *soient rappelés dans un ordre identique*'.[33] The fact that the proverb is a repetition of a given sequence of signifiers also defines it as a *quotation*, but it is characteristic of the proverb that it is impossible to assign a first utterance of it by appending to the sequence an author's signature: the proverb is in this sense always an anonymous utterance.

Further, the apparent specificity of the sequence means that its being labelled 'proverb' rather than 'culinary tip' involves a metaphorical reading. This has to be programmed into the recognition of the sequence as a proverb in cases where it is read in isolation from a given pragmatic 'scene', or, within that scene, provoked by an incongruity between context and literal meaning. This versatility of the proverb with respect to its situation of utterance (which is not a necessary condition of proverbial discourse: Meleuc's example, 'Pauvreté n'est pas vice', does not apparently exhibit this feature) evidently allows an indefinitely wide range of applications, and the notorious fact that almost any proverb can be matched with another

16

which contradicts it allows proverbs to form the basis of an infinitely recuperative discourse, always able to reduce the new to the known, or to repeat the statement 'life's like that', where 'that' already means 'life'. It is here that Rodegem's general comments about sententiousness are most valid.

The particular discourses with which I am here concerned (twentieth-century critical discourse as well as those of the eighteenth century) are irremediably separated from what it would be tempting to think of as a 'living' use of the proverb; but that very idea of a separation between 'life' and 'death' of proverbs may encourage the type of nostalgia displayed by Barthes, who in *Mythologies* opposes the active rural proverb to the 'reflexive' bourgeois maxim. This simply creates another myth.[34] Any attempt we might make to recover a 'true' use of the proverb is always already contradicted by our recognition of the given sequence *as* proverb, as something *other* within a discourse, something to be, precisely, extracted and placed in a list, or analysed in terms of its internal structure.[35] This recognition and labelling of the proverb (which in the process gathers semes such as 'rusticity', 'naïvety', 'picturesqueness', and so on) is not only a modern process: well beyond the twelfth-century French collection which duly notes after each example, 'ce dit le vilains',[36] this type of labelling can be detected in ancient societies.[37]

This activity is evidently a political one, carried out by a dominant discourse on a discourse which it dominates. Insofar as the novel can be regarded as a 'bourgeois' form, it is therefore to be expected that the occurrence of proverbs will be linked to this type of labelling, and subject to ironic distancing.[38] And this is of course the case at least since *Don Quixote*, and is consistently so whenever proverbs appear in eighteenth-century France. That they may be allowed a certain privilege of speaking the 'truth' (already the case for Cervantes's Sancho, similarly for Marivaux's Jacob)[39] does not alter this process of labelling, but exploits a familiar structure of 'naïvety'.[40] Paulhan's text is a useful and amusing account of this 'sophisticated' view of the proverb faced with a community which refuses to accept this type of extraction and labelling. Their insistence that proverbs be replaced in context will support my later critique of 'anthologizing readings' of sententiousness in novels.

A final point about proverbs: despite my opening remarks, it is clear that my example cannot so simply be separated from the problem of narrative; something like an explanatory story of why too many cooks spoil (or once spoiled) the broth seems to be implied. This connection between sententiousness and narrative can no doubt be

17

postulated in general.[41] This possible *solidarity* of sententiousness and narrative is an important preliminary step in the attempt to read 'sententiousness and the novel'.

3.3. The Law

The third example, 'Every body continues in its state of rest, or uniform motion in a straight line, unless it is compelled to change that state by force impressed upon it', is of course a statement which can be labelled 'Newton's First Law of Motion'. The sentence is here not of my own invention, as was example 1, nor an anonymous collective quotation, as was the case with the proverb. In a very obvious sense it is a quotation, signed 'Newton', but this status is not simple, and in any case not so simple as in examples 5, 6 and 7. The definition as a 'sequence of signifiers' is here not so clear, and it is perfectly possible to imagine different formulations of the 'same' truth (if only in different languages: the sequence I have given is already a 'revised translation').[42] 'Newton's First Law' is not so much a quotation from Newton as a formulation (subject to certain controls, but in principle formalizable and repeatedly applicable) of 'what Newton discovered'. Further, the attributive signature is in no way essential to the statement which, after the general fashion of modern scientific discourse, grounds its 'scientificity' partially in the erasure of the subject of the enunciation, or the signatory, from its utterances. Again, where the proverb happily accepted contradiction by what was simply a different proverb, a statement such as this must be able, if it is to maintain its claim to scientific truth, to exclude contraries and contradictories. In an apparently simple sense, such a statement is in principle verifiable or falsifiable; and this simplicity distinguishes it from all of the other examples. The apparent purity of such an example seems to make of it a limiting case of sententiousness. Insofar as such a statement is not about a 'moral' question, nor, apparently, about 'Man', it would be easy to argue for its exclusion from the field of sententiousness; and insofar as the analyses to come are concerned with 'sententiousness and the novel', there will indeed be a general *de facto* exclusion of sententiousness in scientific discourse. But this exclusion is not in principle grounded in any necessity; scientific discourse has its rhetoric, and can be analysed in terms of types of sentence.[43] And most importantly, the apparent autonomy of the sentence can be challenged, and its links with the narrative– descriptive complex are easy enough to imagine in a variety of forms. I should like here to stress a point which I shall investigate at length in the third part of this book, and which concerns the term 'law'. A scientific truth is a descriptive statement, a 'law' in the sense of a 'correct statement of invariable sequence between specified conditions and specified phenomena' (OED): but in achieving this status, it also *lays down the law*, and becomes a source of authority, a ground for exclusions and repressions. In its ambiguity, the notion of 'laying down the law' perhaps best describes sententiousness in general.

3.4. Rules

The idea that sententiousness 'lays down the law' involves an important ambivalence concerning descriptions and prescriptions, and this ambivalence is made clearer in example 4. This type of sentence is difficult to locate in terms of a polarity between 'invented' statements on the one hand, and 'quotations' on the other. It would be distinctly odd to claim that I have 'invented' this sentence, but strange to present it as a quotation. This type of sentence is perhaps best regarded as an *actualization* of an item of 'social competence', here a 'rule' of etiquette. This sentence 'lays down the law' in describing at once a verifiable state of affairs in a definable social domain (and thus involves a notion of closure), but also has prescriptive weight when actualized for purposes of 'initiation' or 'therapy', that is, in order to introduce a subject into the closure, and to enforce that closure against deviant behaviour which threatens it with invasion from 'outside'.[44] It can be assumed that the actualization of such sentences (except when they are re-quoted in the type of meta-discourse which I am writing here, the status of which I do not yet wish to question) implies a pragmatic 'scene' which I shall call a 'scene of education': this immediately implies a certain relationship between the *destinateur* and *destinataire* of such a statement, and their relative positioning with respect to the closure implied in its use. I shall exploit these features at length in later analysis of the eighteenth-century 'novel of worldliness'. It should be noted that this suggested pragmatic scene cannot be identified simply with the notion of the transmission of a cultural heritage, as suggested by Rodegem, which underplays the power-relations involved in such a scene, nor with Meleuc's notion of the maxim as being a teacher's 'reply' to a pupil's error. Rather it involves both of these notions and, beyond them, allows for the possibility of what Lyotard calls an 'agnostics',[45] which retains both doxal and paradoxal sententiousness within its problematic.

With this relatively trivial example, we have reached a level which can be said to correspond broadly to a certain sense of the term 'maxime' prevalent in the eighteenth century.[46]

3.5. Maxims

The remaining examples are all quotations in a much simpler sense than any of those discussed so far, and I have indicated this by writing them within quotation marks and by adding the author's name in each case. All of them are overdetermined as 'maximes' by being taken from texts including that word in their title.[47] We are here then at a crossing-point in the notion of genre between on the one hand discursive genre (assuming still that 'sententiousness' is a sufficiently unified phenomenon to be specified in such terms), and on the other literary genre, where certain literary and institutional marks and frames tell the reader that these are maxims. Of these examples, I include number 5 to suggest again that although Meleuc's 'propositional grammar' is helpful in an attempt to define sententiousness, his 'interpropositional transformation' is not a necessary feature. It is simply not interesting to generate a sentence such as 'Les sots comprennent les gens d'esprit' and to suggest that this be attributed to the reader, and that the maxim draws its strength from its negation of that utterance.[48] Example 6 is more complicated because it in fact involves two sentences, the first of which is not sententious, and the second of which is so only in the context of the first (the pronominal 'ce' is anaphoric). Sententiousness is here a product of the juxtaposition of two sentences, neither of which in isolation could be described as sententious (imagine, for example, a case in which the 'ce' was the substitute for a proper name). It is, of course, easy enough to perform an intuitive transformation and produce the sentence 'Un philosophe est un homme . . .' And this further suggests that it would be possible to apply the same transformation in reverse to maxims of the general type represented here, producing a series of 'question and answer' sequences. This 'question and answer' (and not 'error and correction') structure, which is applicable to a considerable number of sententious statements (even within La Rochefoucauld), again suggests that Meleuc's emphasis on the model examined above is partial. This general type of maxim is evidently linked to the form of the *definition*. It may be possible to provide a historical argument to explain this link,[49] but this would still leave unanswered an essential structural problem which I have already hinted at above: if definitions are to be considered as sententious, then how is it possible for a discourse on sententiousness to define its object without repeating that object? It is in principle impossible for me to write anything like a theory of sententious propositions without producing more sententious propositions. This impossibility of making a clear structural distinction between object-language and meta-language (whatever the apparent empirical facility of deciding which is which) is a problem which affects the genre of *this* writing, whether that genre be considered to be that of the thesis, that of 'theory', or that of 'literary history'. In other words, in writing about sententiousness I am 'laying down the law' *about* laying down the law. Beyond the pragmatic 'scene of education', this emphasizes the need to consider too a 'scene of legislation', and this will be the object of Part III of this book.

Although the 'ne . . . que' in example 7 suggests that it be analysed in Meleuc's terms, we can now also change those terms slightly in view of what has just been said about definitions. In this case, the 'paradoxal' maxim involves problems of (re)definition which push it to the edge of paradox. Here the presupposed statement negated by the maxim would be close to a dictionary definition of the term 'modestie'. No doubt the effect of this type of threat to accepted definition provokes a reading which places the term 'modestie' in notional quotation-marks, and describes it as 'false' modesty, opposed to the 'true' modesty as defined by dictionaries. However, this importation of an imagined prefatory 'Ce qu'on appelle . . .' after the model provided by other maxims in La Rochefoucauld, implies a reduction in the play of the maxim, justified by a worried attachment to a sort of semantic law of identity. If, in this type of maxim,[50] the reader does not exercise this sort of control or censorship, and resists the temptation (ever-present in La Rochefoucauld) to stabilize meaning with the help of quotation-marks placed around key terms,[51] then the self-identity of the stock terms of the moralists is placed in doubt, and the possibility of extracting final meanings threatened. This type of play in sententious discourse depends on the isolation of the statement, its separation from contexts which would clarify and reduce it; and it is to be expected that sententious propositions in narrative contexts will be in general less vertiginous, in this respect at least.

4. Sententiousness as Genre (III): Wholes and Fragments

In the discussion so far I have accepted the idea that sententiousness be approached as a genre, here conceived as a type of sentence considered in its grammatical completion and isolation. At a number of points, however, it has seemed necessary to challenge the efficacity of this type of approach (characteristic of classical structural and transformational linguistics), and to look proleptically towards the 'new' linguistics of the enunciation or towards pragmatics for more adequate models.[52] I now want to suggest that in the case of the maxim, still considered as a sentence, this problem can be linked to its status as paradoxically both a whole and a fragment. Maxims appear to offer independent assertions which can be read on their own terms: the maxim seems to be, as Pascal says of the law, 'toute ramassée en soi'.[53] However, at least in my later examples which I described as 'overdetermined' by their 'framing' as a literary genre, the maxims discussed are also fragments of books, parts of a greater 'whole' from which I have detached them. It is this double property which allows Barthes to open his essay on La Rochefoucauld with the idea that there are two distinct ways of reading the text, one in terms of the individuality of each maxim, the other in terms of the book as a collection.[54]

On the one hand, the succession of the maxims in the texts of La Rochefoucauld, Vauvenargues or Chamfort can be seen to be contingent; on the other, it is possible to argue that there is a certain *necessity* of the texts of these 'collections', and this tendency (almost inevitably espoused in critical writing, even if that writing would like to stress the fragmentary nature of those 'collections') leads to the grouping of maxims, the establishment of indexes by authors or editors,[55] the attempt to find some general coherence in which the individual maxim becomes an example of a theme or a form. The apparent autonomy of the maxim is thus again threatened. In simple cases, a maxim is read in terms of others with which it is associated in some way, perhaps with the help of an index of 'themes'. This type of activity provides a reassuring way of gathering up the fragments and redistributing more satisfactorily the whole of the book. In this way, individual maxims become integrated into a more continuous text (that of reader or critic), and this text will tend to belong 'essentially' to the narrative–descriptive complex. A good example here is provided by Jean Starobinski, who in his article, 'La Rochefoucauld et les morales substitutives',[56] writes a brilliantly argued narrative of the text, leading through a consideration and rejection of moral systems based on simple oppositions of virtue and vice or strength and weakness to a social ethic of 'honnêteté', which is in fact an aesthetic as much as an ethic.

It seems then that it is possible to postulate two tendencies, once the literary maxim is considered in the book from which it was extracted: one of these is a tendency towards plenitude, the other towards fragmentation.[57] These tendencies can of course be marked in the texts themselves: in La Rochefoucauld it would be particularly difficult to choose between them. But in the work of Vauvenargues and Chamfort, the two major eighteenth-century practitioners of the maxim as genre, the tendencies are much clearer, and nicely complementary.

4.1. Vauvenargues: the Book

If we consider certain affirmations made by Vauvenargues, he would seem to be the last author from whom to expect fragmentary texts: a consistent desire throughout his work is to gather fragments together, to make them into a system or a body, a Book. This desire is clear in the opening sentences of the *Introduction à la connaissance de l'esprit humain*, the preface to the second edition of which[58] opens with a misquotation of a famous statement from Pascal: '*Toutes les bonnes maximes sont dans le monde*, dit Pascal, *il ne faut que les appliquer*'.[59] But whereas Pascal is making a point about the application of maxims (presupposing an opposition between what one says and how one actually behaves), Vauvenargues immediately diverts the quotation towards a problem of totalization and reconciliation:

Ces maximes n'étant pas l'ouvrage d'un seul homme, mais d'une infinité d'hommes différents, qui envisagent les choses par divers côtés, peu de gens ont l'esprit assez profond pour *concilier tant de vérités* et les dépouiller des erreurs dont elles sont mêlées. Au lieu de songer à réunir ces divers points de vue, nous nous amusons à discourir des opinions des philosophes, et nous les opposons les uns aux autres, trop faibles pour *rapprocher ces maximes éparses*, et pour en *former un système raisonnable*.[60]

Similar assertions are to be found in posthumous texts, and, more importantly from our point of view, in the first two of the *Réflexions et maximes*, the first of which reads, 'Il est plus aisée de dire des choses nouvelles que de concilier celles qui ont été dites', and the second, 'L'esprit de l'homme est plus pénétrant que conséquent, et embrasse plus qu'il ne peut lier'. Vauvenargues never wrote the Book projected by his fragments (the link with Pascal is obvious, but the status of a text interrupted at a contingent point in the notional progress from fragment to Book is unclear), but the *Introduction à la connaissance de l'esprit humain* shows clearly enough the difficulties inherent in Vauvenargues's project, for in this text there is a constant tendency towards a new fragmentation of the whole into sequences which could stand separately as maxims. This inevitable consequence of an analytical movement working against a synthetic project is occasionally visible even in the typography of the text, notably in the chapter 'Du sérieux' (pp. 79–80), and especially in the penultimate chapter of the work, entitled 'Du courage' (pp. 110–12), which breaks off with the assertion 'Je voudrais pouvoir parcourir ainsi en détail toutes les qualités humaines: un projet si long ne peut maintenant m'arrêter. Je terminerai cet écrit par de courtes définitions.'[61] This dispersion of the text into innumerable definitions (of 'la probité', 'la droiture', 'l'équité', etc.) does not seem to be an accidental difficulty, but a result of the tendency of each abstract quality defined to generate new definitions, and so on. Vauvenargues comments here, 'Observons néanmoins que la petitesse est la source d'un nombre incroyable de vices; de l'inconstance, de la légèreté, la vanité, l'envie, l'avarice, la bassesse, etc.' (pp. 110–11). The 'etc.' is revealing: Vauvenargues's attempt to collect and bind together maxims supposed already to exist explodes into an endless list of new maxims caught up in a search for ultimate elements at last beyond definition, and ready for reintegration into the Logos.

This already suggests that the apparent opposition between the tendency towards the plenitude of the Book and the tendency towards fragmentation is not rigorous. But if the drive to plenitude brings its own fragmentation, the totalizing capacity of the maxim is also threatened in a more humdrum fashion. In the 'Avertissement' to the *Réflexions et maximes*, Vauvenargues disingenuously suggests an essential limitation of the maxim as a form: 'Mais il n'y a personne qui ne sache que toutes les propositions générales ont leurs exceptions. Si on n'a point pris soin ici de les marquer, c'est parce que le genre d'écrire que l'on a choisi, ne le permet pas.'[62] The problem is made more acute by the fact that the first sentence here must presumably *itself* have its exceptions, and this (subsequently quite banal) paradox can only suggest a fundamental criticism of the maxim itself and the constraints which define it, and its dispersal, this time, towards the particularity of facts and events in their individual differences. This is where Chamfort enters the problematic, and complains about the falsity of over-generalization:

Les moralistes, ainsi que les philosophes qui ont fait des systèmes en physique ou en métaphysique, ont trop généralisé, ont trop multiplié les maximes. Que devient, par exemple, le mot de Tacite: *Neque mulier amissà pudicità, alia abnuerit*, après l'exemple de tant de femmes qu'une faiblesse n'a pas empêchées de pratiquer plusieurs vertus?[63]

24

4.2. Chamfort: the Fragment

Where Vauvenargues thought at least that he was moving towards a general systematization of moral truth, Chamfort is explicitly critical of such an enterprise. The pressure of this criticism is such that the text just quoted in part (although one 'collected' under the title 'Maximes et pensées') abandons sententiousness for the space of a sentence, and allows in both a proper name and a pronoun which would be excluded by the grammar of the maxim.[64] The fragment continues:

J'ai vu madame de L. . ., après une jeunesse peu différente de celle de Manon Lescaut, avoir, dans l'âge mûr, une passion digne d'Héloïse. Mais ces exemples sont d'une morale dangereuse à établir dans les livres. Il faut seulement les observer, afin de n'être pas dupe de la charlatanerie des moralistes.

The principle of this type of observation can of course itself be generalized, as in the following maxim: 'Dans les choses, tout est *affaires mêlées*; dans les hommes, tout est pièces de rapport. Au moral et au physique, tout est mixte. Rien n'est un, rien n'est pur' (No. 126, p. 77; the image of the *pièce rapportée* introduced here will be of some importance later). But a maxim such as this tends to accentuate the criticism of the form as such – and this is amply supported by the tendency in Chamfort's writing towards the anecdote or the 'caractère', towards minimal examples of narrative–descriptive texts, dominated by an implicit 'J'ai vu'.[65] In fact this tension does not prevent Chamfort from producing quite 'classical' maxims, but it tends to change their status somewhat, and to engage with a number of epistemological problems. This change in the status of the maxim is in fact announced in the first of 'Maximes Générales', which is worth quoting in full:

Les maximes, les axiomes, sont, ainsi que les abrégés, l'ouvrage des gens d'esprit, qui ont travaillé, ce semble, à l'usage des esprits médiocres ou paresseux. Le paresseux s'accommode d'une maxime qui le dispense de faire lui-même les observations qui ont mené l'auteur de la maxime au résultat dont il fait part à son lecteur. Le paresseux et l'homme médiocre se croient dispensés d'aller au-delà, et donnent à la maxime une généralité que l'auteur, à moins qu'il soit lui-même médiocre, ce qui arrive quelquefois, n'a pas prétendu lui donner. L'homme supérieur saisit tout d'un coup les ressemblances, les différences qui font que la maxime est plus ou moins applicable à tel ou tel cas, ou ne l'est point du tout. Il en est de cela comme de l'histoire naturelle, où le désir de simplifier a imaginé les classes et les divisions. Il a fallu avoir de l'esprit pour le faire. Car il a fallu rapprocher et observer des rapports. Mais le grand naturaliste, l'homme de génie voit que la nature prodigue des êtres individuellement différents, et voit l'insuffisance des divisions et des classes qui sont d'un si grand usage aux esprits médiocres ou paresseux; on peut les associer: c'est souvent la même chose, c'est souvent la cause et l'effet.

I do not here wish to take up the notion of the 'homme supérieur', although it could evidently be situated in a tradition,[66] except to note the change which this represents with respect to La Rochefoucauld's 'nous'. But the positioning of the maxim and axiom at the end of a process of induction is clearly of some importance. The maxim is no longer so much a starting-point as a result, the end of a narrative rather than its beginning. And the result is not final (even if it erases the traces of the narrative which produces it); it cannot be invoked dogmatically as absolute truth. No longer 'ramassée en soi', the maxim is always dependent on particular observations and has no particular epistemological privilege: it becomes a sort of heuristic shorthand. Questions of method and directions of narrative are involved here, and these are far from simple.[67] In the next chapter I shall examine some of the effects of this shift in pedagogical discourse as evidence of an 'enlightened' position; here I shall attempt to show how it can lead to a dramatization of the antagonism between sententiousness and narrative in some texts by Voltaire.

4.3. Hard Facts: Voltaire

The protagonists of *Memnon ou la sagesse humaine* (1749) are types of sentence. The *conte* opens with the positioning of a sententious proposition:

Memnon conçut un jour le projet insensé d'être parfaitement sage. Il n'y a guère d'hommes à qui cette folie n'ait quelquefois passé par la tête. Memnon se dit à lui-même: 'Pour être très sage, et par conséquent très heureux, il n'y a qu'à être sans passions; et rien n'est plus aisé, comme on sait'.[68]

This general maxim (which could easily be detached from its context and read in isolation) leads to three resolutions: Memnon decides not to be affected by women, to live in sobriety, and to retain his financial independence, thus avoiding the need to 'faire (sa) cour'. After the monologue in which this maxim and these resolutions are formulated, narrative sentences take over and challenge Memnon's pretensions. He attempts to help a damsel in distress, fails not to be affected by her beauty, and is forced to give up all his money to avoid death at the hands of a fictitious jealous uncle. The second resolution, that of sobriety, goes next, when Memnon is invited to dinner; here there is a simple juxtaposition of narrative and sententious propositions:

26

Un peu de vin pris modérément est un remède pour l'âme et le corps. C'est ainsi que pense le sage Memnon; et il s'enivre. On lui propose de jouer après le repas. Un jeu réglé avec des amis est un passe-temps honnête. Il joue; on lui gagne tout ce qu'il y a dans sa bourse, et quatre fois autant sur sa parole.
(p. 83)

There is of course, strictly speaking, nothing in the narrative propositions to invalidate the truth-claims of the preceding sententious propositions, but the narrative plays on a constitutive paralogism (the *post hoc ergo propter hoc*)[69] to discredit the general 'truth' of the maxim by means of the contingent events recounted.

The contingency and particularity of the event is intensified, as is typical in Voltaire, by the tendency of events to be of the order of catastrophes – events hurt, and here Memnon loses more than his money: 'l'un de ses amis intimes lui jette à la tête un cornet, et lui crève un oeil' (p. 83). A further catastrophe occurs, although this time its contingency is not reduced by any narrative 'logic': Memnon's debtor goes bankrupt, and this leads to the breaking of the final resolution – Memnon goes to court to plead his case, without success. The relentless and painful nature of events is condensed in a series of narrative propositions:

Memnon, ayant ainsi renoncé le matin aux femmes, aux excès de table, au jeu, à toute querelle, et surtout à la cour, avait été avant la nuit trompé et volé par une belle dame, s'était enivré, avait joué, avait eu une querelle, s'était fait crever un oeil, et avait été à la cour, où l'on s'était moqué de lui. (p. 84)

The 'easy' nature of wisdom seems to be thoroughly discredited, and the abstraction of the maxim proclaiming it made ridiculous by the concrete events.

It is of course in *Candide* that this antagonism of types of sentences is most brilliantly exploited. The immobile, sententious 'Tout est bien' is simply enough placed against the movement of events, of which the Lisbon earthquake is perhaps emblematic: 'La terre trembla à Lisbonne' would be perhaps the paradigmatic narrative proposition for Voltaire, and the absolutely punctual, arbitrary, accidental, and catastrophic nature of the event would be enough to cause philosophical *remous*.[70] Events seem stubbornly to resist being subsumed under Pangloss's generalization, and the humour of the story is often a result of the incongruous juxtaposition of sententious and narrative sentences: 'Tout est bien; soit, mais j'avoue qu'il est bien cruel d'avoir perdu mademoiselle Cunégonde et d'être mis à la broche par des Oreillons' (p. 173). The final practical prescription, 'Il faut cultiver notre jardin', is issued in opposition to a tendency to reduce the sum of the text's narrative propositions to any controlling and totalizing sentencious proposition.

This primacy of the event in Voltaire's *Contes* is, however, still contained by a certain narrative logic which requires sententiousness in order to operate. In *Memnon*, the parts of the text discussed so far are framed by the opening narrative discourse on the one hand, and by the intervention of the 'esprit céleste' on the other, in which the nature of the attack on sententiousness is made clearer. What the opening sentence describes as 'insensé' in Memnon's project is not 'sagesse' as such, but the 'parfaitement' which qualifies it, and it is this qualifier which is taken up by the 'esprit':

Il est vrai que tu seras toujours borgne; mais, à cela près, tu seras assez heureux, pourvu que tu ne fasses jamais le sot projet d'être parfaitement sage. – C'est donc une chose à laquelle il est impossible de parvenir? s'écria Memnon en soupirant. – Aussi impossible, lui répliqua l'autre, que d'être parfaitement habile, parfaitement fort, parfaitement puissant, parfaitement heureux. (p. 85)

We can read this attack on the 'parfaitement' as a summary of narrative's attack on sententiousness, which pretends to propose truths 'parfaitement' and exclusively, and in so doing leaves itself open to catastrophic refutation by particular narrative propositions. But the summary of this attack on sententiousness is itself sententious (Voltaire's *Contes* have a moral), and might be rewritten as 'Il est (parfaitement) impossible d'être parfaitement sage'. The authority for such a proposition is of course removed from the human subject and placed on a cosmic scale through the familar argument that 'Il faut que tout soit en sa place';[71] but even if the human 'philosophe' remains in ignorance, he can retain the pleasure of being sententious about it. The fact that Voltaire's attack on sententiousness produces sententiousness none the less can evidently be linked to the possibility at work in Vauvenargues and Chamfort, that of attacking sententiousness sententiously. This may seem to be a frivolous point, but in fact it involves a considerable problem in the eighteenth century (and for any attempt to discuss sententiousness 'in general'), one which I shall now attempt to link to certain philosophical anxieties about the status of language.

5. Sententiousness, Language, Knowledge

5.1. 'Universal Propositions'

This ambiguous critique of the maxim in Chamfort and Voltaire can be placed in the philosophical tradition of Locke's *Essay Concerning Human Understanding*.[72] Locke both admits a drive towards the production of general propositions,[73] and exhibits a good deal of reticence as to their epistemological value. This reticence is of course consistent with Locke's general theory of the acquisition of knowledge from necessarily *hic et nunc* sensations. The chapter of the *Essay* entitled 'Of Maxims' (IV, VII) denies this type of proposition all epistemological priority and reduces it, significantly, to pedagogical and rhetorical use.

The apparently simple nature of this position is complicated by the fact that, in this chapter, Locke assimilates 'Maxims' and 'Axioms' (as did Chamfort), and has in mind (unlike Chamfort) propositions of the type 'whatever is, is', or 'it is impossible for the same thing to be, and not to be':[74] in other words, logical principles, and not the type of generalizing proposition which I have been discussing. But elsewhere, Locke's work contains valuable indications for the notion of 'sententiousness'. The chapter immediately preceding 'Of Maxims', entitled 'Of Universal Propositions, their Truth and Certainty', is much more helpful. This chapter follows that dealing with 'Truth in general', which sets up the framework for the discussion.

For Locke, truth is a question of propositions. A proposition can be 'Mental' or 'Verbal', the first involving the 'joining or separating' of 'Ideas' (conceived of as the signs in the mind of, in simple cases, things which are outside the mind), the second the transcription in verbal signs of those ideas (IV, V, 3). In this transcription, the 'joining' and 'separating' of ideas become the 'affirming or denying words one of another' (IV, V, 6). True propositions are those in which this transcription conforms to the mental proposition transcribed. If, however, the mental proposition is not true with respect to the 'real world', then the truth involved in its transcription will be 'chimerical' or 'barely nominal', and the 'truth' involved, trivial:

Though our Words signifie nothing but our *Ideas*, yet being designed by them to signifie Things, the *Truth* they contain, when put into Propositions, will be only *Verbal*, when they stand for *Ideas* in the Mind, that have not an agreement with the reality of Things. And therefore Truth, as well as Knowledge, may well come under the distinction of *Verbal* and *Real*; that being only *verbal Truth*, wherein Terms are joined according to the agreement

29

or disagreement of the *Ideas* they stand for, without regarding whether our *Ideas* are such, as really have, or are capable of having an Existence in Nature.

(IV, V, 8)

This question is by no means simple for Locke and for other theorists of language of the time. Any theory based on the atomistic unity of individual elements ('ideas') has a difficult task in advancing from the level of those ideas in their isolation to a level at which they are placed in relationships with each other. For Locke and for classical language-theory in general, language 'begins' in a sort of infra-language which would simply be an indefinitely large collection of proper names, each attached to one such simple idea; but as Locke himself is aware, such a collection would not in fact constitute a language.[75] Language proper can only begin, for a theory of this type, with a drift from the propriety of such a collection, by comparing at least two ideas and being able to affirm their at least partial identity in a proposition of the type 'X is Y'. This simplest of affirmative propositions poses the problem on the one hand of the nouns here replaced by 'X' and 'Y', and on the other of the copula linking them.

The nouns can clearly no longer be absolutely proper names, for if this were the case no identity between them could be posited. The nouns involved, and the ideas they represent, have to be allowed to lose their propriety, and this occurs through a process of abstraction, thus making the names and ideas 'general': '*Ideas* become general, by separating from them the circumstances of Time, and Place, and any other *Ideas*, that may determine them to this or that particular existence' (III, III, 6). This immediately opens up an *écart* with respect to the atoms of experience, a gap which is at once the condition of possibility of language and the cause of its abuse. This is why theorists such as Du Marsais and Condillac are so concerned to provide genetic accounts which attempt to tie abstraction to the propriety of the proper name.[76]

The copula (and in classical language-theory verbs in general tend to be reduced to the single form 'est' by a process of rewriting which has its roots in Scholastic philosophy)[77] is the mark of affirmation, of the subject's ability to do things with his ideas, and thus again marks a certain separation from 'reality', which is the cause of some concern to Rousseau, for example.[78] On the other hand, the duality of this 'est', split between its copulative function and a tendency to assert the reality of the representations which it links,[79] introduces what is, for Locke and his followers, perhaps the major sin of the Scholastics, namely the 'realization' of abstractions, which is tirelessly denounced.[80]

But this 'est', with its dual function, is absolutely necessary to language, insofar as the process of abstraction, which seemed to make the proposition possible, can in fact be said to depend on an implied prior proposition: a 'general idea' can only be produced by the use of a proposition affirming the link of two proper names (which can thus always be said to be already improper).[81] It could, I think, be shown that this surreptitious priority of the proposition over the terms which it links ruins the coherence of classical theories of language and psychology by denying the very possibility of the isolated unity of the 'ideas' on which such theories rest.[82] It also implies that language is of more importance to 'perception' than classical philosophers (with the possible exception of Condillac) will admit.[83] This problem is nowhere more in evidence than in types of proposition involving the abstract terms habitually employed in maxims, in which the apparent difficulty of 'truth's' being anything *but* verbal determines Locke's problems.

This framework introduces the discussion of 'universal propositions', and, specifically, the following passage, which I shall consider in some detail:

Now because *we cannot be certain of the Truth of any general Proposition, unless we know the precise bounds and extent of the Species its terms stand for*, it is necessary we should know the Essence of each *Species*, which is that which constitutes and bounds it. This, in all simple *Ideas* and Modes, is not hard to do. For in these, the real and nominal Essence being the same; or which is all one, the abstract *Idea*, which the general Term stands for, being the sole Essence and Boundary, that is or can be supposed, of the *Species*, there can be no doubt, how far the *Species* extends, or what Things are comprehended under each Term: which, 'tis evident, are all, that have an exact conformity with the *Idea* it stands for, and no other. But in Substances, wherein a real Essence, distinct from the nominal, is supposed to constitute, determine, and bound the Species, the extent of the general Word is very uncertain: because not knowing this real Essence, we cannot know what is, or is not of that *Species*; and consequently what may, or may not with certainty be affirmed of it.   (IV, VI, 4)

The terms which require elucidation here are, on the one hand, simple ideas, modes, and substances, and, on the other, real and nominal essences. Simple ideas are the atoms of experience, beyond which the analysis of sensation and reflection cannot go, and the names of which cannot be defined (III, IV, 4). These simple ideas are, in Locke's account, received passively by the mind. The mind can also, however, be active, and by combining simple ideas in various ways, produce complex ideas, of which the two types that concern us here are 'modes'

31

and 'complex ideas of substances'. Insofar as simple ideas are received from 'reality', the names attached to them 'intimate some real Existence' (III, IV, 2), and this is also the case with the names of 'complex ideas of substances', in that the idea of substance, of which Locke is critical but which he cannot do without, implies a real referent of which the idea is the sign. Modes are either simple (i.e. produced by the combination of the same simple idea: thus the idea of 'a dozen' is the result of the combination of the idea of a unity (II, XII, 5)), or 'mixed', and it is this latter category which is of interest here. Mixed modes are combinations of simple ideas of different kinds, and here the mind is at its most active, and as far from 'real existence' as Locke will allow it to go. There is, Locke argues, no 'pattern' in nature for such complex ideas (whereas there is for complex ideas of substances), and their production (the selection of which simple ideas to put together) is therefore arbitrary (III, V, 2–3).[84] Names of mixed modes are words such as 'Justice', 'Adultery', 'Incest', 'Murther', and so on (Locke has a predilection for names of crimes, and the problem of mixed modes is often discussed with reference to problems of law, which is of some importance given later developments in this book;[85] but he also gives such examples as 'Beauty' and 'Gratitude'):

When we speak of *Justice*, or *Gratitude*, we frame to our selves no Imagination of any thing existing, which we would conceive; but our Thoughts terminate in the abstract *Ideas* of those Vertues, and look not farther; as they do, when we speak of a *Horse*, or Iron, whose specifick *Ideas* we consider not, as barely in the Mind, but as Things themselves, which afford the original Patterns of those *Ideas*.   (III, V, 12)

It is worth pointing out immediately that the abstract moral vocabulary current in maxims would be described by Locke in terms of mixed modes, and this would also be the case, in moral discourse, for a term such as 'Man' (see III, XI, 15–16).

The distinction between the 'real' and 'nominal' essence is now relatively simply explained. The 'real essence' can be linked to a total knowledge or circumscription – and in the case of substances, this is impossible. The real essence is an inaccessible substratum on which the observable properties of the substance are seen to depend. This would be something like the 'goldness' of gold, to use Locke's favourite example: the assumed support for the various properties of gold. The real essence is in a sense negatively determined as what escapes the nominal essence:

By this *real Essence*, I mean, that real constitution of any Thing, which is the foundation of all those Properties, that are combined in, and are constantly found to co-exist with the *nominal Essence*; that particular constitution, which every Thing has within it self, without any relation to any thing without it . . . Supposing the nominal Essence of *Gold*, to be Body of such a peculiar Colour and Weight, with Malleability and Fusibility, the real Essence is that Constitution of the parts of Matter, on which these Qualities, and their Union, depend. (III, IV, 6)

The real and nominal essences can be said to be the same in simple ideas and mixed modes because there is not this type of remainder or substratum: in the case of simple ideas, because the idea is just a given in its assumed elementarity and distinction; in the case of mixed modes, because the bundle of ideas made by the mind presupposes nothing more outside it.

This explains the different status of universal propositions concerning the names of substances and those of mixed modes. For the names and 'species' of substances are in fact determined by their 'obvious appearances' rather than their 'internal real Constitutions' (III, VI, 25), and this always leaves open a margin for the uncertain and the unknown. Here men are 'incurably ignorant' and as we do not 'really' know what a term such as 'Gold' stands for, we can be certain of no general proposition concerning it. Gold as such is always in excess or default, with respect to the limits which its name places on the simple ideas which enter into the complex idea designated by that name. This type of excess or default is not possible in the case of mixed modes, insofar as it is the mind which has decided exactly which simple ideas have gone into them. Only a more Platonic perspective, such as that adopted by Leibniz in the *Nouveaux Essais sur l'entendement humain*,[86] could reinstate the possibility of excess or default for the mixed mode.

It might be said that Locke fences rather unhappily with the problem of language throughout the *Essay*, and is constantly worried that it might take precedence over the notional purity of ideas. For Locke, things come first, ideas next, and language last, and any reversal of the direction of this model constitutes a perversion.[87] But in the theory of mixed modes language takes on a worrying importance, for what is to maintain the unity of the bundle of simple ideas involved if not the abstract noun? Locke does indeed have language intervene only at the last stage of the production of the mixed mode: 'Wherein the Mind does these three things: First, It chuses a certain number [of simple ideas]. Secondly, It gives them connexion, and makes them into one *Idea*. Thirdly, It ties them together by a Name' (III, V, 4), but the role of the noun is recognized to be vital to the maintenance of the unity of the mode, its 'essence':

It is the Name that seems to preserve these *Essences*, and give them their lasting duration. For the connexion between the loose parts of those complex *Ideas*, being made by the Mind, this union, which has no particular foundation in Nature, would cease again, were there not something that did, as it were, hold it together, and keep the parts from scattering. Though therefore it be the Mind that makes the Collection, 'tis the Name which is, as it were the Knot, that ties them fast together.   (III, V, 10)

And at other points Locke allows the name to come first (even in children's acquisition of these ideas), and relegates the previous genetic account to a notional 'beginning of Languages' (III, IV, 15). This repeats a much earlier suggestion that 'now that Languages are made, and abound with words standing for such Combinations, *an usual way of getting these complex* Ideas, *is by the explication of those terms that stand for them*' (II, XXII, 3). Such a priority of the word is something of a scandal for Locke's theory of language, and seems only too vulnerable to the general danger of psittacism which Locke, along with the other theorists of his age, elsewhere strongly condemns.[88] It could probably be shown by careful reading that this priority of words over things is a repressed undermining force in Locke's philosophy in general, beginning with the founding opposition between 'sensation' and 'reflection'.[89] For present purposes, it is enough simply to note the avowed priority of words in the description of mixed modes.

5.2. Definitions

Locke's general worry about words being used without being backed up by distinct ideas is faced, in the case of the mixed mode, with a danger and an opportunity. The danger is that such terms cannot be tied to reality in the way that the names of simple ideas can; the opportunity is that they are susceptible, unlike complex ideas of substances, to exhaustive definition, insofar as their real and nominal essences coincide. This possibility of definition brings us back to the type of proposition with which we are concerned here. Locke himself recognizes the particular relevance of these observations to 'moral words', and asserts, 'a *Definition is the only way, whereby the precise Meaning of moral Words can be known*; and yet a way, whereby their Meaning may be known *certainly*, and without leaving any room for any contest about it' (III, XI, 17). This position allows Locke to claim that morality could be 'demonstrated' in the same way as mathematics, and this again depends on the fact that here the 'precise real Essence of the Things moral Words stand for, may be perfectly

34

known' (III, XI, 16). Definitions will apparently simply untie the bundle of simple ideas, rather like one of the projects of the Academy of Lagado in *Gulliver's Travels.*[90]

All is, however, not so simple in this question of definitions, nor in the alleged coincidence of real and nominal essences, to which the problem is linked. Leibniz is worried by Locke's notion of a 'nominal essence', no doubt because it gives too much to language, and invokes the more traditional distinction between real and nominal *definitions*, certainly implied by Locke, but never clearly articulated.[91] This distinction is, however, the object of careful discussion in the so-called Port-Royal *Logique.*[92] I give three examples of sententious propositions taken from practitioners of the maxim as genre, against which the discussion can take place: 'La sincérité est une ouverture de coeur' (La Rochefoucauld, Maxim 62); 'La patience est l'art d'espérer' (Vauvenargues, 251); 'La conviction est la conscience de l'esprit' (Chamfort, 151). The question is that of knowing how such sentences can be situated with respect to the Port-Royal distinction.

For the Port-Royal logicians, nominal definition involves an implicit demonstration of the dominance of thought (ideas) over words, and is in a sense a radical statement of the 'arbitraire du signe'. The speaking subject is allowed to attach to his ideas whatever signs he likes, so long as he warns his interlocutor(s) of the departure from ordinary usage:

Car chaque son étant indifférent en soi-même & par sa nature apte à signifier toutes sortes d'idées, il m'est permis pour mon usage particulier, & pourvu que j'en avertisse les autres, de déterminer un son à signifier précisément une certaine chose, sans mélange d'aucune autre.   (p. 121)

That this type of argument can be placed in the perspective of a projected ideal language, and that it is aporetical, has been admirably shown by Louis Marin.[93] The important thing for the discussion here is that such definitions, being entirely arbitrary, cannot be contested and can be used as 'principles' for further propositions. The nominal definition is concerned only with the connection between my idea and what I choose to call it, and in no way implies that my idea represents anything real beyond itself.

The second type of definition, the 'définition de la chose', is quite different. Here the word and idea are left in their 'normal' relationship, and the definition implies a claim about reality, insofar as it suggests that other ideas are 'really' contained in that to be defined:

Dans la définition de la chose, comme peut-être celle-ci: *L'homme est un animal raisonnable: le temps est la mesure du mouvement*, on laisse au terme qu'on définit comme *homme* ou *temps* son idée ordinaire, dans laquelle on prétend que sont contenues d'autres idées. (p. 120)

Whereas the form of the nominal definition is 'I call X "Y"', that of the 'définition de la chose' is 'X is Y'. This type of definition is thus a proposition in the sense that its truth can be contested:

Les définitions des choses ne peuvent point du tout être prises pour principes, & sont de véritables propositions qui peuvent être niées par ceux qui y trouvent quelque obscurité, & par conséquent elles ont besoin d'être prouvées comme d'autres propositions, & ne doivent point être supposées, à moins qu'elles ne fussent claires d'elles-mêmes; comme des axiomes. (p. 122)

In terms of the Port-Royal distinctions, it would seem that the three examples quoted above must be 'définitions de choses', in as much as they are not simply statements as to how the author intends to use the term defined. On the other hand, transposing this distinction into Locke's terms, if the words involved are, as seems to be the case, names of mixed modes, then the definition must be nominal as well, insofar as such terms do not have real 'choses' as referents. It does not help very much to invoke a Platonic notion of the reality of even such ideas for Port-Royal, a more nominalist position for Locke, and to leave the matter at that. Rather, by playing the two models against each other, it is possible to advance a little in the description of sententiousness. What is needed here is a mediating category, and it is to be found in the notion of usage. This notion intervenes in the Port-Royal text and considerably reduces the euphoria implied in the first discussion of the nominal definition. Insofar as language is not a private affair (and in the logic both of Port-Royal and of Locke, the fact that thought can in principle do without signs emphasizes the primarily public character of language), but involves a community whose aim in using language is to communicate without confusion, then the pretensions of individuals to impose their idiosyncratic usage of terms is to be repressed. A certain respect is implied here, and this limits the subject's power over his language, which is no longer really his:

Il ne faut point changer les définitions déjà reçues, quand on n'a point sujet d'y trouver à redire . . . quand on est obligé de définir un mot, on doit autant que l'on peut s'accommoder à l'usage. (p. 126)[94]

And this respect for a language no longer that of the subject in isolation leads to a different type of definition, linked to a different kind of truth:

Mais comme les hommes ne sont maîtres que de leur langage, & non pas de celui des autres, chacun a bien droit de faire un dictionnaire pour soi, mais on n'a pas droit d'en faire pour les autres, ni d'expliquer leurs paroles par les significations particulières qu'on aura attaché aux mots. C'est pourquoi quand on n'a pas dessein de faire connoître simplement en quel sens on prend un mot, mais qu'on prétend expliquer celui auquel il est communément pris, les définitions qu'on en donne ne sont nullement arbitraires; mais elles sont liées & astreintes à représenter non la vérité des choses, mais la vérité de l'usage, et on les doit estimer fausses, si elles n'expriment pas véritablement cet usage.   (p. 129)

And turning back to Locke, who has no very clear discussion of the matter, it is possible to find traces of an awareness that individuals cannot be considered to be entirely free in their naming and defining of mixed modes (III, VI, 44–5); indeed this is already strongly implied in the fact, noted earlier, that Locke's examples of mixed modes often involve questions of law. Possibly one could defend Locke's assertion that mixed modes do have a 'real' essence by invoking this indirect consideration of their practical (social, ethical, political) effectiveness.[95]

On the other hand, it seems clear that *none* of the various types of definitions discussed provides an adequate description of our three examples. The oblique awareness that the subject is in practice alienated in a language which is that of the Other rather than his own can help, however, and it seems possible to situate the definition-maxims *between* real and nominal definitions on the one hand, and, on the other, *between* a nominal definition of *personal* usage (for the attributive signature marks at least a pretension to leave a trace on the language) and a definition of *social* usage. The maxim, in this form, becomes a product neither of pure solipsism nor of subservience to social pressure, but becomes something like an *event*, an attempt to play a 'move' in a language-game displaced (following a suggestion of Lyotard's) from considerations of communication to those of an *agonistics*.[96]

5.3. Rhetoric and Meta-language

This will become clearer if I now give the full maxim from La Rochefoucauld of which the sentence quoted above is only a part:

La sincérité est une ouverture de coeur. On la trouve en fort peu de gens; et celle qu'on voit d'ordinaire n'est qu'une fine dissimulation pour attirer la confiance des autres.

The maxim at once defines usage and attacks it. The analysis of 'sincérité' produces two contradictory components, both of which might be described in terms of 'définition de la chose', once that 'chose' is seen as social: both types of sincerity exist, are observable, in complementary distribution. Both sentences might also be considered to reflect 'la vérité de l'usage', if we allow that within the mixed mode, social practice has prised open again the identity of real and nominal essences, and used the one to conceal the other (see Locke, III, XI, 9).

Finally, it might be tempting to suggest that a nominal definition is at work here too, insofar as one of the justifications for such definitions is the clarification of ambiguity (see *Logique*, p. 126). This is not the case, however. La Rochefoucauld is not simply attempting to clarify usage, and 'sincérité' really does mean *both* 'une ouverture de coeur' *and* 'une fine dissimulation', if we assume that language is always already taken up by social usage; it is not clear that the 'real' meaning of sincerity is that first given, nor that the term can henceforth be understood to mean 'une fine dissimulation'. Rather there is a play between these two definitions.

The space of this play, which is characteristic of paradoxal sententious propositions, is complex. On the one hand it is the space opened by words which can no longer be relied on to communicate transparently, and is thus the space in which meta-language can be situated. Locke and the Port-Royal authors both write meta-languages which are made possible, necessary and insufficient by this gap, which they vainly try to patch over. I have suggested that, in terms of classical language theory, once language has progressed beyond the level of an infinite list of proper names (which would not in fact constitute a language), this gap is inevitably opened by the process of abstraction which allows for the formulation of propositions. This gap allows meta-language to lay down the law about language: in a sense La Rochefoucauld's maxims of the type 'Ce qu'on appelle X n'est que Y' are doing just this. On the other hand, this gap is also one of *rhetoric*, which depends on the possibility of non-propriety in order to function.[97] The social 'perversion' of language is a rhetoric. But then, so is the maxim, and this is what in the end distinguishes the maxim as a *literary* genre.[98] La Rochefoucauld's maxim is a meta-lingual condemnation of social rhetoric, and a rhetorical challenge to meta-lingual domination. This duality, which is constitutive of La Rochefoucauld as moralist disapproving of social practice and discourse and simultaneously as advocate of social play,[99] opens up the problem of sententiousness beyond the epistemological questions addressed by Locke, for this socio-rhetorical dimension of language (which inhabits language originally, and is not an accident which befalls some notional 'pure' pre-rhetorical language), means that it is impossible to 'know the precise bounds and extent of the Species its Terms stand for', and therefore attain certainty of the truth of its general propositions. Locke cannot help the enquiry further at this point, as for him rhetoric is simply the ruin of Truth and Knowledge:

> 'Tis evident how much men love to deceive, and be deceived, since Rhetorick, that powerful instrument of Error and Deceit, has its established Professors, is publicly taught, and has always been in great Reputation: And, I doubt not, but it will be thought great boldness, if not brutality in me, to have said this much against it. *Eloquence*, like the fair Sex, has too prevailing Beauties in it, to suffer it self ever to be spoken against. And 'tis in vain to find fault with those Arts of Deceiving wherein Men find pleasure to be Deceived.
>
> (III, X, 34)

6. Sententiousness in the Text: Rhetoric

This much is enough to suggest that it will be as well to turn now from philosophy to rhetoric for help in the characterization of sententiousness. It may be said immediately that this move to rhetoric does not necessarily imply that truth has been abandoned and 'play' adopted: books on rhetoric reduplicate within themselves the split between meta-language and rhetoric located above. The meta-language of Rhetoric (which I distinguish by capitalizing the first letter) is concerned not so much to give free rein to the rhetorical in language as to control it in the interests of truth. Insofar as eloquence recognizes the pragmatics of language, it must take account of its addressee's potential resistance to truth.[100] Far from presenting itself as an 'instrument of Error and Deceit', Rhetoric defends its service of truth. This position is admirably argued by Bernard Lamy:

> Si les hommes aimoient la vérité, il suffiroit de la leur proposer d'une manière vive & sensible pour les persuader; mais ils la haïssent, parce qu'elle ne s'accorde que rarement avec leurs intérêts, & qu'elle n'éclate que pour faire paroître leurs crimes; ils fuyent donc son éclat, & ferment les yeux de crainte de l'appercevoir. Ils étouffent cet amour naturel que nous avons pour elle . . . L'éloquence ne seroit donc pas la maîtresse des coeurs, & elle y trouveroit une forte résistance, si elle ne les attaquoit par d'autres armes que celles de la vérité.[101]

Within this framework, sententiousness will no longer claim an epistemological value, but a persuasive one. Further, Rhetoric will not attempt to treat maxims and so on as a genre (although this is not reason enough to claim that Rhetoric somehow 'missed' the maxim),[102] but as an element to be included in a broader discourse. This inclusion tends to split sententiousness, or to consider it at two different levels: as we shall see, insofar as rhetorical argumentation is based on the *enthymeme*, sentientiousness is *essential* to Rhetoric. But as Rhetoric drifts from its forensic origins and becomes increasingly concerned with *elocutio*, then sententious propositions become largely stylistic elements. On the one hand, they are linked to the persuasive *force* of the discourse, and on the other, to its *elegance*.

6.1. Aristotle: Persuasion and the Doxa

Aristotle discusses the maxim (*gnomè*) in the context of two forms he considers to be 'common to all kinds of oratory', namely the Example and the Enthymeme.[103] The maxim is immediately removed from the type of self-sufficiency which I have accorded it so far, in that Aristotle states that it is 'part of an enthymeme' (1393a), the enthymeme being not a syllogism in which not all the steps are made explicit (as it seems to be most often after Quintilian),[104] but a type of syllogism depending on premises which are probable rather than true (1355a). Aristotle defines the maxim as follows:

It is a statement; not about a particular fact, such as the character of Iphicrates, but of a general kind; nor is it about any and every subject – e.g. 'straight is the contrary of curved' is not a maxim – but only about questions of practical conduct to be chosen or avoided.   (1394a)

This type of statement is at once part of the rhetorical argument and apparently separable from it. Earlier Aristotle has said that the maxim is part of the enthymeme, here he nuances that affirmation: 'It is . . . roughly true that the premises or conclusions of Enthymemes, *considered apart from the rest of the argument*, are Maxims' (1394a, my emphasis). Later this tension will be neutralized in a description of the best type of maxims, those which 'have the essential character of Enthymemes, but are not stated as part of Enthymemes; these latter are reckoned the best; they are those in which the reason for the view expressed is simply implied' (1394b).

Further, Aristotle considers the working opposition I have suggested between 'doxal' and 'paradoxal' sententiousness, but thinks of this in terms of supplements (*epilogoi*):

Proof is needed where the statement is paradoxical or disputable; no supplement is wanted where the statement contains nothing paradoxical, either because the view expressed is already a known truth . . . this being the general opinion: or because, as soon as the view is stated, it is clear at a glance.   (1394b)

The 'known truth' is indeed a 'truth' derived from the doxa, and this is an advantage to the orator, who can thus exploit without proof that which is taken to be the case: 'just because they are commonplace, every one seems to agree with them, and therefore they are taken for truth' (1395a). On the other hand, the paradoxal maxim will achieve a greater 'effect'.

But the two major advantages of the maxim to the orator are to be linked to the enunciation of the statement rather than to its content. On the one hand, the use of the maxim can display a certain virtuosity in the orator: 'One great advantage of Maxims to a speaker is due to the want of intelligence in his hearers, who love to hear him succeed in expressing as a universal truth the opinions they hold themselves about particular cases' (1395b). On the other, and this is more important here, the maxim is linked to the *ethos* of rhetoric:

There is another [advantage] which is more important – [using maxims] invests a speech with moral character. There is moral character in every speech in which a moral purpose is conspicuous: and maxims do always produce this effect, because the utterance of them amounts to a general declaration of moral principles: so that, if the maxims are sound they display the speaker as a man of sound moral character.   (1395b)

Filtered through the tradition of Horatian poetics, it is this 'moral purpose' which will become the 'précepte' dear to theorists of the novel in the eighteenth century. But this moral aspect also raises the question of the ambivalence of sententiousness with respect to the descriptive/prescriptive opposition,[105] and this becomes clearer in the examples which Aristotle gives. On the one hand, maxims can be descriptive or constative, as in the examples 'There is no man in all things prosperous' and 'There is no man among us all is free' (both of which might require a supplement, viz., 'for all are slaves of money or of chance' (1394a–b)). On the other, we have a modalized prescription, 'Never should any man whose wits are sound/ Have his sons taught more wisdom than their fellows' (which can also be – descriptively – supplemented, viz., 'It makes them idle; and therewith they earn/ Ill-will and jealousy throughout the city' (1394a)).

Clearly the second example can the more easily be linked to the notion of the maxim as concerning 'questions of practical conduct to be chosen or avoided'. There is an implied prescription here, which can be rewritten as '(O, men whose wits are sound) do not have your sons taught more wisdom than their fellows', and the supplement explains the ground for the prescription. On the other hand, there is also an implied definition: 'Men whose wits are sound are those men who (among other things) do not have their sons taught more wisdom than their fellows'. If you *do* have your sons taught more wisdom than their fellows, on the one hand they will suffer, and on the other you will not, after all, be a man of sound wits. The orator indeed makes a

41

statement of his 'moral principles' (implying something like 'choose men whose wits are sound'), but in so doing lays down the law about that category of men.

Shifting levels, it seems possible to assert that a further implication of any maxim is something like 'I am a man whose wits are sound', no longer because of what I do with my sons, but because I have formulated a maxim: as we have seen, this gives the orator a certain authority with respect to (less intelligent) listeners. But it also becomes clear why the use of the maxim might be less recommendable if the listeners *are* intelligent: insofar as it is not purely prescriptive, its truth can be contested by the listeners. The definition of the 'man whose wits are sound' might be challenged, for example, and if the challenge were successful, then not only would the maxim no longer be a 'sound' one, but insofar as the orator has, in formulating it, displayed his own 'moral principles', then the attempt to persuade those listeners of his 'sound' character will be a failure. This possibility of successful disagreement with a maxim suggests that the maxim is trying to exploit a formal authority,[106] which is no real guarantee of the speaker's character. This is why Aristotle introduces a further external limitation on their use: 'The use of Maxims is appropriate only to elderly men, and in handling subjects in which the speaker is experienced' (1395a).[107]

However, the 'successful' challenge, insofar as Rhetoric deals with persuasion rather than demonstration (1354a), involves the challenger in the same risk of claiming an authority (as subject of the enunciation) which his utterance might not support.[108] This risk seems to be endless, and this is why the maxim comes to be tied to the doxa. Insofar as the maxim is not rigorously demonstrable, it can only be established as 'sound' by a consensus within a community of speakers and hearers. The 'sound' maxim is prefaced by an implicit 'We (can) all agree that . . .', and only this can consecrate the 'law' which it lays down. This type of consensus brings us back to the notion of a closure, a field within which the maxim can be recognized. This field is at once that of *verisimilitude* and that of a political space. In both cases the problem of the 'first person plural' reappears, insofar as the consensual nature of the maxim implies a *collective* rather than an individual subject of the enunciation. Although the authority of the speaker is established by the consensus of the doxa, his *individuality* is denied by that same consensus; the maxim is spoken by a 'we' and no longer by an 'I'.

On the other hand, the possibility of the paradoxal maxim suggests that the consensus and the closure are not quite so secure and total;

and this is one reason for the possibility of rhetorical argument and of a displacement of the doxa. If this is the case, it is because of a property of the doxa which, after Flaubert, we might call its *stupidity*.[109] This stupidity has nothing to do with the content of the maxims allowed by the consensual subject of the doxa (this would be the position of Chamfort and his 'homme supérieur', for example),[110] but with the structural fact that the doxa consistently and docilely reintegrates paradoxal maxims, and tolerates contradiction while seeming to condemn it: two contradictory maxims are accepted so long as they are not produced by the same speaker in the same context. This feature of the doxa allows Aristotle to suggest that it is easy to argue for *or* against the value of confessions made as a result of torture (1376a), insofar as the aim of the speech is merely to exploit the possibilities of a doxa (and not to establish them), to a particular end – the decision (see 1377b). Similarly, he proposes two possible sententious propositions on the notion of the pleasant: 'To do the same thing often is pleasant, since, as we saw, anything habitual is pleasant. And to change is also pleasant: change means an approach to nature, whereas invariable repetition of anything causes the excessive prolongation of a settled condition' (1371a). This possibility of exploiting 'stupidity' is generalizable at a meta-level: just as the doxa can be said to *contain* the paradoxa, so rhetoric can be said to contain what is apparently outside it. Towards the end of his text, Aristotle advises, 'if you have no enthymemes, fall back upon moral discourse: after all, it is more fitting for a good man to display himself as an honest fellow than as a subtle reasoner' (1418a–b). The implication here is that the most effective form of rhetoric may be an absence of rhetoric (Aristotle does not of course invent this idea: see for example the play that 'Socrates' makes around it in the opening words of Plato's *Apology*); but of course Aristotle states this as a maxim, which could be used in an enthymeme and formalized in terms of rhetorical rules.

This structure can easily be transferred to the problem of verisimilitude, which expands effortlessly to include its contrary, as the *Poetics* points out (1456a). The eighteenth-century novel is able to exploit this structure: the *invraisemblable* becomes the most *vraisemblable*, and often, by implication, 'vrai'.[111] I shall look more closely at this question of the *vraisemblable* in chapter 3; here I want to stress an important structural paradox of the maxim, namely its ability to denounce itself. It is perfectly possible to formulate a maxim of the type 'All maxims are stupid', thus in fact reinforcing the claims of the form.[112] This is the general form of the problem we have already briefly encountered with logical positivism and the empiricism of Locke and Chamfort. It also clarifies the difficulty involved in the juxtaposition in novels of sententious propositions with the narrative–descriptive complex, which cannot fail to resist the totalizing tendency of sententiousness through its particular 'propositions' and 'dispositions', and yet which is subservient to sententiousness in terms of the question of verisimilitude.

6.2. Quintilian: Standing Out

If Aristotle can thus be used to support the idea that sententiousness is necessary to the exercise of rhetoric and to the existence of a doxa, the problem of the formal independence and isolation of sententious propositions remains, and this is the object of concern to later rhetoricians, as the emphasis tends increasingly to be placed on *elocutio*.[113] The relative self-sufficiency of the sententious proposition (producing the necessarily fragmented texts of La Rochefoucauld, Vauvenargues and Chamfort) poses a problem for rhetoric, insofar as it is concerned to produce a continuous text. These problems are addressed by Quintilian in a passage which can be read as a sort of intertextual matrix for subsequent discussions, and which is worth quoting at length:

Rhetoricians are divided in their opinion on this subject: some devote practically all their efforts to the elaboration of *reflexions* (*sententiae*), while others condemn their employment altogether. I cannot agree entirely with either view. If they are crowded too thick together, such *reflexions* merely stand in each other's way, just as in the case of crops and the fruits of trees lack of room to grow results in a stunted development. Again in pictures a definite outline is needed to throw objects into relief (*nec pictura, in qua nihil circumlitum est, eminet*), and consequently artists who include a number of objects of the same design separate them by intervals sufficient to prevent one casting a shadow on the other. Further, this form of display breaks up our speeches into a number of detached sentences; every *reflexion* is isolated, and consequently a fresh start is necessary after each. This produces a discontinuous style, since our language is not composed of a system of limbs, but of a series of fragments: for your nicely rounded and polished phrases are incapable of cohesion. Further, the colour, though bright enough, has no unity, but consists of a number of variegated splashes. A purple stripe appropriately applied lends brilliance to a dress, but a dress decorated with a quantity of patches can never be becoming to anybody (*ita certe neminem intertexta notis vestis*). Wherefore, although these ornaments may seem to stand out with a certain glitter of their own (*licet haec et nitere et aliquatenus videantur*), they are rather to be compared to sparks flashing through the smoke than to the actual brilliance of flame: they are, in fact, invisible when the language is of uniform splendour, just as the stars are invisible in the light of day. And where eloquence seeks to secure elevation by frequent small efforts, it merely produces an uneven and broken surface which fails to win the admiration due to outstanding objects and lacks the charm that may be found in a smooth surface (*quae crebris parvisque conatibus se attollunt, inaequalia tantum et velut confragosa nec admirationem consequuntur eminentium et planorum gratiam perdunt*). To this must be added the fact that those who devote themselves solely to the production of *reflexions* cannot avoid giving utterance to many that are trivial, flat or foolish. For their mere number will so embarrass their author that selection will be impossible . . . Against these persons, on the other hand, must be set those who shun and dread all ornament that is not plain, humble and effortless, with the result that by their reluctance to climb for fear of falling they succeed merely in maintaining a perpetual flatness. What sin is there in a good epigram (*sententia*)? Does it not help our case, or move the judge, or commend the speaker to his audience? . . . For my own part I regard these particular ornaments of oratory to be, as it were, the eyes of eloquence (*Ego vero haec lumina orationis velut oculos quosdam esse eloquentiae credo*). On the other hand, I should not like to see the whole body full of eyes, for fear that it might cripple the functions of the other members, and, if I had no alternative, I should prefer the rudeness of ancient eloquence to the license of the moderns. But a middle course is open to us here no less than in the refinements of dress and mode of life, where there is a certain tasteful elegance that offends no one.[114]

Here *sententiae* are given a rich figural description as crops in a field, fruit on a tree, objects depicted in a painting, fragments or limbs of a body, stripes or patches on a dress, sparks in a smoky fire, stars in the sky, elevated regions of an otherwise flat surface, and eyes in the body. Briefly, sententiousness *stands out*, literally (high points with respect to a surrounding plain) or figurally (the apparent relief of the picture, or the standing out of light in darkness: the *sententia* is an element of *brilliance*) – at a meta-level of the literal and figural, as these are figures of figures. This is the source of its value and the reason for the difficulty of its integration into discourse. If the separation of *sententia* and discourse is *total* (Quintilian describes the *sententia* as 'detached sentences', 'incapable of cohesion', 'nicely rounded and polished' wholes in themselves), then their use is a problem. If the separation is *partial* (*sententiae* are *in* the picture from which they stand out, sparks *in* the smoke, stripes *on* the dress, eyes *in* the body), then there is a place for sententiousness, and the problem of its integration is less serious.

6.3. Lamy: the Patch

These figures of the *sententia* are figures of figures, insofar as the *sententia* is itself a figure of discourse. The 'sentence' appears in the list of figures in, for example, Bernard Lamy's *Rhétorique*. A definition in the 'ne . . . que' style of La Rochefoucauld affirms that 'Les sentences ne sont que des réflexions que l'on fait sur une chose qui surprend, et qui mérite d'être considérée' (p. 161). But the situation of the *sentence* as a figure among others cannot be so simple, insofar as it has an important privilege with respect to the general classical desire to subordinate language to 'things': Lamy refers to *sentences* as 'ces expressions ingénieuses, qui renferment en peu de paroles de grands sens, ou qui disent plus de choses que de paroles' (p. 161).[115] This privilege of the *sentence* allows it to characterize a style, the sublime, much later in the text:

Le stile sublime demande aussi des réflexions sérieuses, des sentences; c'est-à-dire, des manières de s'exprimer ingénieuses, courtes, vives, qui par un tour non commun excitent l'attention. (p. 322)

But if the *sentence* has a privilege among figures, it is also the site of a danger attendant on all figures. For Lamy, figures are the mark in language of the passions, of desire (see p. 119); the fact that men in general are affected by passions and desires is the ground of rhetoric's necessity and efficacity, but only insofar as the orator exploits figures *against* the passions of which they are the mark. The only passion allowed to the orator (who, insofar as he is a man, is necessarily passionate), is the passion for the truth; but this easily becomes inflected into the desire to *appear* eloquent, the moment the love of truth turns round on the orator and becomes *amour-propre*.[116] Lamy thematizes this danger by distinguishing between 'natural' and 'artificial' ornaments, and by suggesting that these latter can degenerate into 'false' ornaments. Natural ornaments are the flowers of discourse, which bear witness to the natural healthiness and fecundity of the plant bearing them;[117] but those orators who are not naturally fecund (whose figures do not appear as an immediate effect of their unreflected desire for truth) betray the nature of rhetoric through the displacement of desire towards *amour-propre*: 'La fécondité est une marque de grandeur; l'ardeur qu'ils ont de paroître féconds, fait qu'ils étouffent leurs pensées par une trop grande abondance de paroles' (p. 353). This is evidently particularly reprehensible in the case of the *sentence*, in which the excess should be that of things over words. The false fecundity of the bad orator produces too many *sentences*, with results similar to those noted by Quintilian:

Les sentences trop fréquentes troublent aussi l'uniformité du stile. Par sentences on entend ces pensées relevées qu'on exprime d'une manière concise, ce qui leur fait donner le nom de pointes. Je ne parle point de ces sentences puériles et fausses qui ne contiennent rien d'extraordinaire & de particulier qu'un tour forcé, & qui n'est point naturel. Les plus belles, si elles sont placées trop près-à-près, s'étouffent, & rendent le stile raboteux: & comme elles sont détachées du reste du discours, on peut dire d'un stile qui est chargé de ces pointes, qu'il est hérissé d'épines. Ces pensées détachées sont comme des pièces cousues & rapportées, qui étant d'une couleur différente du reste de l'étoffe, font une bizarrerie ridicule; ce qu'il faut éviter avec grand soin; *Curandum est ne sententiae emineant extra corpus orationis expressae, sed intexto vestibus colore niteant.* On aime à parsemer ses ouvrages de sentences, parce qu'on croit qu'on passera pour un homme d'esprit.

(p. 355)

This is a very dense piece of writing. Although this passage is quoted from the chapter entitled 'Des faux ornements' (Livre IV, Chapter 19), the play involved between the natural, the artificial and the false is not simple: Lamy makes it clear that he is *not* talking about 'bad' *sentences*, which are 'unnatural' in a simple sense of not respecting the economy of 'words' and 'things' which, as we have seen, distinguishes the *sentence*. The object of the critique is not the orator's ability to formulate *sentences* individually, for even the most beautiful examples are subject to the defect in question (the sense of the fourth sentence of the passage is evidently 'même les plus belles'). These are the *best sentences*, if we can derive this positive value from the double negative of their not being not natural. This defect is not due to the intrinsic quality of the *sentence*, but to the fact which troubled Quintilian, here noted laconically in the subordinate clause, 'comme elles sont détachées du reste du discours'. Within Lamy's text, this means that good, healthy *sentences* can degenerate into the class of 'faux ornements', because of their relationship, or lack of relationship, with the rest of (the) discourse. This 'devenir-faux' of the *sentence* troubles the distribution of the values 'natural', 'artificial' and 'false', in that *sentences* can thus be both natural (or, at least, not not natural), and false. This paradoxical status is mediated through the first of Lamy's metaphorical series, in the progress from 'flowers' to 'thorns'. The flowers are not stifled (nor are they protected) by the thorns: rather they stifle themselves and become thorns, which are evidently scarcely signs of fecundity and health – thorns are rather a sort of *degré zéro* of nature. On the other hand, thorns are not entirely

47

easily made analogous with 'that which is detached', and the induction 'comme elles sont détachées . . . on peut dire . . . qu'il est hérissé d'épines' is thus difficult to justify fully, and returns to the difficulty in Quintilian with partial and total separation.

This difficulty is more in evidence in the second part of the passage. In the second series of metaphors, the discourse is no longer grounded in nature (as field, orchard, plant etc.), but has become the result of a technical activity, that of weaving (as in Quintilian's dress metaphor):[118] the discourse has become a cloth (see p. 54: 'le discours n'est qu'un tissu de plusieurs propositions'),[119] and the *sentence* a *patch*. It seems difficult to imagine how a patch could ever be a sign of 'fecundity', and the shift from one metaphorical series to the other also implies that the problem with sententiousness is no longer one of *quantity* (where before it was because of an overabundance, a sort of overblown fecundity, that the flowers stifled),[120] but of *quality*. All *sentences* are patches of a different colour from the rest of the discourse, and the problem no longer involves limiting their number, but joining on the patch. Quintilian allowed the odd 'stripe' to be tacked on to the dress of discourse, but the logic of Lamy's metaphorics would seem to exclude even this. Or perhaps a neat job of sewing the patch on (or in) can make it the centre of attention? All of this is condensed and complicated in the unassigned quotation,[121] which constitutes a *mise-en-abyme* of the problems raised by Lamy's description. This sentence is 'rapportée' in that it is a quotation, and of a different 'colour' from the rest of the text in that it is in Latin and printed in italics. The first part of the sentence also imports a metaphor not used by Lamy in his passage, that of the text-as-body, from which the *sentence* should not stand out or protrude; the faint air of priapic obscenity, generated by the fact that this metaphor in fact condenses two of those in Quintilian, that of the text-as-body (in which case the *sententia* was an eye or, precisely, a member), and that of the text as a flat surface (whence the 'literal' notion of standing out) should probably not be neglected. The second part of Petronius's precept connects with Lamy's cloth-series (and see the 'intertexta' in Quintilian), but also returns to Quintilian for the light-image in the verb 'nitere'. The whole of Petronius's sentence involves a compromise between the two aspects of 'standing out' noted in Quintilian: the *sentence* must not stand out in the 'literal' sense, but should stand out 'figurally' as light. The *sentence* must be outstanding but should not stand out.

Further, if the object of tacking the patch of sententiousness on to the cloth of discourse is to let the former shine, then the patch is no longer something to hide, but something to show off. The logic here is that the less the *sentence* protrudes, the better it gleams. Thus the lack of an attribution for the quotation (not the case when it appears in the near-contemporary texts of Le Bossu and Corbinelli, where, however, it is printed in the margin)[122] might be read as a mark of Lamy's desire to 'incorporate' the patch as seamlessly as possible into his own discourse (to *appropriate* it),[123] but it can also be read as a desire to allow this 'pièce rapportée' to shine out the better for its new setting.

I have privileged Lamy's text for the analysis of the logic of the patch because of its exceptional richness, but that logic is not idiosyncratic, as can be judged from this passage from Crévier's *Rhétorique française*:

Les sentences sont un grand ornement dans le discours . . . [Elles] ont pourtant un inconvénient: c'est qu'elles décousent le style, & en altèrent la liaison. Chaque sentence fait un tout, & comme un corps à part, qui arrête la marche du discours . . . Mais il est un art de les enchâsser dans un raisonnement, dans une narration, de manière que, sans rien perdre de leur substance, elles entrent dans le tissu du discours, & ne soient point mises en saillie. (II, pp. 247–8)

All of these texts of Rhetoric seem to consider the patch as an ornament which is a threat to the unity of the cloth on or into which it is to be sewn as seamlessly as possible, against which it has yet to shine. We might of course suspect that the presence of a patch on a cloth is a sign that it is there to patch something, that it both hides and reveals a hole or a tear: a patch might normally be read as a sign of the poverty of the cloth supporting it or supported by it. If this is the case, then the *sentence* would no longer be a secondary, decorative adjunct to the discourse in which it appears, added to something already whole, but a necessary supplement, filling in a gap or a lack, holding the cloth together. This is where the discussion of sententiousness as an element of style becomes inseparable from its role as an essential (if possibly implied) component of the enthymeme, and the logic of the patch maintains this ambivalence neatly. It also allows the reformulation of the dangers of the *sentence* as seen by the rhetoricians: the first is an intrinsic and qualitative danger, namely that the patch *inevitably* disturbs the homogeneity of the cloth. The second is contingent and quantitative: if too many patches are added or inserted, then it will become difficult to recognize the 'original' cloth, to 'follow the thread' of the discourse,[124] and eventually there will come a point at which any homogeneity is lost and the cloth becomes a patchwork. In a patchwork there *is* no 'original' cloth: the patches hide nothing, are both purely 'for show', and at the same time the only constituents of the cloth, and this is why Crévier is able to say that 'Des pensées détachées peuvent faire un livre: elles ne feront jamais un discours' (I, p. 413), and why books of rhetoric do not consider sententiousness in terms of genre, but as a problematic element of a now heterogeneous text. Insofar as sententiousness has become in this discussion a *supplement* to discourse (in the double sense of the term exploited by Jacques Derrida),[125] then it is perhaps possible to describe it as the text's difference from itself.

7. Strategies for Integration

The formal incompatibility of sententious propositions and the narrative–descriptive complex remains a problem, then; it is something of an embarrassment to rhetoricians, and, as we shall see, to poeticians. Two strategies emerge here in the attempt to retain the prestige and authority of sententiousness while diminishing its tendency to break up discourse and to insist on its self-sufficiency: the first of these strategies is that of *marginalization*, pushing sententious propositions to the beginning and/or the end of a discourse. The second involves disguising sententiousness, or making it go 'underground', where it can work surreptitiously. The first strategy attempts to turn the patch into a border, to prevent the cloth fraying at the edges: the second is harder to represent – perhaps it involves putting the patch on the back of the cloth, or weaving it in rather than sewing it on.

7.1. *Epiphonème*

The figure immediately following the *sentence* in Lamy's list (and immediately preceding it in Crévier's) is the 'épiphonème', which is 'une exclamation qui contient quelque sentence ou grand sens que l'on place à la fin d'un discours' (p. 162). Crévier similarly describes the *épiphonème* as a final summarizing *sentence*: 'Il est le fruit de la réflexion: & souvent il ramasse en une expression grave & sentencieuse tout le suc & tout l'esprit d'une suite de propositions, qui avoient été traitées avec étendue'.[126] This placing of a *sentence* at the end of a discourse is also a negative implication of the passage from Quintilian, insofar as a 'fresh start is necessary after each' (VIII, V, 27). The *sentence* concludes (this feature also supports the earlier invocation of Flaubert and stupidity).[127] But if it concludes, it can also open, prepare the ground for the discourse. Lamy accords sententiousness an important place in the *exorde* too: 'La principale chose que doit faire un Orateur dans l'exorde, c'est de prévenir d'abord ses Auditeurs de quelque maxime claire, évidente, qui les frappe, d'où il puisse conclure dans la suite ce qu'il veut prouver' (p. 420). Sententiousness concludes, but also prepares for conclusion. The danger of heterogeneity is still present, if the brilliance of this opening merely shows up the poverty of the discursive cloth to come, as suggested by Gibert: 'Après cet Exorde il faut que le Discours se soutienne & qu'il ne soit pas comme un drap d'or cousu à une étoffe d'une médiocre valeur' (Gibert, p. 406). But a certain solidarity between beginning and end of the discourse can be established by the use of this 'frame' of sententiousness, a solidarity suggested by Lamy when he writes, 'l'Exorde devroit être la dernière chose dans le projet, quoique le premier dans le discours' (p. 421). By coming thus first *and* last, sententiousness adopts a position at the frontiers of discourse, guarding its most vulnerable points, containing particularities and allowing them to communicate with the 'outside' of a recognized truth. This liminal position has a long history: Paul Zumthor, for example, in an article to which I have already referred, but whose title, 'L'Epiphonème proverbial', now seems the more significant, refers to a fourteenth-century precept to the effect that sermons should begin and end on the same biblical text.[128] In a minimal form of the juxtaposition of narrative and sententious propositions, such as the fable, the text will usually begin and/or end with a maxim, as Crévier points out (Crévier, II, p. 244). In a later chapter I shall examine the fable more closely from this point of view, in the light of Rousseau's reading of La Fontaine. La Bruyère can also provide examples of this minimal structure,[129] and the *Caractères de Théophraste* are generally constructed on the model of an opening definition and its narrative exemplification.

This marginal position of sententiousness can also be discovered in prose fiction, in different forms: thus Perrault regularly ends his *Contes* with a 'moralité' (written, however, in verse, and italicized), and the prefaces of novels can become the place for stating the maxims illustrated by the text to come, as in Robert Chasles's *Les Illustres Françoises*.[130] The preface (in general) shares the curious position of the *exorde* as described by Lamy, coming first and last, repeating in advance of a text what that text will already have stated.[131] Chasles is concerned to list what his various narratives 'font voir', and in so doing produces maxims, and when he states: 'Mon roman ou mes histoires, comme on voudra les appeler, tendent à une morale plus naturelle, & plus chrétienne, puisque par des faits certains, on y voit établi une partie du commerce de la vie',[132] this is less a defence of some notion of narrative or descriptive 'realism' than of a certain moral possibility of linking narrative 'facts' and maxims.

7.2. Disguise: d'Aubignac and Le Bossu

The second strategy, in which the sententious proposition is 'disguised', can be exemplified in the theoretical writings of the seventeenth-century poeticians d'Aubignac and Le Bossu. D'Aubignac is of course writing about the theatre, and thus a certain amount of care must be taken in reading his text from the point of view of narrative; but as he tends to oppose maxims to 'action', which it seems possible to associate with the narrative component of novels, his remarks are relevant to our problematic.[133] Moreover, d'Aubignac asserts proudly that he is the first author to deal with the problem in poetics (p. 288), and he does this in a chapter entitled 'Du discours didactique, ou instructions', which he identifies with 'ces Maximes & ces propositions générales qui renferment des vérités communes, & qui ne tiennent à l'Action Théâtrale que par application & par conséquence' (p. 288). Here then is the familiar separation, and it is strong enough to lead to a first movement in which d'Aubignac seems to condemn the use of maxims altogether: they are cold, cerebral, and leave the soul unmoved (pp. 289–90). But d'Aubignac goes on to admit that the theatre should 'instruire' as much as 'plaire', and has grudgingly to re-admit sententiousness in some form. Maxims should be subordinated to *examples*; or else, mysteriously, they should be maintained as the 'nerfs' and the 'plus vives couleurs' of the play (p. 294). Maxims can be disguised by the use of *apparently* particularizing propositions (p. 295), and by the use of figures (and especially figures of syntax (p. 297)). Where maxims *do* remain overt, then the playwright must simply be a genius, like Corneille, at which point theory gives way to the untheorizable:

Ce n'est pas qu'on ne puisse mettre sur le Théâtre des propositions universelles déduites au long, & même en style Didactique: Nous en avons des exemples assez fréquens chez Monsieur Corneille; mais pour en recevoir des applaudissemens comme lui, il faut que les expressions en soient fortes, les vers éclatans, & qu'elles semblent n'avoir jamais été dites que pour le sujet particulier où elles sont appliquées; ce qui demande beaucoup d'étude et beaucoup de génie.   (p. 297)

But d'Aubignac's argument establishes a continuity between 'surface' manifestations of sententiousness and its more concealed forms, which become central to the problem. I shall suggest that this continuity can be transferred to the problem of 'sententiousness and the novel' by turning to a text which can mediate between theatre and novels, Le Bossu's *Traité du poème épique* (1675).[134] Le Bossu's argument in his chapters entitled 'Des Sentences' and 'Des Sentences Déguisées' (Livre VI, Chapters 4 and 5) is by now familiar: too many *sentences* make the poem too dogmatic, they are cold, they bore the spectator, and so on. Although writing about the epic, Le Bossu here invokes the bad example of Senecan tragedy.[135] His remedies are also similar to d'Aubignac's, although he points to the possibility (in Latin rather than in French) of producing sentences which are sententious in isolation but which have a particular diegetical reference in context (pp. 222–3). The ambivalence of the maxim as a surface and depth phenomenon is partially addressed in that Le Bossu suggests that such forms cannot simply be identified with the 'utile' side of the poem, but also belong to the 'agréable': 'Les Sentences rendent donc les Poèmes utiles; & de plus, elles ont je ne sais quel éclat qui plaît' (p. 213). It is this *éclat* which explains the reprehensible drive to fill the text with sententious formulations, but it also suggests, rather as in Lamy, an essential contamination of the *sentence* by the *pointe*, in which formal brilliance takes over from moral content. This is evidently to be condemned, and in the following chapter (Livre VI, Chapter VI), Le Bossu suggests that *pointes* be simply cut out altogether: here he locates them purely on the side of the 'agréable', as opposed to the *sentence* proper which is here replaced purely on the side of the *utile*. As so often in classical theory, Seneca and the Italians (Ariosto, Tasso) are the examples of this type of excessive formal brilliance.[136]

But in the logic of Le Bossu's discussion, it is not clear how any *sentence* could be said to be free of this type of formal contamination: the 'je ne sais quel éclat qui plaît' is *always* an excess. The problem, a version of the classical guilty excess of signifier over signified (and it will be remembered what trouble Locke had with this excess in terms of his mixed modes), is that it is difficult to see how a maxim can be other than a formal, linguistic unit. This means that where Le Bossu can optimistically define the *sentence* as 'une instruction morale exprimée en peu de mots' (p. 213), thus emphasizing the priority of the instruction over its expression, we have to prefer the definition he gives a little earlier, of the second sense of the Latin *sententia*: 'un discours de peu de mots, qui contient un sentiment utile pour la conduite de la vie', which gives priority to the discourse.[137]

But this is the least interesting part of Le Bossu's theory of sententiousness. Much earlier in his text, it has become clear that in some sense the whole theory of the epic poem is here based on a theory of sententiousness, mediated through a theory of the *fable*. For according to Le Bossu, the epic poem is simply the fictional expansion of a single maxim, and the opening chapters of his book constitute at once a discovery-procedure for extracting this maxim from epics, and a recipe for the construction of a poem from such a maxim. This theoretical model allows Le Bossu to derive master-maxims from the *Iliad* ('Que la mésintelligence des Princes, ruine leurs propres Etats' (p. 46)), the *Odyssey* ('Que l'absence d'une personne hors de chez soi, ou qui n'a point l'oeil à ce qui s'y fait, y cause de grands désordres' (p. 67)), and from the *Aeneid* ('le Ciel ne manque jamais de prendre sous sa protection les Héros qu'il choisit pour l'exécution de ses grands desseins' (p. 71)).

We have come a long way from the opening impression of the antagonism of sententiousness and the narrative–descriptive complex. Gérard Genette, whose poetics of narrative is in many ways close to that suggested by the opening comments of Jean Ricardou, suggests that the *Odyssey* can be read as an expansion of the kernel-sentence, 'Ulysse rentre à Ithaque'.[138] This is not only a narrative sentence, but also a fictional one (it will be remembered that Frege also used Ulysses as an example):[139] Le Bossu's kernel-sentence is sententious and pretends to be true and useful; his model is a rigorous formalist elaboration of the basic classical subordination of the *agréable* to the *utile*. The priority of this truth-component is made clear in Le Bossu's account of the 'fable' formed of the union of truth and fiction:

La Vérité est cachée; c'est le point de Morale que l'Auteur veut enseigner . . . La fiction est l'action, ou les paroles dont on couvre ces instructions . . . La première chose par où l'on doit commencer pour faire une Fable, est de choisir l'instruction & le point de Morale qui doit lui servir de fond, selon le dessin & la fin que l'on se propose . . . Cette maxime que je choisis, est le point de Morale & la vérité qui sert de fond à la Fable que je veux faire.

(pp. 35–7)

It is only once the fable has been formed in this way that the author looks for proper names with which to particularize it. Whereas Genette's model begins with the absolute particularity of the proper name, Le Bossu's only ends up with it. Fiction is sternly grounded in truth and particularities in generalities.

Le Bossu's use of the term 'fable' is also torn between surface and depth: on the one hand it is clearly a sort of matrix for the development of the fiction, but on the other, he insists that he is using the term in the same sense as it is used to describe Aesop's texts, and attempts to show this by substituting for the proper names of the *Iliad* designations such as 'dogs', 'sheep' and 'wolf', and arguing that the fable is the 'same' in both cases.[140] The argument here may be confused, but it does suggest the need to modify, or refine, the idea that the problems raised by the relationship between narrative–descriptive sentences and sententious propositions can be examined simply in terms of the surface structure of 'types of sentence'. Le Bossu's generative poetics implies that something like a deep structure must also be taken into account. This opposition between 'surface' and 'depth' is not a version of that between 'form' and 'content', insofar as the 'deeper' levels are also formal. What Le Bossu places as the kernel of texts is not some vague notion of content but a form, the sententious proposition.[141] This type of sentence may indeed appear on the surface of the text (with the attendant dangers which I have analysed), but is also to be taken into account even in cases where there is no 'sententious proposition' in the surface structure at all. The sententious patch or border is thus displaced into the centre of the text or into the weave of the cloth of discourse, and its extraction can no longer be simple.

8. Anthologies

The idea that sententious propositions *can* simply be extracted has however dominated the few attempts that have been made to address the problems posed by their presence in texts. The tendency to lift maxims from texts obeys the sententious proposition's claim to universality, and tries to rescue the eternal from the contingent, to recuperate the 'reste' left at the bottom of Marmontel's crucible. Thus, for example, writing of Crébillon *fils*, Octave Uzanne writes revealingly, 'En tirant du fatras de ses oeuvres complètes les maximes qui s'y trouvent enfouies, on arriverait, non sans étonnement, à constituer un bagage de moraliste très digne de la postérité'.[142] And writing about the same author, Aldous Huxley suggests that 'it would be possible to compile out of the works of Crébillon a whole collection of . . . aphorisms', and proceeds to detach a few examples 'which will deserve to find a place in this anthology of psychological wisdom'.[143]

8.1. Diamonds and Nails

And anthologies really are compiled, of course. The notion seen at work in Lamy returns here: anthologies *concentrate* thought in a small space, they retain the (quint)essential.[144] Thus an anthology of French writers defends in its introduction the possibility of

55

formulating timeless truths about 'Man', and announces that the book offers 'un maximum de substance dans un minimum de lignes'.[145] An impression of the formal 'hardness' of the maxim gives rise to recurrent metaphors of jewellery and treasure:[146] an anthology of maxims is a hoard of jewels or pearls or coins. Thus *A Treasury of English Aphorisms*, which adds to the jewel-like brilliance of maxims ('these scintillations of thought') the metaphor of the hoard of treasure ('In these but half-explored depths we may find – I believe we shall find – a great richness of forgotten treasures'), and the notion that the aphorism is a detachable unit of the economy of wisdom ('[the aphorist's] coins, if they are to be added to the currency of thought, must be minted of the most precious metal').[147] The ambivalence of the maxim returns in these metaphors: it has at once an attractive surface brilliance, but is also made of a substance of the highest value.

At this point it is tempting to make an excursion into psychoanalysis and characterize the drive to anthologize as a manifestation of repressed anality: the precious metal of the maxim is easily enough identified with the faeces, a 'reste' detached from the body. The 'orderliness' of the anthology can also be linked to Freud's description of anal eroticism. Further, my earlier remark about Petronius introduces a phallic element, which can also be accounted for in terms of the chain linking gold and faeces.[148] And the introduction of this phallic element can help to motivate the second metaphorical string habitually used in discussions of sententiousness, linked with violence: the maxim can have, as we have seen, a 'pointe',[149] and it can also be said to be 'striking', to have a 'force de frappe'. Diderot, for example, can liken maxims to 'des clous aigus qui enfoncent la vérité dans notre souvenir'.[150] The two metaphorical series can be linked through the French verb 'frapper': 'Les pensées et les maximes . . . sont autant de médailles frappées à l'usage des hommes'.[151]

8.2. The Rest (II)

Maxims in texts are thus substantial and excessive, the best of the text and the rest of the text, a surplus:

Outre le fond des choses qui y est d'une force & d'une beauté peu commune, on trouve encore je ne sçai quel accessoire, peut-être étranger à tout le reste, & auquel véritablement on n'avait pas droit de s'attendre; c'est un surcroît de richesses, une sur-abondance de biens, dont on se trouve comblé au-delà de ses espérances.[152]

Maxims overflow the text, from which they fall in a disorder the anthologist will rarely respect: maxims in anthologies are usually grouped under headings, 'eternal' truths under 'eternal' rubrics, such as 'Man', 'Love', 'La Vie', 'Le Bonheur', and so on. The anthology has an encyclopedic vocation, and attempts to realize Vauvenargues's dream. 'Ce serait rendre un grand service à la littérature, que de donner au public l'esprit, les maximes & les pensées de nos grands Ecrivains: cette collection deviendroit une espèce d'Encyclopédie.'[153]

Anthologies gather up and monumentalize inscriptions now made lapidary: 'the rest' in peace. Jacques Derrida:

Il y a du reste, toujours, qui se recoupent, deux fonctions.

L'une assure, garde, assimile, intériorise, idéalise, relève la chute dans le monument. La chute s'y maintient, embaume et momifie, monu-mémorise, s'y nomme – tombe. Donc, mais comme chute, s'y érige.

L'autre – laisse tomber le reste. Risquant de revenir au même.[154]

8.3. Detaching the Maxim

But insofar as anthologists want to claim that the fragments which they gather are more than a superficial decoration of the text, they are usually prepared to exercise a certain violence to extract the maxims. We have seen that the logic of the discussion of maxims, at least from Quintilian, involves an ambivalent attachment of the maxim to its surroundings, and the anthologist has sometimes to intervene actively in order to make total a separation that was only partial:

Il y a un grand nombre de pensées qu'il a suffi de transcrire mot pour mot: mais il y en a un plus grand nombre qu'il a fallu détacher des circonstances particulières auxquelles elles étaient liées, pour leur donner un certain tour de généralité qui leur étoit nécessaire.[155]

This work of detachment can be more or less great, depending on how concealed the sententious 'essence' is: Corbinelli's 'reduction' of Livy, for example, involves quite a transformation of the original text, as the text's 'avertissement' points out:

en lisant les Historiens il s'est avisé de remarquer les Maximes qui y sont repandües, & de tourner mesme en Maximes certains Passages qui n'ont rien que d'historique: c'est-à-dire, si j'ose m'exprimer de la sorte, qu'il a mis ces Passages à l'alambic; & que chaque Maxime françoise est comme l'essence & l'esprit du Passage latin qui la suit.

For example, Corbinelli 'derives' the maxim 'On perd plustost le souvenir des bienfaits, que des injures' from the following sentence from Book 8 of Livy: 'Injuriae Samnitium, quam beneficii Romanorum memoria praesentior erat' (Corbinelli, p. 147). The important point is that this type of rewriting is carried out in the interests of the anthology: what counts for the anthologizing reading is the result rather than the operation and its implications. Modern critics have proceeded in similar if less drastic fashion: thus a large part of Silverblatt's book on Duclos (pp. 105–51) is occupied by a supposedly exhaustive anthology of the maxims 'in' Duclos's novels, and the discussion deals either with the internal form of the maxims considered as one genre inserted into another, or with the notion that maxims express ethical choices (of the characters, for example). Similarly, Margot Kruse's book on La Rochefoucauld and his 'Nachfolger' has a chapter on Crébillon *fils*, where it is assumed that maxims can be lifted out of their context (this possibility, indeed, being seen as a defining quality of the presupposed 'genre' studied).[156] In a thesis on the maxims in Retz's *Mémoires*, Monique Bilezikian pays more attention to context, and her assertions bear witness, in the play between a 'pourtant' and a 'néanmoins', to the tension which I have noted between the maxim as essential and the maxim as excessive and detachable:

la plupart des maximes ne sont pas nettement détachées de la phrase narrative; au contraire elles tendent à être incorporées dans la narration même, tributaires logiquement sinon grammaticalement des segments syntaxiques qui précèdent ou qui suivent: *pourtant* dans l'ensemble, comme le montre l'édition des maximes du chapitre IV, elles peuvent être relevées et classifiées par rubriques. *Néanmoins* l'incorporation de la maxime dans le discours narratif nécessite une étude du rôle de la maxime d'après la position qu'elle occupe.[157]

Bilezikian goes on to make some brief remarks about these problems of insertion, arguing for example that maxims prepare or impose an action, register and/or generalize an action, or stand as proof of the correct or erroneous nature of a decision (pp. 161–2). But in general she is more interested in the role of maxims in Retz's (detextualized) life than in his text, and she soon proceeds to a description of the internal structure of the maxim, thus again conceived as essentially separable.

8.4. Rewriting

The anthologizing reading, then, can be said to regard the problem of the imbrication of sententiousness with the narrative–descriptive complex as no more than a provisional obstacle to the extraction of a 'well-formed' maxim, and thus unites the two gestures described by Derrida, in that it saves the maxim which 'falls' from the text as a *reste*, and in so doing 'laisse tomber le reste'. It is not easy to escape from the logic of this type of procedure; but it seems necessary to attempt to escape, in that whether sententiousness or narrative–descriptive elements are retained as essential, the bar of a binary opposition remains, and untheorized appeals to 'incorporation' cannot seriously question the status of that bar. To begin such a questioning, it is now necessary to look at some examples of different types of 'incorporation'. I take these examples from Crébillon *fils*'s *Les Egarements du coeur et de l'esprit*, in preparation for the closer analysis of that text in Chapter 3.[158]

1. On s'attache moins à la femme qui touche le plus, qu'à celle qu'on croit le plus facilement toucher; j'étais dans ce cas autant que personne: je voulais aimer mais je n'aimais point. (p. 14)

2. On imagine quelquefois que c'est une preuve d'amour, que de perdre le respect, et c'est la plus mauvaise façon de penser qu'il y ait au monde: je ne dis pas qu'on ne doive naturellement attendre une récompense de ses soins. (p. 67)

The first of these examples is taken from the narrative discourse of the novel, the second from a dialogue. This alternative for the positioning of maxims (more complicated than that between 'author' and 'character') is evidently a basic contextual complication for anthologizing readings, and I shall deal with the problems which it raises later. The following examples will be taken indifferently from narrative and dialogue. In these first examples, the formal separability of the maxim is reduced only minimally by the fact that the maxim does not form a typographically isolated sentence – no anthologizer would have any scruples about extracting such examples and printing them as whole sentences.[159]

3. Incertaine de la façon dont je prendais le ton sur lequel elle me parlerait, elle n'osait en hasarder aucun. Celui de l'amour ne séduit qu'autant qu'il est employé sur quelqu'un qui aime, et devient ridicule partout où il n'attendrit pas. (p. 120)

This type is familiar from the Chamfort example quoted above, and involves the anaphoric 'celui', which would have to be rewritten as 'Le ton' in order to produce a separable maxim.

4. J'ignorais entre beaucoup d'autres choses que le sentiment ne fût dans le monde qu'un sujet de conversation. (p. 18)

In a sentence such as this, rewriting would require the deletion of the introductory 'j'ignorais que', and therefore would have to change the mood and tense of the verb, to produce 'Le sentiment *n'est* dans le monde . . .' This is already more complicated for the anthology, and the 'loss' involved in the transcription is considerable.

5. Pensez-vous donc, me demanda-t-elle, qu'il suffise d'être aimé pour être heureux, et qu'une passion mutuelle ne soit pas le comble du malheur, lorsque tout s'oppose à sa félicité? (p. 115)

Here the maxim is still further from the surface of the text, and can be produced only by the erasure of the rhetorical question, giving, 'Il ne suffit pas d'être aimé pour être heureux . . .' I am not sure how many anthologizers would be prepared to operate such a transformation. On the other hand, all the transformations so far are grammatical in a fairly simple sense, and any references beyond the unit assumed to 'contain' the maxim easily explained by the immediate context.

6. À l'âge que j'avais alors, le préjugé ne tient pas contre l'occasion.
(p. 81)

This introduces a more complicated class of transformations, involving what I would call *intradiegetical reference*. This means that the sentence can be transformed into a maxim only with reference to information *specific to the text and made explicit by the text*. The maxim 'Quand on a dix-sept ans, le préjugé . . .' (or possibly 'Quand on est adolescent . . .' etc.) requires the information given about Meilcour's age in the opening sentence of the novel, sixty-seven pages earlier.

7. Pour peu qu'on estime les gens, on ne dit point ces choses-là tout haut.
(p. 133)

This is a more complex version of the same type: the 'ces choses-là' requires intradiegetical reference in that it refers in the first instance to Mme de Senanges's previous comment on the possibility of Meilcour's being in love with Mme de Lursay. But the plural complicates matters, and suggests the existence of a whole class of such indiscreet remarks to be avoided, and it is not immediately clear how many of these can be said to be specified within the text. Clearly no anthologizer could retain this type of sentence, despite its manifest sententiousness, because of the practical impossibility of rewriting it adequately as a maxim. Further, the fact that the class of 'ces choses-là' seems to exceed the sum of information provided by this novel makes of this example a bridge between 'intradiegetical' and its corollary, *extradiegetical* reference.

8. . . . elle me paraissait si digne d'être aimée, que je ne pouvais penser que Germeuil, ni qui que ce fût au monde, pût la voir avec indifférence.

(p. 35)

The type of grammatical transformation suggested above might produce here a sententious statement such as 'Quelqu'un qui est si digne d'être aimé ne peut être vu avec indifférence'. But the 'si digne' also gestures in the first instance towards a description of Hortense, and thus requires, to be 'filled up', intradiegetical reference to such a passage. Here we find,

9. Qu'on se figure tout ce que la beauté la plus régulière a de plus noble, tout ce que les grâces ont de plus séduisant, en un mot, tout ce que la jeunesse peut répandre de fraîcheur et d'éclat; à peine pourra-t-on se faire une idée de la personne que je voudrais dépeindre. (p. 33)

Here the reference is clearly diverted beyond the text, into the extradiegetical, which can in principle provide sententious statements specifying the qualities here invoked, and dispersing any apparent autonomy of the text into the type of intertext described by Barthes as 'codes culturels'.[160] I shall argue later that it is this type of reference which grounds the text as *vraisemblable*.

Evidently no anthologizing reading would recognize ('remark') such passages as maxims. Turning to Silverblatt's analysis of Duclos's *Les Confessions du comte de* ***,[161] it is clear that she consistently fails to remark and extract this type of sententiousness: references to 'cette aisance et cette liberté que l'on trouve rarement dans un ordre inférieur' (p. 201), or to 'tout ce que l'égarement de l'amour malheureux inspire' (p. 205), are not included in her list. Even cases where the implied sententious statement is more clearly marked, as in a reference to '[les] ridicules que pouvait lui donner un amour qui, par la disproportion de nos âges, pouvait être regardé comme une folie' (p. 202), are ignored. A consideration of such examples would add to Silverblatt's list of 109 maxims in the novel at least a further seventy passages which must be considered to be sententious, and which in most cases would require little rewriting to produce maxims.

8.5. Force

The point here, however, is not at all to count examples and score points (evidently Silverblatt has missed some examples which her own criteria – however inexplicit those criteria remain – would 'count', and my list of seventy further examples is no doubt incomplete too), but to suggest that sententiousness cannot be cut up in this way, and that its presence in texts cannot so easily be quantified. Anthologizers simply stop rewriting at an arbitrary point. If the preceding analyses suggest that the text 'in' which sententiousness is found becomes dispersed in an intertext of which sententiousness is a significant trace, they also suggest that sententiousness 'itself' is dispersed throughout narratives. The idea that sententiousness can be constituted as a 'genre' which happens sometimes to be inserted into another 'genre' becomes untenable. Sententiousness becomes no longer so much a 'type of sentence' as a *force* in texts, of which the type of examples 'remarked' by anthologies are only the spectacular surface manifestation. This force is not some irrational or metaphysical entity assumed to be at work in texts, but a force of law. If the 'overt' forms of sententiousness lay down the law, the more concealed types briefly indicated above draw their force from a law laid down, or exploit that law surreptitiously. If a novel 'proposes' events and actions and 'disposes' objects and characters, it also *imposes* law through its sententious force.

Once we allow sententiousness to retreat from its obvious surface manifestations in this way, then the problem of 'types of sentences' becomes rather a problem of 'types of presuppositions', or perhaps, in the technical sense suggested by Oswald Ducrot, of types of *sous-entendu*.[162] And with the help of this notion it becomes possible to subvert the opposition which seemed so clear-cut at the outset, between the narrative–descriptive complex and sententiousness, and to reinscribe the notion of sententiousness to involve its apparent other. *All narrative is sententious* insofar as it lays down a certain law, even if it nowhere states that law, and even if that law is in accordance with the reader's desire. This point is made in a polemical context by Jean-François Lyotard:

Le récit est une figure de discours qui emprunte sa forme au mythe et au conte, et . . . a comme eux pour fonction de distribuer les 'données' en une succession toujours édifiante, d'en tirer une 'morale'; de la sorte le récit accomplit toujours le désir; et d'abord, par sa forme même, le désir que la temporalité soit sensée et l'histoire signifiable.[163]

This general laying down of the law of narrative can itself be figured *en abyme* in narratives: I would suggest that a maxim such as Prévost's Des Grieux's 'C'est quelque chose d'admirable que la manière dont la Providence enchaîne les événements' be read as an inscription of this law,[164] and that Jacques's famous references to what is 'écrit là-haut' on the 'grand rouleau'[165] be read against the intertext of narrative à la Prévost (generally lampooned in *Jacques le fataliste*, of course), and as addressing a problem of *narrative* and its laws rather than, or as a prior condition of, a 'philosophical' problematic of, for example, 'fatalism'. In Diderot's radical practice, 'events' in novels both follow and outplay a law which has become undecidably that of chance or necessity, of teleology or of the *après coup*.[166]

On the other hand, if this 'deepest' of sententious statements in novels can indeed be sententiously generalized, a lot goes on in the process of that generalization, as much in the object-text as in the critical meta-language which attempts to perform that generalization. And in that process, narrative and sententiousness can indeed be conflictual, as we saw in the case of *Memnon*. This conflict between sententiousness and narrative, and its apparent resolution, will be the object of Part II, which focusses on the pragmatic 'scene of education' implied by sententiousness, in the context of eighteenth-century 'worldliness'. At this point the power of sententiousness to lay down the law (of narrative, for example) will appear to have become dominant, and the 'truth' of that law to have mastered any threat from fiction. Part III will move on again, and attempt to show that this apparent dominance of the law is not so simple, but is vulnerable to effects of fiction and simulacrum in Rousseau and in Sade. The effect of this analysis will be to move beyond the sententious claim just made (that all narrative is sententious), and to destabilize sententiousness's pretensions to immobility and eternality in the name of fiction, writing and textuality. The law is a text, and will not lie down where it is laid.

Part II
THE SCENE OF EDUCATION

2

SENTENTIOUSNESS AND EDUCATION

1. Worldliness

The 'worldliness' of the worldly novel involves a notion of closure.[1] The 'monde' of high society maintains its existence by drawing limits which separate it from what it is not. Within those limits, complicated rules of conduct and of discourse define 'worldly' behaviour. Up to a point, *le monde* can be thought of as a closed system, a self-regulating homeostat.

Up to a point only, however; no system is absolutely closed and self-sufficient: some input is required if it is to maintain itself.[2] In the case of *le monde* as written in worldly novels, this input is provided simply by the coming of age of the children of the aristocracy, and the 'coming of age' here implies a crossing of one of the frontiers (*clôtures*, fences) defining the space of worldliness. Thus the opening sentence of Crébillon *fils*'s *Les Egarements du coeur et de l'esprit* reads simply, 'J'entrai dans le monde à dix-sept ans' (p. 17):[3] this is where the book and social existence start. But the new member of high society is not immediately in command of the rules governing the discourse of worldliness, and has to be 'educated' – and indeed the account of this education forms the whole novel. Similarly, Duclos's *Confessions du comte de ****, and the *Mémoires pour servir à l'histoire des moeurs du XVIIIe siècle* (1751), begin with the entry into society and a 'scene of education'. This education is a double one, involving simultaneously a training in the rules of speech and action *within* the worldly affair, and in the production of discourse *around* that affair.

In the *Egarements*, Meilcour appears to come into existence only upon entry into *le monde*; but his pre-social existence is hinted at by a reference to his 'éducation modeste' (p. 13). If entry into high society is marked by a scene of education, then what has gone before high society (which I shall refer to as the *pré-monde*) is also a scene of education. Duclos is more explicit on this point in the *Confessions*:

Etant destiné par ma naissance à vivre à la Cour, j'ai été élevé comme tous mes pareils, c'est-à-dire fort mal. Dans mon enfance, on me donna un précepteur

67

pour m'enseigner le latin, qu'il ne m'apprit pas; quelques années après, on me remit entre les mains d'un gouverneur pour m'instruire de l'usage du monde qu'il ignorait. (p. 200)[4]

Worldly education takes place against an 'official' pedagogy which it denounces as inadequate. This is also the case in Louvet's *Faublas*, at the beginning of which the eponymous hero arrives in Paris and is given a ridiculous and ineffectual *gouverneur* (p. 422). Faublas rapidly frees himself from the constraints of this representative of official education, and is soon in bed with a marquise, who takes over the role of instructor: 'Elle aida ma timide inexpérience . . . Je reçus avec autant d'étonnement que de plaisir une charmante leçon que je répétai plus d'une fois' (p. 436). The language of education is tirelessly repeated in the same contexts, with reference to the marquise who has 'formé' Faublas, and later with Faublas himself as teacher (pp. 629, 662, 738, 808, 837–8, 861, etc.). We might suspect that *le monde*, in its fictional representations, perverts the education preceding it: this is of course especially the case in *Les Liaisons dangereuses*, with countless references to the notions of 'former', 'éducation', and to Cécile as an 'élève' or 'pupille'.[5] It will be remembered that Valmont takes that perversion far enough to compose 'une espèce de catéchisme de débauche, à l'usage de [s]on écolière' (Ibid., p. 261). And Sade's *La Philosophie dans le boudoir* (1795), subtitled 'Les Instituteurs immoraux', will take this tendency still further.

Worldly novels, then, exclude official pedagogy from *le monde*: it is situated on the other side of the *clôture*. And yet worldly education is parasitic upon that *pré-monde* too, insofar as it borrows and parodies its vocabulary, and receives from it the subjects of its own counter-pedagogy. The worldly novel can be said to take its revenge on the discourse of official pedagogy, and in this chapter I shall discuss why this should be. The discussion involves a consideration of sententious-ness as implying a 'scene of education', and the relationship of sententiousness with the fictional status of the novels in which it appears. In order to approach the problems at stake here, I shall first look at sententiousness from the *other* side of the worldly *clôture*, the *pré-monde* of official pedagogy, occupied largely with the attempt to establish its *own* closure through the rejection or neutralization of *le monde* and its fictions.

1.1. A Minimal Fiction of a Minimal Pedagogy

The title of *Les Egarements* might, in its commonplace appeal to the opposition between 'l'esprit' and 'le coeur', be read against an enormously influential work by Rollin, which came to be known as the *Traité des études*, and the original title of which is *De la manière d'enseigner et d'étudier les belles lettres, par rapport à l'esprit et au coeur* (1726–8).[6] Although Rollin is concerned to reform the educational practice inherited from the seventeenth century, his work remains in the tradition of a conception of pedagogy which did not hesitate to make use of the sententious force of the pedagogical 'scene'. This tradition is specifically, in Rollin's case, that of the Université de Paris, the same university which in 1624, according to Georges Snyders, 'obtenait du Parlement un édit défendant "à toute personne, à peine de vie, de tenir ni enseigner aucune maxime contre les anciens auteurs et approuvés"'.[7] Rollin himself refers to a more recent *arrêt* of the Parlement (27 June 1703):

Le Parlement, qui veille à l'observation des Statuts de l'Université, dans un Règlement général qu'il a fait pour l'un de ses Collèges, enjoint au Principal de tenir la main à ce que *les Ecoliers ne passent jamais un jour sans apprendre par mémoire une ou deux maximes de l'Ecriture Sainte, suivant l'esprit des Statuts de la faculté des Arts.* (Rollin, I, pp. liv–lv)

This simple transmission of authorized maxims, to be learned by a pupil who passively registers and undergoes that authority of the sententious form, is my fictional minimal education, a sort of *degré zéro* of pedagogy. Although it is unlikely that education ever simply realized this minimal form, which reduces the pupil to the status of a parrot or a machine, my appeal to it as a paradigm of the scene of education is not without historical justification. Jean de Viguerie notes that 'Dans les collèges de la doctrine, le professeur dicte tous les jours une sentence tirée de la Bible, que les écoliers inscrivent en guise d'épigraphe en tête de la composition du jour';[8] and in another highly influential treatise the abbé de Fleury issues the following prescription:

D'abord il ne faut que poser des maximes sans en rendre raison, le temps viendra de le faire: & comme je suppose une morale chrétienne, dont les préceptes sont fondés sur les dogmes de la foy; je voudrois commencer par ces dogmes toute l'instruction d'un enfant.[9]

1.2. Supplements

This minimal structure is immediately complicated, in that the simple transmission of maxims is always subject to supplementation. This is already implied in the remark quoted from Jean de Viguerie, where the *sentence* is the epigraph to further elaboration, a truth stated at the outset to control the pupil's writing, but none the less allowing that writing to proceed. Similarly, in the quotation from Fleury, the maxims are 'posed' *first*, and if they are allowed to remain in their sententious purity for some time, a time of explanation and justification is nonetheless implied at the time of their posing. In Rollin, this explanation or explication of the maxim is suggested immediately after the passage quoted, this time in the form of the teacher's *viva voce* comments (Rollin, I, p. lv).

This more complicated structure, comprising maxim and supplement(s), appears too in Jesuit education, in the Classical rhetorical exercise known as the *Chria*, a form of *amplificatio* based on a sententious statement. This exercise is codified in Jouvancy's *Candidatus Rhetoricae* (1712):[10] starting with a kernel-maxim, the pupil produces an elaborate and regulated discourse involving a eulogy of the maxim's author, a paraphrase of the maxim, a motivation of its truth, its confirmation by similar and contrary arguments, its exemplification, its support by reference to the writings of the Ancients, and an epilogue amounting to a repetition of the basic maxim. In such an exercise the maxim stands at beginning and end of the discourse, as epigraph and epilogue, controlling the text throughout its elaboration, and subordinating the pupil's activity to the repetition of the imposed truth. There can be no production of truth in such an activity, and the eighteenth century, perhaps taking its cue from Locke, in general condemns this type of exercise.[11]

One of the 'supplements' involved in the *Chria* is the example, and examples and maxims are often linked in pedagogical discourse. Rollin, for example, suggests that one should

se servir adroitement de tout ce qui se rencontre de maximes, d'exemples, & d'histoires remarquables dans la lecture des auteurs, pour inspirer aux jeunes gens de l'amour pour la vertu, & de l'horreur pour le vice

(Rollin, I, p. xxiv)

The passage from the 'maxime' through the 'exemple' to the 'histoire remarquable' implies a certain narrativization of the maxim. Elsewhere Rollin even inverts the hierarchy here implied between maxim and example and gives precedence to the latter: 'pour la vertu, aussi bien que pour les sciences, la voie des exemples est bien plus courte & plus sûre que celle des préceptes' (Rollin, I, p. lxx); and in a meta-pedagogical reflection on the teaching of rhetoric he asserts (sententiously, according to a now familiar paradox): 'ici, comme dans tout le reste, les exemples ont infiniment plus de force que les préceptes', and supports or repeats this assertion with a (sententious) quotation from

Quintilian: 'In omnibus fere minus valent praecepta quam experimenta' (*Institutio Oratoria*, II, 5; Rollin, II, p. 2).

The primacy of the example here finds an echo in Locke:

Particularly in Morality, Prudence and Breeding, Cases should be Put to [the pupil], and his Judgement asked. This opens the Understanding better than Maxims, how well soever explain'd, and settles the Rules better in the Memory for Practice. (Locke, §98)

As we should expect in an empiricist account of the acquisition of knowledge, the emphasis here is on particular experience; Condillac will stress the same point.[12] Similarly, Crousaz asserts in his *Traité de l'éducation des enfants* (2 vols., 1722), 'les hommes ne sont venus à établir des Règles générales que par les réflexions qu'ils ont faites sur divers cas particuliers qui les ont amenés aux mêmes conclusions' (Crousaz, II, p. 20), and contests the idea of having the young child learn maxims by heart: 'Lui remplirez-vous la mémoire de Règles & de sentences? Il refusera de vous seconder' (I, p. 245). And Pesselier seems to be making the same point in his *Lettres sur l'éducation* (1762), addressing fathers, masters and philosophers as follows: 'substituez les *faits* aux *préceptes*; parlez moins bien; agissez mieux; écrivez moins, pratiquez; diminuez le nombre des savantes *instructions*; & multipliez les bons *exemples*'.[13]

The use of the *sentence* comes to characterize the old-style scholastic preceptor. Crousaz again:

Rien n'est plus propre à gâter l'esprit des jeunes gens qu'un pédant qui ne parle que par sentences . . . Il est capital que les jeunes gens ne se fassent pas un plaisir de remplir leur mémoire de belles sentences, pour les en tirer, & s'en faire honneur dans l'occasion. (I, pp. 320–1)[14]

Crousaz presents this learning by heart as the common pedagogical practice of the day, and a little later bemoans this type of bad substitute for the study of the Humanities: 'L'étude des Humanitez . . . à quoi se réduit-elle encore, & que donne t'on à sa place? Des mots, des phrases, quelques vers, quelques sentences détachées à apprendre par coeur' (I, p. 341).

This strong movement away from the maxim and the *sentence* finds its most eloquent expressions in Rousseau's *Emile*, which would apparently like to free education from what I have suggested to be its paradigmatic structure: 'Jeune instituteur, je vous prêche un art difficile; c'est de gouverner sans préceptes et de tout faire en ne faisant rien' (IV, p. 362); 'L'éxemple, l'exemple! sans cela jamais on ne réussit à rien auprès des enfans' (IV, p. 722). Often, indeed, Rousseau seems to be attempting to move beyond discourse altogether, and to make of the example not so much a text, as was the case in Rollin, as an action: 'Je ne me lasse point de le redire: mettez toutes les leçons des jeunes gens en actions plustôt qu'en discours' (IV, p. 546). It is this attitude which determines, among other things, Rousseau's relative disregard for Socrates, who merely formulated as 'leçons' what others before him had silently practised as 'exemples' (IV, p. 626), and the general devalorization of books and reading in favour of observation and induction.

It would seem that this emphasis on concrete 'facts' marks a break with the structures of pedagogy I am describing here. The fact or the 'thing itself' seems to displace the maxim, and more generally, to escape from a primarily discursive, and *a fortiori* from a sententious, scene of education. But however strongly the empiricists insist on experience and things and facts, they cannot prevent such individual atoms from being taken up, necessarily and no longer empirically, in discourse. In Rousseau, this necessity is figured within the text by the recurrent image of nature as book,[15] and is confirmed, at a different level, by the necessarily sententious way in which Rousseau recommends a lack of sententiousness. This problem will reappear later in the discussion of Rousseau's remarks on historical texts. The essential difference between a writer such as Fleury and the 'enlightened' pedagogues of the eighteenth century is that whereas for the former, the maxims are stated as dogma at the outset of the teaching programme, for a pedagogue such as Rousseau, the maxim comes only at the end of the process.[16] This displacement suggests a terminological change ('j'appelle plustôt gouverneur que précepteur le maître de cette science; parce qu'il s'agit moins pour lui d'instruire que de conduire. Il ne doit point donner de préceptes, il doit les faire trouver' (IV, p. 266)), but still implies a certain dominance of the maxim, and a certain leading of the pupil towards it.

1.3. The Maxim's Return

This fact that facts cannot subsist in a pristine, pre-discursive purity implies that the condemnation of maxims and generalizing statements in education cannot take the form of a simple historical progress, as seemed to be the case. Most pedagogical writers in the century seem to promote facts and examples over maxims and *sentences*, but this promotion is untenable, as we can see by re-examining those same texts. In Locke, for example, the maxim re-enters the text in connection with the exercise of memory, and this goes a long way towards contradicting the emphasis previously placed on the individual 'case':

A good short collection of *Proverbs* out of *Solomon*, and the Proverbs of each single Nation (wherein their Wisedom consists) such as respect *God, Religion, good Manners, civil Breeding* and *Duty* in all Relations, as well digested into a Method, and under *proper Heads*, to be judiciously explained to the Child at leisure times, would be of incomparable use . . . And when he has this Catechism perfectly by heart, so as readily and roundly to answer any Question in the whole Book, it may be convenient to lodge in his Mind the remaining Moral Rules scattered up and down in the Bible, as the best *Exercise of his Memory*, and that which may be always a Rule to him, ready at hand in the whole Conduct of his life. (§157)

And this type of recommendation seems blatantly to contradict an earlier passage:

But pray remember, Children are not to be taught by Rules, which will be always slipping out of their Memories. What you think necessary for them to do, settle in them by an indispensable Practice, as often as the Occasion returns. (§66)

The tension involved here reappears later in a curious argument to the effect that the child should not memorize bits of the great authors . . . but should memorize them anyway:

For what can be more ridiculous, than to mix the rich and handsome Thoughts and Sayings of others, with a deal of poor Stuff of his own; which is thereby the more exposed, and has no other grace in it, nor will otherwise recommend the Speaker, than a threadbare russet Coat would, that was set off with large Patches of Scarlet, and glittering Brocard[17] . . . Such Wise and Useful Sentences being once given in charge to their Memories, they should never be suffer'd to forget again, but be often call'd to an account for them. (§§175–6)

It might here be possible to risk a generalization and suggest that any pedagogical discourse involves this type of tension between the particular and the general, and that the invocation of memory (and what pedagogical method can do without memory?) implies that *any* particular fact is taken up in a movement of generalization by being memorized,[18] and that this movement of generalization will move the particular fact from its particularity to the status of example, and will eventually produce a maxim. The apparent movement away from the maxim in the eighteenth century necessarily results in its reinstatement, and the sententious nature of meta-pedagogical discourse itself figures the end term of the movement of generalization described in its object. The only difference with the traditional valorization of the maxim as a starting-point for teaching is that teaching is here, in a very rigorous way, made theoretically imposs-ible, as will be seen when we consider the problem of entry into *le monde*; and I would suggest that the fact that *Emile* presents itself tirelessly as a 'negative' education (e.g. IV, p. 323), and ends up as a novel, is a symptom of this impossibility of education.

The maxim returns, then: just as in Locke, so in Crousaz, in the same context of the Bible, and with the same unresolved tension. First the valorization of the example: 'Les Exemples frapent plus que les idées générales, & leur impression se conserve tout autrement' (Crousaz, II, p. 260), then the reinstatement of the maxim or *sentence*:

Les sentences qui expriment également la beauté de quelque vertu, ou qui font sentir, sous des tours ingénieux, le ridicule de quelque vice, produisent d'excellens effets quand on les présente à propos de la jeunesse; c'est une nourriture dont leur ame tire de la force & de la grandeur. On en trouve depuis un bout de l'Ecriture à l'autre. On peut utilement y joindre les sentences des Payens . . . Quand des Enfans auront appris un certain nombre de belles sentences détachées, on pourra leur proposer d'en faire un recueil où elles soient rangées par ordre.   (Crousaz, II, pp. 262–3)[19]

Pesselier shows perhaps most clearly the hierarchy involving fact, example and maxim, and the ambivalent valorizations involved in that hierarchy:

Comme la *mémoire* & *l'imagination* sont les premières facultés qui s'exercent chez les jeunes gens, les préceptes & les instructions fondés sur des exemples, font nécessairement le plus d'impression, parce qu'ils sont établis sur des *faits*, & que pour la plûpart, ils forment des images, que l'on se plaît à saisir, à retenir, à se rappeler.   (Pesselier, I, pp. 184–5)

The maxim is, then, in no way supplanted by the fact or the thing itself, even if its position in pedagogical method undergoes a displacement towards the end point of a process of induction, rather than the starting-point of dogmatic indoctrination. After this preliminary characterization of the importance of sententious statements in pedagogical discourse I shall now turn to the elements 'narrative', 'fiction' and 'worldliness', which link the 'scene of education' to the worldly novel.

2. Narrativization and Fiction

2.1. History

Quatres cents ans après, les témoins des choses ne sont plus vivants; personne ne sait plus par sa connaissance si c'est une fable ou une histoire.

(Pascal, *Pensées*, 436 (Lafuma))

Insofar as traditional pedagogy is concerned to transmit the 'truth', it would be reasonable to assume that the narrativization of maxims would imply the study of historical texts in which, in principle, narrative is still tied to the truth of particular events. History also has the advantage of recounting events from the past, and thus helps to distract the pupil from a present world universally decried for its corruption. Snyders summarizes this attitude:

Le monde, tout ce qui n'est pas la relation pédagogique, est menace à la droiture qu'on essaie de conférer à l'enfant – et le monde n'est que cette menace . . . Tout moment du monde constitue une menace à l'enfant.

(Snyders, p. 43)

And Rollin gives direct support to such an assumption:

Pour les préserver ou les guérir de la contagion du siècle présent, il faut les transporter dans d'autres pays & d'autres tems, & opposer au torrent des fausses maximes & des mauvais exemples qui entraîne presque tout le monde, les maximes & les exemples des grands hommes de l'antiquité, dont les auteurs qu'ils ont entre les mains leur parlent.   (Rollin, I, p. xxvii)

The historical bias here is evident, but does it imply the study of history? There is a distinction to be drawn here between the Ancients and their history: in the first instance, the Ancients are valued because their language is Latin,[20] and because of their distance from the *monde* of the present. Snyders shows that history is in fact a neglected discipline in traditional pedagogy, being reduced to the study of 'maximes' and 'exemples', as Rollin implies: and Snyders goes on to make what is by now a familiar formal point about sententiousness and narrative: 'les réflexions et les maximes, même incarnées en quelques grands hommes du passé, s'enchaînent difficilement en une histoire' (Snyders, p. 94). And, in the tradition of classical poetics, it is difficult for history to be valued in the face of Aristotle's famous comparison of particular and general truths in the *Poetics* (1451a–b).

It is in fact only as the novel itself comes more and more to take history as its theoretical model, and to abandon the epic poem, that history emerges among the *opponents* of the novel as a possible antidote to fiction, with the emphasis now placed on its truth-value rather than its particularity. The terms of the debate can become particularly crude here, if the history/novel opposition is simply associated with that of truth/lie; thus the *Journal de Trévoux*: 'Le Roman n'est inventé que pour détruire ou déguiser la vérité; l'histoire est uniquement destinée à l'enseigner',[21] or more generally in the Abbé Jacquin's *Entretiens sur les romans* (1755), where novels are defined in opposition to history simply according to the opposition of the false and the true: 'La vérité a assez de charmes pour parvenir jusqu'[au coeur], sans l'envelopper des ténèbres du mensonge, & du voile de la fiction' (Jacquin, p. 153). Such remarks lead Jacquin to prefer Fléchier's history even to *Télémaque*, which is nonetheless 'le plus parfait & le moins dangereux des romans' (Jacquin, p. 143). This attempt to disqualify the novel on the very theoretical ground which the genre was occupying in an attempt to legitimate itself provokes more subtle replies from its apologists. The possible arguments here are thoroughly worked out in Lenglet-Dufresnoy's two contradictory books *De l'Usage des romans* (1734) and *L'Histoire justifiée contre les romans* (1735). If the problem is simply one of truth and lies, as the reactionary argument here represented by Jacquin asserts, then it is history that can be disqualified on precisely those grounds – it pretends to provide truth about events, and in fact presents mistakes and biassed interpretations as the truth.[22] By presenting itself as false, the novel is thus making a true statement about its own status: 'En commençant à lire, je sçai que tout est faux . . . *Voilà donc* le premier avantage du Roman sur l'Histoire. Je n'y suis point trompé, ou je ne le suis qu'à mon profit' (*De l'Usage des romans*, pp. 59–61). The novel can moreover provide exhaustive motivations for the events it recounts, whereas history is reduced to conjecture and probability in its causal explanations; if this 'second-level' truth of the novel implies trickery, this can be seen in terms of a 'profit' insofar as the production of verisimilitude engages with the reader's practical desire to make the world correspond to the *vraisemblable* of the novel: 'Je sçai que tout est faux dans les avantures qu'ils me racontent, mais on me les donne pour telles; & cependant tout y est si vraisemblable, que je voudrois que tout en fut vrai' (Ibid., p. 62). The moral instruction (the apologists of the novel here remember at an opportune moment the classical preoccupation with Horace) is ensured precisely by the fact that the novel does not represent the immorality of most humans, and the disturbingly regular triumph of vice over virtue; in this light, the question of falsity is trivial: 'Je sçai que tout est faux, plus faux même qu'on ne le pense encore; mais rien n'est plus vraisemblable, & c'en est assez pour mon instruction' (Ibid., p. 115). The obligation to 'tout dire' which hangs over the historian will, as Marmontel points out towards the end of the century, always work at the expense of morality,[23] and the novel, far from providing a 'realistic' account of how things are, opens a gap between an 'is' and an 'ought' which, in this theory, appeals to the reader's desire to close that gap, to 'realize' the *vraisemblable* and make it *vrai*: this gap prefigures the possibility of narrative's inhabiting sententiousness itself.

On the other hand, Lenglet's second book, written with the aim of proving that he could not possibly be the author of the first, seems simply to sweep aside this set of problems, and to anticipate the hard line of a Jacquin. This text states from the outset that 'il n'y a que le vrai qui saisisse l'esprit',[24] and that 'L'Amour du vrai est si naturel à l'homme, que son esprit n'est satisfait que quand il est persuadé qu'il possède la vérité' (Ibid., p. 5). But in fact – and this is what makes Lenglet's exploration of this field so much more interesting than that of Jacquin – the defence of history is constantly undermined by the types of problem which beset fiction. Although here Lenglet is able to offer a definition of history as follows:

Qui dit histoire dit un narré fidèle, un récit exact & sincère des événements, appuyé sur le témoignage de ses propres yeux, sur des actes certains & indubitables, ou sur le rapport de personnes dignes de foi.   (Ibid., p. 28)

his later criteria for acquiring certainty of the truth of the facts recounted in a historical text are all immediately problematical, setting up long chains of reporters leading back to an original eye-witness, and then requiring that each stage of the reporting series be marked by traces of sincerity and truth, the nature of which marks one is, apparently, expected to know already. This comes down to appealing to criteria of what is *vraisemblable* to establish what is *vrai*: only appearances of truth are accessible, while the 'truth itself' is always already absent.[25]

The enlightened pedagogues' phantasy of teaching through an experience of the 'facts themselves' now returns as a problem. Rousseau turns to the reading of history as a moment of Emile's passage into society and adulthood. The logic of the appeal to the Ancients is here more complicated than that at work in Rollin: Emile's reading of history is a detour aimed at facilitating his judgement of men, for any immediate direct exposure to modern man in society involves the risk that Emile will hear words rather than see actions. Paradoxically, the 'real life' of society will be more textual and linguistic than the text of history, which is theatrical and inaccessible to untimely intervention: 'je voudrois lui montrer les hommes au loin, les lui montrer dans d'autres tems et d'autres lieux, et de sorte qu'il put voir la scéne sans jamais y pouvoir agir' (IV, p. 526).

But there are two important problems in this appeal to history. The first is that history tends to show only the bad side of men; history begins, as it were, only when Rousseau's ideal of self-sufficiency is compromised, when men begin to interfere in the business of others (IV, pp. 526–7). This failing appears to be irremediable, and could be linked in Rousseau's thought to the structural problem of the catastrophe which ends the state of nature and sets in motion the declining processes of history, society and writing.[26] History can only show evil, insofar as history and evil each imply the other: 'Nous ne savons donc que le mal, à peine le bien fait-il époque' (IV, p. 527).

The second problem is more directly relevant here, and concerns the possibility of recounting 'the facts'. This is what Rousseau wants from historians, especially when they are to be read by a young man. This desire is linked to Rousseau's general devalorization of the maxim, which he here suggests to be beyond the range of a young man, thus returning, at the level of reading, to Aristotle's strictures on the use of maxims (see above, Chapter 1, §6.1): 'Les pires historiens pour un jeune homme sont ceux qui jugent. Les faits, et qu'il juge lui-même' (IV, p. 528); 'il faut savoir lire dans les faits avant de lire dans les maximes. La philosophie en maximes ne convient qu'à l'expérience. La jeunesse ne doit rien généraliser' (IV, p. 529).[27] The model of the historian from this point of view is Thucydides,[28] who, in a sort of generalized hypotyposis, presents the 'thing itself':

Il rapporte les faits sans les juger, mais il n'omet aucune des circonstances propres à nous en faire juger nous-mêmes. Il met tout ce qu'il raconte sous les yeux du lecteur; loin de s'interposer entre les événements et les lecteurs, il se dérobe; on ne croit plus lire, on croit voir. (IV, p. 529)

And this would seem to represent an ideal of objectivity, an erasure of the presence of the subject of the *énonciation* from his *énoncés*, a realization of the ideal formulated as early as 1683 by Du Plaisir and still discussed as a problem by Bérardier de Bataut in 1776.[29]

What makes Rousseau's apparently simple position interesting is the fact that, even in the immediate context of the discussion of history in Book IV, the ideal *empirically* realized by Thucydides has been, at least implicitly, declared to be impossible *in principle* two pages earlier, and this disturbs the simple desire to 'see' facts. This is the second problem announced above. Rousseau begins by complaining that historians in general alter the appearance of the facts according to their own interests and prejudices, or else (and this seems to be an *a priori* problem rather than an accidental one) an unavoidable perspectival ignorance leaves gaps in the facts and distorts the reader's judgement of them. The 'facts themselves', which seemed important in themselves, here turn out to be no more than the evanescent support of judgements which will in turn be subordinated to generalization and maximization as 'experience' is acquired:

Qui est-ce qui sait mettre exactement le lecteur au lieu de la scène pour voir un événement tel qu'il s'est passé? L'ignorance ou la partialité déguisent tout. Sans altérer même un trait historique, en étendant ou resserrant des circonstances qui s'y rapportent, que de faces différentes on peut lui donner! Mettez un même objet à divers points de vue, à peine paroîtra-t-il le même, et pourtant rien n'aura changé que l'oeil du spectateur. Suffit-il pour l'honneur de la vérité de me dire un fait véritable, en me le faisant voir tout autrement qu'il n'est arrivé? Combien de fois un arbre de plus ou de moins, un rocher à droite ou à gauche, un tourbillon de poussière élevé par le vent ont décidé de l'événement d'un combat *sans que personne ne s'en soit apperçu*? Cela empêche-t-il que l'historien ne vous dise la cause de la défaite avec autant d'assurance que s'il eut été par tout? *Or que m'importent les faits en eux-mêmes, quand la raison m'en reste inconnüe, et quelles leçons puis-je tirer d'un événement dont j'ignore la vraie cause*?   (IV, p. 527, my emphasis)

The argument is powerful enough to cast doubt on the possibility of 'good' historical writing, and the subsequent invocation of Thucydides cannot in principle answer the problems raised here. Immediately after this passage – and this will bring us back to Lenglet-Dufresnoy – Rousseau makes an explicit connection between this necessarily bad history and novels, citing *Cléopatre* and *Cassandre*, and suggesting in passing the possibility of a moral advantage in novels.[30]

The novel, then, stages something of a return even in texts which appear to condemn fiction. In *L'Histoire justifiée*, Lenglet refers to

les puériles imaginations du Roman, incapables d'élever l'homme à des sentiments raisonnables, mais très capables d'abaisser l'esprit, de détruire les principes de la morale, & d'énerver le courage des âmes les plus généreuses, en leur faisant passer les plus beaux jours de leur vie dans une molle oisiveté ou dans les occupations les plus frivoles   (pp. 344–5)

but the logic of the primacy of the *vraisemblable* over the *vrai* determines less dismissive remarks about fiction:

Le Roman même qu'on regarde avant que de le lire, comme un amas de chimères et d'imaginations, n'est recevable, qu'autant qu'il imite l'histoire. C'est de la vraisemblance & du rapport qu'il peut avoir avec les véritéz historiques qu'il tire son mérite principal . . . C'est même par la vérité des moeurs que le Roman le plus sage se soutient auprès des personnes sensées, & raisonnables.   (Ibid., pp. 21–3)

There is, then, a certain slippage and play linked with the difficult notion of historical truth.[31] This play is important in its implications for sententiousness, insofar as fiction may well be recognized as the better bearer of truth and instruction than history. Although Lenglet deals (or fails to deal) with this question in terms of the history/novel opposition, for pedagogues and theorists of fiction in general, the slippage from truth passes through the intermediary stage of the *fable*. This stage is in fact in evidence in *L'Histoire justifiée*, at first, curiously, derived from the love of truth: 'Cet amour du vrai, est tellement gravé dans l'esprit et dans le coeur, que c'est à la faveur des véritéz historiques et theologiques, que les fables anciennes ont été autrefois reçues' (p. 15). This leads to the proposition that fables were not only read because of some attachment to truth, but that ancient fables actually *contain* truth: 'il n'y a point d'ancienne Fable qui ne contienne quelque vérité; & c'est ce qui leur a donné cours', and finally to the idea that all fables are supported by truth: 'il n'y a point de Fable qui ne soit appuyée sur quelque vérité' (p. 20).[32]

All of this is in the *Histoire justifiée*, a work which was accepted as an attack on the 'scandalous' *Usage*. Marian Hobson points out that contradictions in Lenglet take place not merely between the two texts, but also within them.[33] In the progress of my own argument, this instability suggests that as soon as the fictional *degré zéro* of pedagogy is supplemented by narrativization, then there is the danger of a drift towards fiction. Pedagogy accepts this in some measure insofar as it accepts the fable.

2.2. Fables

2.2.1. Truth before Fiction

The extension of the word 'fable' in the classical age is greater than it is now, and tends to cover what might be called 'myth' and 'legend'. This does not imply that it is possible, with hindsight, simply to cut up the field of application of the term and dismiss as irrelevant to the enquiry any parts of that field which fail to correspond to the narrow sense of 'fable' as a literary genre practised by La Fontaine, for example. The whole of that field is important, insofar as it concerns, in classical discussions, a sort of originary inflexion of truth.

The long history of the fable gives rise to some concern: Rollin, for example, is clearly concerned to give truth a historical privilege over fable, which he conceives of as a secondary corruption, referring ambivalently to 'la fable, moins ancienne que la vérité, mais qui l'a suivie de près, & qui en a tiré sa naissance en l'altérant & la corrompant'.[34] Huet locates this priority of truth in the Greek *logos*, and describes fiction, in the form of the fable, as an infiltration from the Orient.[35] For Huet, fiction and falsehood go together and are assigned a common origin among the Arabs and the Persians: 'Les Perses n'ont point cédé aux Arabes en l'art de mentir agréablement' (Huet, p. 27); they produced the 'aventures fabuleuses' of the legislator Zoroaster, who provided his disciples with 'des préceptes de morale enveloppez de fictions'. The false/fictional nature of the texts of the Orient is revealed by comparison with the Greco-Roman tradition, which Huet's account presupposes to be the bearer of truth: the Persians, for example, 'ont tellement défiguré [les histoires] dont nous savons la verité par les relations des Grecs & des Romains, qu'on ne les reconnoit pas' (p. 33). And this *a priori* disqualification of the truth of the Persian texts can be used at a second level to ensure the verisimilitude of Huet's own historical account of origins: 'il est assez vray-semblable qu'ils ont esté fabuleux en parlant de l'Auteur et de l'origine des Fables, comme en tout le reste' (p. 30).

Huet has to recognize that this original distribution of truth and falsehood has not survived, and has to account for the entry of fiction into the Greek world of truth. Here appears what will come to seem an all but necessary link between fiction and *volupté*, love, and eroticism: these essentially Oriental values penetrate the Greek tradition via the Ionians and the Milesians, and this first infraction can be seen to determine Huet's own definition of the novel as 'des histoires feintes d'aventures amoureuses' (pp. 46–7). Once this original contamination of truth by fiction has taken place, Huet can revert to a more linear historical account, based on the simple notion that fiction became dominant during periods when the state of civilization was such as to prevent the perception of truth: thus in the barbaric decline which followed the fall of the Roman Empire, 'on fit alors des Histoires fabuleuses, parce qu'on n'en pouvait faire de véritables, faute de savoir la vérité' (p. 111), and the logic of this argument is later bizarrely generalized in terms of nature and necessity:

Comme dans la necessité, pour conserver nostre vie, nous nourrissons nos corps d'herbes et de racines, lors que le pain nous manque; de mesme lorsque la connoissance de la verité, qui est la nourriture propre & naturelle de nostre esprit, vient à nous manquer, nous le nourrissons du mensonge qui est l'image de la vérité. (pp. 185–6)

Insofar as Huet is writing a history of the novel, he would evidently wish to have his own discourse read as the truth of the matter: we have seen how he attempts to support, in an indirect way, his own claims to accuracy by dismissing those of the Persians. This implies that fictions need not be read in terms of their falsehood, to the extent that true statements can be made about them (if only the statement that they are false); and the logic of this leads Huet, towards the end of his text, to distinguish two types of readers of fiction, the first composed of readers who are 'grossiers' and who 'aiment la fausseté, à cause de la vérité apparente qui la cache', the second composed of more sophisticated readers (like Huet himself, one imagines), who 'se rebutent de cette image de vérité, à cause de la fausseté effective qu'elle cache' (p. 199). This alternative seems to leave Huet in some difficulties given that his enterprise is essentially that of providing a measured *defence* of novels (his essay was published as an introduction to Mme de Lafayette's *Zaïde* (1670, signed of course by Segrais)): it is difficult to see how any defence is possible in terms of the argument as analysed so far. There is however a point of tension in that argument: in setting up a paternal position for the Greek *logos*, Huet (Bishop of Avranches) has nevertheless to admit that 'L'Ecriture sainte est toute mystique, toute allégorique, toute énigmatique' (p. 46), and thus in some sense fictional, and although Huet himself never makes such a connection, it seems that this not insignificant infraction of fiction into a new, non-Greek truth dominating his own text prepares the ground for a certain rehabilitation of the fable.

This is of course not the only account of the fable, and Huet's typically 'Ancien' position (truth comes first and is corrupted) is contested by the 'Moderne' Fontenelle in *De l'origine des fables* (published in 1724, but written perhaps forty years earlier).[36] Fontenelle is certainly aiming at Huet when he writes, 'On attribue ordinairement l'origine des fables à l'imagination vive des Orientaux; pour moi, je l'attribue à l'ignorance des premiers hommes' (pp. 29–30). Early philosophers, far from being in contact with truth, wrote fables in that they invented causes to explain perceptible effects they were not in a position to understand fully.[37] There is no Greek privilege here, and Fontenelle is able effectively to undermine Huet's hellenocentrism by suggesting, in a sketch of comparative mythology, that there are important similarities between Greek and Amerindian 'fables'. This position puts Fontenelle on even more difficult religious ground than Huet: he has to make an arbitrary exception to his picture of generalized ignorance in the ancient world for the 'chosen people', 'chez qui un soin particulier de la providence a conservé la vérité' (p. 33). On the other hand, his argument against a Greek privilege removes a common justification for interest in fiction (and especially Homer), and the parting shot against the *Anciens* runs: 'que ne peuvent point les esprits follement amoureux de l'antiquité? On va s'imaginer que sous ces fables sont cachés les secrets de la physique et de la morale' (pp. 38–9).[38] The invocation of a 'fol amour' is malicious: we have seen that Huet links love precisely to the novel, and the implication is that the *Anciens*' attachment to antiquity as truth leads them in fact to write (amorous) fictions. Fontenelle thus neatly places Huet in the same position as the latter had placed the Persians. The corollary is that novels themselves become relatively unproblematic, insofar as they do not pretend to be other than fictional (this anticipates Lenglet's argument); but the fables of Greeks are to be condemned for pretending to deliver the truth (p. 11). Fontenelle can thus calmly suggest that an enlightened man can take an innocent pleasure in fiction recognized as such, which simply appeals to his imagination rather than to his reason.

This is a strong position which is hardly exploited in subsequent discussion: even Lenglet, as we have seen, is unable to allow fiction this unpretentious position, separated from all considerations of morality. Pedagogues and theorists of the novel are in general much too concerned with the ethical problem of truth and lies (of Truth as law) to dismiss the problem of fiction so blithely.

We left Huet having some difficulty in justifying his interest in fiction; later in his text, when he comes to write his apologue for novels proper, the fable returns, but this time as a controllable supplement to truth, and a useful one. Typically in Huet, the argument involves the invocation of Classical precedents:

Horace disoit que l'Iliade d'Homere enseigne mieux & plus fortement la Morale, que les Philosophes les plus habiles: si l'on ne peut pas dire la mesme chose des Romans, je crois qu'on peut du moins leur appliquer ce que Plutarque a dit de la poësie, que quand les préceptes de la Philosophie sont revestus de ses ornemens, ils trouvent une entrée bien plus libre dans l'âme des jeunes personnes, que quand ils se présentent avec toute leur austerité. Aussi la pluspart des Philosophes ont employé le ministère des fables pour l'établissment de leurs dogmes, & ont excessivement vanté l'utilité de ces impostures qui nous trompent à notre profit

. . . La Politique mesme, qui est une partie de la Philosophie, & qui en tire ses règles, a fait honneur aux fables avant la Poëtique, car Strabon écrit . . . qu'elles ont esté plutost receuës des législateurs que des Poëtes, en veuë de leur utilité, & du naturel des hommes, en qui le désir d'apprendre & d'entendre des choses nouvelles se déclare dés l'enfance, par l'inclination qu'ils ont aux Fables: que si le merveilleux se joint à la nouveauté, il augmente le plaisir, qui est le grand charme de l'instruction; qu'il est donc important de se servir de cet appas et de frotter de ce miel les bords du verre, pour leur faire avaler la medecine amère des enseignemens, qui doivent les purger de leurs mauvaises humeurs.   (pp. 217–220)

If the fable is still on the side of falsehood, then that falsehood is controlled and forms an *economy* with truth. It is on these grounds that the fable can be recuperated for serious pedagogical discourse. But it is still not entirely clear why this fictional supplement to the truth of the 'précepte' is necessary, if truth is, as we have seen, the 'nourriture . . . naturelle de l'esprit humain'. The point is that there is an equally natural aversion, not to truth itself (although that strong line was taken by Bernard Lamy in his defence of rhetoric, as we saw in Chapter 1), but to that truth when presented pedagogically or legislatively. The possibility of this argument for the necessity of fiction and deceit is in fact to be read in Huet's opening remarks about the novel, in which this problem of the prescriptive–pedagogical presentation of truth is explicitly discussed:

La fin principale des Romans ou du moins celle qui le doit estre, & que se doivent proposer ceux qui les composent, est l'instruction des lecteurs, à qui il faut toûjours faire voir la vertu couronnée, & le vice puni. Car comme l'esprit de l'homme est naturellement ennemi des enseignemens, & que son amour propre le révolte contre les instructions, il le faut tromper par l'appas du plaisir & adoucir la sévérité des préceptes par l'agrément des exemples, & corriger ses défauts en les condamnant dans un autre.   (p. 4)

The drift from the *degré zéro* of the scene of education is thus determined by a 'natural' aversion in the pupil *to that scene itself*. The fable now becomes acceptable as a means of *staging* the pragmatics of that scene, and this staging involves the apparent reversal of the relationship of supplementarity which obtains between truth and fiction. From the point of view of the pedagogue, as for Huet, the fiction is the supplement, the honey on the edge of the cup or the sugar on the pill.[39] From the point of view of the pupil, the fiction is the primary attraction, and the moral truth accompanying it no more than an adjunct. Crousaz, for example, recommends the use of fables with children before they learn to read, in order to exploit their 'natural' inclination towards the 'merveilleux', but only as a provisional detour made in the interests of a return to 'le chemin de la Vérité & de la Vertu' (Crousaz, I, p. 243). The teacher is there to ensure that this return takes place: 'Les Livres de Fables accompagnés de figures feront des occasions de leur conter la Fable & dès là d'ajouter quelque chose d'instructif sur le but de celle qu'on leur aura contée & sur son sens moral' (I, p. 229). Crousaz later generalizes this structure to include men in general, suggesting that most men are children when it comes to the transmission of rules and laws, and that they too need the fictional supplement (I, p. 245). He links this to a sort of primal scene of legislation in which God is described in terms of a skilful *metteur en scène*, and Jesus as making use of fictional supplements in the parables. This staging of legislation is something which will return in

Chapter 4; what is important here is that with the fable, fiction is introduced not only into the content of teaching, but into the scene of education itself.

2.2.2. Truth after Fiction

The fable is the minimal case of the conjunction of fictional–narrative and sententious propositions, and the narrative is subordinated to the maxim, *whether or not that maxim is stated explicitly*. This rule of the fable, namely that it must somehow present a maxim even if it does not state a maxim, is well expressed by La Fontaine in the preface to the *Fables* (1668), where he establishes a clear hierarchy between two possible generic rules:

> Cette règle [i.e. that of having only animals in fables] est moins de nécessité que de bienséance, puisque ni Esope, ni Phèdre, ni aucun des fabulistes, ne l'a gardée, tout au contraire de la moralité, dont aucun ne se dispense. Que s'il m'est arrivé de le faire, ce n'a été que dans les endroits où elle n'a pu entrer avec grâce, et où il est aisé au lecteur de la suppléer.[40]

And so most of the *Fables* do contain a recognizable maxim, and it is indeed not difficult to 'supply' a maxim where none is given. It may be, of course, that the reader prefers not to do so, and a modern reader, whose 'literary competence' tends to devalorize didacticism and moralizing, may well prefer a fable such as 'Le Loup et le chien' (I, V), precisely because of a certain open-endedness which loosens the grip of the sententious statement over the narrative, this loosening being figured in the closing narrative proposition, 'maître Loup s'enfuit, et court encor'. This does not of course alter La Fontaine's point. The use of the verb 'suppléer' in the Preface is precious, and returns us to the problem of the patch as elaborated à propos of Lamy. As in Derrida's use of the word *supplément*, the maxim indeed supplements the fable in both senses of the term: it is the additional element which comes to 'fill up' a lack in the narrative and complete the fable, and yet it remains an addition which the reader may have to 'supply' from outside. And on the other hand the maxim tends to *supplant* the fable, to stand in for it once the fiction has gone. This relationship is thematized at the opening of the sixth book of the *Fables*, in a famous passage:

> Les fables ne sont pas ce qu'elles semblent être;
> Le plus simple animal nous y tient lieu de maître.
> Une morale nue apporte de l'ennui:
> Le conte fait passer le précepte avec lui.

En ces sortes de feinte il faut instruire et plaire,
Et conter pour conter me semble peu d'affaire.[41]

This is the classical justification for fiction: it *looks* frivolous, it *is* serious; and behind the animal stands a master, the preceptor. This structure also governs the letter which dedicates the *Fables* to the (six-year-old) Dauphin:

Vous êtes en un âge où l'amusement et les jeux sont permis aux princes;[42] mais en même temps vous devez donner quelques-unes de vos pensées à des réflexions sérieuses. Tout cela se rencontre aux fables que nous devons à Esope. L'apparence en est puérile, je le confesse; mais ces puérilités servent d'enveloppe à des vérités importantes. (Ed. cit., p. 3)

And this suggests that the structure of supplementarity is reversible: here it is rather the fiction, the *jeu*, the *feinte*, which is the non-essential supplement, the 'enveloppe' – the essential element is the truth, the *précepte*, the *réflexion*. There is every appearance of a sort of enlightened pedagogy here: the object is to get the (prescriptive) truth across *effectively*, and this involves a detour through fiction, insofar as moral truth presented directly is boring or simply rebarbative, as we have seen.

As modern readers who might prefer to let the wolf keep running, we may of course suspect that this type of justification is itself a supplementary fiction elaborated to justify, and recursively to reinforce, a guilty pleasure in fiction; this suspicion would reverse again the structure of supplementarity, and make of the moral and the maxim no more than a tribute paid to seriousness, and of the concealed 'master' no more than a simulacrum of a super-ego (or a simulacrum offered to the super-ego). The type of theoretical discourse we are dealing with would then be merely a gesture made *après-coup*, a supplementary 'envelope' hiding the 'important truth' of a guilty libidinal investment in the *feinte*. But if we were to make of this suspicion a truth we should simply be supplying a rival maxim and setting up another master behind the animal, foreclosing the implications of both simulacrum and *après-coup*. Let the Wolf(-Man) keep running.[43]

Classical pedagogy does its best to prevent this type of pleasure in fiction, however, by placing another master beside the pupil to keep the reading-process under surveillance. Here is Crousaz again:

Ce qu'ils renferment de plus estimable c'est quelque chose de bien au-dessus de la beauté de leur stile & de l'élégance de leurs expressions; il faut leur [i.e. the pupils] faire remarquer qu'ils sont remplis d'exemples & de maximes propres à nous rendre sages, pour devenir heureux. Dès qu'on rencontre quelqu'une

86

de ces maximes il faut bien prendre garde que les jeunes gens ne s'accoûtument à la laisser passer sans la faire servir à leur utilité & sans en faire application à eux-mêmes & aux circonstances dans lesquelles ils peuvent se trouver. C'est une des plus fatales habitudes qu'on puisse prendre que de laisser passer des règles sans en faire cet usage.[44]

The *conte* might 'faire passer le précepte', but the master is there to make sure it does not pass too fast or too far.

2.2.3. *Feinte, Fable, Faute*: the Reading-Machine

In some of the most famous pages of *Emile*, Rousseau mercilessly exposes the insufficiency of this argument in favour of the fable, showing how the child is much more likely to be attentive to the 'maître Renard' than to any 'maître' standing behind the animal or beside the book (IV, pp. 351–7). But in the later treatment of the fable, which is in fact much more interesting from the present point of view, it becomes clear that this demonstration must not be allowed to work in the interests of what I have called the 'guilty pleasure in fiction'. Emile's reading of this type of fiction intervenes after his reading of history, and corresponds with his first direct contact with the trickery of man-in-society. Emile is now in a position to understand the moral questions involved; the reading of fables will not simply be a pointless exercise in memorizing a text the child has not understood, but a supplement to experience which will allow the pupil to 'draw out' the maxim for himself and to profit from it:

Le tems des fautes est celui des fables. En censurant le coupable sous un masque étranger, on l'instruit sans l'offenser, et il comprend alors que l'apologue n'est pas un mensonge, par la vérité dont il se fait l'application. L'enfant qu'on n'a jamais trompé par des loüanges n'entend rien à la fable que j'ai ci-devant examinée; mais l'étourdi qui vient d'être la dupe d'un flateur conçoit à merveille que le corbeau n'étoit qu'un sot. Ainsi *d'un fait il tire une maxime*, et l'expérience qu'il eut bientôt oubliée se grave, au moyen de la fable, dans son jugement. Il n'y a point de connoissance morale qu'on ne puisse acquérir par l'expérience d'autrui ou par la sienne. Dans les cas où cette expérience est dangereuse, au lieu de la faire soi-même on tire sa leçon de l'histoire. Quand l'épreuve est sans conséquence, il est bon que le jeune homme y reste exposé. Puis au moyen de l'apologue on rédige en maximes les cas particuliers qui lui sont connus.   (IV, pp. 540–1, my emphasis)

The notion of 'tirer une maxime' describes, in this context, the movement of generalization, going from fact to maxim, which has already been noted. Drawing the maxim out implies the passage of the fact through the stage of the example; and this process denies the

87

singularity of the fact, which becomes defined as fact only insofar as it is susceptible to exemplification. The maxim thus appears at the end of a dialectical process of maximization[45] which involves the cancelling of the fact as such; the fact 'as such' or the subject's singular experience of it is not even strictly necessary to the process: 'on tire sa leçon de l'histoire' even if one has not been through the experience oneself. In this case the activity of the subject has nothing directly to do with the 'experience', but involves a process of reading and writing; and in principle this is the case even when the pupil *does* experience the fact himself – *in itself*, as Rousseau admits, the experience is eminently forgettable, and what is important is its generalized inscription (the use of the verb 'graver' is not without significance).[46] This is not to suggest that the structure here is the same as that described earlier, in which the pupil simply received passively the maxim dictated to him, but rather to displace the apparent emphasis which Rousseau places on experience towards an activity of writing as exemplification and maximization.

What must be 'experienced' by the pupil becomes, then, the activity of reading and writing; and this is what motivates a new, and apparently paradoxical, criticism directed by Rousseau against the use of maxims in fables. The text continues from the passage quoted above:

Je n'entends pas pourtant que ces maximes doivent être développées ni même énoncées. Rien n'est si vain, si mal entendu que la morale par laquelle on termine la pluspart des fables; comme si cette morale n'étoit pas ou ne devoit pas être étendüe dans la fable même de manière à la rendre sensible au lecteur. Pourquoi donc en ajoûtant cette morale à la fin lui ôter le plaisir de la trouver de son chef? (IV, p. 541)

So with respect to La Fontaine, Rousseau would like the guiding maxim of the fable *always* to be 'suppléée' by the reader. The notion of pleasure intervenes in the argument here, but is now displaced on to the supplementing activity itself, and not located in the fiction as such – the passivity of the pupil is what prevents his enjoying his education, and so the work of producing the maxim reunites the functions of the 'utile' and the 'agréable', which are separated in the type of classical discourse here represented by La Fontaine. The fiction is no longer the sweet supplement to the bitter moral pill of the maxim: rather the work of producing that pill brings its own sweetness, a necessary supplement to education which passes through a controlled flattering of the pupil's *amour-propre*. In short, by arguing for the suppression of the maxim from the text, Rousseau sets in place a powerful reading-machine which is able to recuperate and exploit the negativity residually attached to the fiction in the classical model, and in so doing to turn to positive use the *amour-propre* which is the general target of moralizing sententious discourse in the classical period.[47]

Here is Rousseau's description of the process:

Le talent d'instruire est de faire que le disciple se plaise à l'instruction. Or pour qu'il s'y plaise il ne faut pas que son esprit reste tellement passif à tout ce que vous lui dites qu'il n'ait absolument rien à faire pour vous entendre. Il faut que l'amour-propre du maître laisse toujours quelque prise au sien; il faut qu'il se puisse dire: je conçois, je pénètre, j'agis, je m'instruis.   (IV, p. 541)[48]

There is evidently a danger here, inherent in the absence of an explicit maxim: this lack in the text of the fable (signalled by the fable *as* a lack, a gap indicated by the narrative as its 'meaning' or 'import', a carefully defined empty square waiting to be filled by the supplement), allows the possibility of a hiatus in the production of meaning, an uncertainty in the resolution of fiction into truth. The danger is of course simply that the pupil will read badly and generate the 'wrong' maxim for the text – and it is essentially this possibility which motivated Rousseau's condemnation of the use of fables with children. On the other hand, and this is what makes the theory of reading proposed here interesting, this lack and its attendant danger (reduced by the master's control over the moment at which his pupil is to be exposed to this 'experience' of reading) are necessary – for if the text reads itself and produces its own maxim, thus aspiring to totality in its reflexivity, then, paradoxically, this closing-off of the lack produces a greater and more worrying lack by preventing the full possibilities of generalization and maximization which the explicit maxim should in principle guarantee. The drive to 'tout dire', which commands the scene of writing in other texts by Rousseau, is here condemned because the 'tout', the total meaning which the explicit maxim aspires to present, is always still too particular and limited:

Il faut toujours se faire entendre, mais il ne faut pas toujours tout dire; celui qui dit tout dit peu de choses, car à la fin on ne l'écoute plus.[49] Que signifient ces quatre vers que Lafontaine ajoûte à la fable de la grenouille qui s'enfle? A-t-il peur qu'on ne l'ait pas compris? A-t-il besoin, ce grand peintre, d'écrire les noms au'dessous des objets qu'il peint? Loin de généraliser par là sa morale, il la particularise, il la restreint, en quelque sorte, aux exemples cités et empêche qu'on ne l'applique à d'autres.   (IV, p. 541)

This carefully constructed reading-machine can now suggest the mutilation of La Fontaine's texts in order to produce the salutary lack which makes the fable whole. It should be noted that *this* operation is not left to the pupil–reader but is the privilege of the master, who should proceed to excise the maxim 'avant de mettre les fables de cet auteur inimitable entre les mains d'un jeune homme'. The master here is the final controlling instance of reading: he has read the whole text before and knows what it means; the hiatus located above, and the possibility of 'play' which, in principle, it introduces, is rigorously controlled by the master's control over the reader. This scene can be re-applied to the reading of the text of *Emile* itself. The master of Emile's reading of La Fontaine, *within* the scene of reading which I have been describing, also dominates the scene in which that scene is presented – *Emile* is not a text for Emile to read, but a text which tries to teach how to teach other Emiles to read. But the master also places the reader of *Emile*, the aspirant teacher, in a position homologous to that of Emile: 'Je montre de loin, car je ne veux pas non plus tout dire, les routes qui détournent de la bonne afin qu'on apprenne à les éviter' (IV, p. 542).[50]

3. Fiction and Worldliness

It is, I think, no accident that this *mise en scène* of scenes of reading should intervene in Rousseau's text at the moment of Emile's direct exposure to *le monde*; and I would also suggest that this moment can be linked to the inflexion of the text of *Emile* towards fiction. The growing complexity of the discursive status of the text will eventually lead, some 230 pages later, to a final self-righteous attempt to retain the master's mastery over the reader and to salvage the ultimate truth-value of the text. A lot of motifs converge here, linking this problem of fiction to the 'crisis' of Emile's becoming adult, which crisis of sexuality is deferred as long as possible by Rousseau.[51] The text itself announces the importance of this moment:

On nous donne dans les traités d'éducation de grands verbiages inutiles et pédantesques sur les chimériques devoirs des enfans, et l'on ne nous dit pas un mot de la partie la plus importante de toute l'éducation: savoir la crise qui sert de passage à l'état d'homme. Si j'ai pu rendre ces essais utiles par quelque endroit, ce sera surtout pour m'y être étendu fort au long sur cette partie essencielle, omise par tous les autres, et pour ne m'être point laissé rebuter dans cette entreprise par des difficultés de langue.   (IV, p. 777)

Previously Rousseau was concerned to excise parts of texts which said too much; here he fills in the essential part omitted by his predecessors in pedagogy. Without a break, the text continues with the problem of its own possibly fictional status:

Si j'ai dit ce qu'il faut faire, j'ai dit ce que j'ai dû dire, il m'importe fort peu d'avoir écrit un roman. C'est un assés beau roman que celui de la nature humaine. S'il ne se trouve que dans cet écrit, est-ce ma faute? Ce devroit être l'histoire de mon espèce: vous qui la dépravez, c'est vous qui faites un roman de mon livre. (Ibid.)[52]

What Rousseau has been tirelessly deferring, throughout the pages separating the scene of reading from the passage just quoted, is precisely the 'crise' which he repeatedly invokes. The general inability of pedagogy to deal with worldliness and its fiction needs to be explored before any serious attempt could be made to explain the 'devenir-roman' of *Emile,* or the 'return of the repressed' in that curious supplement, *Emile et Sophie ou les solitaires.*

3.1. Rejecting the Novel

We have seen that a certain regular and coherent progression leads from the maxim as such, through its narrativization in historical texts, to a certain acceptance of fiction in the form of the fable. The novel itself, however, remains in general outside pedagogy. It is well known, for example, what pressure was put on the novel at certain times in the early eighteenth century, and Georges May has put forward some evidence for the existence of an actual proscription of the genre.[53] I do not intend to go into this in detail here, but rather to pursue briefly the links between the novel, women, sexuality and worldliness, which I have so far only hinted at. We might add to this the importance of the fact that novels are written in French (the 'vulgar' language, traditionally the domain of women, as are novels, and linked to the novel by the etymology – recognized at least from Huet – of the term 'roman'). In Jesuit education, for example, a certain wariness of French is still present at the end of the seventeenth century: François de Dainville summarizes part of Jouvancy's *Ratio discendi* (1692, itself of course still written in Latin), as follows,

Il ne sera jamais licite de goûter à 'la lie des livres français': contes dangereux, comédies, entretiens ou romans. Tous ces écrits affaiblissent l'esprit ou corrompent les moeurs. Si l'on peut soutenir que les hommes mûrs peuvent parfois goûter à ces frivolités, personne ne niera qu'on ne doive les interdire aux jeunes gens. En dépit de ces réserves si raisonnables . . . le principe était admis, et c'était là par voie de conséquence, le point de départ d'une révolution scolaire.[54]

Far from being admitted as part of pedagogy, it would seem as if novels represent precisely the opposite of pedagogy: that against which the pedagogues are concerned to protect their pupils. This is certainly the case for Fénelon, one of whose reasons for recommending that girls be given a more serious education is that otherwise idleness will leave them the time to read novels: 'Celles qui ont de l'esprit s'érigent souvent en précieuses et lisent tous les livres qui peuvent nourrir leur vanité; elles se passionnent pour des romans . . .' But a later prescription introduces a slight doubt into this apparent condemnation: 'on voit que le moyen de les dégoûter des fictions frivoles des romans, est de leur donner le goût des histoires utiles et agréables'.[55] It is not entirely clear what such 'histoires' might be, but an idea of their nature might be derived from the Abbé de Saint-Pierre's *Projet pour perfectionner l'éducation* (1728), which includes novels in education and makes of them the object of the tenth of the 'exercices journaliers':

> Lecture de Romans vertueux, politiques, & moraux, les Voyages de Télémaque de M. Fénelon Archevêque de Cambrai; il faut que ces Romans soient les uns pour les basses classes, les autres pour les hautes; il faut qu'ils contiennent plus souvent des vertus recompensées, & des vices punis . . . A propos d'erreurs & de mensonges, il faut montrer aux Ecoliers, que les Romans vertueux ne sont ni erreurs ni mensonges, puisqu'ils ne sont point donéz come veritéz, ni comme des faits existans ou qui aient existés.[56]

On the other hand, with the exception of *Télémaque* it seems as if such 'romans vertueux' are no more than a virtuality, and the Abbé goes on to suggest how the writing of such novels might be organized, with one author to provide the approved moral content, and another to integrate that content into a fiction. It is clear that such a process returns to the structure of the fable, in which the narrative elaboration was rigorously subordinated to the maxim or *précepte*: the generative model here is essentially that of Le Bossu, described above.

Crousaz also praises *Télémaque* as 'L'*Homère* moderne',[57] but it is in a separate section of his treatise that he considers novels 'proper'. Novels are situated here in the margins of pedagogy, discussed in a late section entitled 'Des recréations' (II, pp. 510ff). Novel-reading is acceptable, so long as licentious works are avoided. But the motivation for this border-line inclusion of novels is essentially negative: the logic here is that if novels are loudly condemned as instruments of perdition, then they are given an importance and an attractiveness that only increases the pupil's desire. This argument is also present in Mme de Lambert's *Avis d'une mère à sa fille* (1728):

> La lecture des Romans est plus dangereuse, je ne voudrois pas que l'on en fît un grand usage; ils mettent du faux dans l'esprit. Le Roman n'étant jamais pris sur le vrai, allume l'imagination, affoiblit la pudeur, met le désordre dans le coeur, et, pour peu qu'une jeune personne ait de la disposition à la tendresse, hâte et précipite son penchant. Il ne faut point augmenter le charme, ni l'illusion de l'amour: plus il est adouci, plus il est modeste, et plus il

est dangereux. Je ne voudrois point les défendre; toutes défenses blessent la liberté, et augmentent le désir.[58]

This type of measured, apparently reasonable argument in fact breaks the pedagogical closure, and lets in fiction and worldliness: not only in that some novels are tolerated, but in that the logic at work accepts, if only at a meta-level, the structure of desire which is basic to worldly fiction itself. The notion that veiling increases desire is the basis of the worldly discourse of seduction,[59] and placing novels behind just such a veil which both allows and forbids them places them in a position structurally identical to that of women in worldly fiction. By admitting the principle of desire into the scene of education, pedagogy inevitably opens itself up to fiction and worldliness.

3.1.1. *Télémaque*

This complex knot of the motifs of desire, fiction and worldliness can be seen at work in *Télémaque* itself, which has a curious position in all of these discussions of the novel. Fénelon's text seems to realize the apparently oxymoronic ideal of being a 'roman vertueux', and this is the cause of some concern to pedagogues and theorists of the genre. Faced with this anomaly, a standard strategy is simply to deny that *Télémaque* is a novel at all, and to accord it honorary status as an epic poem.[60] The problem of *Télémaque* is not only that it is written with an avowed pedagogical aim, but that it is constituted by a representation of the scene of education itself, and can thus hardly be condemned. The novel also, however, faces the problems of desire and seduction, and these problems occur in the context of telling stories. Télémaque excites Calypso's desire by his skill as a narrator, and the scene of desire turns on a scene of narration, as Mentor explains at the beginning of Book 4:

Le plaisir de raconter vos histoires vous a entraîné . . . elle a trouvé le moyen de parler longtemps sans rien dire, et elle vous a engagé à lui expliquer tout ce qu'elle désire savoir: telle est l'art des femmes flatteuses et passionnées.

(p. 123)

Mentor chides his pupil for including in his narrative elements which bear witness to his courage and 'virtue' (in a broad sense, to his virility), and instructs him to continue in more modest tone – but when Télémaque completes his story, it is with the Cypriot episode of 'mollesse' and 'volupté', from which he has to be rescued by Mentor, just as, two books later, when the time of Télémaque's *récit* has caught up with that of its *narration*, Mentor has to save him from Calypso

93

and the nymphs.⁶¹ Télémaque's escape from Calypso and the devirilizing effects of passion coincides with his escape from story-telling and his return to a story in which he acts, but which he no longer narrates. But by including this scene of seduction in his scene of education, Fénelon ensures that its closure cannot be complete, and it is no accident that the presence of his novel in *Emile* is a determining feature of that text's inability to sustain its pedagogical mode of discourse.

3.2. Rearguard Actions

It seems, then, that even a measured acceptance of the novel into education threatens pedagogical discourse, most insidiously by imposing a certain logic of desire on writers who would like to refuse it. In the light of this, the hard line of the Abbé Jacquin is at least lucid and coherent; but we can see now that in his statement to the effect 'La vérité a assez de charmes pour parvenir jusqu'[au coeur], sans l'envelopper des ténèbres du mensonge, & du voile de la fiction' (Jacquin, p. 153), the metaphor of the veil implies the logic of seduction inherent in fiction and worldliness; and it should be noted that this remark is made in the context of a discussion of *Télémaque*.⁶²

The veil of fiction implies the veils of seduction, and the burden of Jacquin's rejection of the novel involves the complicity of novels and love: 'Les Romans nous offrent à eux seuls, tout ce que l'amour a de plus séduisant, & en même temps de plus criminel' (p. 305). Worldli-ness, novels and love go together in that they all imply seduction: 'On ne connaît que trop tôt ce monde corrompu, que les Romans célèbrent, sans se hâter d'en faire chérir les maximes, avant qu'on se soit mis en garde contre sa séduction' (p. 356).

The question is thus also, explicitly, one of maxims: maxims to avoid, which are those of worldliness, maxims to adopt, which are those of morality. 'Les maximes du monde étonnent une âme timorée: on s'y accoûtume par degrés; l'exemple commence par faire adopter ce qu'on n'admettroit d'abord qu'avec répugnance' (p. 344). But it seems reasonable to suppose that, just as in fables, where the maxim prevented any dangerous fictional excess, so in novels maxims might escape the veil, and control seduction by the fiction and its referents. This point of view is expressed in Jacquin's text by a comtesse (the *Entretiens* involve a – fictional – framework in which a pedagogical role is played by an Abbé, who demonstrates to the comtesse that all novels are pernicious, in the interests of a young chevalier who is just entering *le monde*), who defends the possibility of an anthologizing reading of novels: 'Je m'étois du moins imaginé, Monsieur, que vous auriez séparé du corps de l'ouvrage, les sages maximes qui se trouvent répandues dans quelques Romans' (p. 125). It will be remembered that the pedagogues' appeal to the example implied a useful narrativization of the maxim; the Abbé uses this fact to insist that the anthologizing reading would forget this power of the example, which means that even 'good' maxims in novels are contaminated by their context:

Dangereuses & inutiles maximes que celles qui se trouvent quelquefois dans les Romans, où elles sont si souvent contredites! . . . L'exemple, qui, de toutes les leçons, est toujours la plus efficace, fait bientôt oublier ces vaines déclamations d'une sagesse empruntée: on s'arrête aux actions, elles persuadent. (pp. 122–3)

The point is again that the general context of 'love' contaminates even the most virtuous maxims, and this because love is essentially to be repressed: 'Il est toujours pernicieux de découvrir les mystères de l'Amour, dût-il se mêler beaucoup de vertu dans les leçons qu'on en donne' (p. 319).[63]

3.3. The Fence

Jacquin's is a rearguard action, an attempt to reinforce the closure of a pedagogical discourse which has, as we have seen, been infiltrated by the fiction and worldliness which it would like to deny. Jacquin comes, as it were, too late: his comtesse is already in *le monde*, she is already a great reader of novels, and she is already a fictional character in the text. Traditional pedagogy's attempt to preserve its pupils from *le monde*, into which they inevitably enter, is a type of *politique de l'autruche* which is subject to a good deal of criticism from more enlightened pedagogues, who are prepared to recognize the structural duplicity of the closure, which is also necessarily a point of passage into what is beyond it. The attempt to ignore the existence of *le monde* simply increases the problems involved in that passage. Pesselier, for example, asserts that 'l'ignorance où l'on est, en entrant dans le monde, des choses qu'il faudroit savoir le mieux, expose à plus d'inconvéniens que l'on ne pense, & l'inexpérience y met le comble'.[64] The problem with closing off the *pré-monde* from the *monde* is simply that education must begin all over again, as it does in Crébillon *fils*, Duclos, and Louvet, once entry into *le monde* takes place. This problem is both one of narrative roads and one of generating maxims, as Fénelon was aware:

Le chemin que je représente, quelque long qu'il paroisse, est le plus court, puisqu'il mène droit où l'on veut aller; l'autre chemin, qui est celui de la crainte, et d'une culture superficielle des esprits, quelque court qu'il paroisse, est trop long; car on n'arrive presque jamais par là au seul vrai but de l'éducation, qui est de persuader les esprits, et d'inspirer l'amour sincère de la vertu. La plupart des enfans qu'on a conduits par ce chemin, sont encore à recommencer quand leur éducation semble finie; et après qu'ils ont passé les premières années de leur entrée dans le monde à faire des fautes souvent irréparables, il faut que l'expérience et leurs propres réflexions leur fassent trouver toutes les maximes que cette éducation génée et superficielle n'avoit point su leur inspirer. (*De l'éducation des filles*, p. 597)

Traditional education simply allows *le monde* to carry out its own empty pedagogy on the basis of the vacuity of the first, and this is true even of 'la bonne société', as La Condamine points out: 'C'est à cette école qu'il commence à s'instruire, il recueille les lieux communs de la conversation, il les assaisonne de quelques platitudes qu'il tire de son propre fond; il débite le tout avec confiance; il se croit un oracle.'[65]

These more enlightened pedagogues accept as inevitable the passage into society; traditional pedagogy attempted to deny that necessity. There are two sides here to what I would call a 'pas au-delà mondain',[66] which share at least the presupposition that there is a discontinuous passage between education and the 'real life' of society. If the fence has to be got over, then it seems reasonable that pedagogy should help in the crossing.

The passage into society coincides with a sort of coming of age, the coming into adulthood which remains, according to Rousseau, an untheorized lack in previous pedagogical writing, and which allows the perverted form of education provided by *le monde* to produce 'des hommes doubles' (IV, p. 250). But Locke does in fact have some considerations on this, which set up a scene of some interest to the worldly novel:

He will pass from a boy to a Man; which is the most hasardous step in all the whole course of Life. This therefore should be carefully watch'd, and a young Man with great Diligence handed over it; and not, as now usually is done, be taken from a *Governour's* Conduct, and all at once thrown into the World under his own, not without manifest danger of immediate Spoiling; there being nothing more frequent, than Instances of the great Looseness, Extravagancy and Debauchery, which young Men have run into as soon as they have been let loose from a severe and strict Education; Which I think may be chiefly imputed to their wrong way of Breeding, especially in this Part: for having been Bred up in a great ignorance of What the world truly is, and finding it a quite other thing, when they come into it, than what they were taught it should be, and so imagined it was,[67] are easily perswaded, *by other*

kind of Tutors, which they are sure to meet with, that the Discipline they were
kept under, and the Lectures were read to them, were but the Formalities of
Education, and the Restraints of Childhood; that the Freedom belonging to
Men, is to take their Swing in a full Enjoyment of what was before forbidden
them.   (Locke, §94, my emphasis)

The 'step' into manhood, if left in its hazardous discontinuity, is also a
step into worldly education and debauchery, the discourse of the
worldly novel. Locke evidently does not leave things at that, but is
eager to propose a solution to the problem, and this consists
essentially in an attempt to reduce the discontinuity of the passage
into 'the World'. Two arguments attempt to achieve this reduction:
the first suggests a prior *representation* of the world, the second an
introduction into it *gradually*. In fact these two arguments are linked,
the first being placed in the service of the second, which appears more
frequently. The words of the text immediately preceding the passage
quoted are 'by safe and insensible degrees', and after the passage the
text continues:

The shewing him the World, as really it is, before he comes wholly into it, is
one of the best means, I think, to prevent this Mischief. He should *by degrees*
be informed of the Vices in fashion . . .   (Ibid., my emphasis)[68]

It would probably be a mistake to underestimate the survival of the
theological idea that the world is essentially a place of vice and
depravity, just as it is for Rollin: the difference is that for Locke
ignorance is no defence ('it is not possible now (as perhaps formerly it
was) to keep a young Gentleman from Vice, by a total ignorance of
it . . .'). The young man has to cross the fence into that area of vice,
but if the argument 'by degrees' tends to minimize the fence-like
nature of the *clôture* (the 'degrees' form a ladder over the fence, the
young man has no longer to be 'thrown' but 'handed' over it), this is
also in the interests of preserving that fence as a sort of portable
protection: 'The only Fence against the World is, a thorough
Knowledge of it; into which a young Gentleman should be enter'd by
degrees, as he can bear it.'[69]

An aporia is at work here, however: in accordance with Locke's
general epistemological tenets, knowledge is derived only from
experience, and this argument is later adduced to support the idea that
the *tutor* can only have learned about the world through first-hand
experience of it. Logically this must be the case for the pupil too.
Locke is able to do no more than attenuate the discontinuity of the
passage into society; the fence remains. The brusque opening of *Les
Egarements du coeur et de l'esprit*, 'J'entrai dans le monde à dix-sept

ans' (p. 13), marks against Locke a type of accession to social experience which pedagogy is unable to theorize, and the maxim to which this discussion might be read as an approach, 'Les leçons et les exemples sont peu de chose pour un jeune homme; et ce n'est jamais qu'à ses dépens qu'il s'instruit' (p. 16), makes a tolerably Lockean point against Locke. As I have suggested above, Locke's general position condemns him to an untenable attempt to teach the unteachable.[70]

It is not difficult to link this blind spot, the crossing of the *clôture*, to sexuality: the entry into the world is essentially an entry into a social existence determined by sexuality and seduction. As a good anal empiricist, Locke is prepared to take pains to discuss the training of children in 'going to Stool' (§23), but represses the genital question altogether.

This is where the novel returns, as discourse of love. The novel *in* education is denounced because it occupies this domain of sexuality; the novel *as* education triumphs precisely by this occupation.

3.3.1. The Novel as Education

Traditional pedagogy tended to assume that maxims and examples were necessarily objects of adherence and imitation: Locke's simple idea of presenting the pupil with examples to *avoid* is relatively scandalous in such terms. And this would seem to allow the possibility that novels, even though they represent love and seduction, need not in fact seduce the reader. The arguments of Jacquin against this possibility have in fact already been anticipated and answered by Huet, who, at the beginning of the tradition which I have been discussing, already anticipates its end in the recognition of fiction, seduction and worldliness within education. Here the *pas au-delà mondain* becomes a *pas périlleux* which 'n'est pas périlleux', but necessary:

Si l'on dit que l'amour y est traité d'une manière si délicate et si insinuante, que l'amorce de cette dangereuse passion entre aisément dans de jeunes coeurs: je répondray que non seulement il n'est pas périlleux, mais qu'il est mesme en quelque sorte necessaire que les jeunes personnes du monde connoissent cette passion, pour fermer l'oreille à celle qui est criminelle, & pouvoir se démesler de ses artifices; & pour savoir se conduire dans celle qui a une fin honnête & sainte. Ce qui est si vray que l'expérience fait voir que celles qui connaissent moins l'amour en sont les plus susceptibles, et que les plus ignorantes sont les plus dupes. Ajoustez à cela que rien ne dérouille tant un esprit nouveau venu des Universitéz, ne sert tant à le façonner & le rendre propre au monde, que la lecture des bons Romans. Ce sont des précepteurs muets, qui succedent à ceux du College & qui apprennent aux jeunes gens, d'une méthode bien plus instructive & bien plus persuasive à parler et à vivre, & qui achevent d'abbattre la poussiere de l'école, dont ils sont encore couverts.

(Huet, pp. 215–16)

3.4. Conclusion

In this chapter I have tried to show that, starting from a *degré zéro* of education located in the passive absorption of the maxims of received dogmatic truth, the sententious discourse of pedagogy is progressively supplemented.[71] In the first instance this supplementation takes the form of narrative formations called 'examples'. The movement away from sententiousness towards narrative, or even beyond discourse altogether to 'facts' or 'things', is largely illusory, insofar as such particularities are always taken up in a movement of exemplification and maximization. Further, the appeal to *historical* narratives is disturbed by the difficulty of determining the truth of narrative propositions, and by an essential moral lack in historical truth. The fable allows pedagogy to fill this lack, and, apparently, to avoid any danger involved in the introduction of fiction into a discourse concerned to remain in the truth, in that the fictional narrative is rigorously controlled, at least in theory, by the maxim which directs the text. On the other hand, the introduction of fiction into education is dangerous, in that fiction is consistently linked by pedagogical writing to worldliness, women and seduction. Because pedagogical discourse is concerned in general to repress these aspects, it is generally unable to theorize adequately the necessary passage from the closure of education into the closure of worldliness. Rousseau's attempt to face this problem leads to the fictionalization of his own pedagogical discourse.

It is now time to take the *pas périlleux* into fiction and worldliness, and to examine the construction of closure from the other side of the fence.

3

SENTENTIOUSNESS, EDUCATION, WORLDLINESS: *LES EGAREMENTS DU COEUR ET DE L'ESPRIT*

1. Novels

In the last chapter I suggested that pedagogical discourse faced certain difficulties when forced to consider worldliness and novels, and that it generally associated these two terms with the notion of seduction.[1] In the present chapter I shall look more directly at these two repressed elements and the term which links them.

This change of scene, brought about by the crossing of the fence separating education from *le monde*, brings with it a number of methodological difficulties, insofar as in discussing 'worldliness' I shall be reading 'fictional' texts, which was not, in principle at least, the case in the previous chapter. On the other hand, the example of *Emile* in itself suggests that the separation between 'truth' and 'fiction' here is not simple, and the fact that we have seen the distinction between true and false sentences and fictional ones to be not immediately pertinent to the analysis of sententious formulations further complicates any apparently simple classification of types of discourse.

The question is made the more complex by the fact that worldly novels themselves make reference to novels, as well as to education. We saw that despite the apparently 'radical' character of Meilcour's entry into society, his existence in the *pré-monde* was suggested by a reference to education. It is also hinted that the *pré-monde* is a time of novel-reading, although in the *Egarements* this hint is again discreet. When Meilcour sees Hortense for the first time, he is convinced that he is in love with her because of an experience of novels: 'je retournais chez moi et d'autant plus persuadé que j'étais vivement amoureux que cette passion naissait dans mon coeur par un de ces grands coups de surprise qui caractérisent dans les romans les grandes aventures' (p. 36).

Again, *Faublas* is a useful parallel, and is more explicit; Faublas sees

Sophie at his sister's convent (the convent being the figure of the *pré-monde* for women), and recalls the event on his return home:

Revenu de ce premier transport, je me souvins d'avoir vu dans plusieurs romans les effets prodigieux d'une rencontre imprévue; le premier coup d'oeil d'une belle avait suffi pour captiver les sentiments d'un amant tendre, et l'amante elle-même, frappée d'un trait vainqueur, s'était sentie entraînée par un penchant irrésistible. Cependant j'avais lu de longues dissertations dans lesquelles des philosophes profonds niaient le pouvoir de la sympathie, qu'ils appelaient une chimère . . . L'espérance entra dans mon coeur; il me parut très possible qu'en fait de tendresse, la philosophie radotât, et que les romans seuls eussent raison. (p. 421)

A step has been taken: within the work of fiction, a claim is made for a truth of fiction not present in philosophy, and the insufficiency of education is implied. And as we have seen, Faublas's *gouverneur* arrives too late (Faublas has already read novels and is already in love).

The similar disqualification of education at the beginning of Duclos's *Confessions du comte de* *** occurs in the immediate context of a reference to novel-reading (see p. 67–8 above), and of the introduction to worldly education:

La marquise de Valcour, qui n'était plus dans la première jeunesse, mais qui était encore extrêmement aimable, saisit avec vivacité les plaisanteries que l'on faisait sur moi, et, sous prétexte de plaire à la maîtresse de la maison qui paraissait s'y intéresser, elle voulait que je fusse toujours avec elle. Bientôt elle me déclara son petit amant; j'acceptais cette qualité . . . Je m'y prêtais de meilleure grâce que l'on n'eût dû attendre d'un enfant *qui n'avait aucun usage du monde*; cependant je commençais à sentir des désirs que je n'osais témoigner, et que ne démêlais qu'imparfaitement. *J'avais lu quelques romans*, et je me crus amoureux . . . Mes désirs n'échappaient pas à la marquise, elle s'en apercevait mieux que moi-même, et ce fut sur ce point qu'elle voulut *entreprendre mon éducation*. (p. 201, my emphasis)

1.1. Novels in Novels

It would seem, then, that whereas the 'official' education received in the *pré-monde* is of no use to the subject entering society, the reading of novels in the same period is more helpful. On the other hand, if the novels of the *pré-monde* were adequate educators, there would be no need for worldly novels to stage such elaborate scenes of education. Further, it is clear from the passage just quoted from Duclos that, whatever the value of the novels he has read, the comte has not received from them the same type of education as that offered by the marquise. There is a certain inadequation between the expectations derived from novels and the 'reality' of the 'world' in which their prior reading is noted.

This inadequation is made clear in a comment from *Les Egarements*, again in connection with Hortense. After overhearing her in conversation in a maze, Meilcour wants to find a pretext to meet her, and comments, 'Je me rappelai alors toutes les occasions que j'avais lues dans les romans de parler à sa maîtresse, et je fus surpris qu'il n'y eût pas une dont je pusse faire usage' (p. 54).

These examples suggest that the novels read before access to *le monde* are not themselves worldly novels. The nature of this second type of novel is suggested in comments in Crébillon's first novel, the *Lettres de la marquise de M*** au comte de R**** (1732); the comte is apparently complaining that he is ill through unrequited love, and the marquise replies as follows:

Hé quoi! mon pauvre comte, vous êtes malade, et malade d'amour! le cas est singulier! mes rigueurs vous coûteront la vie! je ne me croyais pas si redoutable . . . D'ailleurs, en mourant pour moi, quelle récompense exigez-vous? Voulez-vous avoir le plaisir de me faire répandre des pleurs dont vous ne jouiriez pas? et quelle satisfaction auriez-vous, quand désespérée de votre mort, j'irai sur des roches désertes fatiguer les échos de mes regrets, et me plaindre aux dieux cruels de la perte de Tircis?[2]

Later in the novel the marquise refers to the attentions of a *magistrat* in terms of the same code: 'je viens de faire emplette d'un petit magistrat si doux, si respectueux, qu'en un besoin il effaceroit feu Céladon; il m'a même assurée que s'il était assez heureux pour me plaire, il auroit pour moi, malgré le feu qui le consume, un respect éternel'.[3] And in the *Egarements* itself, Versac denounces the same code; with reference to Madame de Senanges, Meilcour asks him: 'A propos de quoi peut-elle croire que je lui dois mon coeur?', to which Versac retorts: 'Votre coeur! . . . jargon de roman. Sur quoi supposez-vous qu'elle vous le demande? Elle est incapable d'une prétension si ridicule' (p. 149).

1.2. Novels and Novels

In making this type of explicit reference to novels, the worldly novel is not, then, making some sort of gesture of solidarity with a unitary genre condemned by pedagogy, but rather attempting to split that genre, and to take a polemical distance from seventeenth-century pastoral or heroico-sentimental models, which remain insufficient pedagogical preparation for *le monde*. A terminological vagueness is being exploited here: in the previous chapter I followed the practice of the pedagogical texts under discussion and assumed that the word 'roman' had a stable referent; it is this that the worldly novel calls into question. Whereas eighteenth-century English could exploit the opposition between the terms 'romance' and 'novel', in French this was not the case, and the term 'roman' tends to refer primarily to seventeenth-century practice.[4] It is partly this linguistic conservatism which allows Bougeant's *Fan-Férédin* still to take as the object of its satire largely obsolete seventeenth-century novelistic codes.[5]

So if worldly education takes place against the official pedagogy of the *pré-monde*, it also depends on a disqualification of the notion of 'love' derived from 'les romans'. This is of course an ideological move, but also a technical one: this type of labelling and expulsion of a fictional other within a fictional text has as its corollary an attempt to persuade the reader that the text in which such operations take place is more 'realistic' than those it denounces.

On the other hand, insofar as 'the novel' is associated with something like 'real love', it stages a return in worldly novels where these novels project the possibility of a return to self-possession after the passage through worldliness. This possibility is at its most dramatic in *Faublas*, where the eminently 'novelesque' love for Sophie (mediated with explicit reference to *La Nouvelle Héloïse*)[6] triumphs in the end, although not before its clash with worldly practice has produced the passage through violent death and madness at the end of the book. But Hortense in *Les Egarements* and Mme de Selve in Duclos's *Confessions* also represent this tendency, and the Présidente in *Les Liaisons dangereuses* can be given a similar reading.[7] The real in the worldly novel tends to return in the form of the 'romanesque', but the writing of the novels as such depends on a provisional exclusion of that 'romanesque'.

2. Education

2.1. Ignorance and Instruction

Meilcour is in need of education just as much as is Duclos's comte. But whereas in Duclos's novel that education is in many ways completed in two or three pages of text, from the marquise's maxim to the obtaining of the *dernière faveur*, the *Egarements* expands this first scene of education to fill the entire novel in its reputedly unfinished form.[8] I recapitulate briefly to set the scene of this scene of education: Meilcour enters *le monde*, is concerned only with 'l'idée du plaisir', does not know how to procure that pleasure because of his ignorance of worldly discourse and practice. A series of generalizing paragraphs about that discourse and practice, to which I shall return, ends with the following paragraph, which itself ends with a maxim already quoted:

Loin que je susse la façon dont l'amour se menait dans le monde, je croyais, malgré ce que je voyais tous les jours, qu'il fallait un mérite supérieur pour plaire aux femmes; et quelque bon opinion que j'eusse en secret de moi-même, je ne me trouvais jamais digne d'en être aimé: je suis même certain que, quand je les aurais mieux connues, je n'en aurais pas été moins timide. Les leçons et les exemples sont peu de choses pour un jeune homme; et ce n'est jamais qu'à ses dépens qu'il s'instruit. (p.16)

We shall see that despite this assertion, which seems to deny the pedagogical value of, for example, sententious discourse, 'leçons' and 'exemples' are singularly important in this novel. The apparent rejection of education at the end of this paragraph is contradicted by the end of the next: 'Je fus six mois dans cet embarras, et j'y serais sans doute resté plus longtemps, si une des Dames qui m'avait le plus vivement frappé n'eût bien voulu se charger de mon éducation' (p. 16). It is this educational undertaking which suggests that the particular 'jeune homme' has not learned very much at his own expense during his six months of 'embarras', and which also rescues the narrative from its own 'embarras' by orienting its progress. Sententiousness is essential both to the progress of the education narrated, and to the progress of the narration of that education; conversely, narratives are essential to the understanding of the importance of sententiousness.

2.1.1. The Syntagm of the Affair: Sententiousness and Indirection

Meilcour's ignorance is of 'la façon dont l'amour se menait dans le monde'; he does not know how to construct the essentially narrative syntagm of an 'affair'. The education which he receives in the first instance from Mme de Lursay is in the rules of such narratives. As I have suggested elsewhere,[9] the worldly affair begins with the performance of a preliminary figure of 'choice', and proceeds with the figure of 'declaration of love'. In the present case, the first of these two figures, usually performed by the man, is largely the work of Mme de Lursay. Her first educational task is to communicate to Meilcour that the choice has been made, and to bring him to perform the second figure himself: '[elle] jugea qu'il était temps . . . de me faire penser . . .

que j'étais le mortel fortuné que son coeur avait choisi' (p. 19). The first use of dialogue in the novel shows Mme de Lursay's attempt to provoke Meilcour into making his declaration, which the worldly discourse of *décence* to which she adheres forbids her from making herself. Further, that same *décence* prevents her from 'educating' Meilcour directly, with reference to their own situation: she is obliged to proceed indirectly, and this is the first point at which sententious statements are useful to her. She begins by referring to a theatrical performance, and when Meilcour suggests that he is unable to judge its quality, she switches to the sententious mode:

Sans avoir du théâtre une connaissance parfaite, on peut, reprit-elle, décider sur certaines parties; le sentiment par exemple en est une sur laquelle on ne se trompe point: ce n'est pas l'esprit qui le juge, c'est le coeur; et les choses intéressantes remuent également les gens bornés, et ceux qui ont le plus de lumières. (p. 21)

The 'example' of *sentiment* allows her to make a particular reference to a 'déclaration d'amour' within the play, and to praise its execution. Meilcour's reply removes this distancing by insisting not on the *représentation* but on its *représenté*: 'je crois cette situation difficile à bien manier' (p. 21); and although he is also speaking sententiously, the fact that his statement, unlike Mme de Lursay's, is tied to its context by the deictic 'je'[10] is the mark of a man not yet in command of a certain social style.

Meilcour continues in attenuated sententious form: 'je ne crois pas qu'il soit facile de dire qu'on aime' (p. 21). This attenuation must of course be taken into account in the reading: Mme de Lursay erases from her utterance any marks of the presence of the subject of its enunciation (this being a necessary condition for its being considered a 'detachable' maxim), and thus at once gives the statement a certain legislative force, and implies that it is to be understood not as *her* opinion, but as Opinion, the doxa. The formal marks in Meilcour's 'je ne crois pas que . . .' are sufficient to situate him outside the collective subject of the enunciation of that doxa, and the context of education is enough to confirm that his position outside that collective subject is due to ignorance rather than defiance.

2.1.2. The Doxa's Sex

Mme de Lursay is able to exploit a partial agreement with Meilcour, and to separate the generalized 'on' into two classes of men and women:

Je suis persuadée, dit-elle, que cet aveu coûte à une femme; mille raisons, que l'amour ne peut absolument détruire, doivent le lui rendre pénible; car vous n'imaginez pas qu'un homme risque quelque chose à le faire?   (p. 21)

Here the 'je' stresses Mme de Lursay's belonging to the class of women; but the weakening of the power of the doxa it implies is important too, suggesting not only two classes of object for the generalizing statements of that doxa, but also two classes of subjects of it. This implication complicates the status of all of her maxims, marking them not as individual or subjective, but as belonging to a collective subject not identical with *le monde* as a whole. The possibility that there might be an antagonistic masculine doxa will later be realized in the discourse of Versac. The antagonism also determines the progression of worldly narratives towards their final figures, those of the 'rupture' and of 'médisance'.[11] The antagonism is not of course total, but forms an economy.

Meilcour, meanwhile, continues in his personal disagreement: 'Je ne trouve rien de plus humiliant pour un homme que de dire qu'il aime' (p. 21); and this provokes Mme de Lursay to irony:

C'est dommage assurément, reprit-elle, que cette idée soit ridicule; par sa nouveauté peut-être elle ferait fortune. Quoi! il est humiliant pour un homme de dire qu'il aime!   (p. 21)[12]

A further restriction from Meilcour ('Oui, sans doute, dis-je, quand il n'est pas sûr d'être aimé' (p. 21)) constitutes not so much an error on his part as a *pétition de principe* in the terms of the doxa, and as such would preclude the possibility of narrative progress (hence Meilcour's six-month *embarras*), and Mme de Lursay is now able to proceed with what is more directly a statement of a rule of the worldly affair:

Et comment, reprit-elle, voulez-vous qu'il sache s'il est aimé? L'aveu qu'il fait de sa tendresse peut seul autoriser une femme à y répondre. Pensez-vous, dans quelque désordre qu'elle sentît son coeur, qu'il lui convînt de parler la première, de s'exposer par cette démarche à se rendre moins chère à vos yeux, et à être l'objet d'un refus?   (pp. 21–2)

2.1.3. Economy, Incompetence and Masculinity

The following exchanges turn around the legitimation of the rule here laid down, and specifically around its economic motivation (Mme de Lursay: 'vous cesseriez de sentir du goût pour celle qui vous en aurait inspiré le plus, dans l'instant qu'elle vous offrirait une conquête aisée' (p. 22)).[13] But when Meilcour attempts to reparticularize the

106

discussion a new complication arises: 'Eh! comptez-vous pour rien, Madame, repris-je, l'embarras de le dire, surtout pour moi qui sens que je le dirais mal?' (p. 22). Mme de Lursay suggests that elegance in a declaration is not always desirable: this seems to weaken the closure of the discourse in a serious way, for the implication is that a 'bad' performance is in fact the 'best' performance, and that the height of 'competence' in the declaration lies in pure incompetence. In fact, any opening of the worldly discourse of love to an 'outside' (of pure sentiment, say) is itself rigorously controlled and codified.[14] When Meilcour asks if the persuasive effect of incompetence is always reliable, Mme de Lursay, still sententiously, refines on the previous generalization (which had left open a space for such refinement in the 'pas toujours'):

Non, répondit-elle; ce désordre dont je vous parlais, vient quelquefois de ce qu'un homme est plus stupide qu'amoureux, et pour lors on ne lui en tient pas compte: d'ailleurs les hommes sont assez artificieux pour feindre du trouble et de la passion pendant qu'ils sont à peine animés par le désir, et souvent on ne les croit pas. Il peut arriver aussi que celui à qui vous inspirez de l'amour n'est point celui pour qui vous en voudriez prendre, et tout ce qu'il vous dit ne vous touche pas. (pp. 22–3)

Of these three disqualified possibilities, only the second creates complications for the worldly affair, and the masculine doxa can be located fairly precisely here in the possibility of the *feinte*, the fiction of love and the simulation of its privileged signs.[15] The implication that there *is* a possibility of something like 'real love' in the worldly novel (associated with women), and that it is men who are apt to deal in simulacra of passion, is difficult to sustain, as will become clear when Mme de Lursay comes to re-write the narrative of her affair with Meilcour. It is this problem of the real and the simulated (the true and the fictional) which suggests a perspective beyond worldliness, and which Rousseau will try to exploit. Such a perspective is, however, also figured *in* worldly novels, by the character of Hortense in *Les Egarements* and by Mme de Selve in *Les Confessions du comte de ****: it is essentially linked with the narrative instance of these novels, and will be considered in its place. In recognizing this perspective, and denouncing the possibility of its simulation by men, Mme de Lursay is attempting to reinforce her own claim to sincerity, in a gesture homologous with that of the novel as a whole (with respect to other novels). Versac's pedagogical discourse will unmask this type of claim as no less a simulacrum than the simulacra from which it attempts to distinguish itself.

107

In the context of this dialogue, however, the immediate effect of this series of generalizations is to weaken the force of the earlier 'L'aveu [qu'un homme] fait de sa tendresse peut seul autoriser une femme à y répondre', and to suggest to Meilcour that he might do better to keep silent rather than risk having his declaration fail to provoke a favourable reply. But Mme de Lursay does manage to make Meilcour admit that he has a declaration to make, and to suggest that she might be the object of it. Two further sententious formulations intervene before the effective performance of the declaration. In the first, prescriptive weight is dominant, but the link to the particular situation also sketches out an enthymeme: 'que vous importerait que je ne vous aimasse pas? On ne doit souhaiter d'inspirer de l'amour qu'à quelqu'un pour qui l'on en a pris: et je ne vous soupçonne point du tout d'être avec moi dans ce cas-là; du moins, je ne le voudrais pas' (p. 24). 'If you're interested in my loving you, you must, ought, or (perhaps most importantly) *owe* it to me (or to the doxa) to (say that you) love me.' The final particularized statements are simply dictated by the demands of order or the ordering of *demandes*, but this is what Meilcour takes to be most important, and he sees in it a 'peur étrange'. This provokes the second sententious statement, still linked to a *dénégation*:

Non, reprit-elle, ce n'est pas que j'en aie peur; craindre de vous voir amoureux serait avouer à demi que vous pourriez me rendre sensible: l'amant que l'on redoute le plus est toujours celui que l'on est le plus près d'aimer; et je serais bien fâchée que vous me crussiez si craintive avec vous.   (p. 25)

And now the declaration takes place:

Ce n'est pas non plus ce dont je me flatte, répondis-je: mais enfin, si je vous aimais, que feriez-vous donc?

Je ne crois pas, reprit-elle, que sur une supposition vous ayez attendu une réponse positive.

Oserais-je donc, Madame, vous dire que je ne suppose rien?

A cette déclaration si précise de l'état de mon coeur, Madame de Lursay soupira, rougit, tourna languissamment les yeux sur moi, les y fixa quelque temps, les baissa sur son éventail et se tut.   (p. 25)

The figure 'declaration' has now been performed and named; the qualification of it as 'si précise' can be read as an ironic antiphrasis, but is not only that – the lack of 'precision' in Meilcour's declaration does not of course prevent its being, very precisely, a declaration, and Mme de Lursay's 'reply', exploiting paralinguistic signs which the young Meilcour is unable to read correctly, already inaugurates the next figure, that of 'defence'.

2.1.4. Doxa and Indirection: the Veil

I have suggested above that, in this passage from *Les Egarements*, sententiousness has two functions: first to state or quote a body of accepted 'truths' (a doxa), in the interests of initiating a 'pupil', and secondly to refer indirectly to a particular situation. It might be assumed that the second of these two functions is simply a convenient way for Mme de Lursay to avoid committing herself in a difficult psychological situation; but this type of reading concedes too much to some notion of 'individuality' in the characters – which is precisely what the use of sententiousness casts into doubt. Any notion of psychological individuality which the reader might invoke to explain this second function is challenged within the text itself by its first function, which aims precisely at the elimination of individual differences: Meilcour has no *right*, for example, to insist that he, personally, would find a 'déclaration' difficult to perform. Such an idea is 'ridicule' precisely because it cannot be generalized as a rule in the doxa for the construction of narrative syntagms. The problem is one not of psychology but of discourse and its rules.

This would suggest that the 'two functions' of sententiousness are not distinct, but are rather two sides of a single function, which I shall describe as one of *veiling*. Generalizations are used to veil the inevitable particularity of the aim of the worldly syntagm (the apparent *telos* of the worldly narrative being the sexual act, the 'dernière faveur'), but in fact the narrative proceeds beyond any such particularity insofar as the 'rupture' and consequent 'médisance' ensure the reintegration of that particularity into the general circulation of worldly discourse – this part of the economy is most clearly exemplified, perhaps, in *La Nuit et le moment*. Worldly discourse could be described as formalist in that it tends to the reduction of individual differences and to the erasure of deviations from the order which it prescribes for narratives.

2.2. Sententiousness and Narrativization

The implication of this suggestion – that the function of sententiousness is to state the rules of the discourse of love, and is essentially linked to its use as a mode of indirect reference – is that any apparently absolute separation of sententious and narrative propositions is illusory. The sententious statements do not stand outside narrative propositions, and simply intervene from a position of structural exteriority to comment on, correct, or draw descriptive generalizations from 'individual' events. Rather, sententiousness tends to make general the narrative itself, to make it exemplary in a strong sense: a string of sententious propositions can form a sort of 'ideal' narrative. This type of narrative could be that of a critic's commentary on worldly novels, the extraction from them of elements taken to be structurally necessary; when referring earlier to 'figures' in the worldly love affair, I was implying this sort of general narrative. However, it is also written *within* the worldly novel, and is indeed implied by the presence of sententious formulations in the text. The narrative of the worldly affair is thus, to some extent at least, its own commentary and interpretation: narrative elements are always caught in a movement of generalization, sententious elements in a movement of narrativization. This possibility is made clear in just such an 'ideal narrative' in *Les Egarements*.

Meilcour has caught sight of a beautiful 'inconnue' (Hortense) at the Opéra, and falls in love with her; this 'coup de foudre' complicates the progress of the affair with Mme de Lursay, and leads Meilcour to avoid a *rendez-vous* with her, and to take a solitary walk in the Tuileries. In the maze, Meilcour overhears a conversation between two women, who turn out to be the 'inconnue' and an anonymous older 'Dame'. This conversation is in fact another 'scene of education', in which the 'Dame' warns the younger woman about the dangers of love, and produces the following sententious sequence:

L'amour dans un coeur vertueux se masque longtemps, repartit la Dame. Sa première impression se fait même sans qu'on s'en aperçoive; il ne paraît d'abord qu'un goût simple, et qu'on peut se justifier aisément. Ce goût s'accroît-il, nous trouvons des raisons pour excuser ses progrès. Quand enfin nous en connaissons le désordre, ou il n'est plus temps de la combattre, ou nous ne le voulons pas. Notre âme déjà attachée à une si douce erreur craint de s'en voir privée; loin de songer à la détruire, nous aidons nous-mêmes à l'augmenter. Il semble que nous craignions que ce sentiment n'agisse pas assez de lui-même. Nous cherchons sans cesse à soutenir le trouble de notre coeur, et à le nourrir des chimères de notre imagination. Si quelquefois la raison veut nous éclairer, ce n'est qu'une lueur, qui, éteinte dans le même instant, n'a fait que nous montrer le précipice, et n'a pas assez duré pour nous en sauver. En rougissant de notre faiblesse, elle nous tyrannise; elle se fortifie dans notre coeur par les efforts mêmes que nous faisons pour l'en arracher; elle y éteint toutes les passions, ou en devient le principe. Pour nous étourdir davantage, nous avons la vanité de croire que nous ne céderons jamais, que le plaisir d'aimer peut être toujours innocent. En vain nous avons l'exemple contre nous: il ne nous garantit pas de notre chute. Nous allons d'égarements en égarements sans les prévoir ni les sentir. Nous périssons vertueuses encore, sans être présentes, pour ainsi dire, au fatal moment de notre défaite; et nous nous retrouvons coupables sans savoir, non seulement comment nous l'avons été, mais souvent encore avant d'avoir pensé que nous puissions jamais l'être.

(p. 51)

The subjects of these sententious formulations are either abstracts, such as 'amour', 'goût' and 'faiblesse', or else the general 'nous', which, as in Mme de Lursay's statements, is the general subject of a feminine doxa. Here the situation is different, however, insofar as the *destinataire* of the statements is also a woman: this implies that the deictic 'nous' is of a somewhat different order, implying or inviting or enforcing the inclusion within it of the *destinataire*.[16] Whereas Mme de Lursay wanted to instruct Meilcour in how to deal with women correctly, the 'Dame' is telling Hortense both how women (or a certain class of women) behave, and how Hortense, as a woman, should behave. Again there is a temptation to read this passage as a piece of psychological analysis, as a pseudo-scientific account of how a 'coeur vertueux' really experiences love; but this reading, which would lead one to extract a 'theory of love' from the text, would ignore again the prescriptive weight of sententiousness, and, crucially, would erase the pragmatic situation of the utterance.

2.2.1. Description, Prescription, Ambivalence

The prescriptive weight becomes clearer from the fact that, as a description, the passage involves a contradiction. Apparently describing how a 'virtuous heart' experiences love, it in fact leads to the conclusion that the experience of love by such a heart leads, apparently inevitably, to the loss of its virtue. Love and virtue, or the values accorded to those terms in this passage, are therefore incompatible, and the opening expression, 'L'amour dans un coeur vertueux' is, we might say, an unacceptable sentence in the grammar the rules of which are here laid down. The logic of the passage does not however collapse as a result of this contradiction, but rather exploits it to imply a prescriptive proposition which we might gloss as, 'If you wish to be considered virtuous (by the *nous* of whom I am here the mouthpiece), you must not fall in love'. The narrative of the progress of love is accordingly marked negatively by terms such as 'erreur . . . trouble . . . chimères . . . précipice . . . faiblesse . . . tyrannise . . . étourdir . . . vanité . . . chute . . . égarements . . . périssons . . . fatal moment de notre défaite . . . coupables'. Everything in the passage leads the reader to allow such terms and expressions to retain an 'original' axiological force, and imply the prescriptive statement 'Don't choose this'.[17] And Hortense's own reading of the passage

111

figures this reading: 'Juste Ciel! s'écria l'inconnue, quel portrait! Qu'il me cause d'horreur!' The pragmatic situation of the passage (its structure as a 'scene of education') also supports this view.

On the other hand, the contradiction implied between the two major terms of the passage, the fact that the 'erreur' is 'douce', and a certain inevitability implied by the narrative sequence, might suggest the possibility of a more complex reading, as insidious and compelling in this 'virtuous' passage as is love in a 'virtuous' heart. This insidiousness might be linked to the use of the verb 'masquer' in the opening statement: the 'Dame''s moral vocabulary also 'masks' a possible inflection of her logic towards love, or love's use of logic to 'mask' its presence and to facilitate the justification of its progress.[18] The 'Dame''s use of 'nous' might indeed imply that she herself, and all the individuals indicated by that pronoun, have experienced the love the progress of which is described so carefully. Perhaps 'virtue' here has no existence before its contamination by 'love'; 'virtue' might seem to perish at the hands of love, but 'nous périssons vertueuses encore', and survive the 'fatal moment' to produce sententious formulations guaranteed by 'virtue'. In any case, the passage gives no indication as to how 'virtue' might combat love, insofar as '[la faiblesse] se fortifie dans notre coeur par les efforts mêmes que nous faisons pour l'en arracher'.

So two distinct interpretative possibilities are in play here. The first is that of Hortense herself: its possibility depends on her being, like Meilcour, a newcomer to *le monde*, and thus standing, as it were, before any possible split between 'virtue' and 'love' (see pp. 33 and 50). The second, more complicated, possibility would rely on the ambiguities and equivocations indicated above, and would reason backwards from the experience of love to the reality of virtue. A woman already in *le monde* and already in love could take the doxa laid down in this passage as the basis for a reasoning of the type, 'I am in love, I have "fallen"; but this passage describes exactly the progress of my feelings, and as it is concerned with "l'amour dans un coeur vertueux", then I can reasonably claim to be virtuous in spite of my love'. The second of these possibilities suggests that any purity of virtue is, in this discourse, always already compromised by the necessary possibility of this second type of reading: this 'compromise' of virtue splits its doxa and allows it to be constituted in worldly terms, always permitting a Hortense to become a Mme de Lursay, and a Mme de Lursay to remain, in some sense, a Hortense. The play between the possible readings of 'virtue' here can be designated within the worldly code as *décence*.[19]

Insofar as the feminine doxa relies on this originary drift away from any purity of 'virtue', it evidently moves towards the problems of the *feinte* and of fiction earlier characterized by Mme de Lursay as being an essentially masculine possibility. This implies that the feminine doxa cannot be considered in isolation as a separate discourse, but must be read in conjunction with the masculine doxa apparently opposed to it. The apparent opposition is most clearly to be read in the confrontation of sententious discourse between Versac and Mme de Lursay, and the 'pure' masculine doxa in the novel's most important 'scene of education', in which Versac instructs Meilcour in 'la science du monde'.

2.3. Paradoxa and the Subject of Demystification

Versac's first appearance in the novel prepares the confrontation with Mme de Lursay which opens Part 2: he is immediately characterized as 'le plus audacieux petit-maître qu'on eût jamais vu' (p. 72), as both exemplary and beyond imitation: 'Personne ne pouvait lui ressembler' (p. 73). But he is also the object of a desire to imitate on the part of the young Meilcour, the object of a self-imposed education: 'Je ne le voyais jamais sans l'étudier et sans chercher à me rendre propres ces airs fastueux que j'admirais tant en lui' (p. 73). This imitation is furtive, forbidden by Meilcour's mother (see p. 72), who had, however, blessed his connection with Mme de Lursay. The relationship between Versac and Mme de Lursay depends on the mutual interference in each other's projects for education/seduction. In the confrontations between them, Versac appears to use sententiousness paradoxally, to demystify the doxa put forward by Mme de Lursay, as in the following passage:

> Voyez-vous, marquise, il n'y a personne qui voulût s'engager, même avec l'objet le plus charmant, s'il était question de lui être éternellement attaché. Loin de se le proposer l'un à l'autre, c'est une idée qu'on écarte le plus qu'on peut (du moins quand on est sage); on se dit bien qu'on s'aimera toujours, mais il est tant d'exemples du contraire que cela n'effraye pas. Ce n'est qu'un propos galant qui n'a que force de madrigal, et qui est compté pour rien quand on veut se donner le plaisir de l'inconstance. (p. 78)

The problem of the sententious subject arises here: the 'on' is clearly not to be identified with either of the sexes, in that it is composed of the 'un' and the 'autre' of the couple. On the other hand, just before this example, Versac has affirmed, 'Comme moi, tous les hommes ne cherchent que le plaisir', and so it seems clear that if the subject of the utterance is the couple, the subject of its enunciation is the male, who can claim that women cannot reasonably complain about men's *indécence* because they collude in the publication of their affairs. Mme de Lursay attempts to attack Versac on just this point, but what she (or the doxa of *décence* from which she quotes) reproaches in him is not his *holding* the beliefs he expresses, but rather his *expression* of them; she refers to 'ces sentiments que vous dissimulez fort peu', and 'l'indécence avec laquelle vous conduisez et rompez une intrigue' (p. 79). The *indécence* resides precisely in the refusal to allow the play located above, which permitted the apparent coexistence of 'love' and 'virtue'. The demystificatory quality of Versac's sententiousness lies in his explicit development of the drift from 'virtue' to 'love', towards a purely functional, and fictional, language of *galanterie*.

When, against these assertions, Mme de Lursay claims to know of examples going against the inevitable publication of affairs, Versac takes up this notion of exemplification in the service both of his sententious assertions, and of their strategic reference to Mme de Lursay. The linking of particular and general through the use of the 'un de ces x' formula is particularly instructive here:

Par exemple, j'étais il n'y a pas longtemps avec une de ces femmes raisonnables, de ces femmes adroites dont les penchants sont ensevelis sous l'air le plus réservé, qui semblent avoir substitué aux dérèglements de leur jeunesse, de la sagesse et de la vertu. Vous concevez, ajouta-t-il, qu'il y a de ces femmes-là. Eh bien! j'étais seul avec une prude de cette espèce. L'amant arriva, l'on le reçut froidement, à peine voulut-on le traiter comme connaissance; mais pourtant les yeux parlèrent, malgré qu'on en eût. La voix s'adoucit: le petit homme, fort neuf encore, fut embarrassé de la situation; et moi, à qui rien n'échappa, je sortis le plus tôt que je pus, pour l'aller dire à tout le monde. (p. 80)[20]

The privilege of male over female in the worldly discourse of love is clearly marked here: Versac has, within worldly discourse, the right both to boast about his own conquests, and to unveil the veiling activity of *décence* which is constitutive of the feminine doxa (just before this passage he refers to 'ces petits commerces tendres si scrupuleusement voilés' (pp. 79–80)). The effect of this is to turn the accusation of the *feinte* back against the woman; but we should be wary of attributing too much critical value to the demystificatory function of Versac's paradoxa, which is still here (and in general, as I shall argue later) caught up in a sort of meta-*décence*: Versac is still sufficiently part of *le monde* to veil his allusions in general terms, to adopt worldly strategy.

2.3.1. Generalization and Individuality

These motifs are condensed in the scene of the *souper* which follows,[21] and which introduces into the novel Mme de Senanges, a rival to Mme

114

de Lursay in the education of Meilcour. In the conversation which takes place over table, Versac again turns to *médisance*, and he is opposed here first by Mme de Théville (Hortense's mother, a representative of 'virtue'), and then by Mme de Senanges. The pretext is a remark about a Mme de ***, who has re-entered the *monde* after becoming a *dévote*; she is blamed for her choice of lover by Versac and by Mme de Senanges, who implies a rule for worldly behaviour: 'après s'être retirée du monde avec tant d'éclat, il y fallait du moins rentrer par une aventure plus sérieuse' (p. 97). Mme de Théville suggests a rule of virtue, 'Qui que ce fût qu'elle prît . . . je ne vois pas qu'au fond elle en eût été moins blâmable' (p. 97). Versac seems to second Mme de Senanges, and makes the rule more explicit:

Oh! pardonnez-moi, Madame, répondit Versac; sur ces sortes de choses, le choix ne laisse pas d'être important. L'on est quelquefois moins blâmée d'un magistrat que d'un colonel, et pour une prude, par exemple, l'un est plus convenable que l'autre: car à cinquante ans prendre un jeune homme, c'est ajouter au ridicule de la passion celui de l'objet. (p. 97)

But in the following exchange the alliance shifts, and Versac and Mme de Théville seem to agree on what is the formal problem of the link between general statements and particular applications of them. Mme de Lursay and Mme de Senanges protest at Versac's 'thèses générales' about women, whereas Mme de Théville agrees with him that any such protest implies secret reasons for self-reproach.

Mme de Théville in fact stands outside the domain of the doxa by refusing the essentially collective nature of worldly discourse, and by defending the claims of individual conscience against the generalization of 'women' both as object of worldly sententiousness and as collective subject of a certain worldly discourse. This defence of a certain individuality again points to the possibility of an escape from the closure of worldliness; it is ambiguously taken up in the novel's narrative discourse, and, more radically, but still ambiguously, in the appeal to conscience in *La Nouvelle Héloïse*. Versac is able to agree with this point of view on sententiousness only insofar as, on the one hand, he is protected from such generalizations by the simple fact of not being a woman, and on the other because he is in fact exploiting his own generalizations to attack, although in no sense from a position of 'virtue', particular examples. But his sententiousness on sententiousness here is more complex in its structure than this would suggest, insofar as he is also attacking, from a position yet to be analysed, the *relationship* between particular and general implied in the position of Mme de Senanges and Mme de Lursay, who are both so eager to identify with a collective subject and to defend it at that level of generality. The logic of Versac's criticism of this position is that such a drive to generalization (and such a tendency to disagree with other generalizations) can only be a sign of individual vulnerability to the unmasking of the feminine doxa. This implies that the movement from particular to general is itself taken up by the notion of veiling: in a paradoxical manoeuvre, Versac's argument uses generalizations to attack those who attack such generalizations only because they exploit *other* generalizations, to veil their particular transgressions of the doxa which they apparently support. A further sententious sequence from Versac makes this clear:

> Il est des femmes dont je pense on ne peut pas plus mal, dont je regarde le manège avec mépris, et auxquelles enfin je ne connais nulle sorte de vertu; qui n'ont pas des faiblesses, mais des vices; toujours les premières à crier sur ce que l'on dit de leur sexe, *parce qu'elles ont toujours à couvrir leur intérêt particulier de l'intérêt général.* Pour celles-là sans doute le moindre trait est cruel: elles perdent tant à être connues, et dans le fond de leur coeur le savent si bien; qu'elles ne peuvent supporter rien de ce qui les démasque ou les définit. Ainsi quand je dirai: *les femmes se rendent promptement, à peine attendent-elles qu'on les en prie*, si je fais un portrait désavantageux de quelques-unes, il me sera permis de croire que celles qui s'élèvent contre pensent qu'il leur ressemble.
>
> Sans doute, Monsieur, dit Madame de Théville, et la colère sur ces sortes de choses prouve seulement qu'on pense mal de soi-même.
>
> (p. 99, first emphasis mine)

Mme de Théville's agreement is in fact, despite appearances, not at all in the spirit of Versac's argument: the notion of 'penser mal de soi-même' has no place at all in worldly discourse, any more than does the idea of the individual supporting it. What she does have in common with Versac, and indeed with worldly discourse in general, is an indifference to the truth of such statements at the level of generality which they invoke. But her position has no use for sententiousness at all, whereas both that of Versac and that of Mme de Senanges and Mme de Lursay require it; in the latter case to veil her veilings, in the former to veil the particularity of his unveilings. Worldly discourse *in general* requires this generalization-as-veiling, insofar as that discourse survives through the repetition of set patterns of conduct (narrative norms) performed by essentially interchangeable individuals, who circulate within this general economy (and in this the term 'égarements' is perhaps misleading, insofar as this economy is far from being uncontrolled) as abstract values (the 'fat', the 'petit maître', the 'coquette', the 'prude', and many other types of commodity)[22] which leave no room for individuality.

2.4. Singularity, Exemplarity, Generality

Versac's position in this economy might be contested, in that he is explicitly presented as exceptional, and seems to attack the discourse which supports the circulation of worldly currency. To show that this is not in fact the case, it is necessary to consider in more detail the final important 'scene of education' in the novel, in which he explains to Meilcour the 'science du monde'.

Here Versac assumes the position of educator with respect to Meilcour, and announces that 'Comme je n'ai d'autre but que celui de vous instruire, je me ferais toujours un vrai plaisir d'éclaircir vos doutes . . . et de vous montrer le monde tel que vous devez le voir' (p. 150). It is worth pointing out here the inflexion of this 'showing', compared with the ideal of Locke and Rousseau, who wanted the young man to see the world 'tel qu'il est':[23] the use of the verb 'devoir' in Versac's formulation implies a type of insertion into worldly agonistics, and, perhaps, an acceptance of fiction, which the 'serious' discourse of pedagogy did not envisage. Meilcour 'ought' to see the world in a certain way because he is destined by this education to act in it and to exploit its discursive strategies.

The 'education' again makes abundant use of maxims and 'préceptes', but, as in official pedagogy, some doubt is cast on the usefulness of such formulations, as Versac recognizes when he says, 'Ce n'est pas du reste que je me flatte que vous puissiez marcher sûrement d'après mes seuls préceptes' (p. 151).[24] Here, however, we can use this doubt as an approach to the most difficult problem posed by Versac's long lecture, which is again that of the relationship between particularity and generality. We have already noted that in the narrator's presentation of Versac, the latter is somehow both exemplary and beyond example or imitation, and the tension which this characterization suggests is now translated by Versac into his instructions to Meilcour.

In the first instance, Versac's advice on how to succeed in *le monde* implies a rigorous subordination of any individuality to the general 'principes' which govern it:

C'est une erreur de croire que l'on puisse conserver dans le monde cette innocence de moeurs que l'on a communément quand on y entre, et que l'on puisse être toujours vertueux et toujours naturel, sans risquer sa réputation ou sa fortune. Le coeur et l'esprit sont forcés de s'y gâter, tout y est mode et affectation. Les vertus, les agréments et les talents y sont purement arbitraires, et l'on n'y peut réussir qu'en se défigurant sans cesse. Voilà des principes que vous ne devez jamais perdre de vue.   (pp. 151–2)

Versac himself can then be the example of these general principles to be imitated: 'ce n'est qu'en suivant mes traces qu'on peut parvenir à une aussi grande réputation' (p. 151). However, this type of generalization, and the practical denial of individuality which it implies, is contradicted in later instructions. The possibility of this contradiction first appears in a remark which juxtaposes the possibility of generalization with the mark of singularity constituted by the proper name:

L'on peut réduire l'art de plaire, aujourd'hui, à quelques préceptes assez peu entendus, et dont la pratique ne souffre aucunes difficultés. Je suppose d'abord, et avec assez de raison, ce me semble, qu'un homme de notre rang, et de votre âge, ne doit avoir pour objet que de rendre son nom célèbre.

(p. 153)

Meilcour must apparently 'disfigure' his individuality by adhering to the precepts of a general 'art de plaire', and accept a 'devoir' imposed by the general categories of rank and age; but that 'devoir' is to return to individuality as a notional 'famous name', and not simply an anonymous virtuoso in the performance of that 'art'. This tension is now explicitly pushed towards aporia:

Il faut d'abord se persuader qu'en suivant les principes connus, on n'est jamais qu'un homme ordinaire; que l'on ne paraît neuf qu'en s'en écartant; que les hommes n'admirent que ce qui les frappe, et que la singularité seule produit cet effet sur eux. On ne peut donc être trop singulier, c'est-à-dire qu'on ne peut trop affecter de ne ressembler à personne, soit par les idées, soit par les façons. Un travers que l'on possède seul fait plus d'honneur qu'un mérite que l'on partage avec quelqu'un. (p. 153)

Meilcour himself is worried by the apparent contradiction here, and points out, 'Si je deviens imitateur, je cesse d'être singulier' (p. 154). Versac attempts to resolve this by invoking a 'souplesse d'esprit'. The point here is that for Versac, 'singularité' does not involve standing outside the closure of worldliness (this possibility is simply excluded), but in, precisely, *maximizing* the general system of worldly discourse, in becoming such a perfect representative of it in its totality that that perfection itself becomes singular, turning back on *le monde* its own general rules in total singular form: 'un génie supérieur sait embellir ce que les autres lui fournissent, et le rendre neuf à leurs yeux mêmes' (p. 154). On the other hand, such singularity is itself precarious in that its constitutive attachment to the worldliness it in part denies tends to re-generalize it by making of it the object of imitation and reproduction. Versac goes on to refer to 'Cette fatuité audacieuse et singulière, qui, n'ayant point de modèle, soit seul digne

118

d'en servir' (p. 157). Versac's singularity is a sort of pseudopod, extended by a worldliness which has become amoebic. We must then assume that, however scandalous Versac may appear in terms of the worldly doxa, he is in fact essentially a representative or delegate of that doxa, and ensures its survival and renewal. The fact that a proleptic remark early in the text informs us that later Meilcour 'parvin[t] à mettre la Cour et Paris entre [eux] deux' (p. 73), is proof enough that the type of 'singularity' represented by Versac involves in its structure its own regenera(liza)tion.

It has recently been suggested that Versac be read as a 'relayed narrator' in the structure of the novel:[25] this analysis of his role can only be tested when we come to discuss the position of narrative discourse in the novel.

2.5. Narrative in Narrative: the *Vraisemblable*

As a bridge between the role of sententiousness in the discourse of the characters and its role in the narrative discourse, I turn now to an apparently hybrid structure in which a character becomes a narrator: not in the sense of a 'roman à tiroirs' (where the structure is relatively simple), but where a character retells the 'same' story in which s/he has been a character narrated by the 'true' narrative instance. This occurs in *Les Egarements* when Mme de Lursay retells to Meilcour the story of her love for him. This narrative is produced not so much with the aim of giving information, as with performing the strategic function of establishing her 'innocence' and sincerity, in the service of seduction. This can be achieved only by providing motivations for actions and events, in short by constructing a system of verisimilitude. In the present case, this involves the production of alibis to protect Mme de Lursay from reproach in terms of the doxa which she has previously been concerned to defend, and to make of the narrative of her love for Meilcour something which approaches the ambiguous 'ideal narrative' recounted by the 'Dame' to Hortense. This type of operation again involves a movement of generalization which takes up particular events:

Eh! quelle apparence en effet que je dusse craindre de vous trop aimer? Quand j'aurais pu prévoir que vous penseriez à moi, devais-je imaginer que vous me rendriez sensible, et qu'un événement si peu vraisemblable dût un jour être compté parmi ceux de ma vie? Je ne l'ai pas cru, et vous ne pouvez pas me le reprocher. Toute autre que moi ne vous aurait pas craint davantage, et, à ne considérer que votre âge et le mien (je laisse à part ma façon de penser), ma sécurité était bien naturelle.   (pp. 177–8)

The construction of a system of verisimilitude requires the generation of what can be termed, after Berger and Luckman, 'plausibility-structures',[26] and the verbalization of such structures implies the construction of sententious propositions. The one governing the passage just quoted may be derived as, 'Il n'est pas normal (naturel, vraisemblable) qu'un jeune homme (de dix-sept ans) tombe amoureux d'une femme de quarante'. This implicit maxim is in contradiction with what has 'actually' happened, and so Mme de Lursay can, by implication, claim that it is *vraisemblable* for her not to have foreseen the *invraisemblable*. This basic plausibility-structure can now govern a thorough reinterpretation of events and signs:

> Vos soins plus marqués, vos visites plus fréquentes et plus longues, et le plaisir qu'il semblait que vous prissiez à me voir, ne me parurent que les effets de notre ancienne amitié . . . Ce que vous me disiez sur l'amour, l'acharnement avec lequel vous m'en parliez et la difficulté que je trouvais à vous faire porter votre esprit sur d'autres matières, ne furent à mes yeux que les suites de la curiosité d'un jeune homme qui cherche à s'éclairer sur un sentiment qui commence à troubler son coeur ou sur des idées qui occupent son imagination. (p. 178)

The process of *vraisemblabilisation* continues: Meilcour must remember how she tried to rid him of his 'fantaisie' of love for her, and if she was not so severe on him as she might have been, this was because of the imperatives of 'Mon amitié . . . votre jeunesse . . . une sorte de pitié' (p. 178). The recognition of her own feelings came too late: 'Je reconnus alors la nécessité de vous fuir, mais je ne le pouvais plus' (p. 178). The most difficult part of naturalization of events is now over, in that the progress of 'love' can now be confided to the eminently 'natural' narrative of love provided by eighteenth-century mechanistic psychology, as it figured in the 'ideal narrative' discussed above. What was *invraisemblable* at the beginning of Mme de Lursay's narrative, namely love between two people of widely different ages, must now become *vraisemblable* by losing its pertinence as a fact: 'Cet affreux intervalle de votre âge au mien, et qui m'avait d'abord si sensiblement frappée, disparut à mes regards. Chaque jour que nous passions à nous voir, me semblait vous donner des années, ou m'ôter des miennes' (pp. 178–9). All that remains is to validate the sentiment by naming it as the operator of the *vraisemblabilisation* of the *invraisemblable*: 'L'amour seul pouvait m'aveugler à ce point, et croire que nous pouvions être faits l'un pour l'autre, était une preuve trop sûre du mien, pour pouvoir le méconnaître' (p. 179).

A circularity implicit in any system of verisimilitude is at work here: it is *vraisemblable* that Mme de Lursay is in love, because love alone can make *vraisemblable* her 'blindness' to the age-difference which made her falling in love *invraisemblable* enough for it to happen. The enthymeme runs as follows: 'Love is inevitable: this feeling was inevitable: therefore it was love'. Mme de Lursay gives herself up to a fatality of narrative, hiding a progress generated by codified strategies of desire behind an apparently impersonal causal sequence.

In doing this, she is writing a novel of her love, and obeying laws of a certain 'realism' by providing motivations for facts and events which are in fact teleologically oriented towards the satisfaction of desire. The narrative of her affair with Meilcour is determined by its ostensible end-point in sexual satisfaction (this occurs a few pages later in the novel), and can be made *vraisemblable*, plausible, acceptable, only insofar as that *telos* is hidden. In doing this, she is reproducing a general structure of fiction, and in using the term 'motivation' to describe it I am borrowing from Genette, who defines motivation as 'la manière dont la fonctionnalité des éléments du récit se dissimule sous un masque de détermination causale . . . La motivation est donc l'apparence et l'alibi causaliste que se donne la détermination finaliste qui est la règle de la fiction'.[27]

Motivation requires for its operation a reserve of maxims, which can generate plausibility-structures for particular events or narrative propositions, which must thus, in order to become *vraisemblable*, be subsumed or subsumable under a sententious proposition. But insofar as the recognition of the operation by the reader unveils this operation, it is clear that the *vraisemblable* must veil not only the finalist determination of the narrative, but must also *veil that process of veiling*,[28] in an infinitely regressive series.

2.5.1. Good and Bad Readers

Mme de Lursay's narrative, which obeys these rules so well, is not of course guaranteed by the final narrative instance of the novel; and if Meilcour the actor in the text is a naive reader of her narrative, then Meilcour the narrator is more sophisticated, at least in his reading of her story. The narrative which frames it exploits the fact that a given narrative proposition can be subsumed under different and contradictory sententious propositions: it is clear, for example, that from the beginning of the novel the reader is encouraged to use the difference in age between Mme de Lursay and Meilcour as the basis of a plausibility-structure which makes her desire for him more rather than less *vraisemblable*. Again, the passage quoted above, beginning, 'Vos soins plus marqués . . .' has been pre-empted by a narrative passage at the beginning of the novel:

> Mon respect pour elle, et qui semblait s'accroître de jour en jour, mon embarras en lui parlant, embarras différent de celui qu'elle m'avait vu dans mon enfance, des regards même plus marqués que je ne le croyais, mon soin toujours pressant de lui plaire, mes fréquentes visites, et plus que tout, peut-être, l'envie qu'elle avait elle-même de m'engager, lui firent penser que je l'aimais en secret.   (p. 17)

This motivation has an advantage over that provided by Mme de Lursay, both in that it appears earlier in the novel, and, more importantly, in that it has the authority of the final narrative instance in the text. What Mme de Lursay writes as 'I failed to discern the possibility of love between us *because* it would be so *invraisemblable*' has already been rewritten for the reader of the novel, as 'Mme de Lursay appeared to fail to recognize the signs of Meilcour's love, *so that* she could legitimate his eventually providing her with sexual gratification'.[29]

Mme de Lursay uses the structure of narrative fiction within the discourse of *décence*, which, we can now suggest, involves the telling of decent stories, the simultaneous veiling of the bare functionality of desire and the bare functionality of narrative. Just as Versac used sententious formulations in a veiled operation of unveiling the veilings of *décence*, so in this case the narrator exploits the sententiousness of his plausibility-structures to unveil the functionality of Mme de Lursay's narrative of seduction, or seduction as narrative. The young Meilcour is a poor reader of narratives, while Versac and the narrator appear to read rather better – but the narrator's reading of Mme de Lursay's narrative also brings into play the *narrataire*[30] of the novel as a whole, who is educated, ordered or seduced into the position of 'good reader' of Mme de Lursay's narrative.[31] We must now look at the role of sententiousness in the narrative discourse of the novel, in order to examine the complicity which this suggests between Versac, Meilcour-as-narrator, and the reader.

3. Narrative

3.1. The Split 'Je'

The narrative discourse of the *Egarements* shares with other first-person narratives a complication affecting the status of the pronoun 'je', which designates, in this case, both Meilcour as actor in the *histoire* of the novel, and Meilcour as narrator of the *narration* of that *histoire*. The nature of this complication will become clearer on a new reading of the passage which served as an earlier example, and which I quote again:

> Loin que je susse la façon dont l'amour se menait dans le monde, je croyais, malgré ce que je voyais tous les jours, qu'il fallait un mérite supérieur pour plaire aux femmes; et quelque bonne opinion que j'eusse en secret de moi-même, je ne me trouvais jamais digne d'être aimé: je suis même certain que, quand je les aurais mieux connues, je n'en aurais pas été moins timide. Les leçons et les exemples sont peu de chose pour un jeune homme; et ce n'est jamais qu'à ses dépens qu'il s'instruit. (p. 16)

The 'je' appears eight times in this passage. As an attempt to decide formally how these deictics might be distributed between the two distinct 'subjects' who share the name 'Meilcour', we might apply, but in reverse, a rewriting test proposed by Barthes in his 'Introduction à l'analyse structurale du récit'.[32] This would involve transforming the text into a third-person narrative, and thus attempting to rewrite each 'je' as an 'il'. This produces an intuitively coherent transformation of seven of the eight pronouns, but creates a curious effect when applied to the phrase, 'je suis même certain que . . .', where the 'je' has as its referent not the subject acting in the 'past' time of the diegesis, but the subject narrating in the 'present' time of the act of narration. It seems reasonable to suppose that what marks this particular 'je' in this way is the use of the present tense. The narrating instance outcrops in the narrative with the present tense, which is here, importantly, the time of certainty, as opposed to the time of (mistaken) belief, which is the time of *égarements*.

3.1.1. Reintegrating the Maxim

We can say, then, that although any use of the pronoun 'je' in the narrative discourse of the novel marks the 'presence' of the subject of the narration of that discourse, that 'presence' is foregrounded especially by the use of the present tense. The present tense marks an *intrusion* into the *histoire* of an instance which that *histoire* usually implies only indirectly. The present tense is also, of course, one of the marks characteristic of the 'detachable' sentious proposition. When detached and anthologized, such propositions display a present tense freed from any cotextual contrast; but when such statements are read in the text, their 'present' enters into an opposition with the past time of the *histoire*, and seems to be assimilable to the present tense of the 'je suis même certain que . . .' This means that it is possible, for the moment at least, to link sententious propositions in the narrative with the time of its narration, and to assign them an enunciating subject (the narrator) within the novel. Such propositions are no longer, then, to be given the attributive signature 'Crébillon *fils*', as would be the case if they were anthologized, but that of 'Meilcour (narrator)'. As Meilcour (narrator) is here identified differentially with respect to Meilcour (actor), then it seems as though we must read the sententious propositions not as detachable evidence of the author's wit or wisdom, as Octave Uzanne, Aldous Huxley, and anthologizers in general would have it (see above, Chapter 1, notes 142 and 143), but as elements with an assignable place within the structure of the text.

Even apparently detachable maxims, then, and *a fortiori* the various types of implied sententiousness, involve a contrast between a 'je croyais (alors)' and a 'je sais (maintenant)'. This suggests that any model for deriving sententious propositions from the text must incorporate the possibility of a negative transformation precisely in those cases explicitly marked by an introductory 'je croyais que . . .', or some equivalent. Thus, in the passage quoted, we can derive simply enough the maxim 'Il faut un mérite supérieur pour plaire aux femmes', but we must take into account the fact that the text marks this as erroneous by attributing it exclusively to Meilcour (actor), as potential subject of an enunciation at the time of the *histoire*. Where no such mark is present, we may take it that the proposition is subscribed to by Meilcour (narrator). Further, in the absence of other marks, it seems that sententiousness thus subscribed to implies that Meilcour (actor) did not know, or could not formulate, the sententious proposition concerned. The apparently timeless present of the sententious formulation thus bears the trace of the whole narrative passage from innocence to experience, or from *égarements* to self-presence, which the novel recounts.

This implication is sometimes made explicit by the text: the dialogue leading to the declaration, analysed at length above, ends with Mme de Lursay's abrupt breaking off of the conversation, and the narrative continues,

J'avais si peu d'usage du monde, que je crus l'avoir fâchée véritablement. Je ne savais pas qu'une femme suit rarement une conversation amoureuse avec quelqu'un qu'elle veut engager; et celle qui a le plus envie de se rendre montre, du moins dans le premier entretien, quelque sorte de vertu.   (p. 27)

The whole structure of initiation and 'education' lies in the space between the explicit 'je ne savais pas . . .' and the 'je sais (maintenant)

que . . .' implicit in the present tense of the sententious formulation. This consideration evidently provides for a consistent and reassuring reintegration of the most detachable maxims into the body of the text.

Such explicit marks of the trace of narrative in sententiousness can also appear on the side of the narration, as it were, as in 'j'ai remarqué que les femmes les plus aisées sont celles qui s'engagent avec la folle espérance de n'être jamais séduites' (p. 38), or 'j'ai compris depuis, par l'impression qu'elle me faisait alors, qu'il est bien plus important pour les femmes de flatter notre vanité que de toucher notre coeur' (p. 60). This last example also suggests that the structure of sententiousness in the narrative, as analysed so far, could be invoked to support the coherence, in terms of this text, of the maxim 'Les leçons et les exemples . . .', which had so far seemed rather to be belied by the 'scene of education' as presented by the novel.

3.1.2. *Enonciation*: the 'Je' Dispersed

However structurally attractive and simple this type of analysis may seem, it over-stresses the singularity of the subject of the enunciation. It may be that the whole notion of a 'subject of the enunciation', despite its usefulness in disrupting certain idealistic tendencies in structural and generative linguistics, is itself too imprecise.[33] In the present case, this imprecision appears in two distinct ways, both of which tend to prevent the confident assignation of sententious formulations to 'Meilcour (narrator)'. The first of these ways concerns the link between the two sides of the 'je': it is not in fact always clear that maxims belong to the narrating side of that 'je' as proof of accumulated experience and wisdom. There is, for example, no reason to believe that, at the time of the action, Meilcour would not have agreed with the long sententious characterization of 'ces femmes philosophes' (p. 87) of whom Mme de Senanges is the representative. Although the young Meilcour is inexperienced enough to let himself be manipulated by Mme de Senanges, he is not taken in by her pretensions. In a case such as this, the specificity of the narrating 'je' is reduced insofar as the ignorance/knowledge opposition is not pertinent here; but it is of course still possible to argue that the narrating 'je' has the privilege of *formulating* the maxim, and that the young Meilcour would be insufficiently in command of language to be able to do so.

But if this is the case, then the specificity of the narrating instance is also threatened, and this is the second type of imprecision mentioned above. Insofar as the ability to formulate maxims appears as a mark of

125

a social style or competence, then the narrator's maxims might be read less in terms of an individual experience and wisdom, than as an expression of, again, a doxa, in which the individuality of the subject of the enunciation is denied, and the maxim becomes a quotation from another discourse.[34] For example, at the beginning of the novel, it is explained that Meilcour has as yet had no opportunity of declaring love to a woman, and that even if he had, 'j'aurais sans doute poussé mon respect au point où il devient un outrage pour les femmes, et un ridicule pour nous' (p. 14). The form of the sentence implies the derivation of an implicit sententious reference to such a 'point' about which narrator, men and women, and the *narrataire*, are in agreement. Similarly, the narrator will on occasion align his sententiousness with a 'truth' recognized by Mme de Lursay: 'Elle savait d'ailleurs qu'avec quelque ardeur que les hommes poursuivent la victoire, ils aiment toujours à l'acheter; et que les femmes qui croient ne pouvoir se rendre assez promptement se repentent souvent de s'être trop tôt laissé vaincre' (p. 18). The narrating instance is in such cases dispersed among any number of subjects who may have 'understood' the economy of love in *le monde*, and adopts a position earlier described as a *degré zéro* of pedagogy: the 'scene of education' here designates the reader as its pupil.

3.2. Educating the Reader

This new and more general 'scene of education' suggests that the narrative be read as no more than a figure of the reading of the text, by a notional reader who docilely accepts the position assigned to him by the structure of the text. As in Aristotle, the use of maxims is particularly persuasive or seductive in that it implies a consensual subject uttering them, and invites the addressee to join in that community, to become a member of the general 'we' and to quote in turn the collective wisdom. The opening words of *Les Egarements*, 'J'entrai dans le monde à dix-sept ans . . .' (p. 13), are thus implicitly doubled by a 'Vous entrez dans le monde (de ce livre) . . .'. The book, just like the 'world' within it, is a relatively closed system into which the reader is introduced by being either 'thrown' or 'handed over' a fence constituted not so much by the empirical edges of the text (first and last page, covers, margins, etc.) as by a (possibly heterogeneous) body of sententiousness, overt and implied, veiling the particularity of its references,[35] quoting a doxa, stating rules.

3.2.1. Closure and Gestures Beyond

It can be shown in various ways that the book is not a totally closed system: it is written in a recognizable natural language, it obeys certain conventions in its material presentation and in the use of certain devices. At the level of sententiousness, this relative permeability of the closure can be identified in the type of gesture towards general categories which I earlier called 'extradiegetical reference' (see above, Chapter 1, §8.4.): to produce the maxim, the reader has to bring to the text information which is nowhere explicitly contained in it. The more information of this type is presupposed in the reader, the more closed the text will appear. Thus, in the classic example from Mme de Lafayette's *La Comtesse de Tende*, the comte discovers that his wife is pregnant by another man, and the text states, 'il pensait d'abord tout ce qu'il était naturel de penser en cette occasion'.[36] The implied maxim ('Tout mari qui trouve que . . . pense naturellement que . . .') requires a good deal from the reader, and manifests a good deal of faith in him or her: there is no evidence of a 'scene of education' in such examples, since the reader's position is understood as being already inside the closure (which of course implies nothing about the position of the empirical reader).

If the hypothesis that the positioning of the reader of *Les Egarements* implies a 'scene of education' is correct, we should expect there to be little evidence of this type of radical extradiegetical reference, and this is indeed the case.[37] Some examples do occur, as in a reference to 'tout ce que les hommes à bonne fortune ont imaginé de plus mauvais en procédés' (p. 77), or another to 'ces petits riens qui font briller dans le monde' (p. 34), but in the great majority of cases the text is careful to back up this type of reference with a good measure of intradiegetical support. The best examples of this structure are provided by references to general categories which make use of demonstratives of the type '(un(e) de) ce(s) . . .': the demonstrative looks like an ostensive deictic[38] gesturing beyond the text to 'ce commerce commode qu'on lie avec une coquette . . .' (p. 38.); 'une de ces femmes philosophes . . .' (p. 87); 'ces principes de pudeur, ce goût pour la modestie . . .' (p. 88). Yet the world indicated by these gestures is not here presupposed as already known to the reader, but shown at the end of the pointing finger, as it were: 'ce commerce commode qu'on lie avec une coquette, assez vif pour amuser quelques jours, et qui se rompt aussi facilement qu'il s'est formé'; 'ces femmes philosophes, pour qui le public n'a jamais rien été . . .'; 'ces principes de pudeur, ce goût pour la modestie que l'on appelle dans le monde sottise et mauvaise honte, parce que, s'ils y étaient encore des vertus ou des agréments, trop de personnes auraient à rougir de ne les point posséder'. The reader–pupil has the way into both world and book carefully pointed out.

3.2.2. Versus Versac

This structure must be borne in mind in any analysis of the relationship between the narrator and Versac, insofar as the latter's sententiousness is produced within the *monde* and is concerned to transmit 'recipe' knowledge as to how to succeed in that *monde*. We have seen that any apparently demystificatory function in Versac's discourse is in fact simply taken up by the doxa which it appears to denounce, and provides for the renewal of that doxa as a relatively closed system. Only the fact that Versac's discourse is enclosed within the narrator's, allows the reader, positioned by the narrative, to dominate that system and to see that Versac is in fact a product of its logic rather than a threat to that logic. As Serge Gaubert has suggested: 'Versac avait compris le monde, le narrateur a compris que Versac était compris dans le monde qu'il comprenait'.[39] Versac educates Meilcour (actor) *in* 'la science du monde': the narrator educates the *destinataire through* that science. The necessity of this difference, which suggests that Versac cannot in fact be considered to be simply a 'relay' in the narrative structure, is marked in the text by Hortense's impermeability to Versac's practical application of his science, and the implication that, through her, Meilcour's pre-social notion of love will re-emerge as a truth beyond worldliness.

This reading accepts the position which the text assigns to the reader, and implies the respect of a certain contract implicit in any text. If the text is to maintain its position of superiority with respect to Versac, it must thus educate its reader to read it in a certain way, and this education cannot in principle remain on the same ground as that offered by Versac. A re-reading of the sententious passages introduced by demonstratives, which were above assigned an 'educational' function in terms of worldliness, shows that such a function is also an alibi for a process of *vraisemblabilisation* susceptible to the same type of analysis, by a reader less docile to his or her positioning by the text, as was Mme de Lursay's narrative analysed above. In that case, the young Meilcour was a figure of that type of 'naive' or respectful reader, the type of reader which I have so far largely accepted to be with respect to the text as a whole. The surrounding text suggested the artificial nature of Mme de Lursay's constructions, thus reinforcing its own claims to a more 'plausible' or 'natural' status. The *destinataire* can feel superior to Mme de Lursay's writing and its sententious supports only by submitting to the sententiousness of the narrative instance, which can now be suggested to have 'educated' the reader primarily in the passive acceptance of the authority of the 'educator'.

3.3. Fiction/Function: Losing Respect

However, just as Meilcour (narrator) has become a better reader by losing his respect for Mme de Lursay and her narrative skill, it is reasonable to suppose that the reader of *Les Egarements* might do well to lose respect for the *destinataire* with whom the text invites identification. This 'loss of respect' does not of course mean a simple attempt to step outside the text and to denounce it as 'fictional', 'morally pernicious', 'trivial' or 'false'. Any such gesture implies simply a failure to read at all. Nor can it involve the simple generation of a new narrative instance, which would pretend to tell the 'true story' which Meilcour (narrator) would have masked. There is no ground on which to base such an instance. Any such loss of respect (which cannot therefore be total) can only work by finding traces within the narrative discourse of its efforts to produce a convincing system of verisimilitude. This again involves an attention to sententious formulations and the coherence of the plausibility-structures which they generate. In this first instance, then, this implies a certain defiance in the face of the educational efforts of the text.

3.3.1. The *Vraisemblable* (II)

Read from the point of view of the problem of verisimilitude, a maxim such as 'Les leçons et les exemples sont peu de chose pour un jeune homme, et ce n'est jamais qu'à ses dépens qu'il s'instruit' (p. 16) is less an effort to formulate a 'truth' than an attempt to provide a motivation for what might otherwise seem an arbitrary stupidity on the part of Meilcour (actor): its aim is that of allowing the narrative to continue, of making it readable. The narrative has to justify the length of the scene of education, which runs the risk of seeming implausible. Similarly, the sententious characterization of 'ces femmes philosophes' serves less to communicate wisdom about 'le monde' than to motivate the actions and discourse of Mme de Senanges, to naturalize them. Any pure narrative proposition, as Valéry pointed out, runs the risk of seeming impossibly contingent:[40] by doubling narrative propositions with sententious plausibility-structures, the text confers on them an appearance of necessity. Insofar as particular actions and events can be supported by general 'truths', then the suspicion that the text is saying simply *n'importe quoi* can be allayed. Evidently this type of grounding often takes place at a level far 'below' the 'surface' of the text, so that there is little danger that the reader will question the plausibility of the action. There is, for example, no need to provide particular motivations for Meilcour's going to the Opéra (p. 33), although we might imagine the possibility of a reader who would require the help of an annotated edition to naturalize this micro-narrative. In fact the power of the contract binding reader to text is such that it seems possible to postulate a tendency to accept as plausible (within certain limits) those actions where no supplementary motivation is given, on the grounds that motivation would have been provided had the writer-as-reader felt it to be necessary. The corollary of this is the suspicion that when sententiousness 'surfaces' in the narrative, this signals a risk that the narrative will appear too arbitrary to be acceptable. Sententiousness still functions here as a patch or a veil, hiding and revealing at one and the same time.

3.3.2. Economy

The economy sketched here has been laid out by Genette in his article 'Vraisemblance et motivation', which is remarkable for being one of the only pieces of 'structuralist' writing to recognize the importance of sententiousness in narrative. For Genette, the 'value' of a unit in the narrative can be calculated by subtracting its motivation (conceived of as an outlay, an unfortunate but necessary expense) from its functional role in that narrative.[41] It would follow from this that motivations should be kept to a minimum, and disguised, veiled, as far as is possible. Thus, when Meilcour arrives at the Opéra, the progress of the narrative requires him to see Hortense, and to be within hearing distance of her; this means that he must take a place in a 'loge', and the motivation for this choice of place is provided as follows:

J'étais de si mauvaise humeur en arrivant à l'Opéra, où d'ailleurs je trouvai assez peu de monde, que, pour n'être pas distrait de la rêverie dans laquelle j'étais plongé, je me fis ouvrir une loge, plutôt que de me mettre dans les balcons où je n'aurais pas été si tranquille. (p. 33)

The reader has to work quite hard on this text to produce from it its motivating maxim, which would be something like, 'Quand on est plongé dans une rêverie, on a envie d'être tranquille'.

Where the motivation is harder to find, the text will, according to this hypothesis, be more likely to resort to the authority of more overt sententious forms. The long 'ideal narrative' which begins 'Une femme quand elle est jeune . . .' (p. 29), is thus no longer an anthologizable piece of psychological analysis, but a means of motivating Mme de Lursay's tenacity in her attempts to 'educate' Meilcour within the demands of *décence*: 'Tout paraît passion à qui n'en a point éprouvé' (p. 44) becomes necessary to allow Meilcour to return towards Mme de Lursay despite being 'really' in love with Hortense, this 'real love' being required to remain on the edge of the action as a risk and a promise if the narrative progress through *le monde* is to take place.[42] In the scene of the 'declaration' analysed above, it is important, for Meilcour (actor)'s reading of events, that Mme de Lursay should appear to turn the conversation to the question of love and declaration by chance; but in the wider framework of the narrative discourse, this chance must be confined to the scene narrated and removed from the narration of the scene, and a sententious sequence, which is also a commentary on strategies of *vraisemblabilisation*, is necessary to achieve this:

Une conversation adroitement maniée amène souvent les choses qu'on a le plus de peine à dire; le désordre qui y règne aide à s'expliquer; en parlant on change d'objet, et tant de fois, qu'à la fin celui qui occupe s'y trouve *naturellement* placé. Dans le monde surtout, on se plaît à parler d'amour parce que ce sujet, déjà intéressant par lui-même, se trouve souvent lié avec la médisance et qu'il en fait presque toujours le fond. (p. 20, my emphasis)

3.3.3. Incompetence

In this type of economic reading, it is clear that just as the narrative must retain certain criteria of consistency if it is to appear coherent, then the sententious formulations invoked to motivate its progress should also form a consistent system. This consistency, dictated by the necessities of the narrative, generates effects of ideological systematization which hasty readings might place in too simple a causal relationship with the text. In fact, the system can sometimes break down, and it is at such moments that the narrative mechanisms determining its production become visible. In difficult moments, the narrative may simply revert to arbitrariness. We have already noted that Meilcour (actor) is given enough penetration to see how distasteful

Mme de Senanges is; but this makes it difficult to provide a motivation for his going to see her. In fact this is done by a purely arbitrary remark, in which Meilcour admits having the words to some 'couplets' and offers to send them to her. Versac now invokes a 'règle' which 'obliges' Meilcour to go personally. A supplementary 'motivation' finally gets him there, in that a lack of tranquillity (after a scene in which he suspects Hortense of being in love with someone else, and quarrels with Mme de Lursay) is assumed to motivate a desire for company, and 'à tout hasard' (p. 123), he thinks of Mme de Senanges. Now previously, when the narrative requires Meilcour to overhear the conversation between Hortense and the 'Dame' in the Tuileries, a similar lack of tranquillity is invoked to justify a desire to avoid company. Contradictions such as this, in the plausibility-structures invoked by the text, display the artificiality of its structures, and provide the narratologist with a certain gratification in return for the labour of analysis.

4. The Return of the Law

This type of reading involves a measured loss of respect for the text. In worldly terms, this is an *indecent* operation, a refusal to accept the veiling of contingent facts under general consensual truths, a rejection of the authority of sententiousness and of the doxa which it supports and quotes. By turning back on the text itself the 'lessons' and 'examples' in modes of reading which it provided in the context of Mme de Lursay's narrative, it has seemed possible to unmask a certain type of 'hypocrisy' implicit in the construction of a system of verisimilitude. The narrative discourse of the novel, in its generalizations, is thus caught up in a number of contradictory functions. It needs in part to quote and support the doxa of a Mme de Lursay, to associate the reader in its collective subject in order to provide a distance from the young Meilcour's innocence. It must also exceed that doxa and denounce its generalizing operations in order to secure its own ground beyond worldliness in virtue and wisdom. In so doing, it draws the reader into a different 'nous', capable of certain operations of unveiling; it can only do this, however, by exploiting the same type of mechanisms which it denounced in the worldly text, and this prepares the reader's loss of respect for the text's own manoeuvres. If at this level the reader was the object of a 'scene of education', then the reader has apparently instructed himself not so much at his own expense as at the expense of the text.

Does this mean that the reader has escaped from the hold of

sententiousness and the authority which it implies? This would be an optimistic claim indeed. If, in the economy of narrative motivation elaborated by Genette, sententious formulations were an expense, then the reader's education has indeed been carried out at his or her own expense insofar as we have been obliged to resort to sententiousness, to lay down the law of that narrative economy, to subordinate sententious formulations in the text to a sententiously-formulated law of narrative.[43] This in turn sets the 'scene' of a further 'education' for the reader of *this* text, implies a consensual subject (of narratologists, say) from whose wisdom I have been quoting. Or, in another metaphorical series, if Versac unveiled the veiled nature of a certain doxa, if the narrator unveiled the veiled nature of those unveilings, and if I have attempted to unveil the whole process in its complexity (with the lack of respect which this implies), then there is nothing in the structure of that 'final' unveiling to suggest any grounds for finality, or respect, once the reader refuses the position urged by *this* text. The law is (still) there to be broken (again).

Part III
THE SCENE OF LEGISLATION

4

SENTENTIOUSNESS AND THE LAW

A la honte des hommes, on sait que les lois du jeu sont les seules qui soient partout justes, claires, inviolables et exécutées.

(Voltaire, *Dictionnaire philosophique*)

La définition de la loi est encore à faire.

(Rousseau, *Emile* (IV, 842))

1. The Law

The analysis of sententiousness in the 'worldly novel' led to the problem of the relationship between narrative fiction and the law. I now propose to consider the problem of the law more directly, and attempt to contest in various ways the dominant position which it appears to have taken on at this point in the discussion. More literal attention to the term 'law' is justified by the intuitive ease with which it can be added to the series 'maxim, aphorism, *sentence*', etc., and can be given historical support: in a famous remark in the preface to *Les Caractères*, La Bruyère writes, 'Ce ne sont point au reste des maximes que j'aie voulu écrire: elles sont comme des lois dans la morale, et j'avoue que je n'ai ni assez d'autorité ni assez de génie pour faire le législateur'.[1]

This remark introduces explicitly the problems of the law, of the legislator and of authority, which have been haunting the discussion at least since my intuitive characterization of sententiousness as 'laying down the law'.

2. Against Worldliness

2.1. Polemic

A transition between the apparently heterogeneous areas of the worldly novel on the one hand, and juridical and/or political writing

137

on the other, can be provided by the work of Rousseau, and specifically by *La Nouvelle Héloïse*, which at once entertains a complex polemical relationship with the worldly novel and poses the political problem of sententiousness. Both of these aspects of the novel are linked to the general problem of the ambivalent devalorization of writing in Rousseau's work.

If, as has been convincingly argued by Jacques Derrida, writing is for Rousseau a 'supplément dangereux',[2] then it is not surprising to find within Rousseau's texts not only explicit arguments against writing, but also the traces of a persistent desire which generates logical and rhetorical machines in order to justify the fact that he does none the less write. In terms of the autobiographical texts, or from a critical position which tends to unify all of Rousseau's writing as grounded in a phenomenological subject, this desire can be described in terms of an unfortunately necessary provisional detour through hiding and writing (writing as a kind of hiding), which is only a preparation for an eventual return to presence, immediacy, speech, and 'transparency'. Jean Starobinski has produced admirable analyses of this structure:

Jean-Jacques se cache, écrit, mais pour créer les conditions d'un *retour*, qui réparera la déception de l'accueil manqué. La rupture n'aura donc pas eu lieu que dans l'espoir d'un retour plus émouvant, et Jean-Jacques n'aura passé par un 'circuit de paroles' que pour se représenter devant les autres et leur demander d'être salué selon sa vraie valeur.[3]

In terms of writing itself, it seems possible to say that Rousseau's texts project their own disappearance into silence and proximity, or desire an effacement of the necessary *spacing* of writing.[4] Naturally this desire is contradictory, insofar as the material persistence or monumentality of the texts in which this desire works is itself proof against its fulfilment.

This desire, in one of its forms, does indeed recognize the existence of writing, but projects an ambivalent phantasy which immediately defines that writing as a polemical activity. Here, within a field of tension where doxa and paradoxa stand opposed, Rousseau dreams of a sort of cancellation-effect, in which writing opposed to writing would not simply add to textual excess, but would erase texts, and in so doing produce a sort of simulacrum of the 'transparency' desired. The logic of this phantasy is made clear in the 'Fragment Politique' entitled 'Le luxe, le commerce et les arts':[5]

Le meilleur usage qu'on puisse faire de la Philosophie, c'est de l'employer à détruire les maux qu'elle a causés, dut-on en même temps détruire le bien, s'il y en a: car dans ce qui est ajoûté aux simples lumières de la raison et aux purs sentimens de la nature, il vaut encore mieux ôter le bon que de laisser le mauvais. Il faudroit pour l'avantage de la société, que les Philosophes distribuassent leurs travaux de telle sorte qu'après bien des Livres et des disputes ils se trouvassent réfutés reciproquement *et que le tout fut comme non avenu.*   (III, p. 516, my emphasis)

This distribution of labour in view of a total absence of productivity might seem absurd (or possibly 'modern'), but it is clearly one way in which the guilt which the act of writing generates in Rousseau can be disposed of, and the detour at once made the theme of the activity of writing which constitutes it, and the better annulled in the end.

Rousseau goes on to situate his own writing in this perspective, with a modesty made suspect by the very logic involved:

Mais comme dans tout ceci je me propose plustôt d'attaquer des erreurs que d'établir de nouvelles vérités j'avoüe de bonne foy que quand les ouvrages de mes adversaires ne subsisteront plus, les miens seront parfaitement inutiles. Sans vouloir être le guide de mes contemporains je me contente de les avertir quand j'en observe un qui les égare et je n'aurois pas besoin de les fatiguer de mes avis si personne ne se mêloit de les conduire.   (III, pp. 516–7)

Rousseau's work will then be (or have been) negative, like Emile's negative education:[6] its function will be to cancel out other writing; and to the extent that this cancellation is successful, it will *cancel itself out too*, and thus destroy the guilt attached to its material excess.

This machine makes Rousseau's writing *paradoxal* and *polemical*. However, if the operation were purely automatic, if the desired cancellation were achieved by a simple reversal of doxa into paradoxa, then the need for long texts by Rousseau would not be clear. 'J'aime mieux être homme à paradoxes qu'homme à préjugés' (IV, p. 323), indeed – but the *paradoxe* is not always the result of a mechanical opposition, and so there must be some play in the machine, marked, for example, in a 'presque' in *Emile*: 'Prenez le contrepied de l'usage et vous ferez presque toujours bien' (IV, p. 324).

Rousseau does not, then, write his texts out of silent inspiration, or on the basis of some pure experience of emotion or sensation, but on the prior ground of texts read and contested. This crucial intertextuality should not be ignored: Rousseau writes because others have written, and if his detour involves hiding, as Starobinski suggests, it certainly does not involve hiding from the conflictual field of contemporary thought. Elucidation of this structure should clarify the position of *La Nouvelle Héloïse* in Rousseau's writing, and avoid psychological or biographical explanations of the work. It would also lead to the rejection of Althusser's tempting suggestion that the recourse to the novel is the result of the theoretical *impasse* reached by the *Contrat social*.[7] I shall argue later that the 'failure' or 'impossibility' of the political text has nothing to do with questions of its application to or confrontation with a relcalcitrant political reality, but with its conditions of textual existence; if this is the case, the recourse to 'fiction' cannot be explained in terms of a simplistic disappointment with 'reality'. Rather, as Paul de Man has convincingly argued, both political and fictional writings can be read as *texts*:[8] and indeed both can be read in terms of a similar structure, in which this type of negative and polemical moment is followed by a compensatory affirmative moment which, however, collapses into aporia.

2.2. Novels

The polemical opponent of *La Nouvelle Héloïse* is quite simply 'the novel'. The justification generated for the text depends on what might be termed 'contextual corruption', as Rousseau emphasizes at the beginning of the work's definitive preface:

Il faut des spectacles dans les grandes villes, et des Romans aux peuples corrompus. J'ai vû les moeurs de mon tems, et j'ai publié ces lettres. Que n'ai-je vécu dans un siècle où je dusse les jeter au feu!   (II, p. 5)

However, any attempt to elaborate this justification in terms of the 'cancellation' model outlined above is faced with a complication, perhaps a contradiction, which surfaces in the so-called 'Seconde préface':

En matière de morale, il n'y a point, selon moi, de lecture utile aux gens du monde. Premièrement, parce que la multitude des livres nouveaux qu'ils parcourent, et qui disent tour-à-tour le pour et le contre, détruit l'effet de l'un par l'autre, et *rend le tout comme non avenu.*   (II, p. 18, my emphasis)

Whereas in the 'Luxe' Fragment the annulment caused by the confrontation of the *pour* and the *contre* was clearly presented as positive, here the same structure, described in identical terms, seems to be condemned as pointless. However, the passage goes on to resolve this apparent contradiction and in so doing clarifies the polemical situation of the novel:

Les livres choisis qu'on relit ne font point d'effet encore: s'ils soutiennent les maximes du monde, ils sont superflus; et s'ils les combattent, ils sont inutiles. Ils trouvent ceux qui les lisent liés aux vices de la société, par des chaînes qu'ils ne peuvent rompre.   (II, pp. 18–19)

So in fact the result of the confrontation of doxa and paradoxa about *le monde* in *le monde* is *not* the type of annulment described above, insofar as the result of the confrontation is simply the survival of the doxa: what is *non avenu* is in fact the cancellation-effect itself. It is clear that if this situation were generalized then the justification for Rousseau's writing would again disappear. Rousseau shifts the ground of the problem by turning his attention to the addressee of the work, appealing to the ubiquitous eighteenth-century opposition between Paris and the provinces, and its more generalized avatar opposing town and country. After complaining about the 'résistance invincible' which greets the *homme du monde*'s attempt to return to moral law and order, Rousseau sets up a sliding scale towards the countryside:

Plus on s'éloigne des affaires, des grandes villes, des nombreuses sociétés, plus les obstacles diminuent. Il est un terme où ces obstacles cessent d'être invincibles, et c'est alors que les livres peuvent avoir quelque utilité . . . On lit beaucoup plus de romans dans les provinces qu'à Paris, on en lit plus dans les campagnes que dans les villes, et ils y font beaucoup plus d'impression: vous voyez pourquoi cela doit être. (II, p. 19)

Whether Rousseau's facts are right, and whether he really wrote the novel assuming that it would be read mostly by country-dwellers, does not matter:[9] what is important is to locate the discursive ruses which Rousseau uses to justify his text. The object of the polemic is not so much *le monde* 'itself' as its representation in *fictional* texts read by people who are *not* members of *le monde*, and the possible moral and political effects produced by that fictional representation:

Les Contes, les Romans, les Pièces de Théatre, tout tire sur les Provinciaux; tout tourne en dérision la simplicité des moeurs rustiques; tout prêche les manieres et les plaisirs du grand monde: c'est une honte de ne les pas connoître; c'est un malheur de ne les pas goûter. Qui sait de combien de filoux et de filles publiques l'attrait de ces plaisirs imaginaires peuple Paris de jour en jour? Ainsi . . . ce frivole éclat, qui frappe les yeux des sots, fait courir l'Europe à grands pas vers sa ruine. *Il importe au bonheur des hommes qu'on tâche d'arrêter ce torrent de maximes empoisonnées.*

(II, p. 20, my emphasis)

2.3. Anti-Novel

'Il importe au bonheur des hommes qu'on tâche d'arrêter ce torrent de maximes empoisonnées.' What is at stake in the first instance here is not the fictionality of fiction, but what I have called its sententious force; and precisely because the 'poison' of that force is carried in novels, Rousseau's polemical writing must be situated on the same ground. In Rousseau's account, the effect of novels is to de-centre the reading subject (carrying the *campagnard* outside himself to the 'plaisirs imaginaires' of the capital), and to centre the nation around the capital, leaving the country 'en friche et désert' (II, p. 20).[10] Rousseau's enterprise will be to transform the centrifugal movement of the reader into the structure of the *detour*, in which the movement into fiction leads to a return to the country and to the contentment of rustic self-sufficiency; and this movement is figured in the novel itself both by Julie's departure from and ambivalent return to 'virtue', and more graphically by Saint-Preux's departure from and return to Julie herself, after a 'detour' taking him round the globe.

Before considering the effects of such structures of departure and ambivalent returns on moral and political law as such, we must be aware of the complications inherent in this strategy for the novel as novel. So far the relationship of *La Nouvelle Héloïse* with 'the novel' (as worldly novel) seems to be quite simple, and its sententious force would be the paradoxa to worldly doxa. This is indeed a familiar structure at the level of the *vraisemblable*:[11] the paradoxa denounces as *romanesque* the doxa which it combats, the better to secure its own readability and verisimilitude. Moreover, this negative construction of a *vraisemblable* can be seen at work within the text itself, where it is figured *en abyme* when Saint-Preux tells Edouard the story of his love and reports the latter's reaction to Julie:

Il n'y a, m'a-t-il dit, ni incidens ni avantures dans ce que vous m'avez raconté, et les catastrophes d'un Roman m'attacheroient beaucoup moins; tant les sentimens suppléent aux situations, et les procédés honnêtes aux actions éclatantes. (II, p. 165)

And of course Edouard's own love-story is excluded from the novel, or at least given a marginal position, precisely because it is too 'romanesque' (see II, p. 625n and p. 729). The aim is to legitimate a 'vrai amour' against the 'préjugés du monde' as represented in novels, and this is again made clear in the text when Julie reproaches Saint-Preux with his unseemly conduct:

Ne vous y trompez pas, mon ami; rien n'est si dangereux pour les vrais amants que les préjugés du monde; tant de gens parlent d'amour, et si peu savent aimer, que la plupart prennent pour ses pures et douces lois les viles maximes d'un commerce abject. (II, p. 138)

Such simple mechanisms are, however, misleading, and further analysis will suggest that the binary opposition of doxa and paradoxa is insufficient to account for the sentential force of *La Nouvelle Héloïse* – rather there seems to be a mutual and transgressive parasiting of one term of the opposition by the other. The increased complexity which this suggests can still be read *en abyme* within the text. For Edouard, the story of Julie and Saint-Preux is admirable insofar as it does *not* constitute a novel; but this gesture of exclusion of the novel is mirrored and inverted, still within the novel, when Saint-Preux describes Parisian women:

Il n'est pas moins essenciel à la galanterie française de mépriser les femmes que de les servir. Ce mépris est une sorte de titre qui leur en impose; c'est un témoignage qu'on a vécu assés avec elles pour les connoitre. Quiconque les respecteroit passeroit à leurs yeux pour un novice, un paladin, *un homme qui n'a connu les femmes que dans les Romans.* (II, p. 276, my emphasis)

The problem here is that the fictional other constructed by Rousseau's fiction, the better to ground its own verisimilitude, performs the same operation on its own behalf, and in the last chapter it was possible to find in worldly novels examples of a formally identical expulsion of the *romanesque* in the interests of the legitimation of the text. A supplementary necessity for Rousseau's novel is, then, that of distinguishing itself from the fictional other of its fictional other; and this is indeed attempted in the 'Seconde préface', which explicitly takes its distance from the pastoral model of l'*Astrée*, a paradigm fictional 'other' for worldly texts.[12]

The specific detour of *La Nouvelle Héloïse* thus implies its being immediately situated in this complex field of mutually denouncing fictional models. However, the analysis so far does not fully explain the incorporation and projected annulment of the worldly novel in Rousseau's text, and this is indeed problematic – the text's detour through worldliness is hardly justified by the simple fact that at a given moment the novel sends Saint-Preux to Paris to describe the corruption of *le monde*. How can the introduction of worldliness be explained? This detour can only begin in the awareness that it has always already begun: in other words, in the recognition of the necessary possibility of being always already corrupted by the discourse of worldliness, which thus cannot be expelled without leaving a remainder. The text solves the problem through the invention of a 'character' who never 'appears', La Chaillot, but who provides it with its prior knowledge of corruption and worldliness, and thus allows its departure. References to La Chaillot in Julie's first letter to Claire are thus of vital importance to the structure of the novel as a whole:

Mais conviens aussi que la bonne femme étoit peu prudente avec nous, qu'elle nous faisoit sans nécessité les confidences les plus indiscrètes; qu'elle nous entretenoit sans cesse des *maximes de la galanterie*, des avantures de sa jeunesse, du manège des amans, et que pour nous garantir des pièges des hommes, si elle ne nous apprenoit pas à leur en tendre, elle nous instruisoit au moins de mille choses que de jeunes filles se passeroient bien de savoir.

(II, p. 43, my emphasis)

Only this prior knowledge of the *maximes de la galanterie* allows the novel to exist. As is so often the case in Rousseau, a given series of events (usually seen as regrettable) is presented as the consequence of a single catastrophic instant: that instant is not in itself a pure event, but depends on prior dispositions.[13] In the numerous readings of the events of the novel presented within the text itself, the single catastrophic instant can be the moment Julie opened Saint-Preux's first letter ('Au lieu de jetter au feu votre premiere lettre, ou de la porter à ma mere, j'osai l'ouvrir. Ce fut là mon crime, et tout le reste fut forcé' (II, pp. 341–2)), the moment of the kiss in the *bosquet* ('Un instant, un seul instant embrasa [mes sens] d'un feu que rien ne put éteindre, et si ma volonté resistoit encore, dès lors mon coeur fut corrompu' (II, p. 342)), or the moment of physical possession ('Sans savoir ce que je faisois je choisis ma propre infortune. J'oubliai tout et ne me souvins que de l'amour. C'est ainsi qu'un instant d'égarement m'a perdue à jamais' (II, p. 96)), but the instantaneous purity of these catastrophes is always compromised by a prior preparation, provided by La Chaillot and her lessons, even if those lessons are presented as salutary.[14]

In terms of the text itself, as text, and of readings no longer presented within the novel but projected by the prefaces, this structure of the fatal instant can be linked to the famous assertion:

Jamais fille chaste n'a lu de Romans; et j'ai mis à celui-ci un titre assés décidé pour qu'en l'ouvrant on sut à quoi s'en tenir. Celle qui, malgré ce titre, en osera lire une seule page, est une fille perdue: mais qu'elle n'impute point sa perte à ce livre; le mal étoit fait d'avance.   (II, p. 6)

The novel is only readable from the position of chastity lost, of a worldliness which determines Rousseau's text even if it cannot touch its signatory's aggressive innocence.

2.4. The Language of Worldliness

To the extent that Rousseau's *paradoxa*, the 'vrai amour', is necessarily elaborated on the ground prepared by La Chaillot and the *maximes de la galanterie*, it is clear that the relationship of *La Nouvelle Héloïse* with the novel of worldliness cannot be as simple as Rousseau's own 'cancellation model' would suggest. The text denouncing worldliness is contaminated by the object of its denunciation. But this situation is also incorporated into the novel in another *mise-en-abyme*, when Julie criticizes Saint-Preux's condemnation of the language of worldliness for precisely this type of contamination:

> Di-moi, je te prie, mon cher ami, en quelle langue ou plutôt en quel jargon est la relation de ta dernière Lettre? Ne seroit-ce point là par hazard du bel esprit? . . . Il y a de la recherche et du jeu dans plusieurs de tes lettres. Je ne parle point de ce tour vif et de ces expressions animées qu'inspire la force du sentiment; je parle de cette gentillesse de stile qui n'étant point naturelle ne vient d'elle-même à personne, et marque la prétention de celui qui s'en sert . . . Non, si l'on anime les conversations indifférentes de quelques saillies qui passent comme des traits, ce n'est point entre deux amans que ce langage est de saison, et le jargon fleuri de la galanterie est beaucoup plus éloigné du sentiment que le ton le plus simple qu'on puisse prendre. (II, pp. 237–8)

Evidently this criticism is included to guide the reading by insisting that Saint-Preux's use of this language is an *exception* which can be located and explained, and, by apparently collecting into one part of the novel the doxa of worldliness, to legitimate the rest as different. The previous analysis, however, makes it clear that this is a strategy designed to neutralize the worldliness which is in fact a condition of existence of the whole novel, and which thus permeates the text to a much greater extent than it allows for in its internal representations of its reading.[15]

The ambivalence generated here can be approached by returning to the notion of *pudeur* and its associated figure, the veil; and the problem can be formulated succinctly by saying that if Rousseau affirms that 'on ne joue point la pudeur' (II, p. 296), it is none the less true that *pudeur* always involves play (the 'recherche' and the 'jeu' which Julie condemns in Saint-Preux's letters), and that if for Rousseau the veil is undoubtedly a figure of opacity and death it is also the common instrument of both the *pudeur* which he valorizes and the *coquetterie* which he condemns. As such it belongs to both sides of the opposition between worldly doxa and Rousseau's paradoxa, mediating between the 'viles maximes d'un commerce abject' and the 'pures et douces lois' of love.[16]

Other readings of Rousseau, and most brilliantly that of Starobinski, have provided abundant evidence of the link of the veil to opacity, evil and death, and this use of the figure could reasonably be related to the desire of an 'Enlightenment' eager to lift or pierce veils.[17] By arguing for an irreducible ambivalence of the veil and thereby of *pudeur*, the present analysis casts doubt on this type of reading.

The central importance of *pudeur* is confirmed by a passage which makes of it the (natural) source of morality in general:

> L'attaque et la deffense, l'audace des hommes, la pudeur des femmes ne sont point des conventions, comme le pensent tes philosophes, mais des institutions naturelles dont il est facile de rendre raison, et dont se déduisent aisément toutes les autres distinctions morales. (II, p. 128)

Morality is then grounded in a play which is the very basis of the discourse of worldliness. It is not difficult to find the relationship with the veil. When Saint-Preux replies to Julie's reproaches about his drunken conduct, he writes:

> L'amour eut couvert mes désirs emportés des charmes de ta modestie . . . Di, si dans toutes les fureurs d'une passion sans mesure, je cessai jamais d'en respecter le charmant object? Si je reçus le prix que ma flame avoit mérité, di si j'abusai de mon bonheur pour outrager à ta douce honte? si d'une main timide l'amour ardent et craintif attenta quelquefois à tes charmes, di si jamais une témérité brutale osa les profaner? Quand un transport indiscret écarte un instant le voile que les couvre, l'aimable pudeur n'y substitue-t-elle pas aussitôt le sien? Ce vêtement sacré t'abandonneroit-t-il un moment quand tu n'en aurois point d'autre? (II, pp. 140–1)

From this point of view, the reproach which Saint-Preux addresses to society women is that of not being veiled enough, or of using the veils of their clothing to lift the veil of *pudeur*.[18] Society women fail to place between desire and its satisfaction the detour of *pudeur*, here located in nature. Their play with the veil promises the removal of all veils, whereas what Rousseau valorizes is the resistance of a final veil to any lifting at all. The dress of the women of *le monde* is thus the mark of an essential nudity, whereas the veil of *pudeur* ensures that nudity is never finally reached, even when the body is naked. This play of the veil throws serious doubt on Starobinski's analysis, which assumes that veils are simply unfortunate obstacles in the way of the transparency of a 'jouissance immédiate' (Starobinski, p. 103); rather it suggests that the veil is a means to the perpetual deferral of that *jouissance*, the moment of which is, moreover, consistently associated in Rousseau's texts with the moment of death.[19] The ambivalence here is further confirmed by the recurrent image of tearing the veil, which although it can be seen as providing access to presence and plenitude,[20] can also signal the death of desire itself, the end of its necessary 'illusion':

Enfin le voile est déchiré; cette longue illusion s'est évanouïe; cet espoir si doux s'est éteint; il ne me reste pour aliment d'une flamme éternelle qu'un souvenir amer et délicieux qui soutient ma vie et nourrit mes tourmens du vain sentiment d'un bonheur qui n'est plus. (II, p. 317)

This poses the moral problem that, whereas in the worldly novel this ambivalence of the veil is incorporated into the strategies of a game, in Rousseau it is presented as constitutive of virtue.

2.5. Veil, Law, Supplement

In Chapter 3 I argued that the generalization implied in the production of maxims could be described as a veiling, and accounted for within the strategies of seduction in worldly discourse. It is to be expected that the complication of the structure of veiling implied in Rousseau's texts will be of importance to the position of sententiousness in his work, and this is indeed in evidence in the denunciation of the *maximes de la galanterie*. The first part of this denunciation is apparently quite simple: maxims are suspect because they repress an essential individuality of *sentiment*. This opposition is made clearest in reflexions on the theatre, where, according to Saint-Preux, 'Presque tout s'énonce en maximes générales. Quelque agités [que les interlocuteurs] puissent être, ils songent toujours plus au public qu'à eux-mêmes; une Sentence leur coûte moins qu'un sentiment' (II, p. 253). A footnote clarifies this with reference to Molière and Racine, the former still full of *maximes* and *sentences*, the latter praised because 'il a su faire parler chacun pour soi'.

Earlier, Saint-Preux has made similar comments on the discourse of high society, referring disdainfully to 'le sentiment mis en grandes maximes générales' (II, p. 249). Clearly the problem is that the *maxime* is a resolutely discursive unit, whereas sentiment should ideally exist in some pre-discursive immediacy. The repeatability and therefore 'quotability' of the maxim cannot but cast doubt on its authenticity, and the sententious statement would here be an extreme example of Rousseau's continual attention to the danger of language being used as coinage, to 'se payer de mots'.[21] This type of economic metaphor returns in Saint-Preux's description: 'Ils dépensent ainsi tout leur sentiment en esprit, et il s'en exhale tant dans le discours qu'il n'en reste rien pour la pratique' (II, pp. 249–50).

However, given the complexity of *La Nouvelle Héloïse*'s relationship with worldliness, it would be surprising if the structure of

147

denunciation here were so simple. And indeed Saint-Preux immediately complicates matters by discussing the prescriptive side of sententiousness, the *bienséances* as expressed by worldly *procédés*. Given the failure of sentiment in society, the legislation of the *bienséances* provides a necessary supplement leading to a sort of simulacrum of the behaviour which real sentiment would provoke:

Heureusement la bienséance y supplée, et l'on fait par usage à peu près les mêmes choses qu'on feroit par sensibilité; du moins tant qu'il n'en coûte que des formules et quelques gênes passagères, qu'on s'impose pour faire bien parler de soi; car quand les sacrifices vont jusqu'à gêner trop longtems ou à couter trop cher, adieu le sentiment; la bienséance n'en exige pas jusques-là. A cela près, on ne saurait croire à quel point tout est compassé, mesuré, pesé, dans ce qu'ils appellent des procédés; tout ce qui n'est plus dans les sentimens, ils l'ont mis en regle, et tout est regle parmi eux. Ce peuple imitateur seroit plein d'originaux qu'il seroit impossible d'en rien savoir; car nul homme n'ose être lui-même. *Il faut faire comme les autres*; c'est la première maxime de la sagesse du pays. *Cela se fait, cela ne se fait pas.* Voila la décision suprême.

(II, p. 250)

Much later in the novel, Rousseau appends a footnote to a letter from Claire: 'Tout est usages et lois dans la bonne compagnie' (II, p. 438n). There is, then, an instance of legislation in *le monde*, and although *maximes* and the rules of *bienséance* are here placed in a series of terms such as *jargon*, *bel esprit*, *usage*, *apparence*, *préjugé*, and so on, as opposed to a positive series containing terms of the type *sentiment*, *amour*, *coeur*, *pudeur*, *lois*, *nature*, if the *usages* which 'naissent et passent comme un éclair' are also in some sense 'lois', then there arises the difficult problem of analysing the status of this legislative instance and the role of the law, which is one of the most consistently valorized terms in all of Rousseau's writing. This will require a long and patient detour through political writing.

3. Law and Nature

3.1. Definitions

Qui sibi persuadent posse multitudinem, vel qui publicis negotiis distrahuntur, induci, ut ex solo Rationis praescriptio vivant, seculum Poëtarum aureum, seu fabulam somnient.

(Spinoza, *Tractatus Politicus*, Chapter I, §5)

The intuitive definition of sententiousness as 'laying down the law', in one sense does no more than defer the problem of definition, provoking the question: 'what is the law?' A reply would involve the same type of contamination of object and meta-language seen earlier. But historically it is possible to find attempts to define the law, and in the eighteenth century one of the most famous of these, albeit a confused one, is undoubtedly that offered by Montesquieu at the beginning of *L'Esprit des Lois*:[22]

Les lois, dans la signification la plus étendue, sont *les rapports nécessaires qui dérivent de la nature des choses*, et, dans ce sens, tous les êtres ont leurs lois; la Divinité a ses lois; le monde matériel a ses lois; les intelligences supérieures à l'homme ont leurs lois; les bêtes ont leurs lois; l'homme a ses lois . . .

Il y a donc une raison primitive; et les lois sont les rapports qui se trouvent entre elle et les différents êtres, les rapports de ces divers entre eux.

(I, p. 530, my emphasis)

What is surprising in this definition is that it makes of the law not a command, a prescription, but a relationship of necessity and nature.[23] Any question of the authority of prescriptive discourse and of justice is subordinated to a pre-given rational order of the universe. This subordination of positive law to Truth is made clear in a later passage in this first chapter:

Les êtres particuliers intelligents peuvent avoir des lois qu'ils ont faites; mais ils en ont aussi qu'ils n'ont pas faites. Avant qu'il y eût des êtres intelligents, ils étaient possibles; ils avaient donc des rapports possibles, et par conséquent des lois possibles. Avant qu'il y eût des lois faites, il y avait des rapports de justice possible. Dire qu'il n'y a rien de juste ni d'injuste que ce qu'ordonnent ou défendent les lois positives, c'est à dire qu'avant qu'on eût tracé le cercle, tous les rayons n'étaient pas égaux. (I, p. 530)

This slippage within the term 'law' from prescriptive to descriptive values, here evident in the juxtaposition of relations of justice and relations of geometry, is perhaps constitutive of eighteenth-century thought on the law, and of the Enlightenment in general.[24]

On historical grounds, it is possible to quote a number of interrelated interpretations or explanations for the formation of this particular 'order of discourse', which, by placing Reason in a position logically prior to Power, can tend either towards a utopian projection of societies in which Reason is (re-)established and Power more or less abolished (as in the work of Morelly, and, with immense complications, Rousseau), or towards what amounts to a justification of certain existing power-relations, which gain legitimacy through the appeal to Reason (Locke, Montesquieu). For example, following Louis Althusser, who comments at some length on the opening definition of the law from *L'Esprit des Lois*, it can be suggested that this rational, 'scientific' sense of the term 'law' is inherited from Galileo and Newton, and is to be set against an older sense in which the law was indeed identified with the idea of a command.[25] Again, we might emphasize the fact that Montesquieu affirms that 'la Divinité a ses lois', to link the conception of the law announced here to the rise of what Groethuysen's classic study calls 'l'esprit bourgeois', replacing an old-style arbitrary incomprehensible God with a laicized God whose existence is accepted only if he is willing to submit to a higher instance of Reason which can regulate justice without his direct intervention.[26] And this would lead to the importance of the Natural Right school, and to Grotius's assertion that natural law is, in a sense, independent of God.[27] It would be difficult to contest the relevance of such explanations on historical grounds; and indeed it would be desirable to link them all to a fundamental structure of the self-representation of eighteenth-century thought, which sees itself as placed in a present world of prejudice and error, the result of a perversion of a prehistorical or *a priori* clarity which it is the mission of the *lumières* to restore.

3.2. Prescription, Description, Nature

Returning to the letter of Montesquieu's text, and specifically to the crucial opening chapters of *L'Esprit des lois*, it becomes clear that Montesquieu is exploiting, or being exploited by, an ambivalence in the term 'loi' between descriptive and prescriptive weight – it is not easy to see how the slippages and redoublings which this involves could be reduced by a historical reading. This problem is prominent in the opening of Book I, Chapter 3:

La loi, en général, est la raison humaine, en tant qu'elle gouverne tous les peuples de la terre; et les lois politiques et civiles de chaque nation ne doivent être que les cas particuliers où s'applique cette raison humaine.

(I, p. 532)

Human reason is both a principle of exploration and description of nature, and an instance of power insofar as it 'governs'. Political and civil laws, which are presumably prescriptions, are also *subject to* the prescriptions (or meta-prescriptions) of that primary instance.

One way of attempting to read this type of passage is to postulate a split between method on the one hand, and the objects of methodological inquiry on the other. According to this type of reading, when Montesquieu writes about particular laws, he is in fact relegating them in their historical contingency to the level of objects or phenomena like any others; and, like all objects or phenomena, they have their laws in the sense of rational relationships. These laws of laws are laws in the 'new' scientific sense of the word, and this sense operates independently of the fact that the object of this discourse happens to be the law in a different sense.[28] This new sense of the word can be linked to the methodological remarks which Montesquieu makes in his preface, and associated with the word 'principe'. When Montesquieu writes: 'J'ai posé mes principes, et j'ai vu les cas particuliers s'y plier comme d'eux-mêmes' (p. 529), or when, much later, he announces triumphantly, 'Tout se plie à mes principes' (XXVIII, VI, p. 726), he is working at this methodological level and engaging with epistemological problems.[29] It is tempting to stress this aspect of Montesquieu's enterprise, and to see in it a decisive progression from the 'old' definition of the law as command to the 'new' Newtonian sense; and this progression is indeed the object of praise from thinkers as apparently different as Auguste Comte and Louis Althusser. It is also, perhaps, praised by Montesquieu himself, and one of the ways of reading the *Lettres Persanes* might be in terms of this type of progression. In Letter 97 Usbek praises the European philosophers in the following terms:

Que les législateurs ordinaires nous proposent des lois pour régler les sociétés des hommes; des lois aussi sujettes au changement que l'esprit de ceux qui les proposent, et des peuples qui les observent! Ceux-ci [i.e. the philosophers] ne nous parlent que des lois générales, immuables, éternelles, qui s'observent sans aucune exception, avec un ordre, une régularité et une promptitude infinie, dans l'immensité des espaces.[30]

This preference for the new sense of the word 'law' seems quite simply to evacuate the problem of prescription and power in favour of a sort of positivism. Auguste Comte locates as the principal force of *L'Esprit des lois*, 'la tendance prépondérante qui s'y fait sentir à concevoir désormais les phénomènes politiques comme *aussi nécessairement assujettis à d'invariables lois naturelles que tous les autres phénomènes quelconques*', and goes on to praise

cet admirable chapitre préliminaire où, pour la première fois depuis l'essor primitif de la raison humaine, l'idée générale de *loi* se trouve enfin directement définie, *envers tous les sujets possibles, mêmes politiques*.[31]

According to this type of reading, then, Montesquieu is looking for descriptive laws which just happen to describe an object composed of prescriptive laws. But the fact that that object is also called 'law' suggests that the issue is not so simple, and that Comte's erasure of the specificity of that object (its reduction to the rank of a 'phénomène quelconque') is not innocent.

I want to suggest that this reading is mistaken, and that in fact there is a constant slippage in these texts between the two senses of the word 'law'. This slippage, which upsets the binary descriptive/prescriptive opposition, and any narrative which might seek to historicize that opposition, seems to take place by means of a third term, that of 'nature', and specifically in the notion of 'natural law'. This position of natural law is figured in the layout of the first three chapters of *L'Esprit des lois*, the first of which offers the definition of laws in general, the second that of natural laws, and the third that of positive laws. The problem with Comte's reading is that it tends to identify 'law in general' (linked, as we have seen, to Montesquieu's method) with natural law. I have already quoted Comte's reference to 'd'invariables lois naturelles', and elsewhere he affirms that, in opposition to contemporary notions that laws can be changed arbitrarily according to the caprice of the legislator, Montesquieu shows that 'les divers phénomènes politiques [sont] comme toujours réglés, au contraire, par *des lois pleinement naturelles*'.[32]

The temptation to identify the rational law which organizes Montesquieu's epistemology, with the 'natural law' which is part of the object of his discourse, can call on details of the text for support, to the extent that it is claimed that the law of Reason is derived from the 'nature of things': 'Je n'ai point tiré mes principes de mes préjugés, mais de la nature des choses', announces Montesquieu in his preface (p. 529). But this 'nature of things' in fact appeals to prescription, to show how things ought to be rather than how they are, and this is, at a different level, the same fundamental ambivalence observed above. There is a radical indetermination of these two realms (these two types of sentence) which frustrates any attempt to divide the notion of law neatly into separable senses linked by historical progress. Law 'in general' *is* human reason, but that reason *governs* all nations (as natural law), and as such *prescribes* what political laws *ought to be*. Althusser's reading, which stressed the novelty of Montesquieu's conception of the law, does have the merit of recognizing that his desire to discover the law of laws is not simple, and proposes two possible readings of the prescriptive elements involved. Either the *devoir* (as in 'les lois politiques ne doivent être . . .', quoted above) refers to an epistemological, enlightening attempt to correct 'la conscience errante par la science acquise', or else it indeed overruns this project and reverts to the notion of *loi-devoir*, of 'lois primitives' linked to a primary debt (*devoir*) of man to God. It is difficult to decide in favour of either alternative, insofar as through the ambivalence of the term 'nature', Reason *itself* comes to occupy a theological position. This retreat from the apparently self-contained rationalism of the natural law position to a theological notion of prescription can also be seen at work in the natural law school itself, and specifically in Pufendorf, for whom the law of the law of nature is that of its own inability to stand without a transcendent authority to ground its prescriptions.[33]

Still in his preface, Montesquieu writes: 'Si je pouvais faire en sorte que ceux qui commandent augmentassent leurs connaissances sur ce qu'ils doivent prescrire, et que ceux qui obéissent trouvassent un nouveau plaisir à obéir, je me croirais le plus heureux des hommes' (p. 529). 'Ce qu'ils doivent prescrire': the law of Reason also commands; the law of laws is not just a law in the 'new' scientific sense; Montesquieu *also* legislates about legislation.

Is it possible still to separate two senses of the word 'law', either to denounce Montesquieu's confusions (of, for example, so-called 'facts' and so-called 'values'), as does John Stuart Mill, or to praise the emergence of the 'new' sense from the 'old', as does Althusser?[34] Any such denunciation relies on a presupposition as to what words 'really' mean, which cannot itself avoid introducing a prescriptive element into its decision about that 'real meaning'; it thus perpetuates a 'confusion' which it purports to clarify. And any such praise implies a redistribution of textual elements according to a historical scheme which is none other than that of the Enlightenment itself. But newly-emergent Reason still prescribes itself as the necessity of its own application, and the appearance of the verb 'devoir' in the text is the trace of that primary prescription.

That 'primary prescription' cannot have come from nowhere, and is, rather, evidence of an element suppressed by Montesquieu's writing. In the eighteenth century itself, Montesquieu was devastatingly criticized by Linguet for repressing the truth that law originates in an originary act of violence which is subsequently given a bogus rationalisation and legitimation by legislation: 'Nos titres de jouissance & de propriété sont les mêmes: c'est-à-dire, une force, une violence primitive, légitimées ensuite par la prescription . . . de sorte que la possession la plus légitime, la plus sacrée aujourd'hui, porte par un bout sur l'usurpation la plus criante'.[35]

Most often, in the eighteenth century, however, the appeal will indeed be to 'des lois éternelles inscrites dans la nature des choses',[36] as the ground of authority for laying down the law. There is a continual play between 'laws of nature' and 'natural laws', and this play can make of nature a legislator. If the Enlightenment wants to lift veils in order to discover the laws of nature, to dissipate darkness so that eyes can see, it also attempts to open ears to nature's *voice*, and that voice is prescriptive. Morelly, for example, opens his *Code de la nature* with a commonplace statement of the first aspect of this process: 'Je développe analytiquement dans cette dissertation, des vérités qui, malgré leur simplicité et leur évidence, sont presque de tout temps demeurées dans l'oubli, ou environnées des ténèbres des préjugés'; and a little later he presents his own epic poem, *La Basiliade*, in terms of the second aspect, declaring that his aim is to 'faire voir que le véritable héros est l'homme même formé par les leçons de la nature, et de saper par les fondements tous les malheureux préjugés qui le rendent sourd à la voix de cette aimable législatrice' (Morelly, p. 35).[37] It seems possible to generalize, and to suggest that as soon as nature is endowed with a voice, or is given the power to 'write in men's souls', it becomes a legislative instance whose prescriptions are legitimated through an unproblematized appeal to truth and reason.

3.3. Models for Authority

In order to specify the position of nature with respect to the law, and to prepare for a reading of Rousseau's political texts, it will be as well to look more closely at 'nature', 'natural law', and 'the state of nature', in terms of the specific polemic which opposed the theory of legislation based on these terms to that which defended the Divine Right of kings. 'Nature' is here involved in a quarrel over the essence and ground of law and authority. Grotius and Pufendorf, soon followed by Locke, constructed a nature which could provide a reply to questions about the right to legislate and the legitimacy of legislation, without having any essential recourse to the idea of authority given by God.[38]

Locke summarizes the Divine Right position (represented by Filmer in England and reaching its apogee with Bossuet in France) as follows:

Men are not born free, and therefore could never have the liberty to choose either Governors, or Forms of Government. Princes have their power absolute, and by Divine Right, for Slaves could never have a Right to Compact or Consent. Adam was an absolute Monarch, and so are all Princes ever since.[39]

What this means for the authority of *sentences* is clear: once the Prince has been identified, then his every word has force of law, by virtue of an authority placed *outside* the system in which that law holds. The Prince by Divine Right is thus, structurally, free in his legislation from any controls of truth or falsity or Reason: the place of the enunciation of his prescriptions makes them valid, whatever their content. The opposition of 'vérité' and 'préjugé' which organizes so much of the discourse of the Enlightenment can have no pertinence here. This language-game is later condemned as tyranny, and exiled, as tyranny had been since the Greeks, to the Orient.[40]

In such a system, the prince's words becomes sentences in a quasi-juridical sense, and the only condition for the felicitous performance of those sentences is that the Prince be recognized as such.[41] The shift from Divine Right to Natural Right involves a shift both in the content of the conditions of such performances, and in the structure of legitimation of those conditions. In the Divine Right system each performance is unique, individual, unpredictable (even though a Montesquieu might attempt to analyse the conditions which can give rise to such a system), and in principle refers beyond itself to nothing but the pure authority of the enunciating subject. In the Natural Right system, the performance of the sentence becomes a technical and mechanical procedure mediated by other considerations, and its legitimacy is internalized in terms of a code. This is why Locke is able to reply to Filmer that 'The pronouncing of Sentences of Death is not a certain mark of Sovereignty, but usually the Office of Inferior Magistrates',[42] and to change the emphasis from the sentence itself to the law which determines the 'happiness' or 'unhappiness' of its performance: '*Political Power* then I take to be *a Right* of making Laws with Penalties of Death, and consequently all less Penalties'.[43]

This change of position, which involves some of the key terms in the field of sententiousness, is made clearer in a text by Beccaria: discussing the indications which justify the imprisonment of a suspect, he affirms,

Ces indices doivent être spécifiés d'une manière stable par la loi, et non par le juge, dont les sentences deviennent une atteinte à la liberté politique, lorsqu'elles ne sont pas simplement l'application particulière d'une maxime générale émanée du code des lois.[44]

The sentence is now strictly subordinated in a hierarchy, and becomes not so much a pure event as a simple application of the maxims of the law, which is a code and itself draws on the 'code de la nature'.

But if the notion of Natural Right implies that it is impossible to leap directly from a transcendent source of authority to particular legal applications which draw their legitimacy purely from that instance of authority, and that on the contrary these applications must be justified in terms of an order grounded in 'nature', the discovery of what laws are dictated by this 'aimable législatrice' is not at all self-evident. If the source of authority is to be denied transcendence, and somehow placed within the system for which it legislates, and has therefore to be rationalized in terms of human convention, then the rationality of those conventions must in turn be grounded in a 'state of nature' from which they both derive and, in some way, break. The notion of a *contract* as the origin of such conventions is constant in political theory from Grotius and Hobbes,[45] and the 'state of nature' a fictional projection of what might have come before. The various rival descriptions of the state of nature as a state of peace or war, of happiness or fear and misery, dispersal or collectivity, depend on retrospective phantasies based on various notions about society as it stands.[46] Locke, for example, decides that property must be natural and so makes it a result of natural law, whereas for Mably and Linguet it seems clear that property is the result of social usurpation and is thus 'unnatural'.[47] These 'liberal' and 'socialist' descriptions are banal enough: they have in common the use of 'Nature' as a legitimating fiction for a political position which is always already situated on the ground of society. It is this uncontrolled invocation of Nature which is denounced by Rousseau, and his lucidity in this matter which leads to his particularly complex notions of the law and the legislator.

3.4. Rousseau

Rousseau's questioning of natural law begins in the preface to the *Discours sur l'inégalité*, which criticizes previous attempts to define such a law, and locates the problem as follows:

> Toutes les définitions de ces savans hommes, d'ailleurs en perpetuelle contradiction entre elles, s'accordent seulement en ceci, qu'il est impossible d'entendre la Loy de Nature et par conséquent d'y obéir, sans être un très grand raisonneur et un profond Metaphisicien. Ce qui signifie precisément que les hommes ont dû employer pour l'établissement de la société, des lumières qui ne se développent qu'avec beaucoup de peine et pour fort peu de gens dans le sein de la société même. (III, p. 125)

A little further on: 'On commence par rechercher les régles dont, pour l'utilité commune, il seroit à propos que les hommes convinssent entr'eux; et puis on donne le nom de Loi naturelle à la collection de ces règles' (II, p. 125), and, finally, 'tous . . . ont transporté à l'état de Nature, des idées qu'ils avoient prises dans la société; ils parloient de l'Homme Sauvage et ils peignoient l'homme Civil' (III, p. 132).

Rousseau's own attempt to depict 'l'homme sauvage' is radical enough to escape from the facility of the other theorists of the law, but is also aporetical; and this aporia affects both the contract which creates society, and the legislator who is ultimately necessary to give it its laws. What it is interesting to do in the present perspective is less to retrace the detail of Rousseau's description of the progression leading from 'nature' to 'society',[48] than to stress that, however paradoxical this may seem, Rousseau recognizes that man is always already a social subject (and not the ready-made subject of the liberal tradition).[49] Rousseau's subject is, *qua* subject, irremediably and originarily separated from 'nature'.[50] On the other hand, and more importantly, natural man is *also* radically separated from the state of nature, although it is 'his' state, precisely insofar as he is totally self-contained, pre-moral and pre-rational. There is an originary split in nature, and the name of this split is 'man'. The consequence of this double impossibility of being 'in' nature is that 'natural law' cannot exist as such.

In the preface to the *Discours sur l'inégalité*, Rousseau lays down two conditions for the existence of natural law as law:

Tout ce que nous pouvons voir très clairement au sujet de cette Loi, c'est que non seulement pour qu'elle soit loi il faut que la volonté de celui qu'elle oblige puisse s'y soumettre avec connoissance; mais il faut encore pour qu'elle soit naturelle qu'elle parle immédiatement par la voix de la Nature.

(III, p. 125)

That this type of immediate proximity with Nature and her legislative voice is impossible is shown in the *Manuscrit de Genève*:

La paix et l'innocence nous ont échappé pour jamais avant que nous en eussions gouté les délices; insensible aux stupides hommes des premiers tems, echappée aux hommes éclairés des tems postérieurs, l'heureuse vie de l'âge d'or fut toujours un état étranger à la race humaine, ou pour l'avoir méconnu quand elle en pouvoit joüir, ou pour l'avoir perdu quand elle auroit pu le connoitre.

(III, p. 283)

Natural law and *jouissance* are simultaneously rendered impossible by this double *décalage*: the split in the subject created by the passage to society and the possibility of law and *jouissance* also makes inevitable the impossibility of that same law and *jouissance*.[51] The difficult situation of Rousseau's writing discussed at the beginning of this chapter is at once a recognition of that impossibility and an attempt to overcome it, and that attempt depends on a rehabilitation of the law (now become positive law), as the (artificial) means by which the impossible freedom and autonomy of nature can be recaptured. The law, which can no longer be 'natural law', becomes

157

necessary to 'patch up' man's difference from his natural self,[52] and Rousseau's thought on the law is perhaps his most sustained attempt to ground theoretically his drive towards auto-affection.[53] This is possible because, if there is a sense in which nature is a state of liberty (in that the only limits on what an individual can do are determined by the limits of strength), there is another sense in which liberty can only be secured through society and its law. In the absence of the reflexive split which founds the social subject (along with language, morality and politics), natural man's 'liberty' is no more than a blind submission to appetite: 'l'impulsion au seul appétit est esclavage', whereas real freedom involves the ability to prescribe laws to oneself and to obey them: 'l'obéissance à la loi qu'on s'est prescritte est liberté'.[54] This constitutive paradox of the law which creates a simulacrum of a 'natural' freedom is fundamental to Rousseau's thought, and produces the following ecstatic paragraph in praise of the law:

Par quel art inconcevable a-t-on pû trouver le moyen d'assujettir les hommes pour les rendre libres? d'employer au service de l'état les biens, les bras, et la vie même de tous ses membres, sans les contraindre et sans les consulter? d'enchaîner leur volonté de leur propre aveu? de faire valoir leur consentement contre leur refus, et de les forcer à se punir eux-mêmes, quand ils font ce qu'ils n'ont pas voulu? Comment se peut-il faire qu'ils obéissent et que personne ne commande, qu'ils servent et n'ayent point de maître; d'autant plus librcs en effet que sous une apparente sujétion, nul ne perd de sa liberté que ce qui peut nuire à celle d'un autre? Ces prodiges sont l'ouvrage de la loi. *C'est à la loi seule que les hommes doivent la justice et la liberté.* C'est cet organe salutaire de la volonté de tous, qui *rétablit dans le droit l'égalité naturelle entre le hommes.* C'est cette voix céleste qui dicte à chaque citoyen les préceptes de la raison publique, et lui apprend à agir selon les maximes de son propre jugement, et à n'être pas en contradiction avec lui-même.[55]

Law, then, returns to Nature, the impossibility of which is the ground of its necessity. This simulacrum of natural equality is obtained by *denaturing* man, and making of him an 'artificial individual'.[56] The relative existence of individuals in society (relative not to other individuals but to the whole) is thus secured only by the *detour* through the law. This unnatural recovery of Nature depends on the law's being impersonal, not the result of any individual's legislation, but of a pure act of reflection of the whole upon the whole, of the *volonté générale* as expressed in the sovereign. This account of legislation realizes the ideal of a coherent, self-regulating system without transcendence, and apparently overcomes the problem of the undecidability of descriptive and prescriptive senses of the word 'law', insofar as 'Le Souverain, par cela seul qu'il *est*, est toujours ce qu'il *doit être*' (III, 363, my emphasis).[57] This abolition of the problem of prescription would, if it were successful, remove the law from the domain of prejudice and passion, and make it not prescriptive but descriptive, not divine but thing-like. This phantasy is put forward in a famous passage from *Emile*:

> Il y a deux sortes de dépendance. Celle des choses qui est de la nature; celle des hommes qui est de la societé. La dépendance des choses n'ayant aucune moralité, ne nuit point à la liberté et n'engendre point de vices. La dépendance des hommes étant désordonnée les engendre tous, et c'est par elle que le maitre et l'esclave se dépravent mutuellement. S'il y a quelque moyen de remédier à ce mal dans la societé c'est de *substituer la loi à l'homme*, et d'armer les volontés générales d'une force réelle supérieure à l'action de toute volonté particuliére. Si les loix des nations pouvoient avoir comme celles de la nature une infléxibilité que jamais aucune force humaine ne put vaincre, la dépendance des hommes redeviendroit alors celle des choses, on réuniroit dans la République tous les avantages de l'état naturel à ceux de l'état civil, on joindroit à la liberté qui maintient l'homme exempt de vices la moralité qui l'élève à la vertu. (IV, p. 311, my emphasis)

'S'il y a quelque moyen . . .': the *Contrat social* seems to suggest that there is. 'Si les loix . . . pouvoient': but in truth they cannot, and it is now necessary to see how this is recognized by the *Contrat social* too.

3.4.1. The Failure of Reflection

The thing-like ideal of positive law generated by the pure reflection of the *volonté générale* and the necessary perfection of the Sovereign seemed to provide for an impersonal collective legislator standing in Nature's place. The refusal of 'natural law', in favour of a simulacrum of 'laws of nature' grounded in a radical conventionality, should allow the social body to revert to a unity and ahistory homologous with that of the natural individual. Rousseau's theory seems to provide for a 'machine'[58] running in a perpetual motion indistinguishable from immobility.

But in fact there are problems attached to Rousseau's enterprise which prevent this type of functioning, and which generate the need, beyond the apparently simple mechanisms of contract and law, for a number of supplementary instances within the theory (notably the instances of the executive, the *tribunat*, and the legislator) – I shall argue that only these problems encountered by the theory account for its being written in the first place. These problems are not a result of some practical or psychological implausibility of Rousseau's ideas, nor do I raise them on the basis of any immediate evaluation of those ideas in political or ethical terms. In attempting to locate and analyse these problems, my reading moves in the interstices of the two most persuasive accounts of the *Contrat social* that I know, by Louis Althusser and Paul de Man.[59] Both of these authors base their readings on the location of one or more 'discrepancies' or *décalages* in Rousseau's text, and some such operator is indeed necessary; but I shall argue that Althusser forecloses the full implications of his findings by an unwarranted or untimely invocation of the domain of praxis or the 'real', and that De Man, who shows convincingly that Althusser's reliance on an opposition between 'theoretical' and 'fictional' texts cannot be sustained, nevertheless conflates a number of essential distinctions, and in so doing elides a number of questions crucial both to the reading of the *Contrat social* and to his own theoretical conclusions.

The 'first' discrepancy has in fact already been located in the account of Rousseau's critique of the notion of natural law. The impossibility of the state of nature's coinciding with itself, and the concomitant impossibility of accounting for society in terms of natural law, leads to the derivation of the social and the political as such, and explains Rousseau's valorization of the law as a means of 'patching up' the effects of that non-coincidence. A prior condition of this role of the law is of course the contract itself, but the logic of the contract already shows that the effect of the 'originary' discrepancy is not so easy to overcome. The nature and complexity involved can be approached via the analyses mentioned above.

De Man is keen to find support, in the law and the contract, for his claims about the radical disjunction within language, between performative and constative functions. He attempts to show that the performative utterances generated by Rousseau's model are subverted by incompatible constative elements. In doing this, he tends to conflate the analysis of the contract with that of the law. For example, he states that the law's 'illocutionary mode is that of the *promise*' (p. 273), but supports this assertion with reference to the *contract* rather than the law as such, and indeed it seems intuitively easier to associate contract and promise than law and promise.[60] On the other hand, De Man's claim that the discrepancy within the contractual model 'will necessarily manifest itself phenomenologically' as *time*, would seem intuitively more applicable to the law. This is not to contest that there *is* a discrepancy in the contractual model, nor to deny that it has to do with temporality. By separating the analysis of the contract from that of the law, however (as does Althusser), it seems possible on the one hand to support some of De Man's assertions about the relationship of performative and constative functions (though in terms rather different from his own), but on the other to argue for the importance of a *prescriptive* function of language in the law, and thereby to displace some of De Man's general conclusions.

That there is an aporia in the contractual model as presented by Rousseau has in fact been pointed out often enough, and it is the first *décalage* noted by Althusser.[61] The problem, which does not arise so acutely in the 'liberal' version of the contract,[62] is that one of the parties to the contract (the social body as a whole), is in fact constituted *as* a possible party to any possible contract only by the performance of the very contract to which it is a party. As has perhaps been less often pointed out, this aporia also affects the other party to the contract (the individual), who, not being the pre-constituted individual of the liberal tradition, can also only be produced as able to contract by that same contract. Both of the parties would have to be before the contract, what only the contract can make them. Rousseau's contract depends on a temporal and causal reversal which is part of a persistent logic of the *après-coup*.[63] This is troubling for Rousseau's theory, as elsewhere he is concerned to establish a correct ordering of cause and effect, and in fact his critique of other theories of the origin of legitimate institutions rests on the location and denunciation of formally identical figures.[64]

The immediate effect of this aporia is to threaten any possible empirical 'happiness' of the performance of the contractual promise by splitting open the instant in which any such performance must be assumed to take place. De Man writes, 'every promise assumes a date at which the promise is made and without which it would have no validity' (p. 273); but the aporia in the structure of the contract makes such dating (and its corollary, signing, not mentioned by De Man) strictly speaking impossible. The contract can only take place within what Jacques Derrida has recently called a 'simulacre de l'instant':[65] the social simulacrum of nature can only be instituted through a simulacrum of 'natural' temporality (a temporality of self-present moments), and this simulacrum is constituted by an undecidability, in the statement of the contract, between performative and constative readings. The statement of constitution of the people is both a description of the people constituted and the performance by which the people is/was/will be constituted.[66] Both readings have to coexist in Rousseau's formulation of the pact: 'Chacun de nous met en commun sa personne et toute sa puissance sous la suprême direction de la volonté générale; et nous recevons en corps chaque membre comme partie indivisible du tout' (III, p. 361). Another way of putting this is that 'chacun' and 'nous' are undecidably both proper names and signatures.

This 'simulacre de l'instant' can now be seen to describe more accurately the temporality of the Sovereign, which was previously accepted as one of a succession of pure (self-)present moments. Each of these moments in fact *repeats* in its division the simulacrum-time of the contract in a series of pseudo-signature–events[67] in which the 'origin' of the state is simultaneously enacted, mimed, and effaced. The apparent 'purity' of the Sovereign's 'present' is always already compromised. This discrepancy can thus be said to produce the phenomenal category of time (as opposed to the eternal present to which the Sovereign aspires) long 'before' any question of 'the passage . . . from "pure" theory to an empirical phenomenon' from which De Man derives time (p. 273). The discrepancy also character- izes the state as non-natural, while accounting for its inability to be non-natural *enough* to return to nature.

I have so far followed De Man at least to the extent of stressing a disjunction between performative and constative functions of lan- guage. But insofar as Rousseau's text is attemping to lay down the *de jure* conditions for a legitimate political institution, rather than attempting to account for how political institutions might (have) emerge(d), then this stress is reductive, and misses the importance of prescription, of, precisely, laying down the law. The importance of the notionally 'pure' temporality of the Sovereign was much less to do with the *intelligibility* of the contract than with the necessary *justice* of the state produced by the contract. The attraction of the 'pure' temporality of the Sovereign was that it seemed to allow for a solution to the problem posed by the disjunction between descriptive and prescriptive sense of the word 'law', and to support Rousseau's phantasy of a positive (prescriptive) law's achieving the inflexibility of the (descriptive) laws of nature. Questioning the purity of that temporality not only suggests that the disjunction cannot be reduced, but also accounts for the possibility of any such disjunction in the first place. According to a paradox which re-appears at every level of analysis, and which we have already encountered at the beginning of this chapter, Rousseau's text owes its existence to that which prevents it from achieving its aim.

We have seen that the law is assigned the task of patching up man's/nature's difference from him/herself. This implies that the law already recognizes the split in nature (and its temporality) which is confirmed in the contract, and which is the only reason for the law's existence. On the other hand, if the law achieved its aim, then the patch would be seamlessly incorporated into the no longer torn natural fabric, and it would abolish itself. And this is indeed the point of Rousseau's phantasy: an implicit meta-prescription demands that the law *lose* its character as prescription in an identity with the descriptive laws of nature. But the fact that the laws of society are, precisely, not natural, and must therefore be formulated and promulgated to have any effectiveness (unlike the laws of nature, in Newtonian cosmology at least), guarantees the failure of that meta-prescription to be obeyed, and ensures that the functioning of the Sovereign and the *volonté générale* is both necessary and necessarily insufficient. Recognizing the need for laws implies the recognition that they can be broken, and this *necessary possibility* ensures that in a sense the law has always already been broken in principle.[68]

The need for laws which prescribe does not derive from the state's not being natural enough, but from its still being too natural, its not being enough of a machine: the individual may be *dénaturé* in the legitimate institution of society, but that denaturing never goes far enough, precisely insofar as the 'artificial individual' can still be said to be an individual. This residue of individuality disturbs the account of the law both in its constitution and in its application (two questions conflated by De Man), in the first case affecting the possibility of the *volonté générale* achieving its generality, and in the second giving rise to supplementary instances within the state.

In a section of the *Manuscrit de Genève* which contests the possibility of a general society of humanity based in natural law,[69] Rousseau states the problem of the relationship between individual and general will in psychological terms:

En effet que la volonté générale soit dans chaque individu un acte pur de l'entendement qui raisonne dans le silence des passions sur ce que l'homme peut éxiger de son semblable, et sur ce que son semblable est en droit d'éxiger de lui, nul n'en disconviendra: mais où est l'homme qui puisse ainsi se séparer de lui même et si le soin de sa propre conservation est le premier précepte de la nature, peut on le forcer de regarder ainsi l'espèce en général pour s'imposer, à lui, des devoirs dont il ne voit point la liaison avec sa constitution particulière?

(III, p. 286)

The problem is evidently supposed to be solved by the production of the artificial individual through the contract, but if this were simply the case, then the *volonté de tous* would simply coincide with the *volonté générale*, and again there would be no need for legislation. Only insofar as the natural individual is *not* completely destroyed can there be any need to postulate a *volonté générale* and a realm of *droit*.[70] In terms of the image of the state as machine, the natural residue would be equivalent to the friction which both allows a machine to operate and also prevents it from achieving perpetual motion.[71]

In a notorious passage seized upon by both Althusser and De Man, Rousseau attempts to ground the whole effectiveness of the *volonté générale* in precisely this natural residue of individuality:

Pourquoi la volonté générale est-elle toujours droite, et pourquoi tous veulent-ils constamment le bonheur de chacun d'eux, si ce n'est parce qu'il n'y a personne qui ne s'approprie ce mot *chacun*, et qui ne songe à lui-même en votant pour tous? Ce qui prouve que l'égalité de droit et la notion de justice qu'elle produit dérive de la préférence que chacun se donne et par conséquent de la nature de l'homme. (III, p. 373)

Althusser uses this passage as part of his argument that Rousseau 'plays' on a good and a bad sense of the 'particular': the good sense (for Rousseau) being that of the *chacun* in this passage, the bad sense that of particular groups or classes within the social totality, which Rousseau needs to suppress. For Althusser, this demonstrates that Rousseau is stuck in a juridical ideology of the individual, which simply founders on the given fact of class-divided society (pp. 32–8). This argument is seductive, but seems to jump too hastily into an assumed extra-textual 'real' against which Rousseau's theory is seen to come to grief. This fails to allow for the full complexity of Rousseau's text, in which the sense of the particular supposedly favoured by Rousseau is in fact *itself* split, and is as 'bad' as it is 'good' for the doctrine of the *volonté générale*. Further, the location of this aspect of Rousseau's text as 'ideological' (as opposed to the 'scientific' version which Althusser implies that he can provide), could quite easily be shown to depend on a phantasy about science which reduplicates Rousseau's phantasy about the law, in the mode of positivism.

De Man, with an apparently greater respect for textual complexity, uses the passage to support his general thesis about performative and constative language: here, the generality of the statement of the law is related to the functioning of grammar (linked to a sort of blind performance in the absence of any specified referent), and the particularity of the *chacun* is linked to the referential/constative moment said to subvert that grammar. The argument is compelling but obscure, and again functions through a reduction of the importance of the law as *prescription*, a reduction which depends on an unwarranted assimilation of the *justice* of the law with the *justesse* of a descriptive statement, and of the question of particularity in the constitution of the law with particularity of application.[72] As a result of this, De Man is unable to read the position of the *executive* in Rousseau's theory, and is reduced to identifying it with the Sovereign, thus destroying what for Rousseau is an essential distinction. If that distinction is to be retained, and its logic respected in its consistency, we must read the passage quoted above, no longer as a key to the text as a whole, but as a local and rather desperate pocket of resistance to that logic (which Rousseau thus cannot be said to control). The passage attempts somewhat hastily to foreclose the effects of the discrepancy from which we started, by 'buckling the buckle' of the analysis into a circular structure (departure and return) grounding the simulacrum of nature (secured by the law) *in* nature (individual self-preference). But that naturally grounded self-preference is also what *prevents* politics, society and justice from returning to nature. The *volonté générale* should indeed 'partir de tous pour s'appliquer à tous' (III, 373), in another movement of departure and return; but if that journey closed into a perfect circle with no danger of accident along the way[73] (if there were not a 'natural' residue, if the law could indeed achieve the status of necessity) then politics would be destroyed in its own transparency or frictionless functioning: 'S'il n'y avoit point d'intérêts différens, à peine sentiroit-on l'intérêt commun qui ne trouveroit jamais d'obstacle: tout iroit de lui-même; et la politique cesseroit d'être un art' (III, p. 371n). The law is thus made possible and necessary by the movement of alienation within the general will, which prevents its departure and return from coinciding in the pseudo-instantaneous present of the Sovereign, and which thus makes the detour inevitable; but as the law is the result of the general will itself (which is thus perpetually legislating on (the ground of) its own inability to be general enough to legislate properly), then its inadequacy for its task is a condition of its activity, and its necessity a product of its imperfection.

As a member of the Sovereign, positioned as *destinateur* of the law, the individual is split by the persistence of the natural residue. As *subject* in the State, *destinataire* of that same law, the individual is re-positioned in what only now might be termed the political 'real', the realm of *fait* as against the realm of *droit*. This realm of factuality is opposed to the realm of the Sovereign (the realm of *droit*), not as 'nature', but as the result of the constitutive inability of the State to make a radical break with nature and thus rejoin it as simulacrum. The separation of these two realms is a predictable consequence of the discrepancy from which we began; and if these two realms were to be identified (as De Man, in his eagerness to link law and performance, suggests they are) the 'the political' as such would again disappear. The *Contrat social* is perfectly lucid and explicit about this: in his chapter on democracy (Book III, Chapter IV), Rousseau allows that it would seem as though legislative and executive powers should be joined, but this would in fact imply that there was no need for the executive in the first place: 'un peuple qui gouverneroit toujours bien n'aurait pas besoin d'être gouverné' (III, p. 404).[74]

Such a radical form of democracy would be practicable only for 'un peuple de Dieux' (III, p. 406), that is, precisely, a people for whom the separation of *droit* and *fait*, or that of description and prescription, could have no pertinence. In a political society, however, any attempt at such an identification would indeed revert to nature, but to a bad, violent nature rather than to the desired simulacrum:

> S'il étoit possible que le Souverain, considéré comme tel, eut la puissance exécutive, le droit et le fait seroient tellement confondus qu'on ne sauroit plus ce qui est loi et ce qui ne l'est pas, et le corps politique ainsi dénaturé seroit bien-tôt en proye à la violence contre laquelle il fut institué. (III, p. 432)

The realm of factuality and the executive are therefore necessary components of Rousseau's theory, consistently derived from the originary discrepancy in nature. As the effects of that split have consistently manifested themselves in the form of the *après-coup*, it is predictable that this figure should reappear with the executive, the institution of which again presents a problem. Rousseau explains that the institution of the executive cannot be the result of a contract (which would destroy the authority of the Sovereign), and so must be the result of a law. We have seen that the operation of the *volonté générale* presupposes its own inadequacy, and that inadequacy is recognized *en abyme* in the specific law which prescribes that there should be an executive power. But this law by itself cannot actually constitute the executive unless it is applied, and for this application to take place the executive would have to pre-exist its own institution. This is the *après-coup*:

> La difficulté est d'entendre comment on peut avoir un acte de Gouvernement avant que le Gouvernement existe, et comment le peuple, qui n'est que Souverain ou sujet, peut devenir Prince ou Magistrat dans certaines circonstances. (III, p. 433)

Rousseau solves the problem by postulating a momentary passage through precisely the state of radical democracy which was previously denounced as a state of dangerous confusion. The operation

> se fait par une conversion subite de la Souveraineté en Démocratie, en sorte que, sans aucun changement sensible, et seulement par une nouvelle relation

de tous à tous, les Citoyens devenus Magistrats passent des actes généraux aux actes particuliers et de la loi à l'exécution.   (III, pp. 433–4)

We saw that it was possible to agree with De Man that the discrepancy within the contractual model produced temporality; now it is necessary to refine on that statement and suggest that two sorts of time are involved. On the one hand, the contract produces the simulacrum of 'natural', ahistorical time. But insofar as this simulacrum is never in fact achieved (because of the need to apply the law, consequent on the necessary possibility of its being broken), then the institution of the government produces a different sort of time, which is that of *history*. Only the derivation of the realm of factuality through the executive allows the State to have a history, and this historicity is a logical consequence of the 'originary' split in nature which determines the necessity and insufficiency of politics. Nor can these two times, strictly speaking, be called the time of ' "pure" theory' on the one hand, and that of 'an empirical phenomenon' on the other, as De Man's analysis, admittedly rather obscure at this point, might imply. The 'factual' realm of the executive is not a 'real' world to be placed against Rousseau's text: the two temporalities are both posited *within* 'theory'. Nor is it easy to see how the relationship between these two temporalities could be usefully analysed in terms of performatives and constatives. But that relationship *can* be formulated in terms of sententiousness and narrative.

Once it has a history, the State can be said to live, and therefore to die. Rousseau plots this life-death as a narrative of decline (Book III, Chapters X and XI). The Sovereign's attempts to lay down the law are thus undermined by the narrative sentences of the realm of government, which lead the State to death and dissolution. This opposition of the government to the Sovereign is not merely an unfortunate accident, but an essential consequence of the logic of Rousseau's theory, insofar as the Sovereign is constitutively incapable of laying down the law adequately.[75] This also means that the progress of history-as-decline cannot be prevented, but only retarded by more or less negentropic instances within the State. The most important of these is the *Tribunat* (Book IV, Chapter V). This is a supplementary body which is not a constitutive part of the State, but which, according to Rousseau, draws its strength precisely from its position of exteriority.[76] But this position of strength is itself paradoxical, for as soon as it begins to impinge *within* the State, as it clearly must if it is to function, whether on Sovereign or executive, it is already too strong, and begins to usurp the very functions it is designed to protect:

167

Le Tribunat sagement tempéré est le plus ferme appui d'une bonne constitution; mais pour peu de force qu'il ait de trop il renverse tout: A l'egard de la foiblesse, elle n'est pas dans sa nature, et pourvu qu'il soit quelque chose, il n'est jamais moins qu'il ne faut. (III, p. 454)

This possible *remède*, then, will in fact aggravate the *mal* from which it springs and which it was supposed to cure.[77] The unspecified source of the *Tribunat*'s redoubtable power can only be transcendent, and this movement out of the immanence of the system of the State is a self-defeating attempt to secure the ability of the law to patch up the originary discrepancy.

3.4.2. The Legislator

But insofar as the necessary insufficiency of the patch, and the inevitable decline of the State, have been consistently derived from that discrepancy, then it is to be expected that some transcendental movement will have taken place much 'earlier' in the deduction of the political sphere. And such a movement is indeed suggested, in the figure of the legislator. We have seen how the very postulation of the need for the general will implies that it can never be general enough to abolish its own functioning; the 'corps politique' is never enough of a body, remaining, if not a *corps morcelé*, at least a *corps sans organes*.[78] This situation places it in need of an originary prosthesis, and this is the role of the legislator, whose necessity can in fact be immediately deduced from the necessity of legislation, as the *Manuscrit de Genève* makes much clearer than the final text of the *Contrat social*:[79]

Les loix sont l'unique mobile du corps politique, il n'est actif et sensible que par elles, sans les loix l'Etat formé n'est qu'un corps sans ame, il existe et ne peut agir, car ce n'est pas assés [que] chacun soit soumis à la volonté générale; pour la suivre il la faut connoitre. Voilà d'où nait la necessité d'une législation.

Les loix ne sont proprement que les conditions de l'association civile. Le Peuple soumis aux loix en doit donc être l'auteur, car il n'appartient qu'à ceux qui s'associent de déclarer les conditions sous lesquelles ils veulent s'associer. Mais comment les déclareront-ils? Sera-ce d'un commun accord et par une inspiration subite? Le corps politique a-t-il un organe pour énoncer ses volontés? Qui lui donnera la prévoyance necessaire pour en former les actes et les publier d'avance, ou comment les prononcera-il au moment du besoin? Comment voudroit-on qu'une multitude aveugle qui souvent ne sait ce qu'elle veut, parce qu'elle sait rarement ce qui lui est bon, put former et éxécuter d'elle même une entreprise aussi difficile qu'un sistème de Legislation qui est le plus sublime effort de la sagesse et de la prévoyance humaine? . . . Les particuliers voyent le bien qu'ils rejettent: le public veut le bien qu'il ne voit pas. Tous ont également besoin de guides; il faut apprendre à l'autre à connoitre ce qu'il veut. Alors des Lumiéres publiques resultera la vertu des particuliers, et de cette union de l'entendement et de la volonté dans le corps social, l'exact concours des parties, et la plus grande force du tout. Voila d'où nait la necessité d'un Legislateur. (III, pp. 310–11)

This shows how erroneous it would be to see in the legislator a merely *de facto* requirement, a concession on Rousseau's part to practical or psychological difficulties with the *de jure* system of the general will.[80] The instance of the legislator is a rigorous consequence of the logic which makes political theory necessary in the first place. But once that necessity is recognized, then the theory has failed to produce the self-legitimating system it desired, and the movement of escape which this implies needs to resort to some theological principle if it is to avoid generating an infinite regress of legitimating instances: 'il faudroit des Dieux pour donner les loix aux hommes' (III, p. 381). The legislator is thus, more radically than the *Tribunat* (because at the roots of the political), neither inside nor outside, both in excess of the State and yet necessary to ensure its closure, not complement, but supplement:[81]

Ce n'est point magistrature, ce n'est point souveraineté. Cet emploi, qui constitue la république, n'entre point dans sa constitution. C'est une fonction particulière et supérieure qui n'a rien de commun avec l'empire humain; car si celui qui commande aux hommes ne doit pas commander aux loix, celui qui commande aux loix ne doit pas non plus commander aux hommes.

(III, p. 382)

The legislator can have no authority to impose the laws he formulates, but neither can he resort to reasoning with the people to have those laws accepted by the legitimating procedures of the *volonté générale*, because of another version of the *après-coup* – in order to understand the legislator's language and accept his wisdom, the people would *already* have to be what they can only become through the laws which the legislator formulates. If uttered *within* the system of the State (in a language which the people could already understand), the law would be drawn into an unrelieved dialectic of doxa and paradoxa, remaining formally indistinguishable from the *préjugé* (III, p. 383). 'Il faudroit des Dieux . . .'; but the legislator's word cannot *be* that of (a) God, for if it were, in Rousseau's theology it would have to be accessible to all, and this would again abolish the need for politics: 'Toute justice vient de Dieu, lui seul en est la source; mais si nous savions la recevoir de si haut nous n'aurions besoin ni de gouvernement ni de loix' (III, p. 378).[82]

As Rousseau's text quite lucidly acknowledges, and as De Man's analysis forcefully reiterates, this situation leads to a recourse to *fiction.* The legislator simply *pretends* that his laws are God-given.[83] But even this fiction cannot arrest the logic of the *après-coup*; for the legitimacy of this appeal to fiction cannot *itself* be decided at the moment when it is made (if it could, it would not be necessary). Whether the legislator is a real genius and good charlatan, or a false genius and bad charlatan, can be seen only through the fate of his system of legislation – the 'grande âme' (III, p. 384) which authenticates the true legislator can only be identified after the event. Laying down the law comes to depend for its possible legitimacy on fiction, but also on the narrative dimension of history which it implicitly denies, on which it depends for its necessity, and which guarantees its insufficiency. And insofar as history is, for Rousseau, inevitably decline and death, then in fact no firm decision can *ever* be made between the true legislator and the charlatan: the founding fiction can never be completely justified, but is never completely exposed. There are only more or less long-lived States, and in any case the longevity of a State is not an infallible guide to its legitimacy.[84] The political is thus implicitly recognized to be a radically inconclusive realm, the prescriptions of the law implicitly described as emanating from an undecidable transcendence, and fictionality and narrative implicitly accepted as a necessary component of the attempt to lay down the law.

It is difficult not to suspect some identification on Rousseau's part with the legislator, or at least with some of the legislator's historical incarnations (Lycurgus, Solon, Moses).[85] De Man, however, denies the pertinence of any such identification, which would, according to him, make of the text 'a monological referential statement . . . since the exposure of the deceit would have to come from outside evidence not provided by the text itself' (p. 275). We should note immediately that in view of the radical inaccessibility of any such outside evidence for *any* legislator, and thereby the impossibility of ever 'exposing' the legislator's fiction as deceit, this can hardly be a conclusive objection. It is true that Rousseau denies himself the divine inspiration which the legislators claim, but this could easily enough be a supplementary fiction of the charlatan in him; moreover, it is clear that Rousseau's writing in general must, insofar as it is sententious and lays down the law, implicitly assert a quasi-theological authority against the declining narrative of history which makes that writing necessary. The fact that Rousseau 'undermines the authority of his own legislative discourse' (p. 275) may give his text an appearance of lucidity compared with the texts of the legislators, but the nature of that lucidity is problematic insofar as the radical nature of the fiction involved deprives it of all certainty. On Rousseau's account, the undecidability of genius and charlatan affects *all* attempts to lay down the law, and it would be quite unwarranted to assume that any legislator could himself *know* whether he was genius or charlatan.

Insofar as the *destinateur* positioned by Rousseau's texts, whom we call 'Rousseau', has its ground of authority *and* lucidity radically undercut by the logic which dictates its own necessity, then the homology with the legislator can be maintained. The continuity between legislator and pedagogue (and meta-pedagogical narrator) in *Emile* would not be difficult to establish. But the 'confessional' texts exhibit the homology clearly enough: Rousseau's contemporaries duly fail to recognize his 'grande âme' and see only the charlatan in him. The attempt to write against this pre-judgement leads only to proleptic appeals (such as the invocation of the Last Judgement at the beginning of the *Confessions* (I, p. 5)), produced by, and at the mercy of, the *après-coup*. Rousseau's final reliance on posterity and providence to clear his name cannot escape this structure, and this explains the irony and the tragedy or – perhaps better – *stupidity* of the measures taken to ensure the survival of the *Dialogues*.[86] The 'originary discrepancy' which gives rise to politics and history, writing and prejudice, also dictates that Rousseau, who 'began' by projecting his own writing towards its own disappearance (just as politics aims at its own demise), should 'end' in anguished concern over the survival of his texts, his signature and his *devise*.[87] Rousseau's 'madness' could be read as an effect of the insistence of the charlatan in the legislator, and this insistence can never be eradicated, insofar as texts cannot be guaranteed by legislation, *devise* or signature, but stand clear of authorial control. There is no end to that 'madness' insofar as Rousseau's texts are still available for new (mis-)readings; no final decision between *grande âme* and charlatan will ever be reached – there is no Last Judgement. The 'madness' which this involves is inherited, with anguish or humour, by any critical attempt to lay down the law about Rousseau's texts.

4. *Monde* and Anti-*Monde*

The pre-text for this lengthy consideration of the law as such was *La Nouvelle Héloïse*'s complex polemical relationship with the worldly novel; I left the novel at the point of recognition of a legislative instance in *le monde*. It is now tempting to read that legislation, and the *usages et lois* which it decrees, as a sort of simulacrum of the *volonté générale* of the State. Indeed, Saint-Preux's comment that in high society 'nul homme n'ose être lui-même' might be construed as a cynical comment on the doctrine of the *Contrat social*, in which the ultimate impossibility of a successful general will was a result of the individual's inability to *stop* being a 'lui-même'. Further, it will be remembered that the temporal structure of the Sovereign was projected as one of a succession of formally independent and self-present moments, but in fact functioned as a simulacrum, thus allowing contradictory investments; the legislative instance of *le monde* can be seen as a parodic exploitation of that same structure:

> Tout est usages et loix dans la bonne compagnie. Tous ces usages naissent et passent comme un éclair. Le savoir vivre consiste à se tenir toujours au guet, à les saisir au passage, à les affecter, à montrer qu'on sait celui du jour. Le tout pour être simple. (II, p. 438n)

An authentic general will would control the potential transience of its punctual decisions by appealing, ultimately, to nature. But insofar as this transience is another necessary structural possibility of the model of legislation, Rousseau here moves away from the political dimension altogether, and begins (only now) to locate the desired homeostasis and transparency in the 'individual', eventually retreating into the apparently radical solipsism of the *Rêveries*.

Such a move leads to a *general* (sententious) devalorization of sententiousness, beyond what were simply the *maximes de la galanterie*. For example, during the exchange of letters between Saint-Preux and Edouard on the subject of suicide, the latter writes:

> Mais laissons les maximes générales, dont on fait souvent beaucoup de bruit sans jamais en suivre aucune; car il se trouve toujours dans l'application quelque condition particulière, qui change tellement l'état des choses que chacun se croit dispensé d'obéir à la règle qu'il prescrit aux autres, et l'on sait bien que tout homme qui pose des maximes générales, entend qu'elles obligent tout le monde, excepté lui. Encore un coup parlons de toi.
> (II, p. 387)

Rules are no longer prescribed for oneself, as in the model of the general will, and the troublesome 'chacun' of the *Contrat social* can here apparently no longer be turned to good account. The problem of the individual, artificial or not, which the *Contrat* failed to reduce, returns. Other examples of praise given to a refusal to generalize are not hard to find.[88]

At the political level of the *anti-monde* of Clarens, this collapse of the *volonté générale* leads to a structure which is this time explicitly thematized in terms of seduction and the veil, and very similar to the manipulations of the pedagogue in *Emile*:

Dans la République on retient les citoyens par les mœurs, des principes, de la vertu: mais comment contenir des domestiques, des mercenaires, autrement que par la contrainte et la gêne? Tout l'art du maître est de cacher cette gêne sous le voile du plaisir ou de l'intérêt, en sorte qu'ils pensent vouloir ce qu'on les oblige de faire.   (II, p. 453)

And morally, the fragmentation of the ideal reflexivity of the general will and self-prescription into a now irreducible individuality (metonymized as 'le coeur') on the one hand, and on the other a more or less dishonest authority of a seducing *maître*, produces the central conflict of the novel. This is most in evidence where Edouard suggests that Julie and Saint-Preux go to live in England, where, precisely, 'nos sages lois n'abrogent point celles de la nature' (II, p. 200). But by now the complication of the invocation of any authority of 'nature' is such that the appeal to this guiding principle produces only contradiction and double bind: although Edouard can claim that the 'loi sacrée de la nature' (II, p. 195) assigns Julie to Saint-Preux, Julie would nonetheless be a 'fille . . . dénaturée' (II, p. 202) if she disobeyed her parents, towards whom her duty is no less 'sacré' (Ibid.). Claire provides the best description of this *impasse*:

Ce que je vois de pire dans ton état, c'est que personne ne t'en peut tirer que toi-même. Quand il s'agit de prudence, l'amitié vient au secours d'une âme agitée; s'il faut choisir le bien ou le mal, la passion qui les méconnoit peut se taire devant un conseil désintéressé. *Mais ici quelque parti que tu prennes, la nature l'autorise et le condamne, la raison le blâme et l'approuve, le devoir se tait ou s'oppose à lui-même*; tu ne peux ni rester indécise ni bien choisir; tu n'as que des peines à comparer, et *ton coeur seul en est le juge* . . . Quelque sort que tu préfères, il sera toujours peu digne de toi . . . je te trahirois en voulant te gouverner dans un cas où la raison même s'impose silence, et où *la seule règle à suivre est d'écouter ton propre penchant*.   (II, pp. 202–3, my emphasis)

This radical impossibility of the appeal to a general maxim to authorize a particular judgement casts doubt on the usefulness of sententiousness *in general*, and contests its ability to lay down the law. It is of course possible to say, with a certain amount of cynicism in hindsight, that Julie's eventual decision ('je ne déserterai jamais la maison paternelle' (II, p. 209)) is in fact eminently subsumable under a general law,[89] but this simply lays down the law from a position of exteriority, duplicating rather than questioning the scene of legislation.

Two possible solutions arise here. One involves a sort of abdication of all responsibility, a blind obedience, accepted perhaps out of the desire to avoid *any* detour through a system of laws – this will be Saint-Preux's position with respect to Julie.[90] The second solution is to

173

carry through Claire's advice, and make the heart the ground for decision and the desired autonomy of prescription: Julie herself says that 'le coeur ne reçoit de loix que de lui-même' (II, p. 212; this at the point when she is in fact obeying her father), and much later Saint-Preux says of Julie that she 'n'eut jamais d'autre règle que son coeur' (II, p. 530).

This retreat into the individual heart is the final attempt to establish a place of transparency and pure reflexivity for prescription. But Julie's heart is not as transparent as might be believed, and this leads instead to that final(?) veil valorized elsewhere in terms of *pudeur*. Wolmar, the 'oeil vivant', who has 'quelque don surnaturel pour lire au fond des coeurs' (II, p. 496; also quoted by Starobinski, p. 105), says of her heart: 'un voile de sagesse et d'honnêteté fait tant de replis autour de son coeur, qu'il n'est plus possible à l'oeil humain d'y pénétrer, pas même au sien propre' (II, p. 509). The veil, figure of seduction, deferral, *différance* and thereby writing itself, returns at the heart of transparency, imposes the *replis* of further detours, and denies the return of reflection.

5. Desire

The heart is the seat of desire as well as of conscience. The desire for homeostasis, self-sufficiency, transparency, and possibly *jouissance*, has led, after the detour through the attempt to build a simulacrum of nature, to the rejection of sententiousness, generalization and law. But the resultant stress on the irreducibility of the individual seems no less fraught with difficulties, and self-presence is always denied through effects of deferral and *après-coup*. A final attempt to account for this inevitable failure of writing and desire to catch up with themselves in immobility, places the *state* of self-sufficiency in the *process* of desire itself, in its unfulfilment. This attempt to make desire into its own object still, however, gives rise to supplement and simulacrum, and sententiousness:

Tant qu'on désire on peut se passer d'être heureux; on s'attend à le devenir; si le bonheur ne vient point, l'espoir se prolonge, et le charme de l'illusion dure autant que la passion qui le cause. *Ainsi cet état se suffit à lui-même*, et l'inquiétude qu'il donne *est une sorte de jouissance qui supplée à la réalité* . . . Malheur à qui n'a plus rien à desirer! il perd pour ainsi dire tout ce qu'il possede. On jouït moins de ce qu'on obtient que de ce qu'on espere, et l'on n'est heureux qu'avant d'être heureux . . . l'illusion cesse où commence la jouïssance. Le pays des chimeres est en ce monde le seul digne d'être habité, et tel est le néant des choses humaines, qu'hors l'Etre existant par lui-même, il n'y a rien de beau que ce qui n'est pas.   (II, p. 693, my emphasis)

This paradoxical move into desire and fiction lays down the law of desire as and in fiction. This suspension of the movement of desire arrests writing in the very process of trying to catch up with itself: these final sententious propositions accept that narrative is not to be stopped, except in a simulacrum of stasis which is in fact a figure of radical instability. In Rousseau, the law, become simulacrum, is infiltrated with narrative, fiction and desire: this infiltration will be taken to the limits of coherence and rationality in the novels of the Marquis de Sade.

5

SADE: THE TRANSGRESSION
OF NATURE

Where no law is, there is no transgression.   (Romans, 4:15)

1. Scandalizing/Moralizing

Considering the work of Sade from the point of view of 'sententiousness and the novel', one is immediately faced with the following
paradox: Sade's writing, so clearly 'scandalous' and 'subversive', is
also, and again very clearly, extremely 'classical' in its use of the types
of proposition which I have called 'narrative' and 'sententious'. All of
Sade's novels are made up of alternating blocks of narrative–
descriptive propositions ('scènes', 'tableaux', and so on), and of
sententious propositions ('dissertations'). The relationship seems
simple enough: the narrative sections are produced as exemplifica-
tions of the 'truths' offered by the sententious propositions, and the
sententious passages generated by the need to draw philosophical
consequences from the narrated events. An immediate and common
reaction to this invariable structure of Sade's writing is to complain of
its uninventiveness, as does Georges May: 'The distinctive mark of
Sade's formula lies in a striking lack of balance between the glaring
originality of his ethical philosophy . . . and the banality, indeed
often the clumsiness of the fictional devices to which he resorted'.[1]
This 'striking lack of balance', negatively marked in May's comments,
is implied too in a much more subtle analysis by Maurice Blanchot,
who begins his essay 'La Raison de Sade' with the affirmation that the
book formed by *La Nouvelle Justine* and the *Histoire de Juliette* is the
most scandalous work ever written, and ends with the remark that 'Il y
a dans Sade un moraliste de pure tradition, et il serait aisé de réunir un
choix de maximes auprès desquelles celles de La Rochefoucauld
paraîtraient faibles et incertaines.'[2]

This mixture of 'scandal' and 'pure tradition' is a starting-point for
any attempt to read Sade, and the tension it creates reappears at all
levels of analysis. Perhaps the *monstrous* nature of Sade's texts, which
are of course monstrous not only in their content but also in their
length and repetitiveness, is the result of this unresolved tension

176

between poles which might be named 'morality' and 'scandal', *interdit* and *transgression* (Bataille), *représentation* and *désir* (Foucault).[3] However, generating this two-pole structure and naming the poles is not enough: an attempt must also be made to define the way in which the poles interact, and how they organize the space in which they are situated (if indeed they can be situated in a homogeneous space), and to decide just how conflictual they are.

2. Limits and Excess

Blanchot's remark immediately engages with the problem of sententiousness, and shows that the anthologizing reading is always a temptation, even for so subtle a critic. For the moment I set against his identification of a 'moralist' in Sade a (sententious) quotation from Sade himself: 'La Nature plus bizarre que les moralistes ne nous la peignent, s'échappe à tout instant des digues que la politique de ceux-ci voudrait lui prescrire'.[4] Perhaps this is one of the maxims which Blanchot would put in his anthology; before proceeding to reinscribe statements of this type in the text, it is worth pausing over this particular maxim, since it condenses a certain scene of writing which is basic to Sade.

The subject of the maxim, 'la nature', immediately engages with an immense intertext, a few of the ramifications of which I have attempted to explore with reference to politics. Here, nature is the object of a representation, designated by the ubiquitous classical metaphor of painting; but that representation is inadequate, says Sade, and, more importantly, governed by a repressive politics which is that of the moralists, the writers of maxims. This politics produces *prescriptive* statements which set limits to nature and its representation. It is not a matter of indifference that Sade presents these limits as 'digues'; this implies that the limits drawn by the prescriptive statements of the moralists are not simply located in some neutral space. Rather they attempt to contain an *energy*, an expanding movement: nature here is a force, and the representation of nature by the moralists involves a limitation of that force. Finally, the moralists' representational *coup de force* fails in its prescriptive aim; nature escapes, overflows, and is always in excess of the representational politics which prescribes its limits.

Sade's pretension will be to provide more accurate readings of the statements of nature, readings which do not leave an unread excess. This programme is that prescribed by a famous imperative from the closing pages of *Juliette*, one which lays down the law of exhaustive representation: 'la philosophie doit tout dire' (IX, p. 586). Nature may escape from the self-imposed limits of the moralists' representation of it, but this does not imply that it escapes from representation altogether: by asserting that philosophy *must* say everything, Sade implies that it *can* say everything (and in so doing be worthy of the name 'philosophy').

This model of an expanding energy (more usually referred to as 'désir' or 'libertinage') encountering and crossing the limits imposed on it, is quite simple, and constant in Sade. Desire is always presented as a movement which overflows *digues* ('Je connais l'impossibilité de captiver une femme comme toi, putain par principe et par tempérament: ce serait, je le sais, vouloir imposer des digues à la mer' (IX, p. 435)), breaks chains ('la volupté n'admet aucune chaîne, elle ne jouit jamais mieux que quand elle les rompt toutes' (VIII, p. 62)), crosses boundaries ('franchir les dernières bornes que voudraient . . . prescrire la religion, la décence, l'humanité, la vertu, tous nos prétendus devoirs enfin' (III, p. 418)). Whereas, in Rousseau, desire followed a movement of *détour* and *retour*, its vector curving round to the extent that in the impossible quest for auto-affection the object of desire became desire itself, in Sade desire moves in a logic of departure, or of a pure expenditure without return. Rousseau's desire obeys an economy of reserve and deferral, is Christian and capitalist; Sade's obeys an 'economy' which is that of the gift, the potlatch, expenditure for nothing.

It should be clear that such an economy entails a number of problems for the type of discourse which I have defined as 'sententious', as it does for any theory of representation. The paradox of Sade's writing (and it is perhaps possible to see something like the end of the 'eighteenth century' in this paradox) is that the imperative to 'tout dire' is situated within a philosophy which also constantly posits the perpetual possibility of exceeding all determined, representable totalities.

This problem is the object of some famous and elliptical remarks in Foucault's *Les Mots et les choses*, where Sade is presented as standing at the limit of a classical age whose *épistémè* is dominated, precisely, by representation:

Cette oeuvre inlassable manifeste le précaire équilibre entre la loi sans loi du désir et l'ordonnance méticuleuse d'une représentation discursive. L'ordre du discours y trouve sa limite et sa Loi; mais il a encore la force de demeurer coextensif à cela même qui le régit . . . Le libertin, c'est celui qui, en obéissant à toutes les fantaisies du désir et à chacune de ses fureurs, peut mais doit aussi en éclairer le moindre mouvement par une représentation lucide et volontairement mise en oeuvre. Il y a un ordre strict de la vie libertine: toute représentation doit s'animer aussitôt dans le corps vivant du désir, tout désir doit s'annoncer dans la pure lumière d'un discours représentatif.

(Foucault, p. 222)

As was the case in Sade's description of the moralists' representation of nature, the model proposed is topological but also dynamic; a space is defined here as that of representation, closed by a limit against which desire opposes a transgressive force, a violence: 'c'est l'obscure violence répétée du désir qui vient battre les limites de la représentation' (Foucault, p. 223). In Foucault's description, desire is restrained by representation insofar as representation manages to represent desire; but the desire of desire is to break through the limits of representation, to escape from the light of rational inspection to the (unlimited?) space beyond. The problem will be that of articulating the 'lawlessness' of desire, with the 'ordre strict' which none the less controls its violence; and the discussion to come will be concerned with this paradoxical order of disorder or law of lawlessness. However, even if Foucault seems to pose the problem accurately in a formal sense, the generalization of the limits imposed on desire in terms of representation by-passes (economizes on) the relationship between desire and the moral/political limits constantly invoked by Sade himself. Some mediations seem to be required before such a generalization could be justified; Foucault does not provide any, and this lack in his analysis is the space for my own.

Returning to Sade's text, the prescriptive 'la philosophie doit tout dire' might be opposed to another statement made by Juliette, to the effect that 'tout est bon quand il est excessif' (VIII, p. 227). It seems possible to transform descriptive and prescriptive weight in these sentences to produce 'la philosophie est le discours qui dit tout', and 'soyez excessif, c'est bon', and to suggest that these statements provide something like a matrix for the generation of Sade's novels, or of the types of sentences which make them up. This move involves re-describing the scene/dissertation opposition as one between sentences describing 'excess' and the pleasure it produces, and sentences which are sententious ('philosophical'), and which attain that status through the claim to exhaustivity and rigour in the formulation of the 'truth'. The prescriptive transformation of the description of the pleasure of excess is justified by the presence of sentences inviting the addressee of the text to experiment with similar excesses, with a view to experiencing similar pleasures.[5] The diegetical excesses described by Sade are to be linked to the demand for philosophical rigour controlling those descriptions: the libidinal excess will be produced by the desire to

179

experience *everything*, and the philosophical whole will be determined as excess with respect to conventional totalizations.

On the other hand, if it is manifestly impossible to posit an identity between the whole and the excess, and if both are prescribed by Sade, then those prescriptions are contradictory, and their juxtaposition is in itself excessive. The demand for excess can only be read as a prescription of the type 'Exceed all totalities', and the demand for totalization as meaning 'Recuperate all excesses'. It is this constitutive aporia which generates Sade's writing as endless.

3. Classical Economy

This unrelieved dialectic between the two poles which structure Sade's writing suggests that the 'scandalous' or transgressive nature of that writing is not simple. A certain amount of attention must be paid to the 'classical' pole of the relationship, especially as Sade's best critics have tended largely to ignore this aspect. From the perspective of 'sentientiousness and the novel', this 'classical' pole is best observed in the stories that make up *Les Crimes de l'amour* and the *Historiettes, contes et fabliaux*, where the relationship of sentientious and narrative elements is often extremely simple and traditional, and not at all transgressive of classical narrative economy. Here sentientious propositions often stand as epigraph and epilogue: the opening maxim states a general truth, the narrative either exemplifies it or dramatizes an exception to it, and the final maxim either repeats the first where this is held to have been proven, or contradicts it where it is held to have been disproven. In this type of structure, the sentientious proposition stands as a summarizing commentary on the narrative, and this is often marked in the text by meta-linguistic signals. For example, *Eugénie de Franval* in *Les Crimes de l'amour* opens with the following passage:

Instruire l'homme et corriger ses moeurs, tel est le seul motif que nous nous proposons dans cette anecdote. Que l'on se pénètre, en la lisant, de la grandeur du péril, toujours sur les pas de ceux qui se permettent tout pour satisfaire leurs désirs. Puissent-ils se convaincre que la bonne éducation, les richesses, les talents, les dons de la nature, ne sont susceptibles que d'égarer, quand la retenue, la bonne conduite, la sagesse, la modestie ne les étayent, ou ne les font valoir: voilà les vérités que nous allons mettre en action.

(X, p. 425)

In *La Double Epreuve*, the opening maxim is marked as a quotation from the doxa (with the characteristic 'on dit'), and the narrative proposes a counter-example (X, p. 69). This type of traditional structure involves a classical narrative economy in which the exception is recuperated as a measurable *écart* from a norm. In the case of the *Double Epreuve*, any possible transgression of this economy (in, for example, the wild expense devoted by Ceilcour to the spectacles and illusions which make up the *épreuve*) is recovered, *rachetée*, by the tragic outcome of the story in death. The final sentSentious proposition poses this economy as exemplary:

Il . . . donna, par cette fin désastreuse et prématurée, le cruel exemple que le plus doux bonheur de l'homme . . . la société d'une femme qui lui convienne, peut le fuir, au sein même de l'opulence et de la vertu.   (X, p. 127)

This relationship of sentSentious and narrative propositions is essentially integrative, and the respect of narrative economy which it implies entails a respect for social and discursive economy in general. This can be illustrated more clearly by the *Historiette* entitled *L'Heureuse Feinte*. Here again the text opens with a sentSentious proposition, a 'truth' which it is the narrative's task to 'prove' (XIV, p. 97). The marquise de Guissac exchanges 'quelques lettres galantes' with the baron d'Aumelas. The husband discovers the correspondence, and offers his wife a choice between being shot and drinking a glass of lemonade which she and the reader assume to be poisoned. She chooses the poison, but the husband prevents her from drinking all of it, and takes the rest himself. In this state the marquise makes her confession of innocence in the presence of her father and mother, and her husband, convinced of her virtue, reveals the trick – the lemonade was not poisoned after all. The ruse is contained in a classical narrative economy of order troubled and restored, of the exchange of controlled doses of 'inquiétude'. The marquise's apparent transgression is balanced by an apparent punishment, but this play of appearances has real effects: the final paragraph of the tale informs us that the marquise 'a tenu parole et a vécu plus de trente ans avec son mari sans que jamais celui-ci ait eu le plus léger reproche à lui faire' (XIV, p. 99). The rebalancing of the contractual nature of the marriage (even if it may be felt that the contract is not particularly equitable insofar as the story says nothing about the husband's extramarital conduct) figures the happy conclusion of the narrative contract between text and reader, between narrative and sentSentiousness, between fiction and the 'truth' it sets out to 'prove'.

4. *La Perte*

All of this is of course not very Sadian, if we wish to reserve that qualifier for the more 'scandalous' elements of Sade's practice. Still within the *Historiettes, contes et fabliaux*, however, *Augustine de Villeblanche* is an example in which the integrative relationship of narrative and sententious propositions is not so easily secured. Again, the text begins with a long sententious sequence, but this time spoken by a character (Augustine herself), rather than by the narrator. This sequence amounts to an apologia of lesbianism, which poses an immediate threat to classical economy, insofar as it is based no longer on the notion of a *return* (return to social order, return on an investment, sexual expenditure in view of procreative return within socially recognized structures), but dominated by *loss* (equivalent to Bataille's *dépense*).[6] The logic of the *perte* leaves explicit traces at two points in the text. The first of these is within Augustine's opening harangue, and is hardly exploited by this text, although the structure of the argument becomes dominant in other texts by Sade. In her argument, Augustine pre-empts the objection that lesbianism leads to a risk of depopulation:

Eh, juste ciel, a-t-on peur que les caprices de ces individus de l'un ou l'autre sexe ne fassent finir le monde, qu'ils ne mettent l'enchère à la précieuse espèce humaine, et que leur prétendu crime ne l'anéantisse, faute de procéder à sa multiplication? Qu'on y réfléchisse bien et l'on verra que toutes ces *pertes* chimériques sont entièrement indifférentes à la nature, que non seulement elle ne les condamne point, mais qu'elle nous prouve par mille exemples qu'elle les veut et qu'elle les désire; et, si ces *pertes* l'irritaient, les tolérerait-elle dans mille cas . . .   (XIV, p. 158, my emphasis)

The other instance of the *perte* comes just a little later, and this time no longer in Augustine's discourse, but in that of the narrator. In some sense this occurrence is much the simpler of the two, in that it inaugurates the integrative function we have already seen at work in other texts. The phrase in question reads simply, 'Augustine était une vraie perte pour les hommes' (XIV, p. 159), and the progress of the narrative leads to the recuperation of this loss: Augustine goes to a ball disguised as a man; Franville, who is in love with her, goes to the same ball disguised as a woman. Augustine attempts to seduce Franville, discovers that he is really a man, and after a little hesitation, decides she loves him anyway, and they are married. The moment of return and repayment is again marked by sententious propositions:

Va, je renonce avec joie pour te plaire à des erreurs où la vanité nous entraîne presque aussi souvent que nos goûts. Je le sens, la nature l'emporte, je l'étouffais par des travers que j'abhorre à présent de toute mon âme; on ne résiste point à son empire, elle ne nous a créées que pour vous, elle ne vous forma que pour nous; suivons ses lois, c'est par l'organe de l'amour même

qu'elle me les inspire aujourd'hui, elles ne m'en deviendront que plus sacrées.
Voilà ma main, monsieur . . .   (XIV, p. 167)

As was the case in *L'Heureuse Feinte*, the figure of successful
integration in narrative terms is a 'virtuous' marriage (or at least a
marriage involving a 'virtuous' wife). The closing *sentence on* the law
of nature is also the *sentence of* the law of nature, whose voice
guarantees the economy of the narrative against the initial *perte* by
returning Augustine to the norm of heterosexuality and marriage.

But if the closure of the narrative does indeed follow the classical
model, balancing a 'force perturbatrice' with a 'force équilibrante', we
may none the less wonder whether this economy functions without
leaving a remainder or a deficit. In *narrative* terms, it is certainly true
that the first *perte* described above, that of the sterility of lesbianism, is
erased by Augustine's final conversion to 'normality'; but the relative
sententious weight accorded to this first, transgressive economy (even
if this weight is calculated only in the relatively crude terms of the
number of sententious propositions devoted to its characterization),
might well provoke a reading less dominated by the purely narrative
progression of the text.

And in fact Augustine's opening harangue has already threatened
this economy by situating homosexuality no longer as an *écart* from
nature, but as an *écart within* nature, a natural *écart* (XIV, p. 157). The
perte is a transgression only of nature as seen by the doxa (even though
here that doxa is restated at the end of the text as its truth); but the
nature defined here, in radical discord with the legislative nature
whose voice dictates not only Augustine's final conduct, but also most
of the philosophy of the century, is, despite its characterization as a
'bonne mère', permissive and indifferent, inaccessible to transgression. This new status of nature, which is no longer able to ground
morality, law, and thereby crime, is vital to the structure of Sade's
writing, and I shall return to it at some length; for if the legislative
weight of sententious propositions can no longer be legitimated as a
transcription, however mediated, of the 'law of nature', then the
position of their enunciation becomes problematic.

The argument that *all écarts, all* desires or 'penchants' can be
located within nature, will dominate the 'philosophical' dissertations
in Sade's major texts. The 'voice of nature' is no longer the voice of
normality and morality (as it is at the end of this story, where however
the ambivalence of the designation 'organe de l'amour' already
suggests a complication), but the voice of the passions, of all passions,
and can thus no longer legitimate the integrative use of sententiousness in narrative, any more than it can ground maxims in morality.

The sense of the maxim from the *Idée sur les romans*, discussed above, becomes clearer in the light of this. If all desires, including the most apparently perverse or cruel, are in nature, then the philosophical project to 'tout dire' is also 'natural'. And just as this reinscribed 'nature' transgresses and scandalizes that of the 'moralistes', so the writing which transcribes that nature will of necessity transgress the norms of writing which appeal for their legitimation to the pseudo-nature of the moralists. This *dispositif* produces a new type of text, addressed to a new type of reader. It seems possible to locate this newness by linking the breakdown of the traditional relationship between sententiousness and the narrative, to the concomitant positioning of an addressee for the text who is no longer the moral subject of the classical tradition.

5. The Addressee

Although this repositioning of the subject of reading is implied throughout Sade's 'scandalous' texts, it is often stressed at a meta-level of the fiction (prefaces and footnotes). The classical addressee is that positioned by, for example, the opening sententious proposition from *Eugénie de Franval*, quoted above. It is also, but more controversially, suggested by the *Idée sur les romans*, and in general wherever the alibi for the writing is truth. In the *Idée*, for example, Sade refers to:

le romancier, dont l'ouvrage doit nous faire voir l'homme, non pas seulement ce qu'il est, ou ce qu'il se montre, c'est le devoir de l'historien, *mais tel qu'il peut être*, tel que doivent le rendre les modifications du vice, et toutes les secousses des passions; il faut donc les connaître toutes, si l'on veut travailler ce genre . . .   (X, p. 12, my emphasis)

Evidently this appeal to truth, which is simultaneously an appeal to a certain morality (although the shift from the depiction of a 'devoir-être' to that of a 'pouvoir-être' is decisive if read in the context of earlier eighteenth-century discussions of the novel), may appear thin justification for the sort of scenes Sade portrays, or for the lengthy immoral speeches he 'quotes' from his characters. When Villeterque pointed this out in a review of *Les Crimes de l'amour* in 1791, Sade's rage in his reply may perhaps be read as a symptom of annoyance at the fragility of his explicit alibi for writing.

In works where the addressee of the text is positioned as looking for moral enlightenment, we may expect to find, and do indeed find, the classical structure of sententiousness and narrative discussed so far.

In Sade's 'public' works (those which he signed and published) this structure, and the economy which it implies, are invariable features. In *La Marquise de Gange* (1813), for example, after the historical situation of the fiction, we find the classical maxim serving its classical function of directing the following narrative according to a balanced economy:

Plus un être est favorisé de la nature et de la fortune, plus on voit bien souvent le sort l'accabler de toutes ses rigueurs: cette *compensation* est une justice du ciel, qui sert à la fois d'exemple et de leçon aux hommes . . .

(XI, p. 190, my emphasis)

But this 'just' divine rigour is carried out through guilty human agents, who must thus themselves be punished if the 'compensation' is not to leave an excess; at the end of the narrative a maxim states: 'c'est à l'instant où le coupable croit échapper à la vengeance céleste qu'elle le poursuit et le frappe' (X, p. 388). *Aline et Valcour*, despite its length and complexity, is still framed in this way: the 'Avis de l'éditeur' asserts that the aim of the book is to 'faire voir avec quel ascendant, et en même temps avec quelle facilité le langage de la vertu pulvérise toujours les sophismes du libertinage et de l'impiété' (IV, p. xxviii), and the end of the novel sees balance restored. Aline and Valcour both die, but the villains do not triumph – Blamont is murdered and Dolbourg converted.

6. *Justine*

However, the best place to observe the passage from this classical positioning of the addressee and classical use of sententiousness is undoubtedly in the three versions of *Justine*: that is, in order of composition and of length, *Les infortunes de la vertu*, *Justine ou les malheurs de la vertu*, and *La Nouvelle Justine*, which really forms a single novel with *Juliette*, under the full title, *La Nouvelle Justine, ou les malheurs de la vertu, suivie de l'histoire de Juliette, sa soeur*. All three versions have a similar introductory passage, often couched in identical terms, and yet with differences which are essential. *Justine* also carries a dedicatory text before this introduction, and *La Nouvelle Justine* replaces this with an 'Avis de l'éditeur'; these texts will also have to be borne in mind.

All three introductions invoke a philosophical legitimation in their opening sentence. In the *Infortunes* (hereafter J1) this reads:

Le triomphe de la philosophie serait de jeter du jour sur l'obscurité des voies dont la providence se sert pour parvenir aux fins qu'elle se propose sur l'homme . . .

(XIV, p. 333)

185

The opening of *Justine* (J2) and *La Nouvelle Justine* (J3) is, with slight differences of punctuation and capitalization, the same:

Le chef-d'oeuvre de la philosophie serait de développer les moyens dont la Providence se sert pour parvenir aux fins qu'elle se propose sur l'homme . . .

(III, p. 55)

All three versions link this desire for enlightenment to a practical project of conduct.

In the second paragraph of all three versions we find a modalized quotation of the discourse which it would be possible to draw from an unhappy experience of this providential obscurity. In J2 this gives:

Si, plein de respect pour nos conventions sociales, et ne s'écartant jamais des digues qu'elles nous imposent, il arrive, malgré cela, que nous n'ayons rencontré que des ronces, quand les méchants ne cueillaient que des roses, des gens privés d'un fond de vertu assez constaté pour se mettre au-dessus de ces remarques ne calculeront-ils pas alors qu'il vaut mieux s'abandonner au torrent que d'y résister? Ne diront-ils pas que la vertu, quelque belle qu'elle soit, devient pourtant le plus mauvais parti qu'on puisse prendre, quand elle se trouve trop faible pour lutter contre le vice, et que dans un siècle entièrement corrompu, le plus sûr est de faire comme les autres?

(III, p. 55)

The modalized presentation of a possible sententious discourse continues for a little longer, but we may note that this discourse should perhaps be read less as an indication of possible conduct, than as a possible reading of the text to come, and in J1 and J2 this potential reading is interrupted by a guide to the 'right' way to read the text (I am not here concerned with the possibility of irony in the presentation): 'Il est donc important de prévenir ces sophismes dangereux d'une fausse philosophie' (III, p. 56). Given this positioning of the addressee of the text, the final paragraph to J2 (unnecessary in J1, where the scenes of cruelty and debauch are much less explicit) can excuse the crudely denotative nature of the writing within the economy already described, 'par amour pour la vérité' (Ibid.). This positioning is made still clearer in the dedicatory epistle 'A ma bonne amie', which precedes the main body of the text in J2. Here the biographical circumstances of the dedication are less important than its significance within the economy of the text: the Constance addressed becomes the ideal addressee, the example of the Right Reader. By presenting his novel as a passage through vice, the better to return to virtue (and thus reproducing a simulacrum of Rousseau's structure of the detour), Sade is able at once to claim the moral usefulness of his text and the novelty of its methods, and to state that it will 'parvenir au but par une route peu frayée jusqu'à présent' (III, p. 52). These texts, from the very opening pages of J1 and J2, already stage the end of the story: Juliette's conversion, provoked by Justine's narrative (and by the lightning-bolt which kills her)[7] is essentially linked to the text's positioning of its addressee, and this necessary parallel is pointed in the sententious sequence which ends these first two avatars of the text, and which I quote in the slightly briefer version of J1,

O vous qui lirez cette histoire, puissiez-vous en tirer le même profit que cette femme mondaine et corrigée, puissiez-vous vous convaincre avec elle que le véritable bonheur n'est que dans le sein de la vertu et que si Dieu permit qu'elle soit persécutée sur la terre, c'est pour lui préparer dans le ciel une plus flatteuse récompense.   (XIV, p. 460)

I am not, of course, attempting to make a case for anything like 'sincerity' on Sade's part in this type of presentation, and it is clear that, despite the structure of the detour, too much is left along the way (this is what Sade calls the 'cynisme de certains crayons') for the classical economy mimed in these perigraphical passages to function without the sort of 'perte' seen at work in *Augustine de Villeblanche*. Sade's contemporaries do not seem to have been convinced by these gestures.[8] On the other hand, even a parodic use of sententiousness and of the positioning of its addressee in this way constitutes a sort of tribute paid to narrative convention; this is no longer the case in J3, where the radical change in the text's economy, and in its own representation of its reading, determines a number of changes with respect to the two earlier versions. Justine no longer recounts her story in the first person, and this allows the narrative discourse to rewrite the scenes in the explicit denotative language which has so excited the commentators. Juliette, although still the addressee of Justine's story, now replies to that story with her own, which we *do* read in the first person (and Juliette's language is just as direct as that of the narrator of Justine's story), and the epigraph–maxim for *that* story simply contradicts those which stood at beginning and end of the narrative in J1 and J2:

Juliette annonça à ses amis qu'elle voulait raconter son histoire à sa soeur, afin, disait-elle, de la faire mieux juger de la puissante manière dont le ciel protège et récompense toujours le vice, quand il abat et contriste la vertu.
(VII, p. 409)

In this final version, then, Justine is dispossessed of her language, and the narrative economy is troubled: the corollary of this is a disturbance of the introductory passage which, while maintaining large portions of the versions J1 and J2, in fact subverts those versions. This is done in the first instance by a few additions to the modalized passage which I have already quoted, in part, from J2. Where in J2 we read, 'Si, plein de respect pour nos conventions sociales . . .' (III, p. 55), J3 has, 'Si, plein d'un respect vain, ridicule et superstitieux pour nos absurdes conventions sociales . . .' (VI, p. 89), and this sets the scene for a quite different position of the enunciation of the text. In the discourse modalized by expressions of the type, 'ne diront-ils pas?', which carried the rhetorical *sous-entendu* 'but they're wrong', J3 introduces explicit statements to prevent the derivation of that *sous-entendu*: we now find, 'ne calculeront-ils pas, avec assez de vraisemblance . . . ne diront-ils pas, avec quelque apparence de raison . . . n'ajouteront-ils pas, avec quelque certitude . . .' (VI, pp. 89–90). And this leads to an explicit adherence to these judgements, replacing the denial of J1 and J2:

C'est, nous ne le déguisons plus, pour appuyer ces systèmes, que nous allons donner au public l'histoire de la vertueuse Justine. Il est essentiel que les sots cessent d'encenser cette ridicule idole de la vertu . . .   (VI, p. 90)

And if it is still 'affreux' to have to present the persecution of virtue, this can be justified, no longer in terms of practical reason (figured by the conversion of the reader to virtue), but in the interests of the truth (Ibid.); and the 'epigraph' maxim is now rewritten to produce:

Tels sont les sentiments qui vont diriger nos travaux; et c'est en raison de ces motifs, qu'unissant le langage le plus cynique aux systèmes les plus forts et les plus hardis, aux idées les plus immorales et les plus impies, nous allons, avec une courageuse audace, peindre le crime comme il est, c'est-à-dire toujours triomphant et sublime, toujours content et fortuné, et la vertu comme on la voit également, toujours maussade et toujours triste, toujours pédante et toujours malheureuse.   (Ibid.)

This reorientation of the writing also determines and is determined by the modification to the fate of Justine, who still dies by lightning, but this time because she is deliberately exposed to it by Juliette and her fellow *libertins*; this rewriting of the end of J1 and J2 is accompanied by a re-reading of those two texts, in that in proposing to send Justine out into the storm, Noirceuil says, 'livrons cette créature à la foudre; je me convertis, si elle la respecte' (IX, p. 583). And because Justine's death no longer marks the ostensible return to virtue, there is no longer any reason for J3, now thoroughly usurped by Juliette, to end here; thus it escapes the constraint of a *retour*, programmed by a detour. Although the text does indeed end soon after this, we are told that the *libertins* continue in their good fortune for a further ten years, and it is only the absence of further narrative from Juliette herself which prevents the publication of the rest of her life. The text remains open-ended.

It is necessary to stress that the reorientation of narrative economy implied by the changes noted in J3 should not be read as a clean and absolute break with the preceding versions, and as a sign of Sade's taking on some true 'nature' or 'authentic' Sadian discourse. Although the 'Avis de l'éditeur' to J3 presents it as the authentic, original version of the text, and denounces J2 as a later mutilated variant, it also repeats a certain justification for the writing in terms of virtue, and retains from the dedication of J2 the idea that any objection to such a work will come from real *libertins* unhappy at the idea that they are being unmasked. This persistent ambivalence is, in fact, basic to the structure of transgression as set out in Sade's texts. On the other hand, this same 'Avis' does move towards the aphrodisiac legitimation of the writing which is implied in a number of the footnotes to *Juliette*, and which dominates *La Philosophie dans le boudoir* and *Les 120 journées de Sodome*. There is also a danger of attempting to see, in the temporal sequence of the three versions of *Justine*, a 'development' in Sade's 'thought'; but the fact that *Les 120 journées* antedates even J1 should be enough to discourage any temptation to read Sade in linear terms.

7. Pornography

Certain footnotes in *Juliette*, which invite the reader to imitate the practices described in the text, suggest an addressee very different from that of the classical narrative. *La Philosophie dans le boudoir* is explicitly addressed 'Aux libertins', and is concerned to further their *bonheur*. Any conversion of the reader will now be to *libertinage*, and sententiousness in the text assumes the pedagogical function announced in the work's subtitle, 'Les instituteurs immoraux'. Eugénie, the 'pupil', is thus the figure of the reader within the text. In *Les 120 journées*, which still, in its organization, mimes a discourse whose object is 'truth' (the encyclopedic *tableau* laying out the perversions to a rational, 'scientific' gaze),[9] the position of the reader as the subject of *jouissance* is made still clearer, and the scientific alibi clearly subordinated to this positioning:

Sans doute, beaucoup de tous les écarts que tu vas voir peints te déplairont, on le sait, mais il s'en trouvera quelques-uns qui t'échaufferont au point de te coûter du foutre, *et voilà tout ce qu'il nous faut*. Si nous n'avions pas tout dit, tout analysé, comment voudrais-tu que nous eussions pu deviner ce qui te convient? C'est à toi à le prendre et à laisser le reste; un autre en fera autant; et petit à petit tout aura trouvé sa place . . . choisis et laisse le reste, sans déclamer contre ce reste, uniquement parce qu'il n'a pas le talent de te plaire. Songe qu'il plaira à d'autres, et sois philosophe . . .   (XIII, p. 61)

This positioning of the reader has been analyzed by Michel Tort, and baptized the 'Effet Sade': Tort writes, 'Chaque signifiant d'une jouissance perverse figuré dans le tableau sadien, autant que par ses rapports aux autres, se définit par la possibilité de venir frapper un sujet . . .'[10] The effect of this 'frappe' is to split the reading subject, and to deny in principle the possibility of any moral condemnation of the text: 'La logique veut que la protestation éthique s'étrangle à un moment ou à un autre dans le signifiant où le sujet s'abîme' (Tort, p. 76). It is clear that in this economy, as Tort suggests, the introduction of perversion into the novel perverts the novel as a genre, and, from our point of view, subverts the status of sententious discourse in its relationship to narrative and to the law. For if, still following Tort, 'la loi sera *jouissance*', then the ultimate subordination of sententiousness to the prescriptive 'jouis!' must shift the focus of our reading from the classical residues which I have so far elaborated. To do this it is necessary to return to the problematic of transgression, in the light of the various possible legitimations for legislative statements within Sade's texts, and to show if possible how those legitimations are denied in the production of the punctual, repeated, but strictly ungeneralizable statement of the law of *jouissance*; for it should be clear that the 'Effet Sade' not only (sadistically) 'strangles' ethical protest about the content of his texts, but also, in its implications for the subject of reading, denies the possibility of any totalizing critical reading of those texts. This effect can reasonably be placed alongside those produced by certain texts which one would qualify as 'modern'.[11] On the other hand, it is no doubt too optimistic to expect the economy of the *perte*, which this effect implies for writing, to be pure and unproblematic, and this is one reason for insisting that texts by Sade are still in massive collusion with classical narrative economy. And if one might be tempted to agree with Sollers's assertion that 'Sade . . . dénonce radicalement le type de lecture que nous continuons à pratiquer et à envisager de façon généralisée',[12] one must balance that desire for radical breaks and subversion against a suspicion, still to be confirmed, that the escape of his writing from classical economy will not, and cannot, be total or clean.

8. Interpellation

The two basic poles which structure Sade's writing are those of an expanding force of desire, and a set of limits to that force. Sade's self-imposed philosophical task seems to be to demonstrate the impotence of the limits and celebrate the power of the force. This task seems to be philosophical insofar as it legitimates itself by an appeal to truth. Following a structure familiar in the eighteenth century, Truth is attained at the end of a polemical activity of writing, through the denunciation of the *préjugé*, in the interests of the voice of nature. This structure is very clear in an early text, published only recently, but probably written in the early days of Sade's imprisonment – the poem entitled *La Vérité*. The text is made up of a negative and a positive moment: the first part denounces God, the second affirms nature. God is error, nature is the truth. In its apparent banality, this text in fact produces what will perhaps be an insoluble problem for all readings of Sade, as becomes clear in the following passage:

> Je prétends expirer au sein de l'athéisme –
> Et que l'infâme Dieu dont on veut m'alarmer
> Ne soit conçu par moi que pour le blasphémer.
> Oui vaine illusion, mon âme te déteste,
> Et pour t'en mieux convaincre ici je le proteste,
> Je voudrais qu'un moment tu pusses exister
> Pour jouir du plaisir de te mieux insulter. (XIV, p. 81)

The complication stems not from the various qualities predicated of the name 'God', but from its being positioned as both referent and addressee of the sentences. Denying reference to a proper name is the source of problems in traditional philosophy of language, but here these problems are pushed into paradox. It is coherent to say, 'God does not exist', but more or less unintelligible to say 'God, you do not exist'. Although in the fourth line quoted, 'vaine illusion, mon âme te déteste' is perhaps readable in terms of elementary rhetorical rules, it is much more difficult to read the following line, where God as addressee is positioned as the *interlocutor* in a rhetorical exchange destined to convince that interlocutor of his own inexistence.

The same structure can be observed in a long footnote in *Juliette*. The context of the note is a dissertation from Clairwil which attempts to demonstrate the proposition 'God does not exist' after the manner of classical dialectics. But in the footnote this structure is troubled, again because God is positioned as addressee and interpellated (VIII, p. 372n). In its paradoxical insistence, this pragmatic organization implies a desire and a frustration, a respect and a scandal, and this is very clear in *La Vérité*:

> . . . l'horreur que je te porte
> Est à la fois si juste, si grande, et si forte,
> Qu'avec plaisir, Dieu vil, avec tranquillité,

Que dis-je? avec transport, même avec volupté,
Je serais ton bourreau, si ta frêle existence
Pouvait offrir un point à ma sombre vengeance,
Et mon bras avec charme irait jusqu'à ton coeur
De mon aversion te prouver ma rigueur.
Mais ce serait en vain que l'on voudrait t'atteindre,
Et ton essence échappe à qui veut la contraindre.

(XIV, pp. 82–3)

In the light of this, it would seem that the 'expanding energy of desire' in Sade is not so much *contained* by the limits imposed upon it, as *created* by those limits. To put this in banal and provisional terms, Sade requires the *fiction* of God if he is to gain the pleasure ('transport', 'volupté', 'charme') of transgression. Sade's fiction grows from the frustration born of the philosophical demonstration that transgression is strictly speaking impossible, there being no transcendent order to transgress. From this point of view, it would be reductive to read the final line of the last quotation simply as a parodic quotation from a certain doxa: if the dialectic of *interdit* and *transgression* is to be made possible and repeatable, then the structure of energy and its limits must be reversible, and God himself (now thoroughly fictionalized) must be able to escape a desire for vengeance which would 'constrain' him as a prelude to destruction. The effect of this is that any attempted legitimation of Sade's writing in terms of truth, is *itself* only a fiction allowing for the production of *jouissance*, through the creation of simulacra of limits to be transgressed.

9. Law, Order, Rules

It seems possible to approach something of the specificity of these simulacra of limits by looking at the notion of 'order' in Sade's novels, and the attendant notion of rules. As Roland Barthes has pointed out, 'la luxure est sans frein mais non sans ordre':[13] for example, in *La Philosophie dans le boudoir*, Mme de Saint-Ange suggests to the assembly, 'Mettons . . . un peu d'ordre à ces orgies; il en faut même au sein du délire et de l'infamie' (III, p. 424); and at the beginning of *Juliette*, la Delbène insists: 'mettons un peu d'ordre à nos plaisirs, on n'en jouit qu'en les fixant' (VIII, p. 18). Such statements are habitually the prelude to the elaborate assemblages of bodies which Barthes has analysed. Similarly, the narrative progress of the novels is subordinated to a principle of order: for example the order of the *historiennes*'s stories in *Les 120 Journées*, and that of the narrative itself in the same novel.

The libertines' scorn for social and moral law has to be set against the constant appeal to order and principles, and their tendency to form groups or societies with strict and explicit rules. The order imposed on the orgy evidently forms part of this larger problem, which seems to be the place of contradictions in Sade's texts. For example, in *Les 120 Journées* the Duc de Blangis affirms: 'Ferme dans mes principes parce que je m'en suis formé de sûrs dès mes plus jeunes ans, j'agis toujours conséquemment à eux' (XIII, p. 8). This consequent action is set against blind subservience to the passions. A little later in the novel, however, the narrative discourse, commenting on the same character, affirms sententiously, 'Rien n'est inconséquent comme un libertin' (XIII, p. 113). In the same novel, narrative propositions about Curval introduce sententious propositions in favour of the principled nature of *libertinage* (pp. 314–15). But earlier, again with reference to Curval, there has been a reference to its 'perpétuelles inconséquences', and this paradoxical tendency can be illustrated by an example where the four masters of the château cheat with the rules which they have imposed on their orgies. Durcet catches two of the victims talking about religion; in the rules transcribed at the beginning of the novel, it is said that 'Le plus petit acte de religion de la part d'un des sujets, quel qu'il puisse être, sera puni de mort' (XIII, p. 55).

This is not the first time that the girls in question have been caught breaking this rule, so the rules have already been broken by the *libertins*, who continue to break them, in defiance of contradiction, as follows:

Le président se ressouvint que, quand il était au palais, ses ingénieux confrères prétendaient que comme une récidive prouvait que la nature agissait dans un homme plus fortement que l'éducation et que les principes, que, par conséquent, en récidivant, il attestait pour ainsi dire qu'il n'était pas maître de lui-même, il fallait le punir doublement; *il voulut raisonner aussi conséquemment*, avec autant d'esprit, que ses anciens condisciples, et déclara qu'*en conséquence* il fallait les punir, elle et sa compagne, dans toute la rigueur des ordonnances. Mais comme ces ordonnances portaient peine de mort pour un tel cas, et qu'on avait envie de s'amuser encore quelque temps de ces dames avant d'en venir là, on se contenta de les faire venir, de les faire mettre à genoux, et de leur lire l'article de l'ordonnance, en leur faisant sentir tout ce qu'elles venaient de risquer en s'exposant à un tel délit.

(XIII, p. 283, my emphasis)

In the relationship between *libertins* and their victims, laws or rules are always instituted, but the institution of those laws and rules involves, as a rule, the possibility of arbitrary decisions as to their application or non-application: this possibility clearly undermines the coherence of the notion of law or rule. This is also the case in *La Nouvelle Justine*, where Omphale dictates to Justine the elaborate rules governing the punishment of victims, and points out both the existence of arbitrary elements in the code, and the arbitrary nature of the existence of a code at all (VI, pp. 361–2).

The *libertin* writes a code of laws, then, which is again a simulacrum, producing a supplementary *jouissance* from the undecidability as to whether his punctual sentences will conform to that code or not. This is part of the general tendency to place the victim in a double bind, in which obeying the law can amount to breaking it; this is an important narrative device in Sade, and is figured most clearly in the text by the torture-machines, in which any effort the victim makes to save his life from one danger means he dies from another.[14] The simulacrum in play here is basically one of contractual relationships, and could be read against the intertext of political theory from Hobbes to Rousseau.

Before looking at the detail of political 'theory' in Sade, however, it is worth considering the structure of criminal associations in his novels. These are of two basic types, the first involving thieves and murderers, the second rich and noble *libertins* who can rely on their power, wealth and influence to protect them from the law of society. Both types seem paradoxical in that they appear to rely on contractual relationships between their members, while at the same time contesting the validity of the contractual relationships upon which society as a whole is founded. Sade is of course not the first eighteenth-century writer to consider the problem of the criminal association, although his treatment of it is the most radical. In the article 'Droit naturel' in the *Encyclopédie*, Diderot had considered and dismissed the problem of the criminal association; according to him, even a band of thieves respects the principle of the *volonté générale*, and therefore that of virtue: 'la vertu est si belle que les voleurs en respectent l'image dans le fond même de leurs cavernes'.[15] In *La Nouvelle Justine*, the criminal leader Coeur-de-fer sweeps away any question of a *volonté générale* in the criminal association, and grounds its existence in pure egoism, in a temporary aggregate of individual wills all convinced that the social contract of the political theorists is fundamentally unjust both to the strong in society (who have no need to give up anything in the interests of their happiness), and to the weak (who ultimately have to give up what they have to the strong). The criminal association can gain a temporary stability insofar as it momentarily unites only the strong *or* the weak, but this model can evidently not be extended to society as a whole, which is always, in Sade's description, composed of strong *and* weak.

In some brilliant pages, Marcel Hénaff has approached this problem by opposing to the founding contract of society the 'pacte-éclair' of the society of *libertins*.[16] In analysing the 'club' formed by the 'Société des amis du crime', he points out that such an association presupposes agreement of its members about desire, external sources of income which solve all material problems, and social power (linked to wealth) already held in society prior to the formation of the club. This consensus can exclude the problem of violence from *within* the club, but the *libertin*'s pact is limited by a *horizon* of violence, a 'jeu avec la mort pour la jouissance'. There is no real contract in that there is no third party (God, the Truth, a legal apparatus) to guarantee its terms. The contract is only mimicked in the sperm-signatures which traditionally mark the institution of the pseudo-pact. The model is really that of the *complot*, Hénaff suggests, which 'porte en soi le principe de sa révocation unilatérale' (Hénaff, p. 281). And this is why Sbrigani, Clairwil and others can die at the hands of their partners in crime.

The opposition between law and rule, as examined recently by Jean Baudrillard, might be able to help with the analysis of this paradoxical situation.[17] The law, in the social form attacked by Sade, is a product of the contract, and guaranteed by a transcendent instance – I argued in the last chapter that Rousseau tried and failed to produce a coherent contractual theory of legislation without such transcendence. As Baudrillard puts it, the law obeys 'un principe qui nous dépasse': it tends to forget its contractual origin and retreat into transcendence and mystery, producing guilt and fear.[18] The rule, on the other hand, depends on no such instance: it is arbitrary and ritualized, it institutes a space which is essentially that of the game, it calls for observance rather than belief, it conceals no mystery and produces no debt. The rule and the game set up a pure system of exchange which requires no justification beyond the desire to play, and which produces neither deficit nor surplus-value. The rule cannot be threatened by transgression, as transgression here means simply that the transgressor leaves the space of the game and falls back, outside the domain of the rule, into that of the law. The 'Société', within its rule-bound structure, would seem to conform to this analysis, and to realize the 'entière circulation des vices' recommended by the surgeon Rodin in *La Nouvelle Justine* (VI, p. 249).

Despite the attraction of this model, it seems that the notion of a homeostatic functioning of the rule-governed society will not do, in that the desire of the Sadian *libertin* is, apparently, precisely to move within the domain of the law and to retain the possibility of transgression. The 'Société' is only a stage in Juliette's progress to 'integral' *libertinage*,[19] and already in its statutes exhibits tensions in the rule/law distinction at the point at which the dividing line is drawn. For the 'Société' cannot institute a pure space in isolation from society and the law, despite Hénaff's analysis. There are inevitably points of contact, and it is these points which trouble Baudrillard's distinction between law and rule and establish a certain communication between the two terms, and thus a transgression of the bar which separates them – Baudrillard's assertion that the ritualized, rule-bound sign can 'deliver' us from meaning is a pious and over-optimistic hope. This communication between the space defined by the *Société*'s rules and that of the surrounding legal system is suggested at a number of points in the text which deals with the statutes of the club. The first of these is in the preamble to the numbered paragraphs:

La Société protège tous ses membres; elle leur promet à tous, secours, abri, refuge, protection, crédit, contre les entreprises de la Loi; elle prend sous sa sauvegarde tous ceux qui l'enfreignent, et se regarde comme au-dessus d'elle, parce que la Loi est l'ouvrage des hommes, et que la Société, fille de la nature, n'écoute et ne suit que la nature. (VIII, p. 401)

Much later, in paragraph 43 of the statutes, this suggestion of communication (in the protection of law-breakers) is made more explicit:

Il est absolument défendu de s'immiscer dans les affaires du gouvernement. Tout discours de politique est expressément interdit. La Société respecte le gouvernement sous lequel elle vit; et si elle se met au-dessus des lois, c'est parce qu'il est dans ces principes que l'homme n'a pas le pouvoir de faire des lois qui gênent et contrarient celles de la nature. Mais les désordres de ses membres, toujours intérieurs, ne doivent jamais scandaliser ni les gouvernés, ni les gouvernants. (VIII, p. 408)

The *Société* does, then, institute a closed space (defined as an interior), but is driven in so doing into a respect for laws which it in principle denies; this troubles the topological organization of the spaces in question. The *Société* is above the laws in that it denies their legitimacy, but below them in that it avoids scandalizing them. Paragraph 17 clarifies what is in play here:

Aucune flétrissure juridique, aucun mépris public, aucune diffamation n'empêchera d'être reçu dans la Société. Ses principes étant basés sur le crime, comment ce qui vient du crime pourrait-il jamais les entraver! Ces individus, rejetés du monde, trouveront des consolations et des amis dans une Société qui les considérera et les admettra toujours de préférence. *Plus un individu sera mésestimé dans le monde, plus il plaira à la Société*; ceux de ce genre seront élus présidents dès le même jour de leur réception, et admis dans les sérails sans noviciat. (VIII, p. 404, my emphasis)

The communication is by now evident, and it is clear that the rules are far from arbitrary. This is also shown by the prescription that each session begin with a speech against morality and religion (§11), and the regular confessions which mimic and invert Catholic practice (§18). The *Société* does indeed attempt to set up a space kept secret from the legal space surrounding it (the only derogation punishable by death is the betrayal of the society's secret (§39)), but within, that space depends on a play between the inversion of the law, and the denial of its reality. This play is condensed in the very opening lines of the statutes, and leads to the problem of the referent of the word 'crime': 'La Société se sert du mot *crime* pour se conformer aux usages reçus, mais elle déclare qu'elle ne désigne ainsi aucune espèce d'action, de quelque sorte qu'elle puisse être' (VIII, p. 401).

So the *Société* is both above the law and below it, a secret enclave within the law which inverts the law but denies its legitimacy. It requires the word crime for its title and identity, it befriends crime, but simultaneously makes of 'crime' a word without reference. It follows that its secrecy is a sham, and that it needs to communicate with the discourse of law (which alone gives a sense to 'crime') to publish its own secret, thereby breaking its own rules in order to preserve its name.

10. The Hiatus

Sade is here working very close to a subversion of the identity-principle. In Sade's discourse, acts such as murder simultaneously are and are not crime. Challenging the identity-principle, thus (inevitably) mediated through language, involves the superimposition of two discourses, that of positive law, and that of a certain 'law of nature' as defined by Sade, and the oscillation of a key term between the one in which it has meaning, and the other in which it is denied meaning. This is the logic of the interpellation of God analysed above, and it can now be extended to the whole abstract vocabulary of moral discourse. *Jouissance* is generated by this endlessly repeatable oscillation, which comes to mark with its trace all propositions which use the language of morality. Or perhaps *jouissance* could be located in the unthinkable silent space *between* the two discourses, a space in which the terms in question would have, radically, no meaning at all (not even that of being deprived of meaning).

The logic of this hiatus can be further illustrated from the argument of the pamphlet *Français, encore un effort si vous voulez être républicains,* and, more specifically, in the light of Maurice Blanchot's reading of that text. Here Sade immediately casts into doubt the very coherence of the notion of the law by denying its generalizing character:

Ce serait ici une absurdité palpable que de vouloir prescrire des lois universelles; ce procédé serait aussi ridicule que celui d'un général d'armée qui voudrait que tous ses soldats fussent vêtus d'un habit fait sur la même mesure; c'est une injustice effrayante que d'exiger que des hommes de caractère inégaux se plient à des lois égales: ce qui va à l'un ne va point à l'autre.

(III, pp. 492–3)[20]

And although the pamphlet goes on to recognize the impossibility of there being as many laws as there are individuals, the threat to the coherence of the concept 'law' is posed. This threat is substantially radicalized at a point where the text is concerned with the problem of the maintenance of its version of a 'gouvernement républicain'. First comes a purely formal definition of the duty of such a government (a formalism which provides the basis of Lacan's attempt to read Sade 'with' Kant),[21] which is simply that of its self-preservation:

Nous ne devons certainement pas douter un moment que tout ce qui s'appelle crimes moraux, c'est-à-dire toutes les actions de l'espèce de celles que nous venons de citer, ne soit parfaitement indifférent dans un gouvernement dont le seul devoir consiste à conserver, par tel moyen que ce puisse être, la forme essentielle à son maintien: voilà l'unique morale d'un gouvernement républicain.

(III, p. 498)

Sade's pamphleteer's reasoning now goes as follows: it is impossible for a republican government to conserve this essential form by moral means, because any moral government would run into trouble with surrounding jealous governments. It will therefore have to resort to war to defend itself, and 'rien n'est moins moral que la guerre' (Ibid.). This makes the state essentially immoral, and it cannot then reasonably pretend to enforce morality on its subjects. Moreover, this immorality is desirable. It is worth quoting the following passage at length:

Les législateurs de la Grèce avaient parfaitement senti l'importante nécessité de gangrener les membres pour que, leur *dissolution morale* influant sur celle utile à la machine, il en résultât l'insurrection toujours indispensable dans un gouvernement, qui, parfaitement heureux comme le gouvernement républicain, doit nécessairement exciter la haine et la jalousie de tout ce qui l'entoure. L'insurrection, pensaient ces sages législateurs, n'est point un état *moral*; elle doit être pourtant l'état permanent d'une république; il serait donc aussi absurde que dangereux d'exiger que ceux qui doivent maintenir le perpétuel ébranlement *immoral* de la machine fussent eux-mêmes des êtres très *moraux*, parce que l'état *moral* d'un homme est un état de mouvement perpétuel qui la rapproche de l'insurrection nécessaire, dans laquelle il faut que le républicain tienne toujours le gouvernement dont il est membre.

(Ibid., my emphasis)

In other words, as Blanchot points out, the state can no more become immobile than can nature in Sade's account; but by resituating Sade's text in an internal history, Blanchot is able to refine on the definition of insurrection or revolution and to produce the following gloss: 'Sade appelle donc régime révolutionnaire le temps pur où l'histoire suspendue fait époque, ce temps de l'entre-temps où entre les anciennes lois et les lois nouvelles règne le silence de l'absence des lois'.[22] This description is precious, but acceptable only if we refuse the quasi-historical dimension which allowed its elaboration: the *entre-temps* is not a temporal gap *between* two régimes of law but, *within* a system of law, the silence in the law between the sense and non-sense of the words, the movement which marks with its trace any legislative statement with a sort of internal transgression. Insurrection is not then positively definable, but is rather the crime posited by the law in the same movement which forbids it, the injustice of justice or the incoherence of coherence. The oscillating trace is *figured* in the evidently unrealizable prescriptions for republican government given by the pamphlet.

11. Nature

It may still be, of course, that this postulated 'silence' in the law might not affect the law of nature, to which Sade appeals constantly in his effort to undermine positive and moral legislation: some examples of this have been seen in the Statutes of the *Société des amis du crime*. Sade's statements on nature are not, in general, particularly 'original', but can be placed in the eighteenth-century materialist tradition. It is not my purpose here to discuss or establish Sade's 'debt' to earlier writers such as La Mettrie and d'Holbach, and indeed a good deal of work has already been done in this intertext.[23] What is perhaps new in Sade is the assertion that the laws of nature bear no relation whatsoever to political or moral law: this is the implication of the maxim quoted from the *Idée sur les romans* at the beginning of this chapter.

This assertion, which can be found throughout Sade's novels, can be illustrated from *La Nouvelle Justine*. Bressac has invited Justine to collaborate with him in the murder of his mother, and Justine's protest provokes a theoretical discourse on crime, law, and nature: 'Tout dans l'univers est subordonné aux lois de la nature' (VI, p. 204), and a little later, 'La vie de l'homme, persuadons-nous-le bien, dépend des mêmes lois que celle des animaux, l'une et l'autre de ces existences sont soumises aux lois générales de la matière et du mouvement' (Ibid.). So much is clear: there is a complete continuity of nature, which recuperates all matter in a process of constant transformation. Man cannot destroy matter, but can merely change its form: 'Le pouvoir de détruire n'est pas accordé à l'homme; il a tout au plus celui de varier des formes, mais il n'a pas celui de les anéantir' (VI, p. 202). Killing someone thus does not destroy that person, but simply changes the formal organization of the matter of which s/he is composed. These changes of form are in no sense directed against nature, but are favourable to her creativity:

> Toute forme est égale aux yeux de la nature; rien ne se perd dans le creuset immense où ses variations s'exécutent: toutes les portions de matière qui y tombent en rejaillissent incessamment sous d'autres figures; et, quels que soient nos procédés sur cela, aucun ne l'outrage sans doute, aucun ne saurait l'offenser. Nos destructions raniment son pouvoir; elles entretiennent son énergie, mais aucune ne l'atténue; elle n'est contrariée par aucune.
>
> (VI, p. 202)

There is thus no destruction, no death, no crime, just nature following her own designs and implanting in man the passions as the instruments of her designs (on herself). Man's desire to harm or kill his neighbour is thus an expression of a natural law, and is therefore good.

It is possible to see at work here (in a refined way) the slippage between prescriptive and descriptive senses of the word 'law' which I have suggested to be typical of eighteenth-century discourse, for Sade appeals to the (descriptive) laws of nature, which are essentially laws of perpetual movement and transformation, to undermine the (prescriptive) laws of society (or of the 'nature' appealed to by the theorists of 'natural law'). But these descriptive laws of nature then become prescriptive laws for action in society, in that they encourage murder and crime. For, if measured by the laws of society or the fictional 'nature' used to legitimate them, nature is herself criminal:

> La première et plus belle qualité de la nature est le mouvement qui l'agite sans cesse: mais ce mouvement n'est qu'une suite perpétuelle de crimes; ce n'est que par des crimes qu'elle se conserve; elle ne vit, elle ne s'entretient, elle ne se perpétue qu'à force de destructions. L'être qui en produira davantage, celui

qui sera le plus parfait, sera donc infailliblement celui dont l'agitation la plus active deviendra la cause d'un plus grande nombre de crimes. (VI, p. 208) One obeys the laws of nature by following all the impulsions of one's passions. The law of society is, on the contrary, defined as that which is inaccessible to passion,[24] and it therefore has no excuse for carrying out punitive action; it is no longer excusable in terms of the 'natural' egoism of the passions. The exercise of the law is thus a crime, whereas crime obeys the law, when that law is that of the nature described by Sade.

This description allows a positive and a negative description of nature: positively, it can be used to legitimate what is called crime; negatively, it denies man the possibility of committing crime. The positive aspect also, from our point of view, grounds the enunciation of sententious discourse, which is thus still the voice of nature transcribed by the 'scélérat' who has the courage to destroy prejudice and listen to that voice. The type of maxim generated by this structure would none the less be classical, and reminiscent of La Roche-foucauld, whose maxims so often take the form, 'Ce qu'on appelle X n'est que Y'. The question is one of *naming*, as it was in the example of God; all living organisms partake of the same general 'variations' of natural forms, 'ne recevant jamais une mort réelle': if the propriety of the term 'death' is thus denied (and with it, by implication, the propriety of the term 'life'), then murder, for example, can only be an 'action improprement appelée criminelle' (VI, p. 203), which in fact *helps* nature to lay down her law.

On the other hand, this is not the same as simply producing the sententious affirmation that 'what we call good is really bad and what we call bad is really good', because of the same apparent paradox noted in the example of God. Because the sententious discourse of Sade's characters uses 'truth' only as a bogus legitimation for *jouissance*, it requires the maintenance of the terms which it undermines in order for transgression to take place. If we remember a maxim quoted at the beginning of this chapter, 'la volupté n'admet aucune chaîne, elle ne jouit jamais mieux que quand elle les rompt toutes', it is now clear that the 'chains' *are* admitted precisely to the extent that they are broken. This point could be illustrated with literally dozens of examples, the most extreme and explicit being no doubt in *La Nouvelle Justine*: 'Non, rien au monde n'est délicieux comme l'existence de ces freins, uniquement réalisés pour se procurer le plaisir de les rompre' (VII, p. 294). This structure can now be extended to take in the structure of language, and we can suggest that Sade's insistent use of the language of morality in his sententious passages, while he no less insistently shows that such language has no referential value, is determined by this logic of the *frein*, which is part of the logic of *jouissance*. Just as Sade interpellates God in order to deny his existence, so he calls on the abstract nouns whose economy founds morality in order to repeat the enjoyment of demonstrating their vacuity.

12. Nature Unvoiced

This play with semantic values still, however, seems to be grounded in an appeal to a redefined 'law', that of nature. This law makes it strictly speaking impossible to commit crime, to find a referent for that word, and it is now possible to summarize the life of the 'integral' Sadian *libertin* (who has gone beyond the mere repetition of a single perversion which characterizes the minor protagonists of the novels) as an endless quest for that lost referent, a quest marked by the imposition of simulacra of laws, and the realization that none of these simulacra can survive the reasoning of the dissertations. La Delbène tells Juliette: 'C'est la loi seule qui fait le crime, et . . . le crime tombe dès que la loi n'existe plus' (VIII, p. 74). Desire desires limits in order to break them in *jouissance*; but the true *libertin* cannot simply repeat this dialectic with the same set of limits, for desire in Sade is historical – it expands, and must discover with each *jouissance* a new, wider set of limits to transgress. This imperative of *jouissance* inevitably becomes a 'manque à jouir', and *jouissance* becomes contaminated by the simulacrum which appeared to be in its service. It is again La Delbène who makes this clear:

L'habitude de tout franchir leur [i.e. 'les scélérats'] fait incessamment trouver tout simple ce qui d'abord leur avait paru révoltant, et, d'écart en écart, ils parviennent aux monstruosités à l'exécution desquelles ils se trouvent encore en arrière, parce qu'*il faudrait des crimes réels pour leur donner une véritable jouissance*, et qu'il n'existe malheureusement de crime à rien. Ainsi, toujours au-dessous de leurs désirs, ce ne sont plus eux qui manquent aux horreurs, ce sont les horreurs qui leur manquent.   (VIII, pp. 93–4, my emphasis)

This lack leads to a frustration which resituates desire on a cosmic level, in which nature, which had previously legitimated crime, becomes an ultimate limit to crime. In *La Nouvelle Justine*, the monk Jérôme, now beyond the *jouissance* of simple crime, wishes he could emulate the privileged example of the *écart* within nature, the volcano.[25] This turns out to be possible, through the good offices of the chemist Almani, but nature constantly absorbs attempts made to violate her (VII, pp. 47–8). The specific frustration which the *libertin* eventually encounters is that provoked by the totalizing capacity of nature, which simply gathers up all expenditure and deficit into an economy at a different level. Almani admits defeat: his imitation is always already condemned to the service of nature. The laws of nature, which legitimated the breaking of the *freins* of social laws, themselves become the *freins* which seem to be unbreakable, the limits on desire rather than its motive force. Sade's logic seems to be stuck in contradiction here, insofar as the law of nature is both, and incompatibly, a law which releases and a law which contains. As a force releasing desire it can be praised in the terms we have seen; as container, it can be cursed. The *pas au-delà* which describes the Sadian exploitation of moral vocabulary in the interests of *jouissance* is here apparently radically blocked, and this situation would appear to justify Lacan's assertion that Sade is ultimately still attached to the law. However, in certain passages of the novels, an attempt is made to overcome this limit by exploiting the *indifference* of nature to man, and by transforming this indifference into an absence of all relationship, or, as can be said more neatly in French, a *rapport du sans-rapport*.

The complex problems raised by this new position are most readily in evidence in the Pope's discourse to Juliette, which precedes the orgy in the Vatican. These pages form what is perhaps the most difficult 'philosophical' passage in the whole of Sade. The first essential element here is that nature's creations or productions are essentially the result of blind forces; man might be the result of the laws of nature, but should not be allowed the dignity of being a creation: 'Ces créatures ne sont ni bonnes, ni belles, ni précieuses, ni créées: elles sont l'écume, elles sont le résultat des lois aveugles de la nature' (IX, p. 171). The creatures of the earth are merely the vapours produced by a process indifferent to them. Nature is entirely independent of her creatures insofar as it is perfectly conceivable that she could continue to exist according to a different set of laws. There are two consequences of this: the first is the *non-rapport* of man and nature; the second is that nature is herself subject to laws. The first of these points is argued as follows:

Les rapports de l'homme à la nature, ou de la nature à l'homme, sont donc nuls; la nature ne peut enchaîner l'homme par aucune loi; l'homme ne dépend en rien de la nature; ils ne doivent rien l'un à l'autre et ne peuvent ni s'offenser, ni se servir; l'un a produit malgré soi: de ce moment, aucun rapport réel; l'autre est produit malgré lui, et, conséquemment, nul rapport. Une fois lancé, l'homme ne tient plus à la nature; une fois que la nature a lancé, elle ne peut plus rien sur l'homme; *toutes ses lois sont particulières.*

(Ibid., my emphasis, and see note 20 above).

In his punctual *lancement,* man receives laws to which he is subsequently bound, although these laws are no longer in relationship with nature. On the other hand (and here is the *rapport* despite the previous assertion of the *sans-rapport*), if man (and the other species) follows the law of this primary launching, notably by propagating, then in fact he blocks the creative faculty of nature, and prevents her from throwing the dice differently:

Vous objecterez peut-être à cela que si cette possibilité de se propager, qu'elle a laissée à ses créatures, lui nuisait, elle ne la lui aurait pas donnée . . . Mais observez donc qu'elle n'est pas maîtresse, qu'elle est la première esclave de ses lois . . . qu'elle est enchaînée par ses lois, qu'elle n'y peut rien changer, qu'une de ses lois est l'élan des créatures une fois fait, et la possibilité à ses créatures de se propager. (IX, p. 172)

The logic at work here provokes a distinction between primary and secondary processes, something which is vital for the structure of the enunciation of the law. The text continues:

Mais que si ces créatures ne se propageaient plus, ou se détruisaient, la nature rentrerait alors dans de premiers droits qui ne seraient plus combattus par rien, au lieu qu'en propageant ou en ne détruisant pas, nous la lions à ses lois secondaires, et la privons de sa plus active puissance. (Ibid.)

Within the space defined by these secondary laws, which is the space of observable reality, of the given, nature operates according to principles of perpetual movement, in which notions such as 'death' or 'destruction' are purely relative, mechanically produced by the logic of the *lancement.* This secondary space denies reference or relevance to the laws of society and morality. Nature, whose power to create *or* destroy is radically limited by the effects of this secondary sphere, nevertheless preserves a *volonté,* which allows her to send out tyrants and *scélérats* whose impossible destination is the destruction of the secondary sphere which they inevitably perpetuate:

Lorsque la nature les envoie sur la terre, à dessein d'anéantir ces règnes qui la privent de la faculté de nouveaux élancements, elle ne commet qu'un acte d'impuissance, parce que les premières lois reçues par ces règnes, lors du premier jet, leur ont imprimé cette faculté productive qui durera toujours, et que la nature n'anéantira qu'en se détruisant totalement, ce dont elle n'est pas maîtresse, parce qu'elle est soumise elle-même à des lois, de l'empire desquelles il lui est impossible de s'échapper, et qui dureront éternellement. (IX, p. 175)

This of course proves far too much, and would tend to suggest the pointlessness of crime, so the Pope resorts to two arguments in its favour. The first is that as nature would like to be free of the laws imposed on her by the secondary sphere, mankind must at least try to please her by going as far in that direction as it can: 'Vous ne pouvez lui plaire par l'atrocité d'une entière destruction, plaisez-lui donc du moins par une atrocité locale' (IX, p. 180). This contradicts the logic of what has gone before, and especially the law of the *non-rapport*. The second argument reproduces, with respect to nature, the structure of transgression and *jouissance*:

Loin de remercier cette nature inconséquente du peu de liberté qu'elle nous donne pour accomplir les penchants inspirés par sa voix, blasphémons-la, du fond de notre coeur, de nous avoir autant rétréci la carrière qui remplit ses vues; outrageons-la, détruisons-la, pour nous avoir laissé si peu de crimes à faire, en donnant de si violents désirs d'en commettre à tous les instants . . . Quand j'aurai exterminé sur la terre toutes les créatures qui la couvrent, je serai bien loin de mon but, puisque je t'aurai servie . . . marâtre! . . . et que je n'aspire qu'à me venger de ta bêtise, ou de la méchanceté que tu fais éprouver aux hommes, en ne leur fournissant jamais les moyens de se livrer aux affreux penchants que tu leur inspires! (IX, pp. 186–7)

It is, of course, tempting simply to reject with impatience this type of passage, to denounce its incoherence and delirious character. On the other hand, these incoherences might be read as traces in Sade's writing of the unpresentable *primary* sphere of nature (although there is probably no particularly good reason for calling it 'nature', nor for assuming that it can be named in any coherent way), which would be the final absence grounding Sade's writing. Gilles Deleuze, describing what I have called the secondary sphere as a space in which it is possible to find *partial* destructions, partial crimes, a space of 'le négatif comme processus partiel', opposes to it this primary nature as 'la négation pure comme Idée totalisante', and 'un délire de la raison comme telle'.[26]

I argued in the previous chapter that for most eighteenth-century thinkers, nature was essentially a voice, and a legislative voice. This is heard in the individual as the voice of conscience, and it is the ultimate ground for the authority of the law in general. In its most rigorous formulation, this voice becomes that of Kant's Categorical Imperative, imposing the formal conditions for what moral action would be. A good deal has been made of the fact that this formalism means that the *object* of the law is never given, but merely the form of its application: Lacan has argued that the object of the law is none other than his *objet petit a* perpetually fleeing the grasp of desire, and has attempted to establish a homology between this and the phantasmatics of the Sadian *libertin*.[27] However attractive it may be to read Sade in terms of Kant, and vice versa, it seems necessary here to stress that, in Sade, the primary nature which we are discussing *has no voice*, and that this seems to place us on 'ground' outside the possibilities of rationalism. In Sade, the two voices which speak in man, that of the *préjugé* and that of the secondary sphere, are undermined by this absence of voice in primary nature. In the Pope's discourse, the threat of this radical silence of nature tends to be averted by a stressing of the secondary sphere:

La nature n'a donc point de voix; celle qui tonne en nous n'est donc plus que celle du préjugé, qu'avec un peu de force nous pouvons absorber pour toujours. Il est pourtant un organe sacré qui retentit en nous, avant la voix de l'erreur ou de l'éducation; mais cette voix, qui nous soumet au joug des éléments, ne nous contraint qu'à ce qui flatte l'accord de ces éléments . . .

(IX, p. 184)

But the voiceless primary nature should not be forgotten, for it should prevent most readings of Sade, even the elegant dialectical readings of Blanchot and Bataille, from 'making sense' of his text. The former, for example, asserts that after the *libertin* has applied negation first to God and then to nature, he 'chooses' to become an 'homme intégral' (Bataille would use the term 'souverain'),[28] and that at this stage he has to turn negation against himself, producing the famous Sadian 'apathy'. But it would seem that the 'presence' of the voiceless primary nature as the logically prior ground for this reading threatens the coherence of any such dialectic.

In terms of the opposition between sententious and narrative propositions, the effect of nature's 'losing her voice' is clear. I have assumed in reading eighteenth-century fiction that the presence of sententious elements in fiction marks a pretension to tell the truth, to lay down the law in so doing, and to situate fiction with respect to that truth-as-law. The classical situation of sententious propositions at the edge of fictional texts ensures both a separation of truth and fiction, and a certain communication between them. The ideological function of this situation is to allow fiction a certain dignity, whilst preserving truth from contamination. A sententious proposition in a novel can still lay down the law of truth against the *préjugé*: with the Enlightenment's subordination of God to the instance of Reason, sententious propositions in novels can be legitimated as a transcription of Reason given by the voice of nature.

In Sade, the ultimate silence of nature destroys this type of legitimation: the consequence of this is that sententious propositions are as 'fictional' as fiction, and any internal legitimations in terms of the 'truth' are fictionalized too. Any 'truths' spoken by the voice of the secondary sphere of nature are used to combat the *préjugé* only on this radically fictionalized ground. Nor can we continue to speak the 'truth' of that radical fictionality from the vantage-point of that 'ground', precisely because it is fictionalized. There is no longer *any* ground on which to stand.

This must be placed against the fact that Sade's novels none the less present the succession of narrative and sententious propositions noted at the beginning of this chapter; a purely formal analysis would see no qualitative difference between these texts and other eighteenth-century novels. But what such an analysis would leave aside as the content of sententious propositions in fact destroys the premises on which the analysis was founded. This of course brings back *jouissance* and the 'Effet Sade', but a *jouissance* which is not beyond the simulacrum as its reward, but inhabited through and through *by* the simulacrum. It now seems possible to say that Sade's various pretences of speaking the truth about perversion, to present 'perversion' as the truth of nature, and so on, always already constitute a perversion of speaking the truth, a perversion of the truth/fiction distinction, which can no longer obey the controlled exchanges of classical narrative economy. In terms of the model of energy and limits, sententious propositions in Sade come to have the status of simulacra of statements of truth, which function as a fictional *frein* to the progress of the energy which I have continued to call 'desire', and for which another name in Sade's case would be 'narrative sentences'. So, where Marcel Hénaff can write of the pamphlet *Français encore un effort* . . ., 'Le paradoxe spécifique de ce texte c'est de faire admettre comme principes de socialité des réquisits libertins qui ne se définissent que de s'y soustraire' (Hénaff, p. 249), this can be applied to the whole of Sade's work, in terms no longer of sociality but of readability. A final problem is that of the status of language in Sade: this is indeed a basic question, if it is justifiable to assert that the quest of the *libertin* is a quest for a referent for the word 'crime'. There is no explicit theory of language in Sade's work, and it is probably unthinkable that he should have elaborated one, as in a certain sense language is impossible in Sade's world. Rousseau, in order to get man out of the isolation of the state of nature, needed to exploit the notion of pity as founding the possibility of an identification with the other, on the basis of which, given the necessary natural catastrophe, language and society could develop. In Sade, 'pity' has no status except for the weak, the victims: it would belong to a series comprising terms such as 'bienfaisance', 'charité', 'remords', etc. The Sadian *libertin* is *isolated* from the other.[29] Given what has been said on the non-general status of the law, and the undermining of contractual relationships, it is now possible to suggest that in Sade there can be no linguistic contract for the *libertin*. Such a contract would be more radical than that of 'keeping one's word', and would involve nomination: for Sade's heroes agreement in nomination (in the use of Locke's 'mixed modes') is a mark of the weak, the *sots* dominated by the *préjugé* and the bogus social contract. If for Nietzsche the 'origin of language', and specifically of moral language, is linked to the power of the 'master' to give names,[30] in Sade this naming is a product of the tendency of the weak to herd together; the *libertin* must contest language and the stability of reference if he is to become the 'souverain'. This is evidently a situation close to madness, but again, any 'escape' from the closure of meaning does not lead to a delirious or non-referential writing, but to a perversion of that writing, a play on its limits. This is dramatized in the only episode in Sade which features madmen, in the *Histoire de Juliette*, where madness is linked to a confusion of proper names (the madmen think they are God, Mary, Jesus: 'tout le paradis est dans cet enfer'), which is of course exploited by the *libertins* in terms of the simulacrum (IX, pp. 385–7). The logic is the same in the general use of moral terms: the madness of society is to assume the meaning of those terms; that of the *libertin* is to play at inverting those terms, in the knowledge that they have no referent.[31]

Sadien cruelty is thus not limited to the body of the victim, if only because this dimension of cruelty depends on a reading based on the referential, denotative function of language, cast into doubt in the texts themselves. In a sense, the only 'real' cruelty in Sade is that worked on the body of language, insofar as 'Sade' here means only a body of writing. Where Bataille, for example, can suppose that 'violence' precedes Sade's texts, which are thus the paradoxical expression of what is essentially silent,[32] it seems necessary to say that nothing precedes the text (not even the voiceless primary nature), but that the text produces violence only because of language, which is not preceded. The problem with Sade is not that he recommends crime, but that, in denying a referent to the word 'crime', he commits linguistic crime. This is not to suggest that Sade escapes from referential meaning, nor even from morality or sociality: there is no such escape. Sade's crime is, rather, to work in and on language an unnamable operation which frustrates *jouissance* as much as it liberates it, in an unassignable oscillation beyond transgression, attracting into its aberrant economy any desire to lay down its law. Any impression of intelligibility which the performance of the analysis might have produced is implacably undermined by its result.

POSTSCRIPT

Toute thèse est une prothèse.   (Jacques Derrida, *Glas*, p. 189)

Certainly not a conclusion, for reasons long clear. Nor the place to gather up missing fragments, cut pages, another 'reste' fallen and discarded.

I have tried to avoid totalization, be it that of a narrative of the 'eighteenth century' inserted into some notional 'history of sententiousness', from the Seven Sages to Jacques Lacan,[1] or of some conclusive theoretical statement. No final sententious 'thesis of the thesis'.

But it is still perhaps possible to look proleptically towards further work, to local testings and modifications of the gestures elaborated here: to Balzac seen not in the naturalized tradition of realism, but as pedagogue and legislator, prescribing reality in the guise of description; to Lautréamont's *Poésies*; and especially to Flaubert, who has haunted this discussion with the corrosive dissemination of stupidity.

More generally, the fact that, in Sade, 'sententiousness' has come to be identified with something like 'the philosophical', suggests the need for closer attention to the deconstruction of oppositions such as truth/fiction, philosophy/literature. No term in these unstable pairs would retain any particular privilege, either as a reliable ground for legislation or as a utopia beyond law and power. The work done in and around them would have to move beyond simple pretensions to theorize or historicize. The desire marked here to avoid the trap of answering the question 'What is sententiousness?' is, in this perspective, only preliminary.

209

NOTES

Foreword

1. Peter Brooks, *The Novel of Worldliness: Crébillon, Marivaux, Laclos, Stendhal* (Princeton University Press, 1969); T.M. Kavanagh, 'The Vacant Mirror: A Study of Mimesis Through Jacques le fataliste', *Studies on Voltaire and the Eighteenth Century*, 104 (Banbury, 1973); Andrzej Siemek, 'La Recherche morale et esthétique dans le roman de Crébillon fils', *Studies on Voltaire and the Eighteenth Century*, 200 (Banbury, 1981); Marian Hobson, *The Object of Art: The Theory of Illusion in Eighteenth-Century France* (Cambridge University Press, 1982).
2. Jonathan Culler, *On Deconstruction: Theory and Criticism after Structuralism* (London: Routledge and Kegan Paul, 1983), pp. 7–11.
3. Fredric Jameson, *The Political Unconscious: Narrative as a Socially Symbolic Act* (London: Methuen, 1981), p. 9.
4. This is one of the aims of Jameson's book: for more detailed discussion see my 'Not Yet', *Diacritics*, 12:3 (1982), pp. 23–32. A good earlier example of this ambition is Jean-Joseph Goux, *Freud, Marx: Economie et symbolique* (Paris: Seuil, 1973), pp. 9–52.
5. Jean-François Lyotard, *Le Différend* (Paris: Minuit, 1984).
6. Jean-François Lyotard, *La Condition postmoderne* (Paris: Minuit, 1979).
7. Robert Pring-Mill, 'Sententiousness in *Fuenteovejuna*', *Tulane Drama Review*, 7 (1962), pp. 5–37.

1 Approaching sententiousness

1. Jean Ricardou, 'Le texte en conflit (Problèmes de la belligérance textuelle à partir de *Madame Bovary*)', in *Nouveaux Problèmes du roman* (Paris: Seuil, 1978), pp. 24–88 (p. 24).
2. Gustave Flaubert, *Madame Bovary*, in *Oeuvres complètes*, edited by Bernard Masson, 2 vols. (Paris: Seuil, 1964), I, p. 575. Quoted by Ricardou, p. 29.
3. *Madame Bovary*, I, p. 575. Quoted by Ricardou, p. 25.
4. Ricardou, pp. 24 and 32. The first of these declarations draws explicitly on G. Genette, 'Frontières du récit', in *Figures II* (Paris: Seuil, 1969), pp. 49–69.

210

5. *Madame Bovary*, I, p. 639. Not quoted by Ricardou.
6. See Jean Dubois, *Grammaire structurale du Français: le verbe* (Paris: Larousse, 1967), section 7.2.2.5, p. 185, subtitled 'Le présent: cas non marqué du système'.
7. I borrow this term from Gérard Genette, who borrowed it from film theory. See his *Figures III* (Paris: Seuil, 1972), p. 280: 'dans l'usage courant, la diégèse est l'univers spatio–temporel désigné par le récit'.
8. For this term, see Jacques Derrida, 'Hors Livre', in *La Dissémination* (Paris: Seuil, 1972), p. 13, and *Limited Inc.* (Supplement to *Glyph*, 2, 1977), pp. 23–6.
9. Jean-François Marmontel, 'Essai sur les romans, considérés du côté moral', in *Oeuvres complètes*, 18 vols. (Paris: Costes, 1819), X, pp. 253–318 (p. 315). Marmontel's comments here are by no means exceptional: see for example d'Argens's 'Discours sur les nouvelles', in *Lectures amusantes, ou les délassements de l'esprit*, 2 vols. (La Haye, 1739), I, p. 3, where d'Argens, writing about the texts which he is presenting, affirms, 'il n'y en a point qui en effet ne tende à prouver une vérité pratique, je veux dire une maxime qu'il est souvent avantageux de ne point perdre de vue dans l'occasion'.
10. Diderot, *Essai sur les règnes de Claude et de Néron, et sur les moeurs et les écrits de Sénèque*, edited by Roger Lewinter, 2 vols. (Paris: Union générale d'édition, 1972), I, p. 45.
11. Fénelon, *Les Aventures de Télémaque* (Paris: Garnier-Flammarion, 1968), pp. 269–70.
12. See Roberto Minguelez, 'Le récit historique: légalité et signification', *Semiotica*, 3 (1971), pp. 20–36 (p. 24).
13. Gottlob Frege, 'Über Sinn und Bedeutung', in *Zeitschrift für Philosophie und philosophische Kritik*, 100 (1892), pp. 25–50. English translation in *Translations from the Philosophical Writings of Gottlob Frege*, edited by Max Black and Peter Geach, third edition (Oxford: Blackwell, 1980), pp. 56–78.
14. In Frege's terms, such sentences still have a 'sense' and convey a 'thought'. He gives the example, 'Odysseus was set ashore at Ithaca while sound asleep' (p. 62), and goes on to comment, 'it is a matter of no concern to us whether the name "Odysseus", for instance, has reference, so long as we accept the poem as a work of art' (p. 63). Earlier Frege has recognized the general impossibility of attaining a 'comprehensive knowledge of the reference' (p. 58). I return to some of the problems which this raises for empiricism below, and for historiography, in the following chapter.
15. On the failure to produce a satisfactory statement of the verification principle, see Ian Hacking, *Why Does Language Matter to Philosophy?* (Cambridge University Press, 1975), pp. 93–102. I am grateful to Stephen Bungay for pointing out to me that the principle would in fact be unable to account for its own validity. This is in fact a version of empiricism's basic difficulty with general propositions, which means among other

things that it is unable to give any philosophical foundation to its own basic generalization that all knowledge is derived from experience. See Jean-François Lyotard, *La Phénoménologie* (1954; eighth edition, Paris: PUF, 1976), p. 11, and Jacques Derrida, *L'ecriture et la différence* (Paris: Seuil, 1967; reprinted collection 'Points', 1979), p. 224: '[L'empirisme] au fond n'a jamais commis qu'une faute: la faute philosophique de se présenter comme une philosophie'.

16. The full title of the 1678 edition of La Rochefoucauld's *Maximes* is, significantly, *Réflexions ou Sentences et Maximes morales*; Vauvenargues's maxims are collected under the title *Réflexions et maximes*.

17. This is the point of view taken by, for example, Bette Gross Silverblatt in her book *The Maxims in the Novels of Duclos* (The Hague: Nijhoff, 1972), p. 1.

18. Hyponymy is 'the inclusion of a more specific term in a more general term . . . We will say that *scarlet, crimson, vermilion*, etc., are co-hyponyms of *red* . . . Conversely, we will say that *red* is *superordinate* with respect to its hyponyms'. John Lyons, *Introduction to Theoretical Linguistics* (Cambridge University Press, 1968), pp. 453–5.

19. F. Rodegem, 'Un problème de terminologie: les locutions sentencieuses', *Cahiers de l'Institut de Linguistique de l'Université Catholique de Louvain*, 5 (1972), pp. 677–703.

20. Serge Meleuc, 'Structure de la maxime', *Langages*, 13 (1969), pp. 69–99.

21. As analysed in terms of the 'tableau' by Michel Foucault in *Les mots et les choses* (Paris: Gallimard, 1966), Chapters 3–6. That Foucault's own analysis is in fact caught up in these same presuppositions is argued polemically by Jean Baudrillard in *Oublier Foucault* (Paris: Galilée, 1977), pp. 12–13, and more didactically by Jacques Derrida in 'L'archéologie du frivole', printed as an introduction to Condillac's *Essai sur l'origine des connaissances humaines* (Auvers-sur-Oise: Galilée, 1973), p. 27. Foucault's oblique reply can be read in *L'archéologie du savoir* (Paris: Gallimard, 1969), p. 19, note 1.

22. See Michel Foucault, *L'ordre du discours* (Paris: Gallimard, 1971), pp. 54–5.

23. 'Un segment de discours est dit anaphorique lorsqu'il est nécessaire, pour lui donner une interprétation (même simplement littérale), de se reporter à un autre segment du même discours'. Oswald Ducrot and Tzvetan Todorov, *Dictionnaire encyclopédique des sciences du langage* (Paris: Seuil, 1972), art. 'Relations sémantiques entre phrases'.

24. On the pronominal deictics, see Catherine Kerbrat-Orecchioni, *L'énonciation: de la subjectivité dans le langage* (Paris: Armand Colin, 1980), pp. 34–44, where the *je* and *tu* are described as 'pure' deictics.

25. Kerbrat-Orecchioni, *L'énonciation*, p. 35, distinguishes between the 'cotexte' (the surrounding utterances), and the broader 'contexte' (including the whole pragmatic scene).

26. Philip E. Lewis, *La Rochefoucauld: The Art of Abstraction* (Ithaca and London: Cornell University Press, 1977), p. 164, note 17.

27. See for example Roland Barthes, *Roland Barthes* (Paris: Seuil, 1975), pp. 126–7. I use the term 'paradoxal' in the eighteenth-century sense as defined by Diderot: 'Le paradoxe n'est donc qu'une proposition contraire à l'opinion commune' ('Pages contre un tyran', in *Oeuvres politiques*, edited by Paul Vernière (Paris: Garnier, 1963), pp. 138–49 (p. 140)).

28. Lewis, p. 172. I return to the problem of the *nous* in §6.1 below, and throughout Chapter 3.

29. Vauvenargues, *Réflexions et maximes*, LII, in Vauvenargues, *Introduction à la connaissance de l'esprit humain*, edited by Jean Dagen (Paris: Garnier-Flammarion, 1981), p. 184.

30. Chamfort, *Maximes, pensées, caractères et anecdotes*, edited by Jean Dagen (Paris: Garnier-Flammarion, 1968), No. 53, p. 62.

31. La Rochefoucauld, *Maximes*, edited by Jacques Truchet (Paris: Garnier, 1967), 'Maximes supprimées', No. 27, p. 141.

32. As does Julia Kristeva in 'La Productivité dite texte', in *Sémiotikè: recherches pour une sémanalyse* (Paris: Seuil, 1969), pp. 208–45.

33. Jean Paulhan, 'L'expérience du proverbe', in *Oeuvres complètes*, 5 vols. (Paris: Au Cercle du livre précieux, 1966–70), II, pp. 101–24 (p. 111).

34. Roland Barthes, *Mythologies* (Paris: Seuil, 1957; reprinted collection 'Points', 1970), pp. 242–3. For Barthes the proverb 'reste la parole d'une humanité qui se fait', whereas the maxim 'n'est plus dirigé vers un monde à faire; il doit couvrir un monde déjà fait, enfouir les traces de cette production sous une évidence éternelle'.

35. See for example the model for classifying proverbs proposed by George Milner, 'De l'armature des locutions proverbiales: essai de taxonomie sémantique', *L'Homme*, 9 (1969), pp. 49–70. Most writing on sententious forms has concentrated on questions of internal form: antithesis, rhythm, and so on; see also, for example, Harold E. Pagliaro, 'Paradox in the Aphorisms of La Rochefoucauld and some Representative English Followers', *PMLA*, 79 (1964), pp. 42–50. Lewis provides interesting summaries of a number of such studies, and an appendix summarizing those summaries (pp. 189–91). Given my concern on the one hand to examine sententious propositions in wider segments of text, and on the other to cast doubt on the possibility of providing a generic definition of such forms, I shall not discuss internal formal features here.

36. Discussed by Paul Zumthor in 'L'épiphonème proverbial', *Revue des sciences humaines*, 163 (1976), pp. 313–32 (pp. 315–16).

37. See for example E.I. Gordon, *Sumerian Proverbs* (Philadelphia: The University Museum, University of Pennsylvania, 1959).

38. This distancing with respect to the proverb can also be found in texts of rhetoric; see Jean-Baptiste-Louis Crévier, *Rhétorique française*, 2 vols. (Paris, 1765), I, p. 81: 'Les proverbes ne sont guères employés par l'Orateur, parce qu'étant le langage du peuple, ils n'ont pas de dignité mais en récompense ils ont souvent un grand sens; & le style familier les admet utilement'. See too II, p. 98. This distancing can occasionally be

taken with respect to sententiousness in general, as in Le Gras's *Réthorique (sic) françoise, ou les préceptes de l'ancienne et vraye éloquence* (Paris, 1671), p. 223: 'On peut encore mettre les Sentences au nombre des choses qui forment l'Eloquence, & la rendent admirable, mais comme chacun sait ce que c'est, & que mesme les Paysans & les ignorans en usent le plus, on n'a pas crû en devoir parler'. See also Méré's comments in 'De la conversation' (1677), in *Oeuvres*, edited by Ch.-H. Boudhors, 3 vols. (Paris: Fernand Roches, 1930), II, pp. 99–132 (p. 120), where however *sentences* are to be avoided for their oracular rather than their popular character. On the other hand, if Furetière's dictionary clearly valorizes the 'Sentence', it is ambivalent in its entry 'Proverbe', and a certain ambivalence can also be detected in statements by Bouhours (*La Manière de bien penser dans les ouvrages de l'esprit* (Paris, 1687), p. 59): 'les sentences sont les proverbes des honnestes gens, comme les proverbes sont les sentences du peuple' – see too Montesquieu, 'Mes Pensées', in *Oeuvres complètes*, edited by Daniel Oster (Paris: Seuil, 1964), No. 898, p. 978.

39. Jacob in fact utters relatively few proverbs, although some can indeed be found, such as 'Qui vit bien ne craint rien', and 'Abondance de vivres ne nuit point': *Le Paysan parvenu*, edited by F. Deloffre (Paris: Garnier, 1969), pp. 119 and 164 respectively.

40. 'The naïve occurs if someone completely disregards an inhibition because it is not present in him – if, therefore, he appears to overcome it without any effort.' Sigmund Freud, *Jokes and Their Relation to the Unconscious*, translated and edited by James Strachey, The Pelican Freud Library, Vol. 6 (Harmondsworth: Penguin Books, 1976), p. 240. Freud goes on to postulate the possibility of 'misleading naïvety' used to gain a liberty which would be denied by the recognition of inhibition: it is this that Jacob exploits.

41. See Jean-François Lyotard, *La Condition postmoderne* (Paris: Minuit, 1979), p. 41: 'Qu'on interroge la forme des dictons, des proverbes, des maximes qui sont comme de petits éclats de récits possibles ou les matrices de récits anciens et qui continuent encore à circuler à certains étages de l'édifice social contemporain . . .'

42. And is in fact taken here from Heidegger's 'Modern Science, Metaphysics, and Mathematics', translated by W.B. Barton, Jr., and Vera Deutsch, in *Martin Heidegger: Basic Writings*, edited by David Farrell Krell (London: Routledge & Kegan Paul, 1978), pp. 243–82 (p. 256).

43. See Bruno Latour and Paolo Fabbri, 'Rhétorique de la science', *Actes de la recherche en sciences sociales*, 13 (1977), pp. 81–95, and, for some problems involved in the claim that science is a form of rhetoric, Jean-François Lyotard, *Le Différend* (Paris: Minuit, 1984), §29, p. 35.

44. These terms are used by Peter L. Berger and Thomas Luckmann, *The Social Construction of Reality* (Harmondsworth: Penguin Books, 1971), especially pp. 130–4.

45. Lyotard, *La Condition postmoderne*, p. 23, notes 34 and 35.

46. By this I mean simply that in the eighteenth century a *maxime* is as much a principle according to which one acts as something one says: see, for example, Condillac's posthumous *Dictionnaire de synonymes*: '*Principe* et *maxime*. Le premier est plus relatif à la théorie, et le second l'est plus à la pratique. Ce qui est un *principe*, quand on raisonne sur la morale, devient une *maxime* quand il faut agir'. It is this sense which Kant will radicalize in the Categorical Imperative, placing the maxim between the action and the moral Law.

47. See notes 17, 31 and 32 above.

48. It could of course be suggested that the fact that this structure seems not to work here is a reason for this particular maxim's apparent banality, but this would perhaps be to move prematurely from description to evaluation.

49. In his introduction to his edition of La Rochefoucauld's *Maximes*, Jacques Truchet suggests that the abundance of definitions is a 'trait d'époque' (p. xlv); Meleuc, p. 77, suggests that this simply shows that the maxim and the dictionary definition share certain constraints, and this is indeed the essential point. A definition, like a sententious proposition, tends to rigidify and *arrest* meaning: De Jaucourt's article 'Sentence' in the *Encyclopédie* describes *sentences* as 'autant d'arrêts en fait de moeurs'. See also Rica in Letter 73 of the *Lettres Persanes*: 'J'ai ouï parler d'une espèce de tribunal qu'on appelle *l'Académie Française*. Il n'y en a point de moins respecté dans le monde: car on dit qu'aussitôt qu'il a décidé le Peuple casse ses arrêts et lui impose des lois qu'il est obligé de suivre'. A modern account of lexicography emphasizes the same feature of the definition, and says of the dictionary: 'Ses énoncés ont force de loi; ses définitions forment un texte juridique . . . Le lexicographe . . . est un *législateur* par procuration' (J. and C. Dubois, *Introduction à la lexicographie: le dictionnaire* (Paris: Larousse, 1971), p. 50). This legal perspective (implied too in the ambiguity of the term 'sentence') is, as I shall argue, of great importance: to anticipate, the fact that sententious propositions are *texts* will mean that that attempt to arrest meaning is doomed to fail – but it will take the novelistic practice of a Sade to dramatize that failure.

50. Similar problems about the identity of the terms involved would be posed by, for example, Lord Chesterfield's maxim, 'Modesty is the only sure bait when you angle for praise', and in general by aphorisms of Oscar Wilde.

51. For a discussion of the problems produced by this temptation, see Jonathan Culler, 'Paradox and the Language of Morals in La Rochefoucauld', *MLR*, 68 (1973), pp. 28–39.

52. The need for such a shift is argued by Henri Meschonnic in 'Les Proverbes, actes de discours', *Revue des sciences humaines*, 163 (1976), pp. 418–30. For a brief summary of what the 'new' linguistics involves, see Kerbrat-Orecchioni, *L'Enonciation*, pp. 5–10.

53. Pascal, *Pensées*, edited by Louis Lafuma (Paris: Seuil, 1962), p. 60.

54. Roland Barthes, 'La Rochefoucauld: "Réflexions ou Sentences et Maximes"', in *Le Degré zéro de l'écriture, suivi de Nouveaux Essais critiques* (Paris: Seuil, 1972), pp. 69–88.

55. This drive to construct indexes as a means of reconstituting wholes is well expressed by Jean Dagen in his 'Note liminaire' to his edition of Vauvenargues: 'L'index nous paraît, en effet, indispensable au lecteur d'une oeuvre toute composée de fragments' (p. 54).

56. *NRF*, 28 (1966), pp. 16–34 and pp. 211–29.

57. For an opposition between maxim and aphorism along similar lines, see Gilles Deleuze and Félix Guattari, *Capitalisme et schizophrénie: mille plateaux* (Paris: Minuit, 1980), p. 467.

58. It is this second edition (1747), as edited by Dagen, which I quote throughout.

59. Pascal, *Pensées*, 540: the original text in fact reads, 'Toutes les bonnes maximes sont dans le monde; on ne manque qu'à les appliquer'.

60. The quotation is from Vauvenargues, ed. cit. p. 59, my emphasis. For the posthumous examples, see the fragment 'Sur la morale et la physique', p. 270, and especially the 'Plan d'un livre de philosophie', p. 281: 'Mais, comme ils (i.e. 'la plupart des grands hommes qui ont écrit dans les derniers temps') n'ont traité que des sujets particuliers, et qu'ils n'ont pas pris soin de faire un corps de leurs principes, il n'est pas aisé de saisir leur vues éparses, et de les rapprocher pour former un système . . . C'est à nous à prendre des vues générales, et à former un esprit vaste de tant d'esprits particuliers, mais excellents, qui nous ont ouvert l'entrée de toutes les sciences . . . il me paraît que c'est un grand défaut dans les ouvrages de réflexion de ne pas faire un tout, car l'esprit saisit avec peine ce qui n'est point un'.

61. The verb 'arrêter' returns (see note 49 above), and might prompt a rewriting of Vauvenargues's problem as 'un travail si long ne peut *s*'arrêter', retaining both the reflexive and passive values of the *se*.

62. Vauvenargues, p. 175. See Maxim 111, p. 193: 'Peu de maximes sont vraies à tous égards'.

63. Chamfort, *Pensées Morales*, No. 293, p. 119.

64. This type of intrusion is extremely common in Chamfort, even in the so-called 'Maximes Générales': see also Nos. 19, 24, 32, 33 etc. Such examples would evidently be excluded by a model such as Meleuc's, but they are none the less placed in a text labelled 'maximes' – the difference between literary and discursive genre here becomes conflictual.

65. As in No. 33, for example. In his introduction to the edition, Jean Dagen attempts to link such forms with history or its absence: 'Depuis plus d'un siècle la France n'a pas d'histoire. Vie politique et vie sociale se résolvent en anecdotes. Cent cinquante ans de la vie d'un pays sont pulvérisés en une multitude de petits faits' (p. 24). Such a view depends on an implied opposition between this type of non-history and a 'real' (narrative) history considered to be more normal. It seems more profitable to

attempt to situate the *devenir-anecdote* of the maxim within a more philosophical problematic.

66. Notably that of Nietzsche. This reference can be linked to the opposition between the prudence of eagles and that of moles (No. 38, pp. 59–60), the slightly surprising characterization of Rousseau as an eagle (No. 284, p. 114), and the desire to be an 'Achille *sans talon*' (No. 97, p. 72).

67. See, for example, Condillac's critique of Descartes's method in the *Essai sur l'origine des connaissances humaines*, especially II, §35, which is explicitly concerned with the placing of definitions at the beginning (Descartes) or the end (Condillac) of the methodical narrative. See also, with reference to Locke, W.S. Howell, *Eighteenth-Century British Logic and Rhetoric* (Princeton University Press, 1971), pp. 282–3.

68. In Voltaire, *Romans et contes*, edited by Henri Bénac (Paris: Garnier, 1960), p. 81. Further page references to Voltaire's *Contes* will be to this edition and will be incorporated in the text.

69. See Roland Barthes, 'Introduction à l'analyse structurale du récit', in *Poétique du récit*, edited by Gérard Genette and Tzvetan Todorov (Paris: Seuil, 1977), pp. 8–57 (p. 22): 'Tout laisse à penser, en effet, que le ressort de l'activité narrative est la confusion même de la consécution et de la conséquence, ce qui vient *après* étant lu dans le récit comme *causé par*'. This paralogism was denounced by Aristotle: see the *Poetics* 1452a and the *Sophistici Elenchi* 167b.

70. Especially of course in Voltaire's poem on the event and in Rousseau's reply: 'Lettre à Voltaire', in *Oeuvres complètes*, edited by Bernard Gagnebin and Marcel Raymond, 4 vols. published to date (Paris: Gallimard, 1959–), IV, pp. 1057–75, and especially p. 1068, where Rousseau defends the possibility of a Providential narrative controlled not by the 'optimistic' maxim 'Tout est bien', but by a modified version of it; 'Le tout est bien', or 'Tout est bien pour le tout'.

71. Voltaire, pp. 85–6. See Arthur O. Lovejoy, *The Great Chain of Being* (Harvard University Press, 1950), Chapter 7.

72. See for example Locke, I, II, 21. These numbers designate book, chapter, and paragraph respectively, and refer to the Nidditch edition of Locke's *Essay* (Oxford: Clarendon Press, 1975). Condillac's *Dictionnaire des synonymes* is again helpful: drawing together the terms 'Principe', 'Maxime', 'Axiome', 'Sentence', 'Proverbe', and 'Aphorisme', Condillac comments, 'L'idée commune à tous ces mots est celle d'un fait ou une observation qu'on généralise, et sous laquelle on renferme en un sistême plusieurs vérités; le sistême se forme en expliquant les idées qui ont moins de généralité, par celles qui en ont davantage, en sorte qu'elles s'expliquent toutes médiatement ou immédiatement par un même *principe*. Je ne connois point de premier *principe*, je n'en connois point qui mène à aucune connaissance. Les meilleurs ne sont que l'expression abrégée des découvertes que nous avons faites.'

73. Locke, IV, V, 10: 'I shall begin with general Propositions, as those which

most employ our Thoughts, and exercise our Contemplation. *General Truths* are most looked after by the Mind, as those that most enlarge our Knowledge; and by their comprehensiveness, satisfying us at once of many particulars, enlarge our view, and shorten our way to knowledge'.

74. See I, I, 20 and IV, VII, 4.

75. Locke, III, III, 1–4. See also Condillac, *Essai*, II, I, §§102–3; Michel Foucault, *Les mots et les choses*, p. 112; Paul de Man, *Allegories of Reading* (Yale University Press, 1979), p. 152; Borges's short story *Funes el memorioso*, in *Ficciones* (Buenos Aires: Emecé Editores, 1956), pp. 117–27, and especially p. 125.

76. Du Marsais defines abstraction as 'le point de réunion, selon lequel notre esprit apperçoit que certains objets conviennent entre eux' ('Logique', in *Oeuvres*, 7 vols. (Paris, 1797), V, p. 314), but insists that the naming of abstract ideas takes place by analogy with the naming of 'les objets des idées qui nous représentent des êtres réels' (*Encyclopédie*, art. 'Article', in *Oeuvres*, IV, p. 197), which naming is necessarily prior: 'Les noms des objets réels sont les premiers noms' (*Encyclopédie*, art. 'Abstraction', in *Oeuvres*, IV, p. 38). See Condillac, *Essai*, II, I, §102.

77. See Arnauld and Nicole, *La logique ou l'art de penser*, edited by Louis Marin (Paris: Flammarion, 1970), pp. 150–5. This type of reduction seems to go back to Peter of Spain: see G.A. Padley, *Grammatical Theory in Western Europe, 1500–1750: The Latin Tradition* (Cambridge University Press, 1976), p. 45, note 2, and p. 105 for some later examples of the same procedure. But whereas for the Scholastics this primacy of the verb 'to be' is linked to the predication of being, in the Port-Royal text it is linked to the act of *affirmation*. This position is inherited by Condillac (*Essai*, I, II, §69) and Du Marsais (*Encyclopédie*, art. 'Construction', in *Oeuvres*, V, pp. 42–3, and 'Logique', in *Oeuvres*, V, p. 317). Later grammarians such as Beauzée, however (Du Marsais's successor at the *Encyclopédie*), make of the *est* the sign of the posited existence of the object: see André Robinet, *Le Langage à l'âge classique* (Paris: Klincksieck, 1978), pp. 68–72.

78. See especially in the *Profession de foi du Vicaire Savoyard*, where Rousseau insists on the activity of the mind in the work of putting sensations together and comparing them, but immediately links that activity more to the danger of error than to the promise of truth: 'Je sais seulement que la vérité est dans les choses et non pas dans mon esprit qui les juge, et que moins je mets du mien dans les jugemens que j'en porte, plus je suis sûr d'approcher de la vérité; ainsi ma règle de me livrer au sentiment plus qu'à la raison est confirmée par la raison même', *Oeuvres complètes*, IV, p. 573.

79. See Emile Benveniste, 'La Phrase nominale', in *Problèmes de linguistique générale*, 2 vols. (Paris: Gallimard, 1966–74), pp. 151–67, and here p. 154: 'Au sein de l'énoncé assertif, la fonction verbale est double: fonction cohésive, qui est d'organiser en une structure complète les éléments de l'énoncé; fonction assertive, consistant à doter l'énoncé d'un prédicat de

réalité . . . A la relation grammaticale qui unit les membres de l'énoncé s'ajoute implicitement un "cela *est!*" qui relie l'agencement linguistique au système de la réalité. Le contenu de l'énoncé est donné comme conforme à l'ordre des choses.' In a later essay, however, Benveniste wants to make a radical separation between these two functions, and allow the 'assertive' (now described as 'lexical') function an autonomy with respect to the 'cohesive' (now 'copulative') function ('"Etre" et "avoir" dans leurs fonctions linguistiques', in *Problèmes*, pp. 187–207). And in the earlier essay, Benveniste seems to want to exclude the verb from what he defines as 'phrases nominales' in which no verbal form is present in surface structure, but which, when translated, tend to yield sententious propositions (see pp. 161–2 for Benveniste's examples from Pindar and his recognition of the sententious nature of such forms). These avatars of the verb 'to be' raise philosophical questions which there is evidently no question of my discussing here: see on Benveniste's confusions Jacques Derrida's essay, 'Le supplément de copule: la philosophie devant la linguistique', in *Marges* (Paris: Minuit, 1972), pp. 209–46.

80. See Condillac, *Essai*, I, IV, §§5, 6, 9 and 14, for representative denunciations of this tendency.

81. In the *Discours sur l'inégalité*, Rousseau recognizes this problem: 'les idées générales ne peuvent s'introduire dans l'Esprit qu'à l'aide des mots, et l'entendement ne les saisit que par des propositions' (*Oeuvres complètes*, III, p. 149). On the necessary impropriety even of the so-called 'proper' name, see Jacques Derrida, *De la grammatologie* (Paris: Minuit, 1967), p. 159.

82. For the difficulties which this raises for the Port-Royal logicians, see Louis Marin, *La Critique du discours: sur la 'Logique de Port-Royal' et les 'Pensées' de Pascal* (Paris: Minuit, 1975), pp. 277–9. I discuss this in more detail with reference to Locke in 'The Perfect Cheat: Locke and Empiricism's Rhetoric', forthcoming in the proceedings of the 1984 Leeds conference on *The Literal and the Figural*.

83. In the *Essai*, I, IV, §§9–10, Condillac recognizes the excess of signs over ideas, and in general stresses the importance of signs to thought and its progress (see I, II, §§35–46). In the first edition of the *Essai*, Condillac went so far as to say that 'les progrès de l'esprit humain dépendent entièrement de l'adresse avec lacquelle nous nous servons du langage' (Ed. cit., note to I, II, §107), but later said, in a letter of 1752, that he had 'trop donné aux signes' (Quoted by Derrida in *L'archéologie du frivole*, p. 62). But in the later *Grammaire* (1775), Condillac seems to suggest that the self-identity of the idea, which should precede its sign in classical theories, in fact depends on language: 'C'est donc à l'usage des mots que vous devez le pouvoir de considérer vos idées chacune en elle-même, et de les comparer les unes avec les autres pour en découvrir les rapports' (in *Oeuvres philosophiques*, edited by Georges Le Roy, 3 vols. (Paris: PUF, 1948–50), I, p. 437).

84. See also Condillac, *Essai*, I, IV, §7.

85. 'And we cannot doubt, but Law-makers have often made Laws about Species of Actions, which were only the Creatures of their own Understanding; Beings that had no other existence, but in their own Minds' (III, V, 5). See Condillac, *Essai*, I, IV, §8. On Locke's choice of examples, see too Paul de Man, 'The Epistemology of Metaphor', *Critical Inquiry*, 5 (1978–9), pp. 13–30.

86. G.W. Leibniz, *Nouveaux Essais sur l'entendement humain* (1765), edited by Jacques Brunschwig (Paris: Garnier-Flammarion, 1966); see on this point especially p. 259. For a general discussion of the differences between Locke and Leibniz on the question of language (albeit one which mobilizes an immense erudition to prove the relatively simple point that whereas Locke thought language was the result of convention, Leibniz thought it could be rooted in nature), see Hans Aarsleff, 'Leibniz on Locke on Language', *American Philosophical Quarterly*, 1 (1964), 165–88.

87. See especially *Essay*, III, II, 6–7. Of course Locke is not alone in this: see also, for example, the Port-Royal *Logique*, p. 60, and Marin's comments in *La Critique du discours*, pp. 43–51.

88. For Locke on parrots, see *Essay* II, XXII, 8. See also d'Alembert's 'Discours préliminaire' to the *Encyclopédie* (Paris: Gonthier, 1965), pp. 80–81, for a commonplace criticism of the Scholastics for getting this priority wrong. But it would seem that, in the case of mixed modes at least, the 'agreement with things', which is a necessary condition for the 'real truth', is simply inoperative.

89. Briefly, it could I think be argued that the priority of sensation over reflection in Locke is illusory in his own terms, and that a prior reflection is necessary to found a space for sensation to take place. For Condillac (*Essai*, I, III, §16), only reflection produces ideas (as opposed to perceptions, a sort of undifferentiated flux common to man and animals) and therefore thought. With duly careful mediations, it would be possible to use here the analyses of Husserl proposed by Jacques Derrida in *La Voix et le phénomène* (Paris: PUF, 1967), leading to the assertion that 'la perception n'existe pas' (p. 49, n. 1), at least not in the sense of a pure originary presentation of an idea to the mind. See also Derrida's 'Freud et la scène de l'écriture', in *L'ecriture et la différence* (Paris: Seuil, 1967; reprinted collection 'Points', 1970), pp. 293–340, especially p. 334. A premonition of this problem in the eighteenth century can be found in Diderot's *Entretien entre Diderot et d'Alembert* (in *Oeuvres philosophiques*, edited by Paul Vernière (Paris: Garnier, 1964), pp. 257–84 (p. 271)), where 'd'Alembert' recognizes the difficulty of thinking at all in terms of the model of the individual idea present(ed) to the mind in the unity of an instant. See also the *Lettre sur les sourds et muets*, edited by Paul Hugo Meyer, *Diderot Studies*, 7 (1965), pp. 60–62.

90. Jonathan Swift, *Gulliver's Travels*, edited by Peter Dixon and John Chalker (Harmondsworth: Penguin Books, 1967), p. 250. See also Vico's

New Science (1747), translated by T.G. Bergin and M.H. Fisch (Ithaca and London: Cornell University Press, 1968), §431.

91. Leibniz, p. 252.
92. *Logique*, pp. 120–35.
93. Marin, pp. 239–58. The project for an ideal language is associated with the names of Mersenne, Leibniz, and Wilkins. See Derrida, *De la grammatologie*, pp. 111–21.
94. The two reasons given for this respect are 1) the difficulty of forgetting the idea traditionally attached to a given word, and 2) the danger of falling into the esotericism of the 'Chymistes', said to change the names of things for a dubious pleasure, and 'sans aucune utilité' (p. 127).
95. Which would suggest that Locke is caught up somewhere between a nominalist and a realist position.
96. *La Condition postmoderne*, p. 23. This is only 'something like' an event, for reasons suggested by Derrida (*La Voix et le phénomène*, p. 55).
97. See my 'Réappropriations', *Poétique*, 48 (1981), pp. 495–512.
98. For the association of the rhetorical and the literary, see Paul de Man, *Allegories of Reading*, p. 131.
99. See Philip E. Lewis, 'La Rochefoucauld: The Rationality of Play', *Yale French Studies*, 41 (1968), pp. 133–47, and, incorporating part of this article, *La Rochefoucauld*, pp. 103–40.
100. See Michel Charles, *Rhétorique de la lecture* (Paris: Seuil, 1977), who describes the orator as someone who 'parle à la place de celui qui écoute' (p. 167), and who becomes an 'analyste du discours de l'autre' (p. 181).
101. Bernard Lamy, *La Rhétorique ou l'art de parler*, fourth edition (Paris, 1701), p. 178. The first edition of Lamy's work appeared in 1675 under the title *De l'Art de parler*, and was extensively enlarged and modified in the editions of 1676, 1688, and 1701. Beware of a false 'fourth edition' (Amsterdam, 1699), which appears to be the same as the third edition and which unfortunately reappears in the 'Sussex Reprint' series in 1969. For more bibliographical details, see Geneviève Rodis-Lewis, 'Un Théoricien du langage au XVIIe siècle: Bernard Lamy', *Le Français moderne*, 36 (1968), pp. 19–50. I quote throughout from the 1701 edition, and incorporate page references into the text.
102. As has been done by Michel Pierssens, in 'Fonction et champ de la maxime', *Sub-stance*, 1 (1971), pp. 1–9 (p. 2): 'La rhétorique paraît avoir négligé la maxime. Ou plutôt, elle ne l'a pas *vue* . . . Non seulement la maxime n'a pas été vue, mais il ne se pouvait pas qu'on la voie, il fallait qu'elle échappe au regard, car en son lieu secret, c'est l'idéologie qui se fonde et la littérature qui se construit.' Pierssens's article has the merit of stressing the importance of sententiousness, but unfortunately the blindness he ascribes to rhetoric in this respect is nonsense.
103. Aristotle, *Rhetorica*, translated by W. Rhys Roberts, in *The Works of Aristotle*, edited by W.D. Ross, 12 vols. (Oxford: Clarendon Press, 1908–52), XI, 1393a. I shall quote from this translation and give paragraph numbers in the text.

221

104. See the *Institutio Oratoria*, V, XIV, 24.
105. That Aristotle was aware of such a distinction is shown by the *De Interpretatione*, 17a.
106. Locke (*Essay*, IV, VII, 20), refers to 'Mistake and Errour, which these Maxims . . . do by their Authority confirm and rivet'.
107. This advice becomes a rhetorical commonplace: see for example Quintilian VII, V, 8; René Bary, *La Rhétorique françoise*, nouvelle édition (Paris, 1659), p. 29; B. Gibert, *La Rhétorique ou les règles de l'éloquence* (Paris, 1730), p. 331.
108. This raises the whole problem of *auctoritas* and quotation: Crévier, for example, includes 'les maximes reçues dans la société' among the 'lieux communs extrinsèques' or 'autorités' (*Rhétorique françoise*, 2 vols. (Paris, 1765), I, p. 80). For all of this from the point of view of quotation, see Compagnon, *La Seconde Main, ou le travail de la citation* (Paris: Seuil, 1979), pp. 127–46.
109. As shown most clearly in the *Dictionnaire des idées reçues* and *Bouvard et Pécuchet*. See also Jonathan Culler, *Flaubert: The Uses of Uncertainty* (London: Paul Elek, 1974), pp. 157–85, and Leslie Hill, 'Flaubert and the Rhetoric of Stupidity', *Critical Inquiry*, 3 (1976), pp. 333–44.
110. As in the famous maxim: 'Il y a à parier que toute idée publique, toute convention reçue, est une sottise, car elle a convenu au plus grand nombre' (No. 130, p. 78): in the *Dictionnaire des idées reçues* this maxim appears as an epigraph, but juxtaposed with '"Vox populi, vox Dei"', Sagesse des nations'. Flaubertian stupidity resides in the juxtaposition in which neither statement has any privilege. See Compagnon, *La Seconde Main*, pp. 337–9, and Vincent Descombes, *L'inconscient malgré lui* (Paris: Minuit, 1977), p. 120.
111. 'What is *invraisemblance* in a fiction is *vrai* in reality and thus, by conversion, becomes *vraisemblance* in fiction' (Marian Hobson, *The Object of Art: The Theory of Illusion in Eighteenth-Century France* (Cambridge University Press, 1982), p. 93).
112. As in Jules Lemaître's 'Les pensées et les maximes sont un genre épuisé et un genre futile' (from *Les Contemporains*, 2e série). The fact that I found this quotation in a dictionary of maxims stresses the paradox.
113. On this progressive reduction of the field of rhetoric, usually associated with the name of Ramus, see Pierre Kuentz, 'Le "rhétorique" ou la mise à l'écart', *Communications*, 16 (1970), pp. 143–57.
114. Quintilian, *Institutio Oratoria*, translated by H.E. Butler, 4 vols. (London: Heinemann, 1920–22), VIII, V, §§25–30, 32, 34.
115. This desire for there to be an excess of things over words can be linked, in Lamy, to a drive to reduce expression to a *single* word; see p. 10: 'c'est une grande faute que de dire plusieurs paroles lorsqu'une suffit', and especially p. 61: 'On voudroit, s'il étoit possible, s'exprimer en un seul mot'.
116. See my article 'Réappropriations', p. 504, and Crévier, II, p. 52: 'Excluons donc de l'Ornement dont nous parlons le retour de l'Orateur

vers soi-même, qui doit paroître, non un avantage, mais un piège, ou un écueil'.

117. See also Crévier, II, p. 74: figures 'ne sont belles & louables dans le discours qu'autant qu'elles sont naturelles'.

118. The painting metaphor in Quintilian would be more complicated, insofar as it involves a technical activity which is yet subordinated to the imitation of nature.

119. This metaphor has also of course been extensively exploited in modern criticism, and notably by Roland Barthes: see his *S/Z* (Paris: Seuil, 1970; reprinted collection 'Points', 1976), pp. 27–8 and 165–6, and *Le Plaisir du texte* (Paris: Seuil, 1973), p. 100.

120. The logic of this catastrophic stifling is formulated sententiously near the beginning of Lamy's text: 'L'abondance cause toujours la stérilité' (p. 6).

121. The sentence is from Petronius, and appears in Eumolpus's discourse on the epic poem in Chapter 118 of the *Satyricon*.

122. Le Bossu, *Traité du poème épique*, 2 vols. (Paris, 1675), pp. 218–19; Corbinelli, *Les Anciens Historiens Latins réduits en maximes: premier volume, Tite Live* (Paris, 1694), in the unpaginated *avertissement* (attributed to Bouhours).

123. For both sides of this operation of appropriation, see 'Réappropriations', passim.

124. See Crévier, II, p. 250, for the insertion of *sentences* 'dans le fil de la narration'.

125. The *sentence* both comes to fill up a lack in the discourse, and appears to be excessive with respect to that discourse. See *De la grammatologie*, p. 208: 'Le supplément s'ajoute, il est un surplus, une plénitude enrichissant une autre plénitude, le *comble* de la présence . . . Mais le supplément supplée. Il ne s'ajoute que pour remplacer. Il intervient ou s'insinue *à-la-place-de*; s'il comble, c'est comme on comble un vide'. To be linked also to Derrida's work on the frame, notably in 'Parergon', in *La Vérité en peinture* (Paris: Flammarion, 1978), pp. 19–168.

126. Crévier, II, p. 241. See also Bary, pp. 352–3.

127. As in Flaubert's famous and conclusively stupid *sentence* 'la bêtise consiste à vouloir conclure' (Letter to Louis Bouilhet, 4 September 1850).

128. Zumthor, art. cit., p. 320.

129. See for example, in *Les Caractères*, No. 81 in the Chapter entitled 'Des Femmes'.

130. Robert Chasles, *Les Illustres Françoises*, edited by Frédéric Deloffre, 2 vols. (Paris: Les Belles Lettres, 1959), I, pp. lix–lx.

131. On the status of the preface, see Jacques Derrida, 'Hors Livre', loc. cit.

132. Chasles, p. lix.

133. D'Aubignac, *La Pratique du théâtre* (Genève: Slatkine Reprints, 1971). I shall give page references to this edition in the text.

134. I am deliberately avoiding the problem of whether there is an essential

difference between sententiousness in verse texts and those in prose, for it may be that sententiousness as a question is logically prior to any such distinction – certain passages of Hegel's *Aesthetics* could be invoked in support of this argument. See for example Part III, Section III, Chapter 3, A, 2, a, where Hegel quotes some (in fact non-sententious) sentences from the Bible, and says that they, along with the 'Golden Verses' of Pythagoras, the Book of Proverbs, and the 'wisdom of Solomon' are 'pregnant sentences which precede, as it were, the difference between prose and poetry': they are poetic in that they are 'enclosed wholes', but not poetic in that they do not involve a 'development' (G.W.F. Hegel, *Aesthetics: Lectures on Fine Art*, 2 vols., translated by T.M. Knox, 2 vols. (Oxford: Clarendon Press, 1975), II, pp. 980–1). This might be a general problem with a form I would provisionally call the 'one-liner'. That Le Bossu can be and was read in terms of a general theory of narrative is suggested by a remark in *Jacques le fataliste*: after the Hôtesse has told the story of Mme de la Pommeraye, the Maître says that she has 'péché contre les règles d'Aristote, d'Horace, de Vida et de Le Bossu'. Diderot, *Oeuvres romanesques*, edited by Henri Bénac (Paris: Garnier, 1962), p. 649.

135. Schwartz and Olsen's statistical analysis in *The Sententiae in the Dramas of Corneille* (Stanford University Press, 1939) shows that Seneca himself averaged 82.5 *sententiae* per tragedy, Jodelle 310, Garnier 201, and Corneille 25.5. I shall suggest later that sententiousness cannot in principle be counted in this way.

136. This is, for example, a constant reference in Bouhours's *La Manière de bien penser dans les ouvrages de l'esprit* (Paris, 1687), where the series Seneca, Tasso is opposed to the series Cicero, Virgil, according to oppositions of the type 'éclat/solidité', 'clinquant/or', and so on; see for explicit statements of this pp. 4 and 392. The characterization of the Italians as producing 'clinquant' is best known from Boileau, *Satire IX*, lines 173–6.

137. The first sense of *sententia* is simply that of 'sentiments' or 'pensées'.

138. *Figures III* (Paris: Seuil, 1972), p. 75.

139. See note 14 above.

140. Le Bossu, p. 51. A contemporary hand has written in the margin of the Bibliothèque Nationale copy of Le Bossu's text: 'Cela est burlesque'.

141. A. Kibédi Varga's discussion of Le Bossu in 'L'invention de la fable', *Poétique*, 25 (1976), pp. 107–15, is vitiated by an unproblematized use of the notions of 'form' and 'content'.

142. Octave Uzanne, in *Petits Conteurs du XVIIIe siècle* (Paris, 1879), Vol. IV, p. lxvii, quoted in Margot Kruse, *Die Maxime in der französischen Literatur: Studien zum Werk La Rochefoucaulds und seiner Nachfolger* (Hamburg: De Gruyter, 1960), p. 163.

143. Aldous Huxley, 'Crébillon the Younger', in *The Olive Tree and Other Essays* (London: Chatto & Windus, 1936), pp. 135–49 (p. 145).

144. See C. de Méry, *Histoire générale des proverbes, adages, sentences,*

apophthegmes, 3 vols. (Paris: Delongchamps, 1828), I, p. 2: '[les proverbes] sont des vérités quintessenciées'; Jean Starobinski, 'Introduction' to an edition of La Rochefoucauld (Paris: UGE, 1964), p. 29: 'Les sentences fixent l'état final d'une expérience: nous trouvons une pensée à son point d'achèvement et qui se formule irrévocablement sous la forme brève de l'aphorisme. L'expérience a eu lieu; elle est devenue langage; la vie est désormais cette comédie révolue dont la quintessence est saisie de loin par un coup d'oeil définitif'; the 'avertissement' (attributed to Bouhours) to Corbinelli's 'reduction' of Livy (see above, note 122): 'il a mis ces passages à l'alambic'.

145. Louis Cario et Charles Régismanet, *La Pensée française; anthologie des auteurs de maximes du XVIe siècle à nos jours* (Paris, 1921), p. 28. It may be possible to generalize this particular phantasy (which is perhaps inscribed into the derivation of the term 'maxim' from 'maxima sententia'): see Gaston Bachelard, *La Psychanalyse du feu* (Paris: Gallimard, 1949; re-edited collection 'Idées', 1966), pp. 84 and 139. See also Gita May, 'Les Pensées détachées sur la peinture de Diderot et la tradition classique de la "maxime" et de la "pensée"', *RHLF*, 70 (1970), pp. 45–63, who refers on p. 46 to 'la tendance qu'a Diderot à recourir à la maxime, procédé qui permet . . . d'exprimer beaucoup de choses en peu de mots . . .'

146. See also the discussion of these metaphors in Lewis, *La Rochefoucauld*, pp. 25–6.

147. Logan Pearsall Smith, *A Treasury of English Aphorisms* (London: Constable, 1928), pp. 15, 3, and 14 respectively.

148. See S. Freud, 'Character and Anal Eroticism' (1908), in *On Sexuality*, Vol. 7 of the *Pelican Freud Library*, translated and edited by Angela Richards (Harmondsworth: Penguin Books, 1977), pp. 205–15, and especially 'On Transformations of Instinct as Exemplified in Anal Eroticism' (1917), Ibid., pp. 293–302. In view of the following chapter, it is interesting to note that pedantry is one of the 'qualities' linked by Freud to 'anal-erotic sources'. The use of psychoanalysis here is less an attempt to discover the 'truth' about anthologizing, than a suggestion of a possible intertext.

149. See too Barthes's 'La Rochefoucauld', pp. 77–9.

150. Quoted by Emilien Cazès, *Pensées et maximes pour la pratique de la vie* (Paris: Delagrave, no date [1902]), p. 7. What I imagine is the 'same' passage from Diderot is quoted as an epigraph to another anthology, as 'Les pensées morales sont des clous d'airain qui s'enfoncent dans l'âme et qu'on n'en arrache point', V. Martel, *Une Bonne Pensée par jour: receuil des pensées et maximes morales, à l'usage des familles et des écoles de tous les degrés* (Paris: Garnier, no date (1895)). I have been unable to locate the 'original' version of this quotation in Diderot.

151. *Dictionnaire des pensées et maximes* (Paris: Seghers, 1963), p. 8.

152. *L'esprit de Fontenelle ou recueil de pensées tirées de ses ouvrages* (La Haye, 1753), p. xxvi.

153. *Esprit, maximes et principes de Fontenelle de l'Académie Française* (Paris, 1788), p. i; see pp. ii–iii: 'Il faut rassembler les vérités ésparses, les réunir, comme dans un foyer commun, pour les faire servir à l'instruction publique'.

154. Jacques Derrida, *Glas* (Paris: Galilée, 1974), pp. 7–8 (right-hand column).

155. *L'Esprit de Fontenelle*, p. li.

156. 'Damit soll jedoch nicht gesagt sein, dass die Maximen in Werk Crébillons sich nur im Hinblick auf die Erzählungen, denen sie angehören, interpretieren liessen. Eine gewisse Eigenständlichkeit ist das "sine qua non" dieser Kunstform, und so kann man auch die Sentenzen Crébillons aus dem Zusammenhang herauslösen und zunächst ohne Rücksicht auf ihre literarische Funktion aus sich heraus deuten' (Kruse, p. 162).

157. Monique A. Bilezikian, 'Les Maximes dans les *Mémoires* du Cardinal de Retz' (unpublished dissertation, Harvard University, 1975), p. 159, my emphasis.

158. Crébillon *fils*, *Les Egarements du coeur et de l'esprit*, in *Romanciers du XVIIIe siècle*, edited by René Etiemble, 2 vols. (Paris: Gallimard, 1960–65), II, pp. 5–188. References will be to this edition and will be included in the text.

159. See for confirmation of this the prefatory comments of Justin O'Brien, *The Maxims of Marcel Proust* (Columbia University Press, 1948).

160. Roland Barthes, *S/Z*, especially pp. 210–12.

161. In *Romanciers du XVIIIe siècle*, II, pp. 195–301. References will be to this edition and will be included in the text.

162. See Oswald Ducrot, 'Présupposés et sous-entendus', *Langue française*, 4 (1969), pp. 30–43, and *Dire et ne pas dire* (Paris: Hermann, 1972), especially pp. 131–7. A similar description might be derived from Neil Smith and Deirdre Wilson, *Modern Linguistics: The Results of Chomsky's Revolution* (Harmondsworth: Penguin Books, 1979), Chapters 7 ('Semantics and Meaning'), and 8 ('Pragmatics and Communication'), although the authors do not seem to know Ducrot's work. According to Smith and Wilson, 'We may regard the meaning of a sentence as a set of *propositions*', and the notion of 'entailment' they put forward corresponds broadly to Ducrot's notion of the 'présupposé'. If it were possible to list the propositions implied as 'sous-entendus' (which would involve taking into account contextual factors ignored in the 'présupposé'), then it might be possible to argue that any sentence implying at least one sententious proposition as a *sous-entendu* can be said to have sententious force. But it is probably impossible to produce any exhaustive list of implied propositions in this way: the domain of the *sous-entendu* is too diffuse. See also, drawing on different work in linguistics, Jonathan Culler, 'Presupposition and Intertextuality', in *The Pursuit of Signs* (London: Routledge & Kegan Paul, 1981), pp. 100–118.

163. Jean-François Lyotard, 'Le 23 mars', in *Dérive à partir de Marx et Freud* (Paris: UGE, 1973), pp. 305–16 (p. 315).
164. Abbé Prévost, *Histoire du chevalier des Grieux et de Manon Lescaut*, in *Romanciers du XVIIIe siècle*, I, pp. 1217–1371 (p. 1297).
165. See Diderot, *Oeuvres romanesques*, edited by Henri Bénac (Paris: Garnier, 1962), pp. 493, 496, 498, 503, etc.
166. Marian Hobson has some suggestive comments on this aspect of *Jacques* (*The Object of Art*, p. 132), although her statement to the effect that 'the theme of fatalism becomes that of authorial power' seems to me to concentrate the problem of narrative law too simply in the hands of an 'author'. Viewed from the side of the *après coup*, the 'author' has no 'power' whatsoever.

2 Sentientiousness and Education

1. For characterizations of worldliness in terms of closure, see Barthes's essay on La Bruyère (*Essais critiques* (Paris: Seuil, 1964), pp. 221–37), and the opening chapter of Peter Brooks's *The Novel of Worldliness* (Princeton University Press, 1969).
2. See for example Edgar Morin, *La Méthode*, Vol. I, 'La Nature de la nature' (Paris: Seuil, 1977; reprinted collection 'Points', 1981), p. 199. Morin goes on to make a precious point about the notion of the closure or the frontier: 'La frontière est à la fois ouverture et fermeture. C'est à la frontière que s'effectue la distinction et la liaison avec l'environnement. Toute frontière, y compris la membrane des êtres vivants, y compris la frontière de nations, est, en même temps que barrière, le lieu de la communication et de l'échange. Elle est le lieu de la dissociation et de l'association, de la séparation et de l'articulation' (pp. 203–4); see too *De la grammatologie*, pp. 96–108, 'la brisure'.
3. Quotations from the *Egarements*, Duclos's *Les Confessions du comte de ****, and Louvet's *Faublas* (comprising *Une Année de la vie du chevalier de Faublas* (1787), *Six semaines de la vie du chevalier de Faublas* (1788), and *La Fin des amours du chevalier de Faublas* (1790)), are taken from the editions provided in *Romanciers du XVIIIe siècle*, ed. by R. Etiemble, 2 vols. (Paris: Gallimard, 1960–65), II, to which page references will be given in the text.
4. The notion of 'destination' is important here: worldly closure opens only to subjects destined to perpetuate that closure, and it is a defining characteristic of worldly novels that principal characters are wealthy and noble – this would be a distinguishing feature in any attempt to define such novels as a sub-genre, as opposed to the novels of Lesage and Prévost for example, where birth and wealth are not taken for granted.
5. Choderlos de Laclos, *Les Liaisons dangereuses* (1782), edited by Yves le Hir (Paris: Garnier, 1961), pp. 10, 42, 78, 112, 129, 157, 188, etc.
6. I quote from the second edition, 4 vols. (1728–31). Rollin also provided a volume of *Maximes tirées de l'écriture sainte* (1697). For an appreciation

of Rollin's importance see P. Mesnard, 'Rollin forge l'esprit de l'enseignement secondaire', in *Les Grands Pédagogues*, edited by Jean Château, third edition (Paris: PUF, 1966), pp. 147–69.

7. Georges Snyders, *La Pédagogie en France aux XVIIe et XVIIIe siècles* (Paris: PUF, 1964), p. 32.

8. Jean de Viguerie, *L'Institution des enfants: l'éducation en France, XVIe–XVIIIe siècle* (Paris: Calmann-Lévy, 1978), p. 52.

9. Abbé Claude Fleury, *Traité du choix et de la méthode des études* (Paris, 1686), pp. 112–13.

10. This remained the standard text-book for Jesuit rhetorical training, and was translated into French as late as 1892. On the importance of the exercise of *amplificatio*, see Peter France, *Rhetoric and Truth in France: Descartes to Diderot* (Oxford: Clarendon Press, 1972), pp. 20–23; for a classical discussion of the *chria*, which includes what is apparently the oldest extant example of the exercise, see the *Rhetorica ad Herrennium*, IV, XLIII, 56 – IV, XLIV, 57.

11. John Locke, 'Some Thoughts Concerning Education' (1693), in *The Educational Writings of John Locke*, edited by James L. Axtell (Cambridge University Press, 1968), §171. See also Jean-Pierre de Crousaz, *Traité de l'éducation des enfants*, 2 vols. (La Haye, 1722), I, pp. 286–7: 'En particulier rien n'est plus fade & plus contraire au bon sens que la plûpart des amplifications que l'on prescrit dans les Ecoles d'Eloquence. On donne pour sujet une *Sentence*, dont la force & la beauté dépend en partie du peu de mots & de mots choisis, dans lesquels elle est énoncée. Mais on recommende de tout gâter, en l'énervant par des tas de synonymes, de paraphrases lâches & peu justes, de similitudes obscures & que le sujet, très clair de lui-même, ne demande point. Au lieu d'apprendre à la jeunesse à penser beaucoup en peu mots (*sic*), on leur apprend à dire peu en beaucoup de paroles, & c'est pour cela qu'on veut qu'ils fassent des efforts'. Marmontel's article 'Chrie' for the *Encyclopédie* ends with the roundly-expressed hope that the *chria* will disappear for ever. (Jean-François Marmontel, *Oeuvres complètes*, 18 vols. (Paris: Costes, 1819), XII, p. 413.)

12. In, for example, the opening of the Introduction to the *Cours d'études pour l'instruction du Prince de Parme*, in *Oeuvres philosophiques*, edited by Georges Le Roy, 3 vols. (Paris: PUF, 1947–50), I, p. 397.

13. Charles-Etienne Pesselier, *Lettres sur l'éducation*, 2 vols. (Paris, 1762), I, p. 24.

14. In the light of this it is interesting that Rousseau's only reference to Crousaz in *Emile* should be to 'le pedant de Crousaz' (*Oeuvres complètes*, IV, p. 371).

15. IV, pp. 351, 421, 430, 624, 736, 826. It is important here from the point of view of worldliness to respect the indeterminacy of the reference to the 'monde' as a book, insofar as the 'monde' can be almost a synonym and almost an antonym of 'nature'. This ambivalence is, significantly, greatest in *Emile*, in the passage which states 'Le monde est le livre des

femmes' (IV, p. 737). I shall suggest that this link of women and worldliness is crucial in *Emile*, and that it is to be read in the context of the work's drift towards fiction.

16. I do not wish to suggest that this change in the position of the maxim is unimportant: it is in one sense clearly vital to the Enlightenment's representation of itself as an oriented narrative *progress*, and can be linked to my earlier remarks about method (Chapter 1, note 67, above). I simply want to point out here that for all their apparent insistence on 'the facts', the enlightened pedagogues cannot in fact do without maxims.

17. The image of the patch of course returns to the problems analysed above with reference to Quintilian and Lamy: here the tensions which were implicit in the earlier works surface in the form of the contradictory arguments of the text.

18. In Condillac, this would imply its integration into a system of institutional signs: this is the prerogative of man, and Condillac concludes from the fact that animals only recognize 'accidental' signs, the fact that they have no memory (*Essai sur l'origine des connaissance humaines*, I, II, §§35–46). This link of signs and memory is fundamental to Condillac's account of knowledge, insofar as only this allows men to master their own attention and imagination, and to make the 'soul' self-sufficient in its reflexivity (Ibid., I, II, §51). In an interesting 'digression', Condillac notes that there is a movement towards the production of 'propositions générales' here, and is concerned to situate any such 'principles' firmly at the end of the process of induction (I, II, §§61–8).

19. Other authors also recommend this type of composition of anthologies: see Ignace Vanière, *Second discours sur l'éducation, dans lequel on expose tout le vicieux de l'Institution Scholastique, & le moyen d'y remédier* (Paris, 1763), p. 72, and Pesselier, I, p. 182.

20. See Snyders, p. 68: 'C'est précisément parce que la vie courante se déroule en français que le collège se donne comme tâche de vivre en latin'.

21. *Journal de Trévoux*, juillet 1735, p. 1217.

22. See also Béliard, 'Discours pour la défense des romans', in *Zélaskim*, 4 vols. (Paris, 1765), I, i–xlvii (p. xv).

23. Marmontel, *Essai sur les romans* (1787), in *Oeuvres complètes*, ed. cit., X, p. 311. The obligation to 'tout dire' also appears in Sade, with explosive effects which I discuss in Chapter 5.

24. *L'Histoire justifiée contre les romans* (Amsterdam, 1735), 'Avertissement', unpaginated.

25. The problem is also discussed in Lenglet's *Méthode pour étudier l'histoire*, 2 vols. (Paris, 1713), and is of course a problem for historiography in general, at least since Thucydides' famous Book I, Chapter 22. Paul Veyne, for example, who insists that History is no more than a narrative with an 'intrigue' chosen by the historian, makes the point forcibly enough: 'en aucun cas ce que les historiens appellent un événement n'est saisi directement et entièrement; il l'est toujours incomplètement et latéralement, à travers des documents ou des témoignages, disons à

travers des *tekmeria*, des traces' (*Comment on écrit l'histoire* (Paris: Seuil, 1971; reprinted collection 'Points', 1979), p. 14). See also Barthes, 'Le Discours de l'histoire', *Social Sciences Information*, 6 (1967), pp. 65–75, who makes an important point about the so-called 'fact': 'On arrive ainsi à ce paradoxe qui règle toute la pertinence du discours historique . . . le fait n'est jamais qu'une existence linguistique (comme terme d'un discours), et cependant tout se passe comme si cette existence n'était que la "copie" pure et simple d'une autre existence, située dans un champ extra-structural, le "réel". Ce discours est sans doute le seul où le référent soit visé comme extérieur au discours, sans qu'il soit possible de l'atteindre hors de ce discours' (p. 73). The 'absence' of the fact is also at the centre of Michel de Certeau's historiography: see *L'absent de l'histoire* (Paris: Mame, 1973), and *L'écriture de l'histoire* (Paris: Gallimard, 1975), and especially in the latter pp. 60, 119, and 274.

26. See Derrida's analyses of the complexities of catastrophe and decline in Rousseau in *De la grammatologie* (Paris: Minuit, 1967), pp. 211–13 and 361–75.

27. This position is complicated by two passages in Book II of *Emile*, of course dealing with an earlier period of the pupil's life. The first of these attacks directly the notion of the 'fact' which is valorized in the passage discussed in the body of my text: 'Par une erreur encore plus ridicule on leur fait étudier l'histoire; on s'imagine que l'histoire est à leur portée parce qu'elle n'est qu'un recueil de faits; mais qu'entend-on par ce mot de faits? Croit-on que les rapports qui déterminent les faits historiques soient si faciles à saisir que les idées s'en forment sans peine dans l'esprit des enfans, croit-on que la véritable connoissance des événemens soit séparable de celle de leur causes, de celle de leurs effets, et que l'historique tienne si peu au moral qu'on puisse les connoitre l'un sans l'autre?' (IV, p. 348). This essential link of 'facts' and morality is further complicated in the second reference to history in Book II, where the status of the 'fact' is further reduced: 'Les anciens historiens sont remplis de vües dont on pourrait faire usage quand même les faits qui les présentent seroient faux: mais nous ne savons tirer aucun vrai parti de l'histoire; la critique d'érudition absorbe tout, comme s'il importoit beaucoup qu'un fait fut vrai, pourvu qu'on en pût tirer une instruction utile. Les hommes sensés doivent regarder l'histoire comme un tissu de fables dont la morale est très appropriée au coeur humain' (IV, p. 415n).

28. This choice of Thucydides as representing a sort of 'degré zéro' of history is interesting insofar as it is, precisely, Thucydides who refers to the *ktema es aei*, the 'leçons à jamais valables de l'histoire', as Veyne rather oddly puts it (Veyne, p. 105). On this complex issue, see R.G. Collingwood, *The Idea of History* (Oxford: Clarendon Press, 1946) pp. 29–30; V. Hunter, *Past and Process in Herodotus and Thucydides* (Princeton University Press, 1982), pp. 119–75, 'Generalization, Process and Event'; J. de Romilly, *Histoire et raison chez Thucydide* (Paris: Les Belles Lettres, 1956), pp. 46–52.

29. Du Plaisir, *Sentiments sur les lettres et sur l'histoire avec des scrupules sur le stile* (Paris, 1683), p. 129; Bérardier de Bataut, *Essai sur le récit ou entretien sur la manière de raconter* (Paris, 1776), pp. 321ff. Bérardier argues that it is in fact impossible for the historian to be totally neutral; but far from being an eighteenth-century version of the modern preoccupation with the inevitable presence of the 'subject of the enunciation', even in utterances which attempt to erase all marks of that presence, Bérardier's concern is a moral one: a historian who provided no moral judgements at all would simply be 'sans principes', and thus at the mercy of the potentially immoral content of his history.

30. It is this notion of an essential *lack* in history which brings the pedagogues to consider fiction as potentially a more 'complete' discourse; thus Vanière, in *Discours sur l'éducation* (Paris, 1760), p. 38: 'La fable, par ses fictions ingénieuses, joint à l'histoire ce qui pouvait lui manquer pour en faire un corps d'instructions des plus complets'. See also Laclos, *Oeuvres complètes*, edited by Laurent Versini (Paris: Gallimard, 1979), p. 440: 'c'est aux romans à suppléer à cette insuffisance de l'histoire'.

31. This type of play has been admirably analysed by Marian Hobson in *The Object of Art*, pp. 90–95.

32. See also Voltaire, *Essai sur les moeurs*, edited by René Pomeau, 2 vols. (Paris: Garnier, 1963), I, p. 228: 'Les Grecs, dans leur mythologie, n'ont été que des disciples de l'Inde et de l'Egypte. Toutes ces fables enveloppaient autrefois un sens philosophique; ce sens a disparu, et les fables sont restées.'

33. Hobson, p. 90. The inconsistency in the reviewer's reaction in the *Journal de Trévoux* would suggest that the ostensible object of the attack (namely the very project of providing moral justification for fiction, which is indeed apparently a mark of 'madness' (*Journal de Trévoux*, avril 1734, pp. 683–4)) is not the real cause of anger. The 'scandal' of Lenglet's book is much more linked to questions of nomination: one of his work's sins is that it 'nomme les personnes par leur nom' (p. 674), and this leads to curious effects, as in the following passage: 'Voilà, dira-t'on infaillible-ment un Ouvrage de ***, c'est là son coin et sa marque. Ainsi n'avons nous pas douté un moment que celui dont il est ici question ne soit cet illustre Auteur; mais plus modérés que lui nous ne voulons pas lui faire le tort de le nommer' (pp. 674–5). This unnamed author is accused of attributing the book to a certain Brossette, and the reviewer (himself of course anonymous), asserts, 'La modération, dont nous faisons pro-fession, ne nous permet pas de *donner à un tel procédé les noms qu'il mérite* . . .' (p. 694, my emphasis). The review in fact ends with the 'word' '***'. In the light of this, the subsequent review of *L'histoire justifiée* (juillet 1735, pp. 1200–35) is more concerned with 'clearing' Lenglet's *name* than with the internal coherence of the book.

34. Rollin, I, p. lxxviii. This does not prevent him from recommending the study of Phaedrus and La Fontaine in the section of his work concerned with rhetoric (II, p. 15). This idea of the fable being a secondary

corruption of a primary truth is taken up and exploited, not without a certain sophistry, by a late eighteenth-century apologist of the novel, Bricaire de la Dixmerie, in his 'Discours sur l'origine, les progrès, et le genre des romans' (in *Toni et Clairette*, 2 vols. (Paris, 1797), I, v–lxxvi (p. v)): 'Le regne de la Fable n'est guere moins ancien que celui de la Vérité, ou, pour mieux dire cette seconde rivale fut bientôt détrônée par la première.'

35. Pierre-Daniel Huet, *Traité sur l'origine des romans* (1670), eighth edition, 1711, critical edition by Arend Kok (Amsterdam: Swets and Zeitlinger, 1942): references will be given in the text to Huet's pagination, indicated in the margins of Kok's edition. The vast erudition of Huet's essay dominates discussion of the novel throughout the eighteenth century, and is still a basic point of reference for La Harpe ('Des Romans', in *Oeuvres*, 6 vols. (Paris, 1778), III, p. 337), and even Sade ('Idée sur les romans', *Edition définitive des oeuvres du marquis de Sade*, edited by Gilbert Lély, 16 vols. (Paris: Au Cercle du livre précieux, 1966–7), V, pp. 3–22). The location of the origin of the genre in the Orient becomes a commonplace.

36. See J.R. Carré's introduction to his critical edition of Fontenelle's text (Paris: Alcan, 1932), to which I refer in the text.

37. p. 15. See also Vico, §§808 and 814. This is of course the problem which upset Rousseau's account of history.

38. This position is that, for example, of Rapin: 'Homère a esté, pour ainsi dire, le premier fondateur de tous les arts et de toutes les sciences, et le modèle des sçavans de tous les siècles' (René Rapin, *Les Réflexions sur la poétique de ce temps et sur les ouvrages des poètes anciens et modernes* (1674), edited by E. Dubois (Genève: Droz, 1970), I, §4 (p. 16)).

39. This commonplace image appears to come from Lucretius, *De Rerum Natura*, I, 935–43.

40. Jean de la Fontaine, *Fables*, edited by Edmond Pilon and Fernand Dauphin (Paris: Garnier, 1960), p. 8.

41. 'Le pâtre et le lion: le lion et le chasseur', ed. cit., pp. 131–2. This assertion might seem to be contradicted by the closing lines of 'Le pouvoir des fables' (VIII, IV):

> Au moment que je fais cette moralité,
> Si *Peau d'Ane* m'étoit conté,
> J'y prendrois un plaisir extrême.
> Le monde est vieux, dit-on: je le crois; cependant
> Il le faut encore amuser encor comme un enfant.

But that this statement is not as simple as it looks ('Les fables ne sont pas ce qu'elles semblent être') is shown by Louis Marin in *Le Récit est un piège* (Paris: Minuit, 1978).

42. The fact that La Fontaine here invokes a general and anonymous prescription should be proof against the temptation to identify the author with any 'master' behind the text. This problem is implied in any invocation of an endoxal sententious statement, and I shall examine it more closely in the following chapter.

43. I certainly do not wish to set up Freud as an ultimate master behind all animals here – as a useful antidote to any such temptation, see Gilles Deleuze and Félix Guattari, '1914 – Un seul ou plusieurs loups', in *Capitalisme et schizophrénie: mille plateaux* (Paris: Minuit, 1980), pp. 38–52. I take up simulacrum and *après-coup* more fully in Part III.

44. Crousaz, I, p. 278, discussing, in fact, not the fable, but the poetry of the ancients, and thus indicating how the structure as described here concerns the whole of 'fiction'.

45. Later Rousseau seems to divide the process of observation and that of its maximization in terms of the difference between the sexes: 'La recherche des vérités abstraites et spéculatives, des principes, des axiomes dans les sciences, tout ce qui tend à généraliser les idées n'est point du ressort des femmes: leurs études doivent se rapporter toutes à la pratique; c'est à elles à faire l'application des principes que l'homme a trouvés, et c'est à elles de faire les observations qui mènent l'homme à l'établissement des principes' (IV, p. 736).

46. The appeal to the experience of others is not simple, and the nature of the 'danger' which motivates that appeal remains unclear: a little earlier, Rousseau has said that he would expose Emile to all 'accidents' and 'dangers' of society, except the 'pièges' of the *Courtisanes* (IV, pp. 537–8). The problem is further complicated by the fact that Rousseau states that the appeal to others' experience involves taking a 'route opposée' to that taken so far (this change of direction corresponding to Emile's first contact with society and its doxa, and the exposure to society is described as 'un cas d'exception à mes propres régles' (IV, p. 537)). Again, this disturbance of the rectitude of rule or road is linked to society and women.

47. And of course in Rousseau himself, for whom *amour-propre* is essentially the bad, social version of the good natural *amour de soi* (see the standard discussion of this in the *Discours sur l'inégalité*, and especially Rousseau's note XV (in *Oeuvres complètes*, III, p. 219)). On the other hand, Rousseau's comment here to the effect that the master's *amour-propre* should give some ground to that of his pupil has been prepared sententiously a little earlier in the text: 'L'amour-propre est un instrument utile, mais dangereux' (IV, p. 536). It is the danger presented by Emile's *amour-propre* that will push Rousseau to make the compensatory exception to the rule noted above, and expose his pupil to the tricks of men in society.

48. For a recent analysis of how this apparent liberality is not all it seems, but in fact involves a fundamental imposition of the master's desire, see Josué V. Harari, 'Therapeutic Pedagogy: Rousseau's *Emile*', *Modern Language Notes*, 97 (1982), pp. 787–809.

49. This is a poignant comment in view of the reaction to Rousseau's reading of his *Confessions* (see *Oeuvres complètes*, I, p. 656).

50. See also IV, p. 387: 'S'il faut tout vous dire, ne me lisez point.'

51. This notion of crisis and its deferral is insistent from the beginning of Book 4 of *Emile*, which opens with the idea of a 'second birth' to sexuality

(p. 489). The production of narrative as the promised and deferred resolution of a sexual encounter is basic to the structure of the worldly novel (see my article 'From Narrative to Text: Love and Writing in Crébillon *fils*, Duclos, Barthes', *The Oxford Literary Review*, 4 (1979), pp. 62–81), and possibly of narrative in general. The importance of this motif in *Emile* may be judged from the following passages: 'quand l'âge critique approche, offrez aux jeunes gens des spectacles qui les excitent' (p. 517: this involves an avoidance, precisely, of high society and 'la parure et l'immodestie des femmes'); 'Nous entrons enfin dans l'ordre moral: nous venons de faire un second pas d'homme' (p. 522: the ambiguity of the 'pas' in this type of formulation is something to which I return below); 'Encore un pas, et nous touchons au but' (p. 536); 'Le vrai moment de la nature arrive enfin, il faut qu'il arrive. Puisqu'il faut que l'homme meure, il faut qu'il se reproduise' (p. 639); 'Ne balancez point à l'instruire de ces dangereux mistères que vous lui avez cachés si longtems avec tant de soin. Puisqu'il faut enfin qu'il les sache' (p. 641); 'Enfin le moment presse; il est tems de la chercher tout de bon' (p. 691).

52. See IV, p. 759: 'mais enfin que risquerai-je d'achever sans détour l'histoire d'une fille semblable à Sophie, que cette histoire pourrait être la sienne sans qu'on dût en être surpris? Qu'on la croye véritable ou non, peu importe; j'aurai si l'on veut raconté des fictions, mais j'aurai toujours expliqué ma méthode et j'irai toujours à mes fins'. This story is of a girl who falls in love with the fictional character Télémaque and appears to die of grief because she is unable to find him in reality. The 'real' Sophie will be a fictional answer to this in that she finds a 'real' Télémaque in the fictional Emile.

53. See Georges May, *Le Dilemme du roman au XVIIIe siècle* (Yale University Press/Paris: PUF, 1963). Despite the rich documentation of May's work, it suffers conceptually precisely from the notion of the 'dilemma' announced in its title: May assumes that the novel evolves under the pressure of the contradictory forces of a drive towards realism and *vraisemblance* and the demands of morality. But no such contradiction can simply be presupposed, and May's version of it depends on a simplistic notion of the *vraisemblable*.

54. François de Dainville, *L'éducation des Jésuites (XVIe–XVIIIe siècles)*, edited by Marie-Madeleine Compère (Paris: Minuit, 1978), p. 217.

55. François de Salignac de la Mothe Fénelon, *De l'éducation des filles* (1687), in *Oeuvres complètes*, 10 vols. (Paris, 1848–52; Genève: Slatkine reprints, 1971), pp. 563–99 (p. 565 and pp. 587–8).

56. Abbé Castel de Saint-Pierre, *Projet pour perfectionner l'éducation, avec un discours sur la grandeur et la sainteté des hommes* (Paris, 1728), pp. 122–5.

57. Crousaz, I, p. 276: 'l'*Homère* moderne, ouvrage où l'agréable est si bien mêlé avec l'utile, & qui est si propre à pénétrer le coeur des jeunes gens de maximes et de sentimens, dont eux-mêmes & le Public profiteront pendant tout le cours de leur vie'.

58. Anne-Thérèse de Lambert, *Avis d'une mère à sa fille*, in *Oeuvres complètes* (Paris, 1808), pp. 1–104 (p. 74). The appeal to 'pudeur' is complicated by

the logic of the veil (see next note), and by seduction; cf. p. 60: 'Les passions même les plus vives ont besoin de la pudeur pour se montrer dans une forme séduisante: elle doit se répandre sur toutes vos actions'.

59. For the essential links between the figure of the veil and the notions of 'pudeur', 'coquetterie' and seduction, see my articles 'From Narrative to Text', art. cit., and 'Les Machines de l'Opéra: le jeu du signe dans le *Spectateur Français* de Marivaux', *French Studies*, 36 (1982), 154–70; see also Chapter 4, below.

60. See for example Baculard d'Arnaud, Preface to *Les Epreuves du sentiment*, in *Oeuvres*, 3 vols. (Paris, 1803), I, p. xiv; Bérardier de Bataut, *Essai sur le récit*, p. 670.

61. *Télémaque*, pp. 187–8. Télémaque duly produces maxims as the result of his experience: 'on ne surmonte le vice qu'en le fuyant', and 'L'amour est lui seul plus à craindre que tous les naufrages' (p. 188).

62. Although, as we have seen, Jacquin compares *Télémaque* unfavourably with Fléchier's history, he does concede that it is the best of novels, on the basis of its maxims: '*Télémaque* est, sans contredit, le plus parfait & le moins dangereux des Romans: les maximes qui en font la baze, sont dictées par la sagesse' (p. 148).

63. See also the *Journal de Trévoux*'s exasperated comment in the review of *De l'usage des romans*: 'N'est-il pas décidé depuis plus de deux mille ans, qu'on ne se garantit de la passion dangereuse de l'amour, que par la fuite des occasions' (avril 1734, p. 690).

64. Pesselier II, pp. 52–3. This is in contrast with an earlier, more complacent remark: '*L'âge mûr* reçoit enfin lui-même une sorte d'éducation qui lui est propre et particulière, *c'est le monde* qui la lui procure' (I, p. 47).

65. Charles-Marie de la Condamine, *Lettre sur l'éducation* (Paris, 1751), p. 15.

66. The ambiguity of the 'pas' in this type of formulation has been exploited by Maurice Blanchot in *Le Pas au-delà* (Paris: Gallimard, 1973), and by Jacques Derrida, 'Pas', *Gramma*, 3–4 (n.d.), 111–215, and *La Carte postale de Socrate à Freud et au-delà* (Paris: Aubier-Flammarion, 1980), pp. 278, 303, 314–15, 317, etc.

67. This play between the 'is' and the 'ought' effectively denounces traditional pedagogy for providing only a *fiction* of worldliness.

68. See in *Emile*, 'S'il ne s'agissoit que de montrer aux jeunes gens l'homme par son masque, on n'auroit pas besoin de le leur montrer, ils le verroient toujours de reste; mais puisque le masque n'est pas l'homme, et qu'il ne faut pas que son vernis les séduise, en leur peignant les hommes peignez-les leur tels qu'ils sont; non pas afin qu'ils les haïssent, mais afin qu'ils les plaignent, et ne leur veuillent pas ressembler' (IV, p. 525). It is in order to do this that Rousseau turns to the reading of history. In neither case is there the type of direct experience of society which would be the 'normal' method of Locke and Rousseau.

69. Following the signifier a little, it is interesting to see what becomes of the sequence 'Fence' within the 'world': 'Certainly a Man of Courage who cannot *Fence* at all, and therefore will put all upon one thrust, and not

stand parrying, has the odds against a moderate Fencer, especially if he has skill in *Wrestling*' (Locke, §199).

70. Marx's famous dictum about 'educating the educators' comes to mind (third of the *Theses on Feuerbach*), as does Kant's earlier formulation of the problem, in §10 of *Der Streit der Fakultäten* (1798), translated by H.B. Nisbet, in *Kant's Political Writings*, edited by Hans Reiss (Cambridge University Press, 1970), p. 189.

71. It should be clear that this 'progressive supplementation' does not imply a historical process, but simply the sequence created by my own narrative on the concepts at work in pedagogical discourse.

3 Sententiousness, Education, Worldliness

1. The importance of seduction in novels of worldliness suggests that some of the claims advanced by Ross Chambers in his *Story and Situation: Narrative Seduction and the Power of Fiction* (Manchester University Press, 1984), p. 10, could in fact be extended beyond the period (the nineteenth century) in which he chooses to locate them.

2. Crébillon *fils, Lettres de la marquise de M*** au comte de R**** (1732), Preface by Jean Rousset (Lausanne: La Guilde du livre, 1965), pp. 49–50. The notion of a 'récompense' introduces an economic motif which will be insistent in the worldly novel.

3. *Lettres de la marquise*, p. 177: here a certain comic effect is achieved by the juxtaposition of an unusually concrete economic reference ('faire emplette'; see too p. 178: 'il est mon conseil dans mes emplettes') with the code of the heroico-sentimental novel.

4. English Showalter Jr. stresses this point in *The Evolution of the French Novel, 1641–1782* (Princeton University Press, 1972), p. 16. Diderot opens his *Eloge* of Richardson wishing that another name were available to designate the type of fiction written by that author.

5. *Voyage merveilleux du prince Fan-Férédin dans la Romancie; contenant plusieurs observations historiques, géographiques, physiques, critiques & morales* (1735). The work is an explicit response to Lenglet-Dufresnoy's *De l'usage des romans*.

6. See for example pp. 428, 706, 471–2 and 1109–10.

7. This reading cannot in principle be claimed to be the 'right' one, depending as it does on what can only be a dogmatic interpretation of a sentence such as Valmont's *sentence* 'on n'est heureux que par l'amour' (Letter 155), and especially of the 'suppressed' letter referred to by the 'editor' in a note to Letter 154.

8. An eighteenth-century opinion was that it was the publishing of Duclos's novel which prevented Crébillon from pursuing his. See Bricaire de la Dixmérie, 'Discours', p. 1. Jean Ehrard thinks that Crébillon was unable to finish the novel because Mme de Lursay had become too dominant a character (see note 31, below).

9. See my article, 'From Narrative to Text: Love and Writing in Crébillon *fils*, Duclos, Barthes', *The Oxford Literary Review*, 4 (1979), pp. 62–81.

For a similar use of the notions of 'code' and 'figure' in Crébillon *fils*, see Andrzej Siemek, *Recherche morale et esthétique dans le roman de Crébillon fils*, printed as No. 200 of *Studies on Voltaire and the Eighteenth Century* (Banbury, 1980), pp. 89–92.

10. I follow Catherine Kerbrat-Orecchioni (*L'énonciation*) in describing personal pronouns as 'deictics', and not limiting the category to 'ostensive deictics'. This goes against the usage of Benveniste, whose essay 'De la subjectivité dans le langage', in *Problèmes de linguistique générale*, 2 vols. (Paris: Gallimard, 1966–74), I, pp. 258–66, is none the less essential.

11. See 'From Narrative to Text', pp. 69 and 73.

12. This is a good example of a limitation on the 'separability' of a maxim: the ironic antiphrasis can only be read in context.

13. This economy is fundamental in the worldly novel, dictating the deferral of the 'conquête' and thus providing the space for the narrative, and dominating the military metaphor of the conquest.

14. This fact would justify a treatment of worldly discourse as a *rhetoric*, and is homologous with a comment at the end of Aristotle's *Rhetoric*, which shows how any 'outside' to rhetoric (such as 'honesty', for example) is recuperated by rhetoric as a ruse among others: see above, Chapter 1, §6.1. For a similar analysis of the structure of *coquetterie* in Marivaux, see my article, 'Les Machines de l'Opéra: le jeu du signe dans le *Spectateur Français* de Marivaux', *French Studies*, 36 (1982), pp. 154–70. It is this totalizing tendency of the discourse of worldliness which programmes the exchanges between Zulica and Nassès in Crébillon *fils*'s *Le Sopha*, briefly analysed in 'From Narrative to Text'.

15. Later Versac will accept this use of the *feinte*: 'Etre passionné sans sentiment, pleurer sans être attendri, tourmenter sans être jaloux: voilà tous les rôles que vous devez jouer, voilà ce que vous devez être' (p. 157). In *Les Heureux Orphelins: histoire imitée de l'Anglois* (1754), the *libertin* Chester is even more explicit on this point: for Chester, men need only the 'art de paroître aimer' (*Collection complète des oeuvres de M. de Crébillon, fils*, 14 *tomes* in 7 vols. (London, 1777), VIII, p. 26), and this 'art' involves, for example, the ability to tremble convincingly (Ibid., p. 41). One of Chester's 'victimes', Milady Suffolk, laments this type of exploitation: 'Pourquoi faut-il que les hommes puissent jouer si facilement la passion, & les mouvements qui peuvent en indiquer une?' (VII, p. 108). I note in passing that some doubt has been cast on the legitimacy of the attribution of this work to Crébillon *fils*: see John P. Kent, 'Crébillon *fils*, Mrs Eliza Haywood and *Les Heureux Orphelins*: A Problem of Authorship', *Romance Notes*, 11 (1969), pp. 326–32. This question is of no importance to the present analysis.

16. 'Nous' is the most complex of the personal pronouns: here it could be analysed as being made up of the components 'je' (la Dame), 'elles' (other women), and, virtually, 'tu' (Hortense). For a summary of the complexities of the 'nous', see Kerbrat-Orecchioni, pp. 40–43.

17. See R.M. Hare, *The Language of Morals* (Oxford: Clarendon Press, 1952;

reprinted Oxford University Press, 1964), especially Chapters 8–11.

18. See too Siemek's comment on this passage: 'En démasquant, dans l'intention de les prévenir, les dangers de l'amour, on constate inconsciemment l'impossibilité de s'y soustraire' (Siemek, p. 168). The ascription of an intention seems misleading here: the ambivalence of the passage is such that it is strictly speaking impossible to separate 'intentional' from 'unintentional' readings, 'conscious' from 'unconscious', 'masked' from 'unmasked'.

19. I think this characterization of *décence* is not incompatible with that given by Michel Foucault: 'Ce qui charge ce langage, ce n'est pas ce qu'il veut *dire*, mais *faire*. Ne disant rien, il est tout animé de sous-entendus, et renvoie à des positions qui lui donnent son sens puisque par lui-même il n'en a pas; il indique tout un monde silencieux qui n'accède jamais aux mots: cette distance indicatrice, c'est la décence' ('Un si cruel savoir', *Critique*, 182 (1962), pp. 597–611 (p. 600)), except insofar as it would stress that the 'monde silencieux' is not so much prior to discourse as hollowed out in and through discourse.

20. Versac exploits the same strategy when he brings the marquis de Pranzi with him to embarrass Mme de Lursay: see p. 90.

21. This scene has been analysed in detail by Philippe Berthier: 'Le Souper impossible', in *Les Paradoxes du romancier: les 'Egarements' de Crébillon*, edited by Pierre Rétat (Grenoble: Presses Universitaires, 1975), pp. 75–88.

22. The link between economic and pedagogical motifs is implied in *Faublas*, when the baronne de Fonrose suggests that Faublas undertake the 'education' of the comtesse de Lignolle: 'A son âge elle fuit le monde: personne ne la rencontre nulle part, et peu de gens ont le bonheur de la trouver chez elle. Je crois bien que ce vilain mari n'est pas fâché de cette économique retraite; mais ce n'est pas lui qui l'exige, car c'est elle qui commande. M. de Faublas, je vous charge de former cette enfant; songez que c'est un effet qu'il faut mettre dans la société' (p. 808).

23. See the discussion of this in Chapter 2, §3.3. Jean Garagnon's analysis of this scene ('Le Maître à penser Versac ou les égarements philosophiques', in *Les Paradoxes du romancier*, pp. 129–49) seems to me to misread this prescriptive element in Versac's discourse.

24. I read the verb 'marcher' as a figure of the elaboration of worldly narratives or syntagms: Versac's comment thus presents *en abyme* the problem of the relationship between narrative and sententious propositions.

25. By Marian Hobson, *The Object of Art*, p. 110.

26. Peter Berger and Thomas Luckman, *The Social Construction of Reality: A Treatise in the Sociology of Knowledge* (Harmondsworth: Penguin Books, 1971), p. 172.

27. Gérard Genette, 'Vraisemblance et motivation', in *Figures II* (Paris: Seuil, 1969), pp. 71–99 (pp. 96–7). This important essay first appeared in a number of the review *Communications* devoted to 'Le Vraisemblable'

(No. 11 (1968)): the issue also contains articles by Todorov ('Introduction', and 'Du vraisemblable qu'on ne saurait éviter', reprinted together as 'Introduction au vraisemblable' in *Poétique de la prose* (Paris: Seuil, 1971), pp. 92–9), Barthes ('L'Effet de réel'), and Kristeva ('La productivité dite texte', reprinted in *Sémiotikè: recherches pour une sémanalyse* (Paris: Seuil, 1969), pp. 208–45), to which the present discussion is indebted.

28. 'On parlera de la vraisemblance d'une oeuvre dans la mesure où celle-ci essaye de nous faire croire qu'elle se conforme au réel et non à ses propres lois; autrement dit le vraisemblable est le masque dont s'affublent les lois du texte, et que nous sommes censés prendre pour une relation avec la réalité' (Todorov, *Poétique de la prose*, p. 94).

29. This is again the problem of the 'post hoc ergo propter hoc': see above, Chapter 1, note 69.

30. This term is used by Gerald Prince, 'Introduction à l'étude du narrataire', *Poétique*, 14 (1973), pp. 178–96; but I use it in a slightly less specialized sense, to mean simply the addressee positioned by the text, not to be confused with any possible addressee within the diegesis, nor with any empirical or phenomenological reader.

31. The implication of this 'education of the reader' seems to be that Mme de Lursay's narrative is somewhat discredited, and that therefore Hortense be tentatively identified with the 'femme estimable' to whom, according to the preface, Meilcour will owe his virtues (p. 11). Although I shall go on to suggest that a passive acceptance of the position assigned to the reader in the text's education is perhaps not the most interesting way of reading, it seems necessary to distinguish productive resistance to that positioning from a failure to notice the structure of narration at all, and an identification with the bad readings of Meilcour-as-actor. This type of naive reading is presented by Peter V. Conroy Jr. in *Crébillon fils: Techniques of the Novel, Studies on Voltaire and the Eighteenth Century*, 99 (Banbury: 1972), especially p. 120: '(Mme de Lursay) struggled with his innocence, and suffered by his pride, but she won and loved him in the end. The novel, having Mme de Lursay as heroine and complete as it stands, is an old man's fond tribute to the first woman who loved him and to the special niche she will always retain in his heart'. A slightly more urbane version of this reading is offered by Jean Ehrard in 'De Meilcour à Adolphe ou la suite des *Egarements*', *Proceedings of the Fifth International Congress on the Enlightenment* (*Studies on Voltaire and the Eighteenth Century*, 200 (Banbury, 1980), pp. 101–17), in which Mme de Lursay is found to be 'sublime' in her final narrative: it should be clear from the above analysis why such a reading is unacceptable.

32. Roland Barthes, 'Introduction à l'analyse structurale du récit', in *Poétique du récit*, edited by G. Genette and T. Todorov (Paris: Seuil, 1977), pp. 8–57 (p. 40). See also Jonathan Culler's comments on this test and its avatars in *Structuralist Poetics: Structuralism, Linguistics and the Study of Literature* (London: Routledge and Kegan Paul, 1975), pp. 199–200.

For an impressive discussion of the complexities of the narrative enunciation in all of Crébillon's novels, see Siemek, pp. 210–22, where, however, no mention is made of the problem of sententiousness.

33. For its usefulness, see Kerbrat-Orecchioni, *L'énonciation*, pp. 5–10, and passim. The notion has also been extensively used by Jacques Lacan, notably in discussions of the Cartesian *cogito*: see for example *Ecrits* (Paris: Seuil, 1966; reprinted collection 'Points', 2 vols., 1970–71), II, pp. 159, 225, 230, and, for a more didactic explanation, *Le Séminaire, Livre XI* (Paris: Seuil, 1973), pp. 127–9. The insistence on the *enunciation* of the *cogito* effectively denies that *cogito*'s reputed ability to affirm the existence of a subject 'present to itself'. That this fragility can be read *in* Descartes rather than simply against him has been persuasively argued by Jean-Luc Nancy in *Ego Sum* (Paris: Aubier-Flammarion, 1979): Nancy also suggests that although the effect of Lacan's work is indeed to question the notion of the subject, that subject nonetheless returns as the *telos* of Lacan's discourse, and psycho-analysis thus falls back into what Nancy would call an anthropology (pp. 11–25). Nancy wants to produce a more philosophical discourse around the question which is no longer one of an enunciation but one of an *énoncer*. This type of work denies a text any substantial grounding in a subject, even for its *énonciation*; the present analysis would like to retain something of the radical implications of this approach.

34. The analysis here comes very close to the notion of a narrative 'code' as a 'perspective de citations' put forward by Barthes in *S/Z*, and specifically to what he calls the 'codes culturels'. From a certain point of view, the whole enterprise undertaken here, insofar as it is concerned to derive sententious formulations underlying even apparently non-sententious sentences, can be read as a contribution to what Barthes formulates programmatically as 'transformational stylistics' (Ibid., pp. 106–7). However, the very notion of 'code' (taken from information-theory and Jakobsonian linguistics) is difficult, insofar as it tends to reduce any individual 'message' (the inevitable correlate of the notion of 'code') to the status of a secondary manifestation of a rigid, pre-existent structure which determines it absolutely. This is inconsistent with comments made by Barthes at the beginning of the text (pp. 9–10) which claim the importance of individual differences. The dilemma can perhaps be resolved by an appeal to the notion of 'play' between message and code (although these terms become displaced, and the opposition perhaps deconstructed), which, in the present case, would imply that the *Egarements* does not merely quote from elements seen to pre-exist it (in a social reality, say), but is active in the constitution of the 'code' of which it is a 'message'. A similar point against Barthes has been made, with reference to Balzac, by Christopher Prendergast in *Balzac: Fiction and Melodrama* (London: Arnold, 1978), pp. 152–4. Prendergast formulates the idea of a 'circular gesture of self-validation' by means of which Balzac's texts create their *own* doxa or code: the same point must be made for the worldly novel. More generally, this difficult and important point

has implications for linguistics and philosophy: see for example the opening pages of Oswald Ducrot, *Dire et ne pas dire* (Paris: Hermann, 1972).

35. This inevitably raises the question of the 'roman à clé', although this is not the type of 'reference' I have in mind here. Marian Hobson has suggested that *Les Egarements* was indeed read in this way (*The Object of Art*, p. 108). I should like to stress that the notion of the *roman à clé* designates no more than one way of *reading* novels, and that the pressure of this reading-strategy can find *à clé* references in any text, as Rousseau found to his cost (cf. *Confessions* (*Oeuvres complètes*, I, p. 512)).

36. Mme de Lafayette, *La Comtesse de Tende*, in *Romans et nouvelles*, edited by E. Magne and A. Niderst (Paris: Garnier, 1970), p. 410. The example is discussed by Culler in *Structuralist Poetics*, p. 134.

37. This prompts my disagreement with the analysis of Benjamin W. Palmer, 'Crébillon *fils* and his reader', *Studies on Voltaire and the Eighteenth Century*, 132 (Banbury, 1975), pp. 183–97. Palmer assumes that Crébillon wrote 'for and about the same people', and that his basic purpose was to 'abuse' his reader.

38. See Kerbrat-Orecchioni, p. 43. Any 'pure' use of such formulas in a text could only give rise to very strange effects.

39. Serge Gaubert, 'Synchronie ou diachronie ou la naissance du narrateur', in *Les Paradoxes du romancier*, pp. 42–60 (p. 49).

40. Valéry's legendary example is, of course, 'La marquise sortit à cinq heures': see Genette, 'La Littérature comme telle', in *Figures I* (Paris: Seuil, 1966; reprinted collection 'Points', 1976), pp. 253–65 (pp. 255–6), and 'Vraisemblance et motivation', pp. 92–4.

41. Genette, 'Vraisemblance et motivation', pp. 98–9.

42. The structure here is the same as in *Faublas*. Compare Duclos's *Confessions*, where Mme de Selve is discovered only at the end.

43. Todorov formulates this same problem in terms of the *vraisemblable*: 'Même indépendamment de ce caractère sérieux et immuable des lois du vraisemblable, auxquelles nous avons affaire, le vraisemblable nous guette de partout et nous ne pouvons pas lui échapper . . . La loi constitutive de notre discours nous y contraint. Si je parle, mon énoncé obéira à une certaine loi et s'inscrira dans une vraisemblance que je ne peux expliciter et rejeter sans me servir d'un autre énoncé dont la loi sera implicite' (Todorov, p. 99). Where Derrida can write, 'La loi exige un récit' ('La Loi du genre', *Glyph*, 7 (1980), pp. 176–201 (p. 188)), it seems necessary also to say 'le récit exige une loi'.

4 Sententiousness and the Law

1. La Bruyère, *Les Caractères*, edited by R. Garapon (Paris: Garnier, 1962), p. 64.

2. See *De la grammatologie*, pp. 203–34.

3. Jean Starobinski, *Jean-Jacques Rousseau, la transparence et l'obstacle*, revised edition (Paris: Gallimard, 1971), pp. 153–4.

4. The predicate 'espacement' is also attached to the notion of writing by Derrida. See, for example, *De la grammatologie*, p. 59.
5. Jean-Jacques Rousseau, *Oeuvres complètes*, edited by Bernard Gagnebin and Marcel Raymond, 4 vols. published to date (Paris: Gallimard, 1959–), III, p. 516. Unless otherwise indicated, all references to Rousseau will be to this edition and will be included in the text.
6. For example, 'j'enseigne à mon élève un art très long, très pénible et que n'ont assurément pas les vôtres, c'est celui d'être ignorant' (IV, p. 370).
7. Louis Althusser, 'Sur le *Contrat social*', *Cahiers pour l'analyse*, 8 (1967), pp. 5–42 (p. 42).
8. Paul de Man, *Allegories of Reading: Figural Language in Rousseau, Nietzsche, Rilke, and Proust* (Yale University Press, 1979), p. 247.
9. The account of the novel's reception given in the *Confessions* stresses the Parisian reception of the work: see I, pp. 545–8, and especially the disingenuous 'Tout au contraire de mon attente son moindre succés fut en Suisse et son plus grand à Paris' (I, p. 545).
10. The passage omitted from the quotation given above reads: 'Ainsi les préjugés et l'opinion, renforçant l'effet des systèmes politiques, amoncellent, entassent les habitants de chaque pays sur quelques points du territoire, laissant tout le reste en friche et désert; et ce frivole éclat . . .' See also III, p. 911, IV, p. 277, and IV, p. 740. The argument is also mobilized in the *Lettre à Voltaire*. Similar language can be found earlier in Montesquieu (*De l'esprit des lois*, XII, Ch. 9), and later in Diderot (*Oeuvres politiques*, edited by Paul Vernière (Paris: Garnier, 1963), p. 307).
11. I continue to use the term 'vraisemblable' as linked to plausibility and acceptability. Both interlocutors in the 'Seconde préface' admit that the novel is not *vraisemblable* in the traditional sense. See De Man, p. 196.
12. II, pp. 18–21. In the *Confessions*, Rousseau's reading is less circumspect; see I, p. 427.
13. The most cosmic example of this structure in Rousseau is the tilting of the earth on its axis and the production of climatic differences, giving rise, on the ground of man's 'perfectibility', to the declining processes of society and language. See the *Essai sur l'origine des langues*, edited by Charles Porset (Paris: Nizet, 1970), p. 109, and III, p. 531. See too Derrida's commentary on this structure in *De la grammatologie*, pp. 361–72. Another important example is that of Diderot's persuading Rousseau to write, after the experience on the road to Vincennes (I, p. 351). In *L'oeil vivant* (Paris: Gallimard, 1961), Jean Starobinski rather dubiously assimilates this structure to that of the expulsion from the Garden of Eden (pp. 142–5).
14. See II, p. 342: 'Vous voyant prêt à m'obéir, il falut parler. J'avais reçu de la Chaillot des leçons qui ne me firent que mieux connoitre les dangers de cet aveu.'
15. This general contamination of *La Nouvelle Héloïse* by the strategies of worldliness has also been argued, within a very different analytical

framework, by Philip Stewart in *Le Masque et la parole: le langage de l'amour au XVIIIe siècle* (Paris: Corti, 1973), pp. 205–15.

16. See the *Lettre à d'Alembert*, edited by Michel Launay (Paris: Garnier-Flammarion, 1967), pp. 168–83, for an extended discussion of the problem of *pudeur*, which involves a number of terms crucial to the economy of Rousseau's writing. The aphrodisiac qualities of *pudeur* are here made explicit: 'Les désirs voilés par la honte n'en deviennent que plus séduisants; en les gênant la pudeur les enflamme: ses craintes, ses détours, ses réserves, ses timides aveux, sa tendre et naïve finesse, disent mieux ce qu'elle croit taire que la passion ne l'eût dit sans elle: c'est elle qui donne du prix aux faveurs et de la douceur aux refus' (p. 170–1). A little later, Rousseau gives the 'natural' example of the courting behaviour of pigeons, and comments: 'l'innocence de la Nature ménage les agaceries et la molle résistance, avec un art qu'aurait à peine la plus habile coquette' (p. 175). See too IV, pp. 703 and 747.

17. Starobinski, Chapter 4, pp. 84–101.

18. See the *Lettre à M. d'Alembert*, p. 173, note 1: 'Je m'attends à l'objection: Les femmes sauvages n'ont point de pudeur: car elles vont nues. Je réponds que les nôtres en ont encore moins: car elles s'habillent.' Rousseau refers the reader to a passage at the end of the text in which he elaborates his notion of the *fête* and invokes the model of Sparta: answering an imaginary objection to the nudity of Spartan girls on such occasions, Rousseau replies that they were 'couvertes de l'honnêteté publique' (p. 246). Here the type of play earlier valorized as natural *pudeur* returns in the bad form of *coquetterie*, without any essential structural difference being made: 'Il n'y a point de vêtement si modeste au travers duquel un regard enflammé par l'imagination n'aille porter les désirs . . . quand on s'habille avec autant d'art et si peu d'exactitude que les femmes font aujourd'hui, quand on ne montre moins que pour faire désirer davantage, quand l'obstacle qu'on oppose aux yeux ne sert qu'à mieux irriter l'imagination, quand on ne cache une partie de l'objet que pour parer celle qu'on expose, *Heu! male tum mites defendit pampinus uvas*' (p. 247). It is not clear to me that nudity *as such* can be said to exist in Rousseau's texts. Starobinski's analysis of the structure of the veil in *L'Oeil vivant* is vitiated by the assumption that veils simply hide and can therefore simply reveal (p. 16); but the structure of the veil cannot be explained in terms of a simple opposition between the visible and the invisible, the present and the absent. The complication of the veil (which can be read as the irruption of writing, in Derrida's sense, into the field of the visible) in fact undermines a basic valorization of the eye and visibility in Starobinski's whole critical enterprise (see for example *L'Oeil vivant*, pp. 24–5).

19. The notion of *jouissance* in Rousseau's writing is complex: although there is an ideal of a tranquil self-present auto-affection, free of any relation to the other, of time and of writing (e.g. 'Le vrai plaisir est simple et paisible, il aime le silence et [le] recueillement; celui qui le goute est tout à la chose, il

ne s'amuse pas à dire: "j'ai du plaisir"' (*Projet de constitution pour la Corse*, III, p. 937)), more often *jouissance* is linked to the split of reflective consciousness and is therefore separated from itself, for example in a movement of temporalization: the fifth of the fragments collected by the Pléiade editors under the title 'De l'art de jouir et autres fragments' reads simply 'En me disant, j'ai joüi, je joüis encore' (I, p. 1174). The same movement can be found in the *Confessions* (I, p. 585), and even in the *Rêveries*, always already compromising the effort towards *recueillement* (I, p. 999). But as Derrida shows, only this movement of separation allows Rousseau to write, and even to live: 'La jouissance elle-même, sans symbole ni supplétif, celle qui nous accorderait (à) la présence pure elle-même, si quelque chose de tel était possible, ne serait qu'un autre nom de la mort' (*De la grammatologie*, p. 223). Numerous examples of the link between *jouissance* and death could be added from the novel: see for example II, pp. 63–4, II, p. 107, and II, p. 145.

20. For example, II, p. 279: 'Julie! . . . O ma Julie! le voile est déchiré . . . je te vois . . . je vois tes divins attraits!'; although here of course what is revealed is only Julie's portrait.

21. See for example II, p. 562 and IV, p. 293.

22. I shall quote from Daniel Oster's edition of the *Oeuvres complètes* (Paris: Seuil, 1964), and give book, chapter, and page references in the text.

23. The question of the relationship between Montesquieu and Spinoza is perhaps best addressed at this point. The possible influence of the latter on the former has been postulated by Paul Vernière (in *Spinoza et la pensée français*, 2 vols. (Paris: PUF, 1954), pp. 447–66), and contested by Robert Shackleton (*Montesquieu: A Critical Biography* (Oxford University Press, 1961), pp. 261–4). Neither postulation nor contestation is particularly convincing. The fundamental difference seems to lie in the fact that in Montesquieu primary Rational Law precedes even the law of nature, whereas for Spinoza the laws of Reason are secondary. The result of this difference is that Spinoza is able to avoid the ambivalence of prescription and description which is such a problem in Montesquieu: for Spinoza, natural laws are prior to any distinction between description and prescription.

24. See for example Locke's desire to demonstrate moral truths in the full mathematical sense: *An Essay Concerning Human Understanding*, III, XI, 16; IV, III, 18; IV, XII, 8. Or, in the immediate area of concern here, Morelly, *Code de la nature* (1755), edited by Albert Soboul (Paris: Editions sociales, 1970): 'Cette science [i.e. 'la morale'], qui *devrait être* aussi simple, aussi évidente dans ses premiers axiomes et leurs consé-quences que les mathématiques' (p. 38, my emphasis). The whole intellectual project of enlightenment (as a basic structure for 'The Enlightenment') can be read in the *écart* separating the 'être' from the 'devoir être', and it is this gap between description and prescription which introduces the space for a narrative into the notion of the law.

25. See Spinoza, *Tractatus Theologico-Politicus*, Chapter 4 (in Benedicti de

Spinoza, *Opera*, quotquot reperta sunt, recognoverunt J. Van Vloten et J.P.N. Land, 2 vols. (The Hague: Nijhoff, 1882–3)): 'Verum enimvero, quoniam nomen legis per translationem ad res naturales applicatum videtur, et communiter per legem nihil aliud intelligetur quam mandatum, quod homines et perficere et negligere possunt, utpote quia potentiam humanam sub certis limitibus, ultra quos se extendit, constringit, nec aliquid supra vires imperat; ideo Lex particularius definienda videtur, nempe quod fit ratio vivendi, quam homo sibi vel aliis ob aliquem finem praescribit.' This passage is also picked out by Louis Althusser, in *Montesquieu, la politique et l'histoire* (1959), fifth edition (Paris: PUF, 1981), p. 30.

26. Bernard Groethuysen, *Les Origines de l'esprit bourgeois en France* (Paris: Gallimard, 1927), especially pp. 99 and 115.

27. Hugo Grotius, *Le Droit de la guerre et de la paix*, translated by Jean Barbeyrac (Amsterdam, 1724), I, I, §X, 5. See also I, I, §XVII, 2. In the 'Discours préliminaire', Grotius locates the first source of *droit* in a natural sociability in man (§§VI–VIII): this *droit* could do without God, but as there *is* a God, His will can be considered to be a second source, if not the source of the first source (§XII).

28. In view of this, the title of the book might have been *Les Lois des lois*, and the specificity of Montesquieu's work would lie in the first occurrence of the word. See also Althusser, p. 35.

29. Whether this epistemology is described as empiricist or rationalist is not of great importance here. For example, Georges Davy seems to show unnecessary concern for the 'facts' in asserting that the statement 'J'ai posé mes principes . . .' is a statement about the order of presentation of the material rather than the order of research ('Note Introductive' to E. Durkheim, *Montesquieu et Rousseau: précurseurs de la sociologie* (Paris: Marcel Rivière, 1953)).

30. Letter 97, *Oeuvres complètes*, p. 113.

31. Auguste Comte, 'Leçon 47', in *Physique sociale* (*Cours de philosophie positive*, Leçons 46–60), edited by J.-P. Enthoven (Paris: Hermann, 1975), p. 85 (my emphasis).

32. Comte, p. 86 (my emphasis). The editor of Comte's text, J.-P. Enthoven, is also suspicious of this passage, suggesting that Comte's reading depends only on a 'jeu de mots', and stating in a note to this page, 'Cette interprétation exemplaire surprend, car chez Montesquieu la loi, qui illustre canoniquement ce rapport nécessaire dérivant de la nature des choses, ne cesse jamais d'être une loi *positive*, c'est-à-dire une loi écrite.' This simply forces the problem in the other direction, and can be given little support from Montesquieu's text. The 'jeu de mots' remains the whole problem.

33. Samuel Pufendorf, *Le Droit de la nature et des gens*, translated by Jean Barbeyrac (Amsterdam, 1706), Book I, Chapter 2, §VI, and *Les Devoirs de l'homme et du citoien tels qu'ils lui sont prescrits par la Loi Naturelle*, fifth edition, translated by Jean Barbeyrac, 2 vols. (Amsterdam, 1735),

Book I, Chapter 5, §VIII. See too Leo Strauss's comments on Locke's need to retain the idea of an identity between Divine Law and Natural Law in *Natural Right and History* (Chicago University Press, 1953), pp. 202–3, provoked by the problem that 'Natural reason is . . . unable to know the law of nature as a law'.

34. John Stuart Mill, 'Nature', in *Nature, the Utility of Religion and Theism* (London: Longman, Green, Reader and Dyer, 1874), pp. 3–65 (p. 14); Althusser, having given his two possible interpretations of the 'devoir', simply decides that the second of the two strands in Montesquieu is regressive, and proceeds to ignore it. Although I would argue that no simple reduction of the two senses of the word 'law' is possible, attempts less confused than Montesquieu's to deal with the resultant problems can certainly be found, notably in the Kant of the second and third *Critiques*.

35. Simon-Nicholas-Henri Linguet, *Théorie des loix civiles, ou principes fondamentaux de la société* (1767), Nouvelle édition revue, corrigée et augmentée in *Oeuvres*, 6 vols. (London, 1774), III–V (III, pp. 78–80). Marx quotes Linguet approvingly in *Capital*: 'Linguet overthrew Montesquieu's illusory *"esprit des lois"* with one word: *"L'esprit des lois, c'est la propriété"*' (Karl Marx, *Capital*, I, translated by Ben Fowkes (Harmondsworth: Penguin Books, 1976), note to p. 766): but in Linguet this original insight in fact leads to a totally reactionary position insofar as the illegitimacy of law and state is seen as necessary. When Linguet suggests that society should remain as close to its source as possible ('ramener tout à la simplicité primitive' (*Théorie*, III, p. 72)), this in fact means adopting the Asian despotic model as the purest form available. Violence and repression are necessary components of society for Linguet: three-quarters of the human race are condemned to suffer as prisoners under the jailors who make up the remaining quarter of the population (for all of this see *Théorie*, V, Chapter 27), and any attempt to restore 'natural' equality would simply produce more violence without any guarantee of compensation: 'Voilà l'emblème naturel de la société. C'est un ouragan qui l'a formée: mais qui de nous voudroit courir les risques du tourbillon qui remettroit les choses dans leur premier état?' (*Théorie*, V, pp. 172–3).

36. Jean Starobinski, *Montesquieu* (Paris: Seuil, 1953), p. 73.

37. See also Mably, *Sur la théorie du pouvoir politique*, edited by Peter Friedmann (Paris: Editions sociales, 1975), p. 193: 'Si on excepte le règne trop court de Charlemagne, jamais les Français n'ont recherché *par quelles lois la nature ordonne* aux hommes de faire leur bonheur' (my emphasis). It would be worth reading such statements in connection with the following comment from the *Grammatologie*: 'Il y aurait beaucoup à dire sur le fait que l'unité native de la voix et de l'écriture soit *prescriptive*. L'archi-parole est écriture parce qu'elle est une loi. Une loi naturelle. La parole commençante est entendue; dans l'intimité de la présence à soi, comme voix de l'autre et comme commandement.'

38. See Robert Derathé, *Jean-Jacques Rousseau et la science politique de son temps* (Paris: PUF, 1950), pp. 27–55, and A.P. d'Entrèves, *Natural Law,*

second edition (London: Hutchinson, 1970), pp. 51–63, for accounts of these positions. The idea that God is not a necessary element in considerations of the legitimacy of legislation is also implied in Montesquieu, of course: see the *Lettres Persanes*, Letter 83.

39. Locke, *First Treatise on Government*, §5. See also Bossuet, *Politique tirée des propres paroles de l'écriture sainte* (1709), edited by Jacques Le Brun (Genève: Droz, 1967), especially Book 3. Bossuet describes royal authority as sacred, paternal and absolute, but also as subject to Reason, and certainly would not wish to identify absolute power and arbitrary power. The controls preventing that identification are, however, entirely dependent on the character of the monarch: this implies that they can be the object of a *pedagogical* project such as Bossuet's book, but not of a *political* theory as such. On the theory of absolutism, see John Plamenatz, *Man and Society* (London: Longmans, 1963), I, pp. 155–208, and Nannerl O. Keohane, *Philosophy and the State in France: The Renaissance to the Enlightenment* (Princeton University Press, 1980), especially pp. 241–61.

40. This is of course the case throughout *L'Esprit des lois*: see also Beccaria, *Des Délits et des peines* (1764) (Paris: Flammarion, 1979), p. 109, for a typical Enlightened comment: 'Mais je n'oserai décider cette question, jusqu'à ce que les lois, devenues plus conformes aux sentiments naturels de l'homme, les peines rendues plus douces, l'arbitraire des juges et de l'opinion comprimé, rassurent l'innocence, et garantissent la vertu des persécutions de l'envie; jusqu'à ce que la tyrannie, réléguée dans l'Orient, ait laissé l'Europe sous le doux empire de la raison, de cette raison éternelle, qui unit d'un lien indissoluble les intérêts des souverains aux intérêts des peuples'. What offends the Enlightened thinkers about the despotic structure is its unpredictability and temporal instability: see *L'Esprit des lois* V, Ch. 16, where the law in despotic government is described as 'la volonté *momentanée* du prince' (p. 554, my emphasis). This precludes the possibility of justice because the prince's will cannot be codified (see Diderot's article 'Représentants' for the *Encyclopédie*, in *Oeuvres politiques*, pp. 40–54 (p. 47): in a despotic state such as Turkey, 'il n'est point de justice, parce que la volonté du maître est l'unique loi'). Diderot is perhaps the most consistent eighteenth-century thinker on this point, in his insistence that this is a *structural* problem, and in his avoidance of the trap of 'enlightened despotism'. See especially in his *Entretiens avec Catherine II* (Ibid., p. 271): 'Tout gouvernement arbitraire est mauvais; je n'en excepte pas le gouvernement d'un maître bon, ferme, juste et éclairé', and in his *Observations sur le Nakaz*, besides a repetition of this point (Ibid., p. 354), his insistence of the need for the sovereign's will to be limited by a body of representatives, and his objection on principle to the royal formula, 'tel est notre bon plaisir' (Ibid., p. 357). This point of view also dictates his *Pages contre un tyran* (Ibid., pp. 135–48), directed at Frederick the Great. Rousseau's *Contrat social* is the most radical attempt in the eighteenth century to solve the problem.

41. See also Louis Marin, *Le Portrait du roi* (Paris: Minuit, 1981), p. 30.

42. Locke, *First Treatise*, §129. See too the *Contrat social* II, V (III, 377).
43. Locke, *Second Treatise*, §3. For an 'economic' interpretation of this shift in the interpretation of power, with specific reference to criminal law, see Michel Foucault, *Surveiller et punir: naissance de la prison* (Paris: Gallimard, 1975), pp. 80–84.
44. Beccaria, pp. 58–9.
45. See Derathé, pp. 41ff.
46. In the *Entretiens avec Catherine II*, Diderot provides a summary of the 'beau texte' of these various imagined origins of society, before going on to suggest that the originary and ongoing war constitutive of society is that *against* nature (*Oeuvres politiques*, pp. 303–4).
47. Mably, *Sur la théorie du pouvoir politique*, in a long footnote pp. 106–11. For Linguet the first human groupings were those of hunters and peaceful farmers, the hunters rapidly turning their activity to the violent appropriation of domesticated animals. Marx again approves of this account (*Capital* I, p. 452, note 20), and there are evident parallels to be drawn between this conception of an originary violence and Marx's account of the primitive accumulation of capital (Ibid., pp. 871–940).
48. This has been done scrupulously by Stephen Ellenburg in *Rousseau's Political Philosophy: An Interpretation from Within* (Ithaca and London: Cornell University Press, 1976), pp. 56–81.
49. The liberal tradition rests on a definition of the subject as being 'naturally' possessed of rights and interests which can determine his calculation of the advantage to be derived from the signing of a social pact. An excellent account of this basic presupposition is given in Ellenburg, Chapter 2, 'Rousseau and the liberal tradition' (pp. 35–55). See also a brief and penetrating discussion in Paul Hirst, *On Law and Ideology* (London: Macmillan, 1979), pp. 153–63. Lester G. Crocker blithely assumes that this notion of the subject is the only possible one in his essay on the *Contrat social*, and this assumption dictates a use of the term 'individual' in the demonstration of Rousseau's supposed 'totalitarianism' which begs all the questions that Rousseau's text raises (Lester G. Crocker, *Rousseau's Social Contract: An Interpretive Essay* (Cleveland: Case Western Reserve University Press, 1968)).
50. This point has been well made by Paule-Monique Vernes: 'L'état social une fois advenu, toute réinsertion de l'homme dans la nature primitive est exclue, tout modèle extra-social de la société est inadéquat . . . La Nature joue le rôle d'un principe, d'un fondement de droit pour un jugement sur la société existante' (*La Ville, la fête, la démocratie: Rousseau et les illusions de la communauté* (Paris: Payot, 1978)), pp. 39–40. Leo Strauss's laconic comment should also be borne in mind: 'Rousseau's thesis that man is by nature good must be understood in the light of his contention that man is by nature subhuman' (*Natural Right and History*, p. 271). See also III, p. 364 and III, p. 123.
51. The contract which coincides with the possibility of recognizing *jouissance* is the act which transforms that *jouissance* into *property*: 'Loin

248

qu'en acceptant les biens des particuliers la communauté les en dépouille, elle ne fait que leur en assurer la légitime possession, changer l'usurpation en un véritable droit, et la jouissance en propriété' (III, p. 367). Strauss argues that a similar problem is at work in Locke's political thought: 'Only such men could know the law of nature while living in a state of nature who have already lived in civil society, or rather in a civil society in which reason has been properly cultivated' (*Natural Right and History*, p. 230).

52. This return of the notion of the patch might be motivated with reference to Plato's *Statesman*, 279b–283a and passim, and linked to Rousseau's own awareness of the danger of the State degenerating into patchwork (III, p. 369).

53. This drive is recognized as fundamental to Rousseau by Marcel Raymond (*Jean-Jacques Rousseau: la quête de soi et la rêverie* (Paris: Corti, 1962), p. 8: 'Se suffire à soi-même, tel est le bonheur dernier qu'il désire'), and accepted as Rousseau's basic desire throughout Derrida's analyses in *De la grammatologie*. The shift here from individual to social self-sufficiency does not affect the basic structure of the drive. The notion of self-sufficiency as a pre-requisite for the existence of the State is a constant in classical political writing: see for example Aristotle, *Politics*, 1252b and 1253a. Self-sufficiency is not synonymous with unity, and this is the burden of Aristotle's critique of Plato (Ibid., 1261b).

54. Rousseau is very close to Spinoza here. See for example the *Tractatus Theologico-Politicus*, Chapter 16: 'At forsan aliquis putabit, nos hac ratione subditos servos facere, quia putant servum esse eum, qui ex mandato agit, et liberum, qui animo suo morem gerit; quod quidem non absolute verum est, nam revera is, qui a sua voluptate ita trahitur, et nihil quod sibi utile est, videre neque agere potest, maxime servus est, et solus ille liber, qui integro animo ex solo ductu Rationis vivit.' (Ed. cit., I, pp. 557–8).

55. *Discours sur l'économie politique*, III, p. 248, my emphasis. The passage also appears (with minor changes of detail) in the *Manuscrit de Genève*, III, p. 310, but is omitted from the definitive text of the *Contrat social*.

56. The term 'artificial individual' is used by Ellenburg to distinguish Rousseau's individual from that of the liberal tradition. The nature of the denaturing is made clearest by a passage from *Emile*: 'Les bonnes institutions sociales sont celles qui savent le mieux dénaturer l'homme, lui ôter son existence absolue pour lui en donner une relative, et transporter le *moi* dans l'unité commune' (IV, p. 249); see also III, pp. 313 and 381.

57. A condition for this identity of descriptive and prescriptive senses of the term 'law' appears to be the peculiar temporality of the sovereign, which is that of a succession of pure present moments, none of which can in principle be prised open into the narrative space implied by the gap between an *être* and a *devoir être*, and which can be seen as a simulacrum of natural (ahistorical) temporality. See for example the *Manuscrit de Genève*, III, p. 296: 'La volonté générale qui doit diriger l'Etat n'est pas

celle d'un tems passé, mais celle du moment présent, et le vrai caractère de la souveraineté est qu'il y ait toujours accord de tems, de lieu, d'effet, entre la direction de la volonté générale et l'emploi de la force publique'; and the *Fragments politiques*, III, p. 485: 'Chaque acte de souveraineté ainsi que chaque instant de sa durée est absolu, indépendant de celui qui précéde et jamais le souverain n'agit parce qu'il a voulu mais parce qu'il veut'.

58. See Keohane, *Philosophy and the State in France*, p. 370: '[The Abbé de Saint-Pierre] asserted that the true goal in political science is to construct a "perpetual-motion machine" that runs smoothly on its own energy. The machine should not depend on the accidental presence of a god-like ruler at its head.'

59. Louis Althusser, 'Sur le *Contrat social* (Les décalages)', *Cahiers pour l'analyse*, 8 (1967), pp. 5–42; Paul de Man, 'Promises (*Social Contract*)', in *Allegories of Reading*, pp. 246–77. None of the following analysis of Rousseau would have been possible without Derrida's *De la grammatologie*.

60. De Man, p. 273. De Man simply asserts that the illocutionary mode of the law is that of the promise, and then quotes a passage from the *Manuscrit de Genève* (III, p. 316) which *denies* that the law depends on a prior commitment, in order to develop an aporia according to which the *Contrat social* is supposed simultaneously to perform an act (the promise, also arbitrarily assigned as the illocutionary mode of Rousseau's text) and to show that any such act is impossible. In the absence of better evidence for the identification of law and promise, it seems simpler to take Rousseau's word for it that the law is not a promise in the first place.

61. Althusser, p. 18. Derathé, p. 172, also points out the aporia, as does Patrick Hochart in 'Droit naturel et simulacre', *Cahiers pour l'analyse*, 8 (1967), pp. 65–84 (p. 70). A recent attempt to justify Rousseau against Althusser has been made by Felicity Baker ('La Route contraire', in *Reappraisals of Rousseau*, pp. 132–62), who argues that Rousseau redistributes the semantic components of the word 'contract' in order to preserve its psychological value. It is difficult to agree with the bias of this argument: on the one hand, it is not clear that the desire imputed to Rousseau to preserve a certain 'psychological' connotation can be presented as an 'exigence théorique' (p. 141), and on the other it is difficult to treat the notion of a contract as no more than a 'word' with certain semantic components.

62. But a very similar problem can be detected in, for example, the American Declaration of Independence: see Jacques Derrida, *Otobiographies: l'enseignement de Nietzsche et la politique du nom propre* (Paris: Galilée, 1984), pp. 13–32.

63. De Man notes this figure of reversing cause and effect only at a much 'later' stage of the analysis, with the appearance of the legislator, where he calls it a metalepsis. I prefer to maintain this term in the usage of Gérard Genette (*Figures III*, p. 243) and Jean-François Lyotard (*Le Différend*

(Paris: Minuit, 1984, pp. 45–6), and shall use the term *après-coup* for the type of figure identified here.

64. The concern for the establishment of causes of course dominates the confessional texts: see I, p. 175: 'Je m'applique à bien déveloper par tout les prémiéres causes pour faire sentir l'enchainement des effets'. The need to find causes for effects is the burden of Rousseau's critique of materialism in *Emile* (see especially IV, p. 576). In the *Contrat social* itself, theories of natural inequality and of the 'droit du plus fort' are refuted on the grounds that they invert the correct order of cause and effect. More generally, this figure evidently justifies Rousseau's general dismissal of descriptions of the state of nature. The most general version of this *après-coup* is no doubt Rousseau's awareness of the necessity that both language and society precede the other. The fullest treatment of this problem is to be found in the second *Discours*: see especially III, p. 151.

65. *Otobiographies*, p. 25.

66. The impossibility of making the contract intelligible in empirical terms might reinforce the serenity with which Rousseau can accept the possibility that no existing *polis* has in fact been instituted according to his theory (III, p. 297).

67. On signatures and events, see Jacques Derrida, 'Signature, événement, contexte', in *Marges*, pp. 367–93, and 'Limited Inc.', Supplement to *Glyph*, 2 (1977). In view of this repetition of the contract, Jacqueline de Romilly is no doubt wrong to suggest a fundamental difference in this respect between Rousseau's contract and that of Socrates, in *L'Idée de loi dans la pensée grecque* (Paris: Les Belles Lettres, 1971), p. 134.

68. This consequence of the 'necessary possibility' is drawn in different contexts by Derrida, in 'Limited Inc.', and in 'Le Facteur de la vérité', in *La Carte postale*, pp. 441–524.

69. The polemical opponent for this section is of course Diderot, and especially his article 'Droit naturel' for the *Encyclopédie*: the first part of the quotation from Rousseau here quotes Diderot's text.

70. This realm of *droit* is itself legitimated by the stipulation of at least one 'unanimous' decision, that of the contract itself, which carries the presupposition that majority decisions will suffice thereafter. See III, pp. 359 and 440.

71. See also III, p. 297: this passage is quoted by De Man (p. 272), who goes on to talk of 'a kind of political thermodynamics governed by a debilitating entropy'.

72. De Man, p. 269: the analysis would need to establish the commensurability of reference in descriptive and prescriptive statements. This might be possible within a juridical model of philosophy, such as Kant's, but then the question would no doubt have to be elaborated in terms of the relationship of law and *case*, and it would be necessary to address the problem raised by the law *itself* becoming a case for judgement: see Jean-Luc Nancy, 'Lapsus Judicii', in *L'impératif catégorique* (Paris: Aubier-Flammarion, 1983), pp. 35–60. Where De Man appears to make the

distinction between 'the elaboration of the law and its application' (p. 269), he is in fact referring to generality on the one hand and particularity on the other, rather than to the two distinct types of particularity involved in elaboration and application.

73. This evidently recalls Derrida's insistence on the necessary possibility of a letter's not arriving at its destination (in 'Le Facteur de la vérité'): in these terms, the 'letter' of the *volonté générale* would of course be a 'circular'. A 'postal' reading of eighteenth-century political discourse is in progress, taking its cue from Montesquieu's assertion: 'C'est l'invention des postes qui a produit la politique' (*Oeuvres complètes*, p. 174).

74. See also the paradox proposed by the 'Discours sur l'économie politique' on the statesman: 'Le chef-d'oeuvre de ses travaux seroit de pouvoir rester oisif' (III, p. 250).

75. See III, p. 421: 'Comme la volonté particulière agit sans cesse contre la volonté générale, ainsi le Gouvernement fait un effort continuel contre la Souveraineté. Plus cet effort augmente, plus la constitution s'altère, et comme il n'y a point ici d'autre volonté de corps qui résistant à celle du Prince fasse équilibre avec elle, il doit arriver tôt ou tard que le Prince opprime enfin le Souverain et rompe le traité Social. C'est-là le vice inhérent et inévitable qui dès la naissance du corps politique tends sans relâche à le détruire, de même que la vieillesse et la mort détruisent le corps de l'homme.'

76. The logic of this strength drawn from exteriority is homologous with that of the 'simple mouvement de doigt' which tilts the earth on its axis in the *Essai sur l'origine des langues*: see Derrida's analysis, *De la grammatologie*, p. 363.

77. I refer to Rousseau's famous comment in the *Manuscrit de Genève*: 'efforçons nous de tirer du mal même le remède qui doit le guérir' (III, p. 288). See also Althusser, p. 17. The logic of this statement could be read in conjunction with Derrida's analyses of the *pharmakon* in 'La Pharmacie de Platon', in *La Dissémination*.

78. Clearly 'corps sans organes' cannot here be taken in a Deleuzian sense. It might in fact be more accurate, were this not still too metaphysical a notion, to characterize the 'corps politique' as remaining at the 'stade du miroir'.

79. The final version of the text in the *Contrat social* (Book II, Chapter 4, 'De la loi') is more concerned with a formal definition of the law than with the deduction of its necessity.

80. For this assumption, see for example Ellenburg, pp. 238–50.

81. Raymond Polin uses the term 'complément' to describe the legislator: see 'La Fonction du législateur chez Jean-Jacques Rousseau, in *Jean-Jacques Rousseau et son oeuvre: problèmes et recherches* (Paris: Klincksieck, 1964), pp. 231–48. For the distinction between 'complément' and 'supplément' see *De la grammatologie*, p. 208.

82. This invocation of God might seem to be regressive in view of the imputed

resistance to transcendence in eighteenth-century political discourse; but read at this point of the analysis, Rousseau's statement could equally be read as a lucid recognition of the inevitability of transcendence in the ethical sphere.

83. Having used the term 'deceit' to describe the appropriation of the 'chacun' in the passage discussed above, De Man goes on to apply the term to the fiction of the legislator. But 'deceit' is an unduly moralistic term here, not because the legislator does what he does 'for their own good', but because there is no available ground from which to identify the legislator's fiction as deceitful.

84. This undecidability is programmed by the ambivalence of the notion of the simulacrum, as shown by the following: 'Comme le régime des gens sains n'est pas propre aux malades, il ne faut pas vouloir gouverner un peuple corrompu par les mêmes Loix qui conviennent à un bon peuple. Rien ne prouve mieux cette maxime que la durée de la République de Venise, dont le simulacre existe encore, uniquement parce que ses Loix ne conviennent qu'à de méchans hommes' (III, pp. 452–3). On this complexity of the notion of *simulacre*, see Patrick Hochart's remarkable article 'Droit naturel et simulacre', pp. 81–4. But whereas Hochart thinks that the *simulacre* involved in Rousseau's political thought is of the natural law he appears to reject, I think it is a *simulacre* of the laws of nature.

85. On Rousseau's special admiration for Moses, see Bronislaw Baczko, 'Moïse, législateur . . .' in *Reappraisals of Rousseau: Studies in Honour of R.A. Leigh*, edited by S. Harvey, M. Hobson, D.J. Kelley and S.S.B. Taylor (Manchester University Press, 1980), pp. 111–30.

86. Posterity and Providence are the two instances to which Rousseau appeals in his attempts to secure the safety of the manuscript of the *Dialogues*: see the 'Histoire du précedent ecrit' (I, pp. 977–89), and Foucault's introduction to the edition published by the Bibliothèque de Cluny (Paris: Armand Colin, 1962). See note 2 to I, p. 982 for information on how the transmission to posterity worked (through Condillac) despite Rousseau's conviction that it had failed.

87. The most economic exposition of the questions raised by this paradox (which I hope to explore in more detail elsewhere) is no doubt to be found in a manuscript note distributed by Rousseau in 1774, printed as 'Déclaration relative à différentes réimpressions de ses ouvrages' (*Oeuvres complètes* I, pp. 1186–7).

88. See Julie on Wolmar (II, p. 369), and on Saint-Preux (II, p. 427).

89. This psychoanalytical line is taken by Tony Tanner in his essay on *La Nouvelle Héloïse* in *Adultery and the Novel: Contract and Transgression* (Baltimore and London: The Johns Hopkins University Press, 1979), pp. 113–78.

90. As when he writes to Julie, 'ta seule volonté me suffit' (II, p. 227), or to Claire of Julie, 'Puisqu'elle commande, il suffit' (II, p. 318), or, in terms of

the detour: 'Parlez-moi sans détour, Julie. A présent que je vous ai bien expliqué ce que je sens et ce que je pense, dites-moi ce qu'il faut que je fasse' (II, p. 686).

5 Sade: the Transgression of Nature

1. Georges May, 'Novel Reader, Fiction Writer', *Yale French Studies*, 35 (1965), pp. 5–11 (p. 9).
2. Maurice Blanchot, 'La Raison de Sade', in *Lautréamont et Sade* (Paris: Minuit, 1963), pp. 17–18 for the scandal, p. 47 for the quotation.
3. Georges Bataille, *L'érotisme* (Paris: Minuit, 1957), passim; Michel Foucault, *Les mots et les choses* (Paris: Gallimard, 1966), pp. 222–3.
4. Donatien-Alphonse-François, marquis de Sade, 'Idée sur les romans', in *Oeuvres complètes*, édition définitive, 16 vols. (Paris: Au Cercle du livre précieux, 1966–67), X, p. 19. All references to Sade are to this edition and will be incorporated into the text.
5. See for example the footnote to VIII, p. 328. I shall return to the implications of this type of text.
6. See especially 'La Notion de dépense' and *La Part maudite* (both texts published together under the latter title (Paris: Minuit, 1967)), and Derrida's essay elucidating this economy; 'De l'économie restreinte à l'économie générale', in *L'écriture et la différence*, pp. 369–407.
7. The role of the lightning-bolt in the three versions has been well analysed by Philippe Roger in *Sade: la philosophie dans le pressoir* (Paris: Grasset, 1976), pp. 146–55.
8. See for example Charles Villers, 'Lettre sur le roman intitulé "Justine"', *Le Spectateur du nord*, IV (1797), pp. 407–14, reprinted as a book in 1877: excerpts of this text are available in F. Laugaa-Traut's excellent *Lectures de Sade* (Paris: Armand Colin, 1973), pp. 75–7.
9. This does not of course imply that one should read the book as a scientific account of perversions: Gilbert Lély falls into this trap, and then criticizes the work for its excessive interest in coprophilia (this excess being measured against the truly scientific standard supplied by the authority of Krafft-Ebbing): see his *Vie* of Sade, *Edition définitive*, II, p. 256.
10. Michel Tort, 'L'effet Sade', *Tel Quel*, 28 (1967), pp. 66–83 (p. 74).
11. See for example Roland Barthes, *Fragments d'un discours amoureux* (Paris: Seuil, 1977), p. 8.
12. Philippe Sollers, 'Sade dans le texte', *Logiques* (Paris: Seuil, 1968), pp. 78–96 (p. 78).
13. Roland Barthes, 'Sade 1', in *Sade, Fourier, Loyola* (Paris: Seuil, 1971; reprinted collection 'Points', 1980), p. 32.
14. An example of double bind as a narrative device is provided in *La Nouvelle Justine*, where d'Esterval calculates on the basis of Justine's virtue that she will not attempt to escape because of a feeling of duty towards the guests she might save by staying. This double bind allows the narrative to continue, but is also a figure of d'Esterval's *jouissance* (VII,

pp. 94–5). See also VII, p. 30, for an example of a torture-machine as a figure of the double bind.

15. 'Droit naturel', *Oeuvres politiques*, pp. 29–35 (p. 34).
16. Marcel Hénaff, *Sade: l'invention du corps libertin* (Paris: PUF, 1978), pp. 243–83: this chapter owes much to Hénaff's masterly work.
17. Jean Baudrillard, *De la Séduction* (Paris: Galilée, 1979; reprinted by Denoël–Gonthier, 1981), pp. 120–4.
18. This argument was used earlier by Gilles Deleuze in his *Présentation de Sacher Masoch* (Paris: Minuit, 1967), p. 67.
19. And not a paradigm of Juliette's *libertinage* in general, as Jane Gallop takes it to be in *Intersections: A Reading of Sade with Bataille, Blanchot, and Klossowski* (Lincoln and London: Nebraska University Press, 1981), p. 20.
20. See too the principles laid down by the monk Sylvestre in *La Nouvelle Justine* (VI, pp. 336–7). It would be possible to argue that this push towards an individual law is in fact within the logic of the political thought of Sade's generation (see Leo Strauss, *Natural Right and History*, p. 14), and it would certainly find an echo in Marxism: see Allen Buchanan, *Marx and Justice: The Radical Critique of Liberalism* (London: Routledge and Kegan Paul, 1983), pp. 68–9 and the attendant quotations.
21. Jacques Lacan, 'Kant avec Sade', in *Ecrits*, II, pp. 119–48.
22. Maurice Blanchot, 'L'insurrection, la folie d'écrire', in *L'entretien infini* (Paris: Gallimard, 1969), pp. 323–42 (p. 336).
23. Pierre Naville, *D'Holbach et la philosophie scientifique au XVIIIe siècle*, second edition (Paris: Gallimard, 1967); Jean Deprun, 'Sade et le rationalisme des lumières', *Raison présente*, 3 (1967), pp. 75–90, and 'Quand Sade récrit Fréret, Voltaire et d'Holbach', in *Roman et lumières au XVIIIe siècle* (Paris: Editions sociales, 1970), pp. 331–40; Paul-Laurent Assoun's presentation of his edition of La Mettrie's *L'Homme machine* (Paris: Denoël–Gonthier, 1981).
24. See III, p. 493 (from *Français, encore un effort* . . .): 'La loi, froide par elle-même, ne saurait être accessible aux passions qui peuvent légitimer dans l'homme la cruelle action du meurtre; l'homme reçoit de la nature les impressions qui peuvent lui faire pardonner cette action, et la loi, au contraire, toujours en opposition à la nature et ne recevant rien d'elle, ne peut être autorisée à se permettre les mêmes écarts . . .' This notion of the law's being inaccessible to passion seems to be Aristotelian – see the *Politics*, 1287a: 'The law is reason unaffected by desire'.
25. Roger has a good chapter on the role of the volcano in *Sade: la Philosophie dans le pressoir* (Paris: Grasset, 1976), pp. 156–65.
26. Deleuze goes on to map this configuration on to the structure described by Freud in *Beyond the Pleasure Principle*: there are on the one hand death *drives*, mingled with life drives, processes which can only be observed as negative moments mingled with positive ones, in which destruction is only presentable as the 'envers' of construction. On the

other hand, the death *instinct*, which can never be presented as such, is pure negativity (*Présentation de Sacher Masoch*, p. 24). I think that it would be unwise to read Freud as the 'truth' of Sade (there is, for example, no reason why the structure of 'nature' as elaborated by Sade should be seen in psychic terms); it may be too that to discuss the ultimate silence of nature in Sade in terms of 'pure negativity' or a totalizing Idea is still too positive and 'philosophical' a description.

27. Lacan, 'Kant avec Sade', art. cit. But the logic of the simulacrum is not that of the phantasm. Sade 'goes further' than Lacan allows in stating simply that 'ça prêche un peu trop là-dedans' (*Ecrits*, II, p. 147): the 'preaching' is in fact undermined by the simulacrum and its associated values of fiction and even humour.

28. Blanchot, 'La Raison de Sade', pp. 34–44; Georges Bataille, 'L'homme souverain de Sade', in *L'Erotisme*, pp. 183–96.

29. See Blanchot, 'La Raison de Sade', p. 19; A.M. Laborde, 'La Notion d'isolisme', in *Sade romancier* (Neuchâtel: La Baconnière, 1974), pp. 157–63.

30. Nietzsche, 'The Genealogy of Morals', in *The Birth of Tragedy and the Genealogy of Morals*, translated by Francis Golffing (New York: Doubleday, 1956), p. 160: 'The lordly right of bestowing names is such that one would almost be justified in seeing the origin of language itself as an expression of the rulers' power. They say, "This is this or that"; they seal off each thing and action with a sound and thereby take symbolic possession of it.'

31. If Sade must be read with Kant, then we might note here how Sade operates in advance the sort of 'linguistic' critique of Kant more usually associated with Schopenhauer and Nietzsche. At this point it also becomes clear that the logic of Sade's language opens up an 'ultimate' Sadian possibility which he never exploits: a *perversity* which would function as a simulacrum indistinguishable from (Kantian) morality.

32. Georges Bataille, 'Sade et l'homme normal', in *L'Erotisme*, pp. 197–218, especially p. 207.

Note to the Postscript

1. See Serge Doubrovsky, 'Vingt propositions sur l'amour-propre: de Lacan à La Rochefoucauld', in *Parcours critique* (Paris: Galilée, 1980), pp. 203–34.

SELECT BIBLIOGRAPHY

The Bibliography lists only those works quoted or referred to in the text. For convenience, I have divided it into four sections: I. Fictional works first published before 1800; II. Non-fictional works first published before 1800; III. Historical and critical studies; IV. General and theoretical works. The following abbreviations are used throughout: *MLN* (*Modern Language Notes*); *MLR* (*Modern Language Review*); *NRF* (*La Nouvelle Revue française*); *OLR* (*The Oxford Literary Review*); *PMLA* (*Publications of the Modern Language Association of America*); PUF (Presses Universitaires de France); *SV* (*Studies on Voltaire and the Eighteenth Century*); UGE (Union Générale d'Edition).

I. Fictional works first published before 1800

Bougeant, Le père Guillaume Hyacinthe, *Voyage merveilleux du Prince Fan-Férédin dans la Romancie; contenant plusieurs observations historiques, géographiques, physiques, critiques & morales* (Paris, 1735)

Chamfort, Sebastien-Roch Nicolas, dit, *Maximes, pensées, caractères et anecdotes*, edited by Jean Dagen (Paris: Garnier-Flammarion, 1968)

Chasles, Robert, *Les Illustres Françoises: histoires véritables*, edited by Frédéric Deloffre, 2 vols. (Paris: Les Belles Lettres, 1959)

Choderlos de Laclos, Pierre-Ambroise-François, *Les Liaisons dangereuses*, edited by Yves Le Hir (Paris: Garnier, 1961)

Corbinelli, Jean, *Les Anciens Historiens Latins réduits en maximes: premier volume, Tite Live* (Paris, 1694)

Crébillon, Claude Prosper Jolyot de (Crébillon *fils*), *Collection complète des oeuvres de M. de Crébillon, fils*, 14 tomes in 7 vols. (London, 1777)

Lettres de la marquise de M*** au comte de R***, edited by Jean Rousset (Lausanne: La Guilde du Livre, 1965)

Les Egarements du coeur et de l'esprit, in *Romanciers du XVIIIe siècle*, edited by René Etiemble, 2 vols. (Paris: Gallimard, 1960–65), II, pp. 5–188.

Diderot, Denis, *Oeuvres romanesques*, edited by Henri Bénac (Paris: Garnier, 1962)

Essai sur les règnes de Claude et de Néron, edited by Roger Lewinter, 2 vols. (Paris: UGE, 1972)

Select Bibliography

Duclos, Charles Pineau, *Oeuvres complètes*, 3 vols. (Paris, 1821)
  Les Confessions du comte de ***, in *Romanciers du XVIIIe siècle*, edited by
  René Etiemble, 2 vols. (Paris: Gallimard, 1960–65), I, pp. 195–301
Fénelon, François de Salignac de la Mothe, *Les Aventures de Télémaque*,
  edited by Jeanne-Lydie Goré (Paris: Garnier-Flammarion, 1968)
La Bruyère, Jean de, *Les Caractères de Théophraste traduits du grec avec les
  caractères ou les moeurs de ce siècle*, edited by Robert Garapon (Paris:
  Garnier, 1962)
Lafayette, Marie-Madeleine Pioche de La Vergne, Comtesse de, *Romans et
  nouvelles*, edited by Emile Magne and Alain Niderst (Paris: Garnier,
  1970)
La Fontaine, Jean de, *Fables*, edited by Edmond Pilon and Fernand Dauphin
  (Paris: Garnier, 1960)
La Rochefoucauld, François, Duc de, *Maximes*, edited by Jacques Truchet
  (Paris: Garnier, 1967)
Louvet de Couvray, Jean-Baptiste, *Les Amours du Chevalier de Faublas*, in
  Romanciers du XVIIIe siècle, edited by René Etiemble, 2 vols. (Paris:
  Gallimard, 1960–65), II, pp. 407–1222
Marivaux, Pierre Carlet de Chamblain de, *Le Paysan Parvenu*, edited by
  Frédéric Deloffre (Paris: Garnier, 1969)
Montesquieu, Charles-Louis de Secondat, Baron de, *Lettres persanes*, in
  Oeuvres complètes, edited by Daniel Oster (Paris: Seuil, 1964), pp. 61–
  151
Perrault, Charles, *Contes*, edited by Jean-Pierre Collinet (Paris, Gallimard,
  1981)
Prévost, Abbé Antoine-François, *Histoire du chevalier des Grieux et de
  Manon Lescaut*, in *Romanciers du XVIIIe siècle*, I, pp. 1217–317
Rousseau, Jean-Jacques, *Julie ou la Nouvelle Héloïse*, in *Oeuvres com-
  plètes*, II, pp. 1–793.
Sade, Donatien-Alphonse-François, *Oeuvres complètes*, édition définitive,
  edited by Gilbert Lély, 16 vols. (Paris: Au Cercle du livre précieux, 1966–
  67)
Swift, Jonathan, *Gulliver's Travels*, edited by Peter Dixon and John Chalker
  (Harmondsworth: Penguin Books, 1967)
Vauvenargues, Luc de Clapiers, Marquis de, *Introduction à la connaissance de
  l'esprit humain; Fragments; Réflexions critiques; Réflexions et maximes;
  Méditation sur la foi*, edited by Jean Dagen (Paris, Garnier-Flammarion,
  1981)
Voltaire, François-Marie Arouet de, *Romans et contes*, edited by Henri Bénac
  (Paris: Garnier, 1960)

II. Non-fictional works first published before 1800

d'Alembert, Jean le Rond, *Discours préliminaire de l'encyclopédie* (Paris:
  Gonthier, 1965)
d'Argens, Jean-Baptiste de Boyer, 'Discours sur les nouvelles', in *Lectures
  amusantes, ou les délassements de l'esprit*, 2 vols. (La Haye, 1739),
  pp. 9–69

Select Bibliography

Aristotle, *The Works of Aristotle translated into English*, edited by W.D. Ross, 12 vols. (Oxford: Clarendon Press, 1912–58)

Arnauld, Antoine, and Pierre Nicole, *La Logique ou l'art de penser* (1662–83), edited by Louis Marin (Paris: Flammarion, 1970)

d'Aubignac, Abbé François Hédelin, *La Pratique du théâtre*, edited by Hans-Jörg Neuschäfer (Genève: Slatkine Reprints, 1971)

Baculard d'Arnauld, François-Thomas-Marie de, 'Préface', in *Les Epreuves du sentiment*, in *Oeuvres complètes*, 3 vols. (Paris, 1803), I

Bary, René, *La Rhétorique françoise. Où l'on trouve de nouveaux exemples sur les Passions & sur les Figures. Où l'on traitte à fonds de la Matiere des Genres Oratoires et où le sentiment des puristes est rapporté sur les usages de nostre Langue, Nouvelle édition* (Paris, 1659)

Beccaria, Cesare, *Des Délits et des peines* (1764), translated by Collin de Plancy, edited by Jean-Pierre Juillet (Paris: Flammarion, 1979)

Béliard, François, 'Discours pour la défense des romans', in *Zélaskim*, 4 vols. (Paris, 1765), I, pp. i–xlvii

Bérardier de Bataut, *Essai sur le récit ou entretien sur la manière de raconter* (Paris, 1776)

Boileau-Despréaux, Nicolas, *Oeuvres complètes*, edited by F. Escal (Paris: Gallimard, 1966)

Bossuet, Jacques-Bénigne, *Politique tirée des propres paroles de l'écriture sainte* (1709), edited by Jacques Le Brun (Genève: Droz, 1967)

Bouhours, Le père Dominique, *La Manière de bien penser dans les ouvrages de l'esprit* (Paris, 1687)

Bricaire de la Dixmérie, Nicolas, 'Discours sur l'origine, les progrès et le genre des romans', in *Toni et Clairette*, 2 vols. (Paris, 1797), I, pp. v–lxxvi

Castel de Saint-Pierre, Abbé Charles Irénée, *Projet pour perfectionner l'éducation, avec un discours sur la grandeur et la sainteté des hommes* (Paris, 1728)

Choderlos de Laclos, Pierre-Ambroise-François, *Oeuvres complètes*, edited by Laurent Versini (Paris: Gallimard, 1979)

Condillac, Abbé Etienne Bonnot de, *Oeuvres philosophiques*, edited by Georges Le Roy, 3 vols. (Paris: PUF, 1947–50)

Essai sur l'origine des connaissances humaines, edited by Charles Porset (Auvers-sur-Oise: Galilée, 1973)

Crévier, Jean-Baptiste-Louis, *Rhétorique française*, 2 vols. (Paris, 1765)

Crousaz, Jean-Pierre de, *Traité de l'éducation des enfants*, 2 vols. (La Haye, 1722)

Diderot, Denis, *Oeuvres politiques*, edited by Paul Vernière (Paris: Garnier, 1963)

Oeuvres philosophiques, edited by Paul Vernière (Paris: Garnier, 1964)

Lettre sur les sourds et muets, edited by Paul Hugo Meyer, *Diderot Studies*, 7 (1965) pp. 60–62

Oeuvres esthétiques, edited by Paul Vernière (Paris: Garnier, 1968)

Du Marsais, César Cheneau, *Oeuvres*, 7 vols. (Paris, 1797)

Des Tropes, postface de Claude Mouchard (Paris: Le Nouveau Commerce, 1977)

Select Bibliography

Du Plaisir, *Sentiments sur les lettres et sur l'histoire avec des scrupules sur le stile* (Paris: 1683)

L'esprit de Fontenelle ou recueil de pensées tirées de ses ouvrages (La Haye, 1753)

Esprit, maximes et principes de Fontenelle de l'Académie Française (Paris, 1788)

Fénelon, François de Salignac de la Mothe, *De l'éducation des filles*, in *Oeuvres complètes*, 10 vols. (Paris 1848–52; Genève: Slatkine reprints, 1971), V, pp. 563–99

Fleury, Abbé Claude, *Traité du choix et de la méthode des études* (Paris, 1686)

Fontenelle, Bernard le Bouyer de, *De l'origine des fables* (1724), edited by J.R. Carré (Paris: Alcan, 1932)

Gibert, Balthasar, *La Rhétorique ou les règles de l'éloquence*, (Paris, 1730)

Grotius, Hugo, *Le Droit de la guerre et de la paix*, Nouvelle traduction de Jean Barbeyrac (Amsterdam, 1724)

Huet, Pierre-Daniel, *Traité de l'origine des romans*, eighth edition (Paris, 1711), critical edition by Arend Kok (Amsterdam: Swets and Zeitlinger, 1942)

Jacquin, Abbé Armand-Pierre, *Entretiens sur les romans. Ouvrage moral et critique, dans lequel on traite de l'origine des romans et de leurs différentes espèces, tant par rapport à l'esprit, que par rapport au coeur* (Paris, 1755)

Jaucourt, Chevalier Louis de, art. 'Sentence', in Diderot et d'Alembert, eds., *Encyclopédie ou Dictionnaire raisonné des sciences, des arts, & des métiers*, 17 vols. (Paris, 1751–65), XV (1765), pp. 55–6

Jouvancy, Le père Joseph de, *Candidatus Rhetoricae* (Paris, 1712)

L'Elève de rhétorique, translated by H. Ferté (Paris: Hachette, 1892)

La Condamine, Charles-Marie de, *Lettre critique sur l'éducation* (Paris, 1751)

La Harpe, Jean-François de, 'Des romans', in *Oeuvres*, 6 vols. (Paris, 1778), III, pp. 337–88

Lambert, Anne-Thérèse, Marquise de, *Oeuvres complètes* (Paris, 1808)

La Mettrie, Julien Offroy de, *L'Homme machine* (1748), edited by Paul-Laurent Assoun (Paris: Denoël/Gonthier, 1981)

Lamy, Le père Bernard, *La Rhétorique ou l'art de parler*, Quatrième édition revue et augmentée (Paris, 1701)

Le Bossu, Le père René, *Traité du poème épique* (1675), Nouvelle édition revue et corrigée, 2 vols. (Paris, 1708)

Le Gras, Sieur, *La Réthorique (sic) françoise, ou les préceptes de l'ancienne et vraye éloquence* (Paris, 1671)

Leibniz, Gottfried Wilhelm, *Nouveaux Essais sur l'entendement humain* (1765), edited by Jacques Brunschwig (Paris: Garnier-Flammarion, 1966)

Lenglet Dufresnoy, Abbé Nicolas, *Méthode pour étudier l'histoire*, 2 vols. (Paris, 1713)

De l'Usage des romans, 2 vols. (Amsterdam, 1734)

L'Histoire justifiée contre les romans (Amsterdam, 1735)

Linguet, Simon-Nicolas-Henri, *Théorie des loix civiles, ou principes fonda-*

mentaux de la société, Nouvelle édition. Revue, corrigée et augmentée, in *Oeuvres*, 6 vols. (London, 1774), III–V

Locke, John, *The Educational Writings of John Locke*, edited by James L. Axtell (Cambridge University Press, 1968)

Two Treatises of Government, edited by Peter Laslett (Cambridge University Press, 1960)

An Essay Concerning Human Understanding, edited by Peter H. Nidditch (Oxford: Clarendon Press, 1975)

Mably, Gabriel Bonnot, Abbé de, *Sur la théorie du pouvoir politique*, edited by Peter Friedmann (Paris: Editions sociales, 1975)

Marmontel, Jean-François, *Poétique française*, 2 vols. (Paris, 1767)

Elémens de Littérature, in *Oeuvres complètes*, 18 vols. (Paris, 1819), XII–XV

Essai sur les romans, considérés du côté moral, in *Oeuvres complètes*, X, pp. 253–318

Méré, Antoine Gombauld, chevalier de, 'De la Conversation' (1677), in *Oeuvres*, edited by Ch.-H. Boudhors, 3 vols. (Paris: Fernand Roches, 1930), II, pp. 99–132

Montesquieu, Charles-Louis de Secondat, Baron de, *Oeuvres complètes*, edited by Daniel Oster (Paris: Seuil, 1964)

Morelly, *Code de la nature: ou le véritable esprit de ses lois, de tout temps négligé ou méconnu*, edited by Albert Soboul (Paris: Editions sociales, 1970)

Pascal, Blaise, *Pensées*, edited by Louis Lafuma (Paris: Seuil, 1962)

Pesselier, Charles-Etienne, *Lettres sur l'éducation*, 2 vols. (Paris, 1762)

Pufendorf, Samuel, *Le Droit de la nature et des gens, ou système général des principes les plus importans de la morale, de la jurisprudence, et de la politique*, translated by Jean Barbeyrac (Amsterdam, 1706)

Les Devoirs de l'homme et du citoien tels qu'ils lui sont prescrits par la Loi Naturelle, fifth edition, translated by Jean Barbeyrac, 2 vols. (Amsterdam, 1735)

Quintilian, *Institutio Oratoria*, translated by H.E. Butler, 4 vols. (London: Heinemann, 1920–22)

Rapin, Le père René, *Les Réflexions sur la poétique de ce temps et sur les ouvrages des poètes anciens et modernes*, edited by E. Dubois (Genève: Droz, 1970)

Rollin, Charles, *De la manière d'enseigner et d'étudier les belles lettres, par rapport à l'esprit et au coeur*, second edition, revised and corrected, 4 vols. (Paris, 1728–31)

Rousseau, Jean-Jacques, *Oeuvres complètes*, edited by Bernard Gagnebin and Marcel Raymond, 4 vols. published to date (Paris: Gallimard, 1959–)

Essai sur l'origine des langues, où il est parlé de la mélodie et de l'imitation musicale, edited by Charles Porset (Paris: Nizet, 1970)

Lettre à M. d'Alembert sur son article 'Genève', edited by Michel Launay (Paris: Garnier-Flammarion, 1967)

Select Bibliography

Vanière, Ignace, *Discours sur l'éducation* (Paris, 1760)

Second discours sur l'éducation, dans lequel on expose tout le vicieux de l'Institution Scholastique, & le moyen d'y remédier (Paris, 1763)

Vico, Giambattista, *The New Science*, translated by T.G. Bergin and M.H. Fisch (Ithaca and London: Cornell University Press, 1968)

Voltaire, François-Marie Arouet de, *Essai sur les moeurs*, edited by René Pomeau, 2 vols. (Paris: Garnier, 1963)

III. Historical and critical studies

Aarsleff, Hans, 'Leibniz on Locke on Language', *American Philosophical Quarterly*, 1 (1964), pp. 165–88

Althusser, Louis, *Montesquieu: la politique et l'histoire*, fifth edition (Paris: PUF, 1981)

'Sur le *Contrat social*', *Cahiers pour l'analyse*, 8 (1967), pp. 5–42

Baczko, Bronislaw, 'Moïse, législateur . . .', in *Reappraisals of Rousseau: Studies in Honour of R.A. Leigh* (see below), pp. 111–30

Baker, Felicity, 'La Route contraire', in *Reappraisals of Rousseau: Studies in Honour of R.A. Leigh* (see below), pp. 132–62

Barthes, Roland, 'La Bruyère', in *Essais critiques* (Paris: Seuil, 1964), pp. 221–37

'La Rochefoucauld: réflexions ou sentences et maximes', in *Le Degré zéro de l'écriture, suivi de Nouveaux Essais critiques* (Paris: Seuil, 1972), pp. 69–88

Sade, Fourier, Loyola (Paris: Seuil, 1972; reprinted collection 'Points', 1980)

Bennington, Geoffrey P., 'From Narrative to Text: Love and Writing in Crébillon *fils*, Duclos, Barthes', *OLR*, 4:1 (1979), pp. 62–81

'Réappropriations', *Poétique*, 48 (1981), pp. 495–512

'Les Machines de l'Opéra: le jeu du signe dans le *Spectateur Français* de Marivaux', *French Studies*, 36 (1982), pp. 154–70

Bilezikian, Monique Araxe, 'Les Maximes dans les *Mémoires* du Cardinal de Retz' (unpublished dissertation, Harvard University, 1975)

Brooks, Peter, *The Novel of Worldliness: Crébillon, Marivaux, Laclos, Stendhal* (Princeton University Press, 1969)

Conroy, Peter V., Jr., *Crébillon fils: Techniques of the Novel*, *SV*, 99 (1972)

Crocker, Lester G., *Rousseau's Social Contract: An Interpretive Essay* (Cleveland: Case Western Reserve University Press, 1968)

Culler, Jonathan, 'Paradox and the Language of Morals in La Rochefoucauld', *MLR*, 68 (1973), pp. 28–39

Dainville, François de, *L'éducation des Jésuites (XVIe–XVIIIe siècles)*, edited by Marie-Madeleine Compère (Paris: Minuit, 1978)

Davy, Georges, 'Note introductive', in Emile Durkheim, *Montesquieu et Rousseau: précurseurs de la sociologie* (Paris: Marcel Rivière, 1953)

Deleuze, Gilles, *Présentation de Sacher Masoch: avec le texte intégral de 'La Vénus à la fourrure', traduit de l'allemand par Ande Willm* (Paris: Minuit, 1967)

Select Bibliography

Deprun, Jean, 'Sade et le rationalisme des lumières', *Raison présente*, 3 (1967), pp. 75–90

'Quand Sade récrit Fréret, Voltaire et d'Holbach', in *Roman et lumières au XVIIIe siècle* (Paris: Editions sociales, 1970), pp. 331–40

Derathé, Robert, *Jean-Jacques Rousseau et la science politique de son temps* (Paris: PUF, 1950)

Derrida, Jacques, 'L'Archéologie du frivole', in Condillac, *Essai sur l'origine des connaissances humaines*, edited by Charles Porset (Auvers-sur-Oise: Galilée, 1973), pp. 9–95

Ehrard, Jean: 'De Meilcour à Adolphe, ou la suite des *Egarements*', *Transactions of the Fifth International Congress on the Enlightenment*, *SV*, 190 (1980), pp. 101–17

Ellenburg, Stephen, *Rousseau's Political Philosophy: An Interpretation from Within* (Ithaca and London: Cornell University Press, 1976)

Foucault, Michel, 'Un si cruel savoir', *Critique*, 182 (1962), pp. 597–611

Les mots et les choses: une archéologie des sciences humaines (Paris: Gallimard, 1966)

Surveiller et punir: naissance de la prison (Paris: Gallimard, 1975)

France, Peter, *Rhetoric and Truth in France: Descartes to Diderot* (Oxford: Clarendon Press, 1972)

Gagnebin, Bernard, 'Le rôle du législateur dans les conceptions politiques de Rousseau', in *Etudes sur le Contrat social* (Paris: Les Belles Lettres, 1964), pp. 277–90

Gallop, Jane, *Intersections: A Reading of Sade with Bataille, Blanchot, and Klossowski* (Lincoln and London: Nebraska University Press, 1981)

Gordon, E.I., *Sumerian Proverbs* (Philadelphia: The University Museum, University of Pennsylvania, 1959)

Groethuysen, Bernard, *Les Origines de l'esprit bourgeois en France* (Paris: Gallimard, 1927)

Harari, Josué V., 'Therapeutic Pedagogy: Rousseau's *Emile*', *MLN*, 97 (1982), pp. 787–809

Hénaff, Marcel, *Sade: l'invention du corps libertin* (Paris: PUF, 1978)

Hobson, Marian, *The Object of Art: The Theory of Illusion in Eighteenth-Century France* (Cambridge University Press, 1982)

Hochart, Patrick, 'Droit naturel et simulacre', *Cahiers pour l'analyse*, 8 (1967), pp. 65–84

The House of Sade, *Yale French Studies*, 35 (1965)

Huxley, Aldous, 'Crébillon the Younger', in *The Olive Tree and Other Essays* (London, Chatto and Windus, 1936), pp. 135–49

Jean-Jacques Rousseau et son oeuvre: problèmes et recherches, Commémoration et colloque de Paris (Paris: Klincksieck, 1964)

Kavanagh, Thomas M., *The Vacant Mirror: A Study of Mimesis Through Jacques le Fataliste*, *SV*, 104 (1973)

Kent, John P., 'Crébillon fils, Mrs Eliza Haywood and *Les Heureux Orphelins*: A Problem of Authorship', *Romance Notes*, 11 (1969), pp. 326–32

Kibédi Varga, A, 'L'invention de la fable', *Poétique*, 25 (1976), pp. 107–15

Select Bibliography

Kruse, Margot, *Die Maxime in der französischen Literatur: Studien zum Werk La Rochefoucaulds und seiner Nachfolger* (Hamburg: De Gruyter, 1960)

Kuentz, Pierre, 'Le "rhétorique" ou la mise à l'écart', *Communications*, 16 (1970), pp. 143–57

Laborde, A.M., *Sade Romancier* (Neuchâtel: La Baconnière, 1974)

Lacan, Jacques, 'Kant avec Sade', in *Ecrits* (Paris: Seuil, 1966; reprinted collection 'Points', 2 vols., 1970–71), pp. 119–48

Laugaa-Traut, Françoise, *Lectures de Sade* (Paris: Armand Colin, 1973)

Lewis, Philip E., 'La Rochefoucauld: The Rationality of Play', *Yale French Studies*, 41 (1968), pp. 133–47

La Rochefoucauld: The Art of Abstraction (Ithaca and London: Cornell University Press, 1977)

Lovejoy, Arthur O., *The Great Chain of Being: A Study in the History of an Idea* (Harvard University Press, 1950)

Marin, Louis, *La Critique du discours: sur la 'Logique de Port-Royal' et les 'Pensées' de Pascal* (Paris: Minuit, 1975)

Le Récit est un piège (Paris: Minuit, 1978)

Le Portrait du Roi (Paris: Minuit, 1981)

Masters, Roger, *The Political Philosophy of Rousseau* (Princeton University Press, 1968)

May, Georges, *Le Dilemme du roman au XVIIIe siècle: étude sur les rapports du roman et de la critique, 1715–1761* (Yale University Press/Paris: PUF, 1963)

'Novel Reader, Fiction Writer', *Yale French Studies*, 35 (1965), pp. 5–11

May, Gita, 'Les "Pensées détachées sur la peinture" de Diderot et la tradition classique de la "maxime" et de la "pensée"', *Revue d'histoire littéraire de la France*, 70 (1970), pp. 45–63

Méry, C. de, *Histoire générale des proverbes, adages, sentences, apophthegmes*, 3 vols. (Paris: Delongchamps, 1828)

Mesnard, P., 'Rollin forge l'esprit de l'enseignement secondaire', in *Les Grands Pédagogues*, edited by Jean Château, third edition (Paris: PUF, 1966), pp. 147–69

Naville, Pierre, *D'Holbach et la philosophie scientifique au XVIIIe siècle*, second edition (Paris: Gallimard, 1967)

Padley, Graham A., *Grammatical Theory in Western Europe, 1500–1700: The Latin Tradition* (Cambridge University Press, 1976)

Pagliaro, Harold E., 'Paradox in the Aphorisms of La Rochefoucauld and some Representative English Followers', *PMLA* 79 (1964), pp. 42–50

Palmer, Benjamin, 'Crébillon *fils* and his reader', *SV*, 132 (1975), pp. 183–97

Les Paradoxes du romancier: les 'Egarements' de Crébillon, edited by Pierre Rétat (Presses Universitaires de Grenoble, 1975)

Polin, Raymond, 'La Fonction du législateur chez Jean-Jacques Rousseau', in *Jean-Jacques Rousseau et son oeuvre* (see above), pp. 231–48

Raymond, Marcel, *Jean-Jacques Rousseau: la quête de soi et la rêverie* (Paris: Corti, 1962)

Select Bibliography

Reappraisals of Rousseau: Studies in Honour of R.A. Leigh, edited by S. Harvey, M. Hobson, D.J. Kelley, and S.S.B. Taylor (Manchester University Press, 1980)

Robinet, André, *Le Langage à l'âge classique* (Paris: Klincksieck, 1978)

Rodis-Lewis, Geneviève, 'Un Théoricien du langage au XVIIe siècle: Bernard Lamy', *Le Français moderne*, 36 (1968), pp. 19–50

Roger, Philippe, *Sade: la philosophie dans le pressoir* (Paris: Grasset, 1976)

Schwartz, William L., and Clarence B. Olsen, *The Sententiae in the Dramas of Corneille* (Stanford University Press, 1939)

Shackleton, Robert, *Montesquieu: A Critical Biography* (Oxford University Press, 1961)

Showalter, English, *The Evolution of the French Novel, 1641–1782* (Princeton University Press, 1972)

Siemek, Andrzej, *La Recherche morale et esthétique dans le roman de Crébillon fils*, *SV*, 200 (Banbury, 1981)

Silverblatt, Bette Gross, *The Maxims in the Novels of Duclos* (The Hague: Nijhoff, 1972)

Snyders, Georges, *La Pédagogie en France aux XVIIe et XVIIIe siècles* (Paris: PUF, 1964)

Sollers, Philippe, 'Sade dans le texte', in *Logiques* (Paris: Seuil, 1968), pp. 78–96

Starobinski, Jean, *Montesquieu* (Paris: Seuil, 1953)

  'Introduction', to La Rochefoucauld, *Maximes et mémoires* (Paris: UGE, 1964)

  'La Rochefoucauld et les morales substitutives', *NRF* 28 (1966), pp. 16–34, and 29 (1966), pp. 211–29

  Jean-Jacques Rousseau, la transparence et l'obstacle, revised edition (Paris: Gallimard, 1971)

  L'oeil vivant (Paris: Gallimard, 1961)

Stewart, Philip, *Le Masque et la parole: le langage de l'amour au XVIIIe siècle* (Paris: Corti, 1973)

Tort, Michel, 'L'effet Sade', *Tel Quel*, 28 (1967), pp. 66–83

Vernes, Paule-Monique, *La Ville, la fête, la démocratie: Rousseau et les illusions de la communauté* (Paris: Payot, 1978)

Vernière, Paul, *Spinoza et la pensée française avant la Révolution*, 2 vols. (Paris, PUF, 1954)

Viguerie, Jean de, *L'Institution des enfants: l'éducation en France, XVIe–XVIIIe siècle* (Paris: Calmann-Lévy, 1978)

Zumthor, Paul, 'L'éphiphonème proverbial', *Revue des sciences humaines*, 163 (1976), pp. 313–28

IV. General and theoretical works

Bachelard, Gaston, *La Psychanalyse du feu* (Paris: Gallimard, 1949; reprinted collection 'Idées', 1966)

Barthes, Roland, *Mythologies* (Paris: Seuil, 1957; reprinted collection 'Points', 1970)

Select Bibliography

Essais critiques (Paris: Seuil, 1964)

Le Degré zéro de l'écriture, suivi de Nouveaux Essais critiques (Paris: Seuil, 1972)

'Introduction à l'analyse structurale du récit' (1966), in *Poétique du récit*, edited by Gérard Genette and Tzvetan Todorov (Paris: Seuil, 1977), pp. 8–57

'Le Discours de l'histoire', *Social Sciences Information*, 6 (1967), pp. 65–75

'L'effet de réel', *Communications*, 11 (1968), pp. 84–9

S/Z (Paris: Seuil, 1970; reprinted collection 'Points', 1976)

Le Plaisir du texte (Paris: Seuil, 1973)

Roland Barthes (Paris: Seuil, 1975)

Fragments d'un discours amoureux (Paris: Seuil, 1977)

Bataille, Georges, *La Part maudite [1949], précédé de la Notion de dépense [1933]* (Paris: Minuit, 1967)

L'erotisme (Paris: Minuit, 1957)

Baudrillard, Jean, *Oublier Foucault* (Paris: Galilée, 1977)

De la Séduction (Paris: Galilée, 1979; reprinted by Denoël–Gonthier, 1981)

Bennington, Geoffrey P., 'Reading Allegory', *OLR*, 4:3 (1981), pp. 83–93

'Not Yet: Fredric Jameson's Political Unconscious', *Diacritics*, 12:3 (1982), pp. 23–32

Benveniste, Emile, *Problèmes de linguistique générale*, 2 vols. (Paris: Gallimard, 1966–74)

Berger, Peter L., and Thomas Luckman, *The Social Construction of Reality: A Treatise in the Sociology of Knowledge* (Harmondsworth: Penguin Books, 1971)

Blanchot, Maurice, *Lautréamont et Sade* (Paris: Minuit, 1963)

L'entretien infini (Paris: Gallimard, 1969)

Le Pas au-delà (Paris: Gallimard, 1973)

Borges, Jorge Luis, *Ficciones* (Buenos Aires: Emecé Editores, 1956)

Buchanan, Allen E., *Marx and Justice: The Radical Critique of Liberalism* (London: Methuen, 1982)

Collingwood, Robin George, *The Idea of History* (Oxford: Clarendon Press, 1946)

Compagnon, Antoine, *La Seconde Main, ou le travail de la citation* (Paris: Seuil, 1979)

Culler, Jonathan, *Flaubert: The Uses of Uncertainty* (London: Paul Elek, 1974)

Structuralist Poetics: Structuralism, Linguistics and the Study of Literature (London: Routledge and Kegan Paul, 1975)

The Pursuit of Signs: Semiotics, Literature, Deconstruction (London: Routledge and Kegan Paul, 1981)

On Deconstruction: Theory and Criticism after Structuralism (London: Routledge and Kegan Paul, 1983)

Deconstruction and Criticism, edited by Geoffrey H. Hartman (London: Routledge and Kegan Paul, 1979)

Select Bibliography

De Man, Paul, *Allegories of Reading: Figural Language in Rousseau, Nietzsche, Rilke and Proust* (Yale University Press, 1979)

'The Epistemology of Metaphor', *Critical Inquiry*, 5 (1978–9), pp. 13–30

Derrida, Jacques, *La Voix et le phénomène: introduction au problème du signe dans la phénoménologie de Husserl* (1967), third edition (Paris: PUF, 1976)

De la grammatologie (Paris: Minuit, 1967)

L'écriture et la différence (Paris: Seuil, 1967; reprinted collection 'Points', 1979)

La Dissémination (Paris: Seuil, 1972)

Marges: de la philosophie (Paris: Minuit, 1972)

Positions (Paris: Minuit, 1972)

Glas (Paris: Galilée, 1974)

'Pas', *Gramma*, 3–4 (n.d.), pp. 111–215

'Limited Inc.', Supplement to *Glyph*, 2 (1977)

La Vérité en peinture (Paris: Flammarion, 1978)

'Living On: Border Lines', translated by James Hulbert, in *Deconstruction and Criticism* (see above), pp. 75–176

La Carte postale de Socrate à Freud et au-delà (Paris: Aubier-Flammarion, 1980)

'La Loi du genre', *Glyph*, 7 (1980), pp. 176–201

'Les Morts de Roland Barthes', *Poétique*, 47 (1981), pp. 269–92

Otobiographies: l'enseignement de Nietzsche et la politique du nom propre (Paris: Galilée, 1984)

Descombes, Vincent, *L'inconscient malgré lui* (Paris: Minuit, 1977)

Doubrovsky, Serge, *Parcours critique* (Paris: Galilée, 1980)

Dubois, Jean, *Grammaire structurale du Français: le verbe* (Paris: Larousse, 1967)

and Claude Dubois, *Introduction à la lexicographie: le dictionnaire* (Paris: Larousse, 1971)

Ducrot, Oswald, 'Présupposés et sous-entendus', *Langue française*, 4 (1969), pp. 30–43

Dire et ne pas dire: principes de sémantique linguistique (Paris: Hermann, 1972)

and Tzvetan Todorov, *Dictionnaire encyclopédique des sciences du langage* (Paris: Seuil, 1972; reprinted collection 'Points', 1979)

d'Entrèves, A.P., *Natural Law: An Introduction to Legal Philosophy* (1951), second edition (London: Hutchinson, 1970)

Flaubert, Gustave, *Oeuvres complètes*, edited by Bernard Masson, 2 vols. (Paris: Seuil, 1964)

Foucault, Michel, *L'archéologie du savoir* (Paris: Gallimard, 1969)

L'ordre du discours (Paris: Gallimard, 1971)

Freud, Sigmund, *Jokes and Their Relation to the Unconscious*, translated and edited by James Strachey, The Pelican Freud Library, Vol. 6 (Harmondsworth: Penguin Books, 1976)

On Sexuality, translated and edited by Angela Richards, The Pelican Freud Library, Vol. 7 (Harmondsworth: Penguin Books, 1977)

Genette, Gérard, *Figures I* (Paris: Seuil, 1966; reprinted collection 'Points', 1976)

Figures II (Paris: Seuil, 1969)

Figures III (Paris: Seuil, 1972)

Hacking, Ian, *Why Does Language Matter to Philosophy?* (Cambridge University Press, 1975)

Hare, R.M., *The Language of Morals* (Oxford: Clarendon Press, 1952; reprinted Oxford University Press, 1964)

Hegel, Georg Wilhelm Friedrich, *Aesthetics: Lectures on Fine Art*, translated by T.M. Knox, 2 vols. (Oxford: Clarendon Press, 1975)

Heidegger, Martin, *Basic Writings*, edited by David Farrell Krell (London: Routledge and Kegan Paul, 1978)

Hill, Leslie, 'Flaubert and the Rhetoric of Stupidity', *Critical Inquiry*, 3 (1976), pp. 333–44

Jameson, Fredric, *The Political Unconscious: Narrative as a Socially Symbolic Act* (London: Methuen, 1981)

Joliet, Jos, *L'Enfant au chien-assis* (Paris: Galilée, 1979)

Kant, Immanuel, *Political Writings*, translated by B. Nisbet, edited by Hans Reiss (Cambridge University Press, 1970)

Critique of Practical Reason, and Other Writings in Moral Philosophy, translated and edited by L.W. Beck (Chicago University Press, 1949)

Kerbrat-Orecchioni, Catherine, *L'énonciation: de la subjectivité dans le langage* (Paris: Armand Colin, 1980)

Kristeva, Julia, *Sémiotikè: recherches pour une sémanalyse* (Paris: Seuil, 1969)

Lacan, Jacques, *Ecrits* (Paris: Seuil, 1966; reprinted collection 'Points', 2 vols., 1970–71)

Le Séminaire, Livre XI: Les quatre concepts fondamentaux de la psychanalyse (Paris: Seuil, 1973)

Latour, Bruno, and Paolo Fabbri, 'Rhétorique de la science', *Actes de la recherche en sciences sociales*, 13 (1977), pp. 81–95

Lyons, John, *Introduction to Theoretical Linguistics* (Cambridge University Press, 1968)

Lyotard, Jean-François, *La Phénoménologie* (1954), eighth edition (Paris: PUF, 1976)

Dérive à partir de Marx et Freud (Paris: UGE, 1973)

La Condition postmoderne (Paris: Minuit, 1979)

Le Différend (Paris: Minuit, 1984)

Martel, V., *Une Bonne Pensée par jour: recueil de pensées et maximes morales, à l'usage des familles et des écoles de tous les degrés* (Paris: Garnier, no date [1895])

Marx, Karl, *Capital: A Critique of Political Economy*, translated by Ben Fowkes, The Pelican Marx Library, Vol. 1 (Harmondsworth: Penguin Books, 1976)

Meleuc, Serge, 'Structure de la maxime', *Langages*, 13 (1969), pp. 69–99

Meschonnic, Henri, 'Les Proverbes, actes de discours', *Revue des sciences humaines*, 163 (1976), pp. 419–30

Select Bibliography

Mill, John Stuart, *Nature, The Utility of Religion and Theism* (London: Longman, Green, Reader and Dyer, 1874)

Milner, George B., 'De l'Armature des locutions proverbiales: essai de taxonomie sémantique', *L'Homme*, 9 (1969), pp. 49–70

Minguelez, Roberto, 'Le Récit historique: légalité et signification', *Semiotica*, 3 (1971), pp. 20–36

Morin, Edgar, *La Méthode* (Vol. I, *La Nature de la nature*) (Paris: Seuil, 1977, reprinted collection 'Points', 1981).

Nancy, Jean-Luc, *Ego sum* (Paris: Aubier-Flammarion, 1979)
L'impératif catégorique (Paris: Aubier-Flammarion, 1983)

Nietzsche, Friedrich, *The Birth of Tragedy and the Genealogy of Morals*, translated by Francis Golffing (New York: Doubleday, 1956)

O'Brien, Justin, *The Maxims of Marcel Proust* (Columbia University Press, 1948)

Paulhan, Jean, 'L'expérience du proverbe', in *Oeuvres complètes*, 5 vols. (Paris: Au Cercle du livre précieux, 1966), II, pp. 101–24

Pierssens, Michel, 'Fonction et champ de la maxime', *Sub-stance*, 1 (1971), pp. 1–9

Poétique du récit, edited by Gérard Genette and Tzvetan Todorov (Paris: Seuil, 1977)

Prendergast, Christopher, *Balzac: Fiction and Melodrama* (London: Edwin Arnold, 1978)

Ricardou, Jean, *Nouveaux problèmes du roman* (Paris: Seuil, 1978)

Rodegem, François, 'Un problème de terminologie: les locutions sentencieuses', *Cahiers de l'Institut de Linguistique de l'Université Catholique de Louvain*, 5 (1972), pp. 677–703

Smith, Logan Pearsall, *A Treasury of English Aphorisms* (London: Constable, 1928)

Smith, Neil, and Deirdre Wilson, *Modern Linguistics: The Results of Chomsky's Revolution* (Harmondsworth: Penguin Books, 1979)

Sollers, Philippe, *Logiques* (Paris: Seuil, 1968)

Strauss, Leo, *Natural Right and History* (Chicago University Press, 1953)

Todorov, Tzvetan, *Poétique de la prose* (Paris: Seuil, 1971)

Translations from the Philosophical Writings of Gottlob Frege, translated and edited by Max Black and Peter Geach, third edition (Oxford: Blackwell, 1980)

Veyne, Paul, *Comment on écrit l'histoire, suivi de Foucault révolutionne l'histoire* (Paris: Seuil, 1971; reprinted collection 'Points', 1979)

INDEX

Index

271

Index

Kristeva, Julia, 213 n32
Kruse, M., 58, 226 n156

La Bruyère, Jean de, 51, 137
Lacan, Jacques, 198, 205, 209, 240 n33, 256 n27
Laclos, P.-A.-F. Choderlos de, 68, 103, 236 n7
La Condamine, Charles-Marie de, 96
Lafayette, Mme de, 82, 127
La Fontaine, Jean de, 51, 80, 85–90, 232 n41
La Harpe, Jean-François de, 232 n35
Lambert, Mme de, 92–3
Lamy, Bernard, 39, 46–50, 51, 55, 84, 221 n101
La Rochefoucauld, François, duc de, 9, 11–15, 20, 21, 22, 23, 26, 35, 37–8, 44, 46, 58, 176
Laugaa-Traut, Françoise, 254 n8
law, the (*see also* prescription), 18–19, 62, 133, 137, 148–75 *passim*, 192–208 *passim*, 255 n24
Le Bossu, René, 49, 52–5, 92, 224 n140
Leibniz, G.W., 33, 35
legislation, 84–5, 148
legislator, 159, 168–71, 215 n49, 253 n83
Le Gras, 214 n38
Lély, Gilbert, 254 n8
Lemaître, Jules, 222 n112
Lenglet-Dufresnoy, Nicolas, 76–7, 79–80, 229 n25, 231 n33
Lewis, Philip E., 14, 15, 212 n26, 213 n28
Linguet, Simon-Nicolas-Henri, 153, 156, 246 n35
Locke, John: *Essay Concerning Human Understanding*, 29–39, 44, 53, 217 n73, 220 n85, 220 n88, 220 n89, 222 n106, 244 n24; on education, 70, 71–2, 74, 96–8, 117, 235 n69; on politics, 149, 154–6, 245 n33, 248 n51
Louvet de Couvray, Jean-Baptiste, 68, 95, 100–1, 103, 236 n6, 238 n22, 241 n42
Lyons, John, 212 n18
Lyotard, Jean-François, xiii, 19, 37, 62, 212 n15, 214 n41, 250 n65

Mably, Gabriel Bonnot, 156, 246 n37, 248 n47
Marin Louis, 35, 232 n41, 247 n41
Marmontel, Jean-François, 6, 55, 228 n11

Marx, Karl, 236 n70, 246 n35, 248 n47
May, Georges, 91, 176, 234 n53
May, Gita, 225 n145
Meleuc, Serge, 9, 11–15, 16, 19, 20
Méré, Antoine Gombauld, 214 n38
Méry, C. de, 224 n144
Meschonnic, Henri, 215 n52
Mesnard, P., 228 n6
Milner, George, 213 n35
Minguelez, Roberto, 211 n12
modes, mixed, 32–4
Montesquieu, Charles-Louis de Secondat, baron de, 149–53, 155, 244 n23, 246 n38, 252 n73
Morelly, 149, 154, 244 n47
Morin, Edgar, 227 n2
motivation, 121, 131

Nancy, Jean-Luc, 240 n35, 251 n72
narrative, 3, 16, 26, 27, 52, 62–3, 74, 85, 104, 109, 175–6, 207–8, 217 n69
Natural Right, 150, 155–8, 163, 251 n69
Nature, 155–6, 156–8, 182–4, 199–208 *passim*, 246 n34, 248 n46
Newton, 18
Nietzsche, F., 208, 217 n66, 256 n30

Padley, G.A., 218 n77
Pagliaro, Harold, 213 n35
Palmer, Benjamin, 241 n37
paradoxa, see doxa
Pascal, Blaise, 22, 23, 74
pas au-delà, le, 96, 235 n66
patch, logic of, 25, 46–50, 130, 158, 168, 229 n17, 249 n52
Paulhan, Jean, 16, 17
Pesselier, Charles-Etienne, 74, 95, 235 n62
Petronius, 47–8
Pierssens, Michel, 221 n34
Plamenatz, John, 247 n39
Plato, 43, 249 n52, 249 n53
Polin, Raymond, 252 n81
Port-Royal, logique de, 35–38
pré-monde, 67–8, 100–1
prescription, 19, 41–2, 111, 149–54, 159, 161, 162–3, 164, 200, 246 n37, 249 n47; *see also* law
Prince, Gerald, 239 n30
proverbs, 13, 16–18, 213 n38
pudeur (*see also* veil), 145–7, 243 n16, 243 n18
Pufendorf, Samuel, 153, 154, 245 n33

272

Index

Rapin, René, 232 n38
Raymond, Marcel, 249 n53
rhetoric, 38–50, 70, 237 n14
Ricardou, Jean, 3–6, 8
Rodegem, François, 9–11, 17, 19
Roger, Philippe, 254 n7, 255 n25
Rollin, Charles, 69, 70, 75, 80, 227 n6
Rousseau, Jean-Jacques, 178, 207;
   Confessions, 171, 242 n9, 242 n12,
   251 n64; *Discours sur l'inégalité*, 156,
   157, 219 n81, 233 n47, 251 n64;
   Emile, 71–2, 73, 77–9, 87–91, 99, 100,
   139, 159, 218 n78, 228 n14, 228 n15,
   230 n27, 233 n45, 233 n46, 233 n48,
   233 n49, 233 n50, 233 n51, 234 n52,
   235 n68, 249 n56; *Essai sur l'origine
   des langues*, 242 n13. on *jouissance*,
   243 n19. *Julie ou la Nouvelle Héloise*,
   103, 107, 115, 117, 138–48 *passim*,
   171–5, 244 n20, 253 n88, 253 n90;
   Lettre à d'Alembert, 243 n16, 243
   n18; *Lettre à Voltaire*, 217 n70;
   political writings, 140, 149, 156–71
   passim, 248 n51, 249 n52, 249 n55,
   249 n57, 252 n75, 252 n77, 253 n84

Sade, D.A.F., marquis de, 63, 68, 175,
   176–208 *passim*, 209, 232 n35
Saint-Pierre, *see* Castel de Saint-Pierre
seduction, 93, 98, 100, 235 n59
Shackleton, Robert, 244 n23
Showalter, English, 236 n4
Siemek, Andrzej, xi, 236 n9, 238 n18,
   239 n32
Silverblatt, Bette Gross, 58, 61, 67–8,
   95, 101, 107
simulacrum, 63, 86, 107, 158, 161–2,
   165, 172, 174–5, 186, 192, 194, 202–
   8, 253 n84
Smith, Neil and Deirdre Wilson, 226
   n162
Snyders, Georges, 69, 75
Social Contract, 156, 160–1, 181, 250
   n61, 250 n62

Socrates, 43, 72
Sollers, Philippe, 190
sous-entendu, 62, 188
Spinoza, Baruch, 148, 244 n23, 244
   n25, 249 n54
Starobinski, Jean, 22, 138, 145–6, 224
   n144, 242 n13, 243 n18
Stewart, Philip, 242 n15
Strauss, Leo, 246 n53, 248 n50, 249 n51
stupidity, 43, 50, 209, 222 n110, 223
   n127
supplement, 50, 69–72, 85, 174, 223
   n125

Tanner, Tony, 253 n89
temporality, 160, 162, 167, 249 n57
Thucydides, 78, 229 n25, 230 n28
Todorov, Tzvetan, 239 n28, 241 n43
Tort, Michel, 190
transgression, 177, 192, 195, 208
Trévoux, journal de, 75, 231 n33, 235
   n63
truth: *see* fiction

Uzanne, Octave, 55, 124

Vanière, Ignace, 244 n23
Vauvenargues, 15, 22, 23–5, 35, 44, 57,
   216 n60
veil, logic of, 93, 94, 109, 114–6, 121,
   130, 145–8, 174, 234 n58, 235 n59,
   245 n18
Vernes, Paule-Monique, 248 n50
Vernière, Paul, 244 n23
Veyne, Paul, 229 n25
Vico, Giambattista, 220 n90, 232 n37
Viguerie, Jean de, 69
Villers, Charles, 254 n8
Villerterque, 184
Voltaire, François-Marie Arouet de,
   26–8, 217 n70, 231 n32

Zumthor, Paul, 51, 213 n36